► STUDENTS! ESSENTIAL ACCESS INFORMATION FOR HOUGHTON MIFFLIN VIDEO CASES

Explore Teaching in Action.

Are you interested in what happens in actual classrooms? Do you want to know how in-service teachers handle a variety of situations in the classroom? Watch the Houghton Mifflin Video Cases and explore how new and experienced teachers apply concepts and strategies in real K–12 classrooms. Integrated into your text, these 4- to 6-minute video clips cover a variety of different topics faced by today's teachers and allow you to experience and reflect on real teaching in action.

To Access the Houghton Mifflin Video Cases:

1. Using your browser go to: **college.hmco.com/PIC/orlich8e**
2. Select the student web site
3. Click on HM Video Cases
4. You will be prompted to enter the passkey below and to choose a username and password
5. Select a video case from the list of options

Passkey: BFF9IC0KFHX7O

Access is provided for free with the purchase of a new Orlich et al., *Teaching Strategies: A Guide to Better Instruction*, Eighth Edition textbook, and will expire 6 months after first use. If you have a problem accessing the web site with this passkey, please contact Houghton Mifflin Technical Support at: **http://college.hmco.com/how/how_techsupp.html.**

Enhance Your Learning Experience.

Houghton Mifflin video cases are integrated with your new copy of Orlich et al., *Teaching Strategies: A Guide to Better Instruction*, Eighth Edition through boxed features in the margins of the text. The cases include video clips and a host of related materials to provide a comprehensive learning experience.

Reflect on the teacher's approach and assess how you might handle the situation by considering the **Viewing Questions.**

Watch textbook concepts come to life through video clips and bonus videos of real teachers applying teaching models and addressing key topics in their own classrooms.

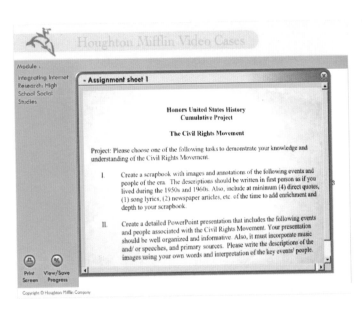

View **handouts and materials** used in the class, and gain ideas for your own portfolio.

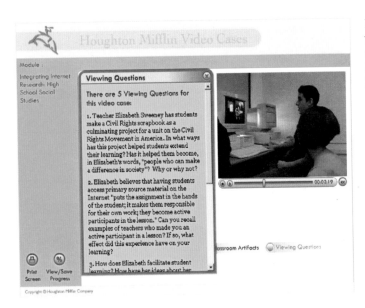

Read detailed **interviews with the teachers** as they explain their approach, how they engage students and how they resolve issues.

eighth edition

Teaching Strategies

A Guide to Effective Instruction

DONALD C. ORLICH
Washington State University

ROBERT J. HARDER
Washington State University

RICHARD C. CALLAHAN
Callahan Associates

MICHAEL S. TREVISAN
Washington State University

ABBIE H. BROWN
California State University, Fullerton

Houghton Mifflin Company   Boston   New York

Editor in Chief: Pat Coryell
Sponsoring Editor: Sue Pulvermacher-Alt
Senior Development Editor: Lisa Mafrici
Development Editor: Janet Young
Project Editor: Andrea Dodge
Editorial Assistant: Kristen Truncellito
Production/Design Coordinator: Jill Haber
Marketing Manager: Elinor Gregory

Cover Photo: © Jonathan Kantor/Getty Images

Printed in the U.S.A.

Library of Congress Control Number: 2005938028

Instructor's Exam Copy:

   ISBN 13: 978-0-618-73017-9
   ISBN 10: 0-618-73017-6

For orders, use student text ISBNs

   ISBN 13: 978-0-618-66071-1
   ISBN 10: 0-618-66071-2

2 3 4 5 6 7 8 9-EB-10 09 08 07 06

Contents

Preface

The institution of education is encountering accelerated change and uncertainty that create new challenges for teachers and students. Both groups must master the tools of the information age and prepare for the unknown opportunities it offers. Teachers must respond to demands for greater professionalism and reform, and they must help an increasingly diverse mix of students prepare for life in an ever more global and competitive world. This edition of *Teaching Strategies: A Guide to Effective Instruction* focuses yet more clearly on improvement of the teaching act. Teachers as leaders are pivotal decision makers in this context and must master techniques that enhance greater student achievement. Each chapter in this extensively revised eighth edition has been condensed and more tightly focused with an emphasis on the classroom teacher's instructional needs. Driving the book throughout is the core belief that teachers have the ability to make a profound difference in their students' lives. *Teaching Strategies* helps all prospective teachers to acquire the professional knowledge that is so necessary to produce learning for all our nation's children. Using this book, practicing teachers also can improve their skills and strategies, and learn to blend technical competence with artistic sensitivity as they change and grow as professionals.

PURPOSE AND INTENDED AUDIENCE

This book has multiple uses. *Teaching Strategies* is designed primarily for use in courses of instruction for those preparing to become elementary, middle, or secondary school teachers. Topics are treated in depth to help prospective teachers master the broad range of competencies required for state and national certification. We strive to contribute to the profession by providing tested and validated theories and methods of classroom instruction, and by showing how best to apply them in today's schools.

The authors illustrate a broad spectrum of instructional methodologies and techniques that work in today's complex classrooms. Novices and experienced teachers alike have found it a valuable source of sound, tested, and humane educational strategies. It is a reliable guide for making logical, effective, systematic instructional choices. In-service teachers have reported that the book is a helpful and easy-to-use resource in areas they previously missed or in which they need some technical brushing up.

NEW TO THE EIGHTH EDITION

As a result of feedback we received from reviewers, changes in education, and new research, we've made several changes to the eighth edition. In several places in the text you will find a *new feature* called "Professional Voices in the Field," which gives first-person perspectives, many by award-winning teachers, on implementing the strategies we discuss. Here are some other highlights.

1. Substantial revisions to Chapters 1, 2, 3, 4, 6, and 10. In response to reviewers' desire for more emphasis on professionalism, we've streamlined Chapter 1, now titled, "The Professional Challenges of Teaching," to focus on four major topics: teaching as a profession, the key contexts of teaching and incentives, diversity in the schools, and the challenge of reflective teaching and decision making. We close with a preview of mandated professional standards.

Chapter 2, now called "The Big Picture in Your Classroom: Focusing the Instruction in a Social Kaleidoscope," provides a holistic view of instruction. Chapter 3, now called "Objectives, Taxonomies, and Standards for Instruction," is also streamlined and contains an expanded section, "Converting Standards to Objectives," which discusses in detail the process of converting state and national standards into concrete learning objectives.

Chapter 4, "Instructional Design" includes two new *Voices from the Field* vignettes on the chapter's theme.

Chapter 6, "Managing the Classroom Environment" has been more tightly focused. At reviewers' request a short section on assertive discipline has been reintroduced.

Finally, Chapter 10, now called "Classroom Assessment," includes an expanded section on formative assessment.

3. Improved pedagogy to facilitate comprehension and recall. This edition includes more reflection questions, sharpened marginal notes to help students study and review, and redesigned chapter-opening graphic organizers.

4. New research and data throughout. The eighth edition has been brought completely up to date with relevant research, data, and sources.

5. Updated technology coverage. "Technology Insight" features have been updated to include new information on topics such as cooperative learning for multimedia technology and gender bias, and using gradebook software.

6. An expanded Online Study Center with Houghton Mifflin Video Cases. Marginal notes throughout the text direct students to our web-based Video Cases, short videos that invite students into the classroom to watch beginning and seasoned teachers use the book's strategies.

WHAT'S COVERED IN THE TEXT

The revised text is organized in three parts. Part 1, titled "Foundations of Instructional Design," examines the culture of the schools and presents the fundamental frameworks within which teachers set goals and make daily instructional decisions. Chapter 1, "The Professional Challenges of Teaching," presents an overview of the school milieu. We discuss teaching as a profession and the contextual factors that affect teaching. The all-important concept of teacher as decision maker is highlighted. The chapter closes with discussion of five different sets of mandated professional standards affecting contemporary teacher preparation.

Chapter 2, "The Big Picture in Your Classroom: Focusing the Instruction in a Social Kaleidoscope," begins with a discussion and graphic organizer of holistic instruction, a contextualizing section that follows the previous chapter's decision-making theme, and then sets the stage for most of the major topics in the remainder of the book. We present three major perspectives that can guide systematic decision making: developmental, behavioral, and cognitive. Highlighted are two themes: diversity and equity. Each of these sections integrates key material.

In Part 2, "Fundamental Tools for Instructional Planning," we vividly illustrate the basic tools and knowledge base for effective instructional planning. Chapter 3, "Objectives, Taxonomies, and Standards for Instruction," continues to focus on the goals and objectives of instruction. The related discussion of student standards is expanded to illustrate samples from various states and how they are converted into daily lesson design. The concept of effect size is introduced here.

Chapters 4 and 5 define and demonstrate the process of instructional design with a variety of useful planning methods, planning resources, and instructional models. Chapter 4, "Instructional Design," contains a strong research-based section that illustrates subsequent topics on planning. It also includes a short section on the construction of individual education plans (IEPs). This coverage reflects the text's emphasis on integrating coverage of special-needs educational issues within related discussions. Chapter 4 concludes with a section on how expert teachers plan, which directly applies the field experiences of award-winning teachers to the knowledge base. The title of Chapter 5, "Sequencing and Organizing Instruction," reflects its emphasis on the two critical planning angles of sequencing and organizing. We show how teachers can adapt their plans using a multimethodological approach, thus meeting the needs of students with diverse learning styles.

Part 3, "Instruction as a Dynamic Process in Classrooms," presents the dynamic and interactive aspects of teaching, and provides the core knowledge base for creating a lively and productive learning environment. Chapter 6, "Managing the Classroom Environment," introduces classroom management as a technique for establishing a positive and supportive environment. We illustrate our presentation of a broad continuum of management systems with practical applications. Throughout, we stress the concept of equity and the need to create classroom routines that foster smooth classroom operations—for example, cell phone management.

Chapter 7, "The Process of Classroom Questioning," continues to provide the most thorough treatment of the questioning process that you will find in any methods textbook. In addition to illustrating the process of classroom questioning, the chapter highlights the essential issue of how teachers can better attend to and develop higher-level questioning, as well as reflective questioning.

Chapter 8, "Small-Group Discussions and Cooperative Learning," explores six basic types of small-group discussion to create exciting lessons and to encourage active student participation. A synthesized section describes in practical terms how to establish and maintain small groups. We also include material on collecting feedback from small groups.

Chapter 9, "Inquiry Teaching and Higher-Level Thinking," opens with a discussion of the nature of thinking and how it can be emphasized. We present in practical detail the two primary avenues for teaching thinking: inquiry-based methods and specific techniques that emphasize problem solving and critical thinking skills.

Chapter 10, "Classroom Assessment," focuses on monitoring student progress. This chapter provides reflections on the all-important contexts for classroom assessments. This includes purposes for and areas of assessment, simple core definitions, and emphasis on the relationship of assessment to planning and instruction. A section on formative classroom assessment stresses feedback as a critical element that enhances student achievement. The entire chapter emphasizes the classroom teacher's needs. Test item writing and grading, as well as other topics of importance to teachers, receive full treatment.

The entire book is tightly focused on instructional strategies and teaching techniques. We provide the prerequisite technical skills needed to be successful in the classroom. Overarching themes, such as the use of technology within the classroom and the instructional needs of diverse students, are integrated in discussions throughout the book. You will find a wide array of ideas from which to select the strategies that best meet your instructional goals and the learning goals of your students.

special Features

A new, user-friendly, two-color format highlights pedagogical features designed to organize and illustrate the content and make the text easier to use. This format encourages readers to engage with the information presented, to make it their own, and to expand their professional horizons.

- **Concept maps** introduce each chapter. The maps identify the key topics in each chapter and serve as handy visual organizational aids.
- **Instructional Strategies** boxes provide up-to-date strategic ideas and techniques for direct application in the classroom.
- **Technology Insight** boxes appear in each chapter, introducing relevant technology-related issues and, in some cases, relevant Web sites.
- **Key Ideas** boxes provide periodic breaks in the chapter to summarize key content.
- **New HM Video Case** boxes appear in the margins and link text topics to short video clips found on the Online Study Center. There are over 25 Video Cases with reflection questions that accompany the text.

- **Reflect boxes**, which appear at the end of major sections, allow the reader to stop and reflect on the previously learned content and place it in an experiential context, thereby enhancing its personal and professional relevance.
- **Marginal notes** throughout the text highlight key concepts.
- **Key terms** are highlighted in bold print to draw the reader's attention to these important building blocks of a professional vocabulary, and the Glossary at the end of the book contains all the key terms with definitions.
- **Professional Voices from the Field** features present the experience of practicing and award-winning teachers who validate the instructional techniques that we highlight.
- **A Closing Reflection** concludes each chapter, providing formative questions for thought on the contents of the chapter.
- **Summaries** at the end of each chapter aid the reader in pinpointing major concepts.
- **Print Resources** at the end of each chapter provide readers with additional resources that can be used for further information on a given topic and to expand their professional competence.
- **Internet Resources** include the URLs for specific Web sites where more information or interactive activities can be found.
- **Standards Correlation charts** on the inside covers connect the text content with INTASC, PRAXIS II, and NCATE standards.

Accompanying Resources for Instructors and Students

- An **online Instructor's Resource Manual** provides the instructor with additional teaching and assessment support materials.
- Our **Online Teaching and Study Centers** at http://college.hmco.com/pic/orlich8eoffers additional information on key topics such as the legal structure of public schools, school reform agendas, lifelong learning, elements of the school culture, and characteristics of children in the K–12 setting. We also offer other features, such as ACE self-testing questions, reflection questions, and additional Web links. As mentioned, *new HM Video Cases* are offered with this edition and are correlated to the text by marginal features. Each video case is a 4- to 6-minute clip that presents actual classroom scenarios depicting the complex problems and opportunities teachers face in the classroom every day. HM Video Cases are accompanied by teacher interviews, classroom artifacts, and reflective viewing questions. Instructors can go to http://college.hmco.com/pic/orlich8e to find instructors' resources, such as model syllabi, activities, PowerPoint slides, discussion starters, and more.
- Support for online courses is available via platform-ready **WebCT and Blackboard cartridges.**

ACKNOWLEDGMENTS

The authors express their appreciation to the colleagues who contributed to earlier editions of this text. These include Dr. Harry Gibson, Olympia, Washington; Dr. Anne Remaley of Washington State University; Dr. Constance H. Kravas of the University of Washington; Dr. Andrew J. Keogh, University of Wisconsin–Marshfield/Wood County; Dr. R. A. Pendergrass, Glenwood, Missouri, public schools; Dr. Donald P. Kauchak of the University of Utah; Dr. Eileen M. Starr of Valley City State University; and Dr. Foster M. Walsh of Gonzaga University. Each helped make the previous editions of the book relevant and useful, and their insight continues to be reflected in the eighth edition.

A number of reviewers critiqued this edition: Cynthia L. Carver, Western Michigan University; Richard A. Giaquinto, St. Francis College; Florette Reven, Tarleton State University; Ann Ross, Arkansas State University. We would like to thank each of them, as well as the many students who offered feedback, for their suggestions. The authors wish to thank Sandra Tyacke for her outstanding job of preparing the many manuscripts necessary for this project, and to express their appreciation to the staff of Houghton Mifflin, including Sue Pulvermacher-Alt, Lisa Mafrici, and Andrea Dodge, and freelance developmental editor Janet Young; their help is more than observable in the final product.

Donald C. Orlich

Foundations of Instructional Design

Part 1 is an overview of the foundations of effective instruction, which we systematically expand throughout the remainder of the book. This part introduces teaching as a profession, the professional contexts of the school milieu as a learning community, and how social factors affect what is taught and how. We also provide a rationale that illustrates the many interacting components of instruction and their cyclical nature. In Chapter 1, we discuss various professional, cultural, and political contexts that have an impact on the ways that you teach. We make a strong plea for reflective teaching, setting the stage for the key role of teacher as decision maker. Chapter 2 establishes the big picture of instruction by illustrating how some sociopsychological perspectives shape our techniques of presentation. We show how meaningful instruction is cyclical, and how all elements of the cycle inform teacher decisions. We stress the need for instructional equity.

The concept map, or advance organizer, that follows highlights the topics to be presented and how they are interrelated. The maps that appear at the beginning of each chapter not only are useful study tools but also provide models that you can adapt in your own instructional planning.

The Professional Challenges of Teaching

1

A SNAPSHOT OF TEACHING AS A PROFESSION

Facilitating the American Dream

Teaching as a Profession

Key Contexts of Schooling

Incentives of the Teaching Culture

Professionalism and Diversity

2

THE CHALLENGE OF REFLECTIVE TEACHING AND DECISION MAKING

Teaching as Art and Science

Decision Making and Responsibility

Selecting Developmentally Appropriate
   Content and Processes

Motivation and Learning

Choosing Technology Wisely

Teaching as Reflection and Problem
   Solving

3

MEETING MANDATED PROFESSIONAL STANDARDS

Dee Ennis, like most college students, has been in the system for over fifteen years. (Make that sixteen, because she attended a full year of kindergarten.) She is now completing a teaching internship in a large urban high school. Along with her master teacher, she spends many free periods analyzing instruction and how to better reach more students. Dee already has observed how things seem to get done and by whom. She is also very much aware of the diversity represented in the student population.

In her quest for greater understanding, she jotted down a few general questions to ask her faculty mentor.

- Do teachers meet the criteria for professionals? If so, how?
- What major instructional decisions and choices do teachers make?
- What kinds of contexts do the schools reflect?
- How do educators attempt to meet current and emerging professional standards?

Dee's mentor examined the list, smiled, handed her a copy of this book, and said, "The answers to all those questions might be addressed in Chapter 1."

Are you ready?

SECTION 1: A SNAPSHOT OF TEACHING AS A PROFESSION

The schools of America are its single largest social service institution. Projected 2007 expenditures for all K–12 schooling are over $500 billion. Add to that an estimated $300 billion for higher education, and the magnitude of our enterprise accounts for a tidy 7 percent of the nation's gross domestic product. Teachers recognize that, as members of this "industry," which serves almost one out of every four persons, they must have a broad understanding of instruction. Teachers and administrators know they need to analyze how they teach in terms of what they are teaching and to whom they are teaching it. In this chapter, we present a rationale that gives a theoretical and practical structure to guide action in the classroom as it relates to education as a professional endeavor. If all one had to do were stand up front and talk, then teaching would be a snap, but there is far more to effective teaching than this.

Education is the largest social service industry in the United States.

Facilitating the American Dream

By and large, surveys show the American public believes that the nation's schools provide students with the knowledge, skills, and competencies they need to be successful. For millions of individuals, public schools have provided the opportunities that have allowed them to realize their own American dream. Most Americans believe that success comes with education—and from an economic standpoint, there is little doubt that this is often true.

This dream is not uniformly achieved, however. Not all individuals in our society profit equally from public education. The reasons vary, from socioeconomic factors to language diversity. Perhaps the best that we can expect from schools is that they assure every student an equal access to opportunity.

Teachers guide all individuals toward being successful in American society.

The chance to achieve one's dream is a great self-motivator. Thus every educator has an ethical and moral obligation to enhance the potential for all students. Embracing those ideals is a professional obligation.

Teaching as a Profession

What is a professional? What do you think of when you hear the term *professional*? You may think of professional athletes, who are paid to perform. What is a professional teacher hired and paid to do?

Criteria for Professionals   What makes a particular livelihood a **profession** rather than a job? While others' lists may differ on a uniform set of criteria, we offer the following six generalizations.

What is a professional?

1. *Learning a profession involves learning, by intellectual endeavor, many concepts and principles.* Medicine, law, and engineering—to list but three widely recognized professions—contain many complex ideas and principles. The field of teaching likewise relies heavily on the findings from social and psychological fields for basic theoretical structures that can be applied to the classroom. Virtually all teachers must complete courses of study that have been approved by state boards of education and national accrediting associations. We'll expand on this in Section 4.
2. *A profession has a body of techniques that are applied in specific situations and that can be transmitted.* An architect understands the principles of design and how form and structure are interrelated. During your preservice phase, you will be exposed to a number of instructional and management strategies that are used by in-service teachers and that will help your students achieve at optimal levels. Many ideas you learn in the professional setting will be brand new to you, even though you have served that thirteen-year apprenticeship in K–12 classes.
3. *A profession is internally organized and contains the apparatus for self-discipline.* The fields of medicine and law have tightly controlled organizations and a published code of ethics. Frauds and quacks are expelled when they are found to have violated the codes of their professions. The Code of Ethics of the Education Profession (National Education Association 1964, 1975) establishes the code of practice for all teachers in regard to students and to other educators.
4. *A profession is altruistically motivated.* One of the reasons people hold such great respect for the medical profession is that it alleviates suffering, and the legal profession because it has a goal of promoting fairness. The emphasis in teaching is also service to fellow humans. People who enter teaching want to work with young children and adolescents. Educators exhibit *pervasive caring,* a sense of attunement to young people's emotional needs and well-being that underscores all decision making. Teachers want their students to succeed. Day by day, they try to provide each student with the best education.
5. *A profession must allow for independence.* The clients of an accountant do not tell that person how to prepare income tax forms. Similarly, teachers with broad professional and subject matter backgrounds know

their fields, and to perform at their top levels, they must work in an environment that offers academic freedom. We will expand on this concept on the section on decision making.

6. *A profession is recognized as such and commands high prestige.* Few would dispute that physicians and engineers command a high degree of prestige. Teachers, likewise, have a particular glow or mystique that surrounds them. How often has someone asked what you're studying in school and then responded, "You're going to be a teacher? How wonderful!" How often have acquaintances or family members told you about teachers who greatly influenced them early in their lives? There is social status in being a teacher, and many teachers receive due recognition for having contributed to the welfare and betterment of children.

These six general criteria for a profession set the stage for *informed decision making.* Study and reflection increase the ability of professionals to act independently. For the most part, as a teacher you will often find yourself "bowling alone," to borrow the title from Robert D. Putman's (2000) popular book that observes the decline of social group associations. Teaching can be a lonely endeavor, especially in self-contained elementary and middle schools. Even in high school, you may be the only art teacher. Your immediate interactions, aside from those with students, are those with colleagues with whom you share professional interests. You are a part of the school organization, but you work independently to plan units and lessons and to carry out those plans.

Independence vs. isolation

However, since 1984 and the publication of *A Nation at Risk: The Imperative for Educational Reform* (National Commission on Excellence in Education 1983), there has been an erosion of teacher autonomy resulting in greater federal and state control in the form of legislated political statements. These statements have established long lists of instructional standards, methods by which to teach—including scripted scenarios for specific lessons, high-stakes tests for all children beginning in the second and third grades, and tests for new and even experienced teachers. Under the rubric of reform, teacher professionalism is being challenged.

Teacher autonomy is being challenged.

How, for example, do you exhibit independence (academic freedom) if you are told that only the content listed on the standards may be taught, and even that must be presented as scripted? What would be the impact on your instruction?

Professional Obligations   In your first years of teaching, you will be in a unique position. As a professional, you have an obligation to provide the best educational services to your students that you know. But as a new teacher, the experiential basis for your actions is limited compared to those with twelve or fifteen years of experience and advanced degrees. That is step one of fulfilling your professional obligation—you must become a lifelong learner. You will expand your intellectual horizons so that difficult classroom situations become less difficult. You will gain the intuition to anticipate tricky situations and transform them into learning experiences for your students.

Your professional obligations are further elaborated in the Code of Ethics. Two main principles set the stage for professional behavior: commitment to the student and commitment to the profession. Says the code: "The educator strives to help each student realize his or her potential as a worthy and effective member of society. The educator therefore works to stimulate the spirit of inquiry, the acquisition of knowledge and understanding, and the thoughtful formulation of worthy goals."

On commitment to the profession, the code states:

> The education profession is vested by the public with a trust and responsibility requiring the highest ideals of professional service.

In the belief that the quality of the services of the education profession directly influences the nation and its citizens, the educator shall exert every effort to raise professional standards, to promote a climate that encourages the exercise of professional judgment, to achieve conditions that attract persons worthy of the trust to careers in education, and to assist in preventing the practice of the profession by unqualified persons.

Each principle is followed by eight recommended actions or prohibitions. (See the website of the National Education Association, **http://www.nea. org/code.html**, for the full code.) Although you may encounter some situations in which the teacher's code of ethics and other requirements in the state or local arena may seem to conflict, developing sufficient technical knowledge will help you cope with many of the dilemmas you'll encounter. In subsequent chapters of this text, you will gain an entry level of technical knowledge that will help you to meet the instructional obligations of our profession.

Being a Professional

- Endorsing an intellectual commitment to teaching
- Caring for all your students
- Practicing ethical standards
- Helping others achieve the American dream

reflect

- During one of your classroom observations, discuss the Code of Ethics with the teacher you are observing.
- Hold a class discussion to define professionalism.

Key Contexts of Schooling

The profession of teaching takes place in a number of contexts that will place demands on your work. Some of these demands reinforce one another; others are sometimes in conflict.

The Social Context   A sign in the Singapore International Airport reads "Welcome to Singapore: Where Our Only National Resource Is Our People." That sign sums what our schools should be all about. Institutions are made up of people. Schools consist of systems and subsystems of individuals who collectively conduct the business of schooling. The human interactions among administrators, teachers, parents, and learners forge bonds of trust and mutual support. As teachers, our goal is to enhance human potential for every person associated with the school. The process of education takes place, for the most part, in structured and well-organized schools. This is true even for parents who home-school their children. Schooling, to be effective, has a group orientation about it. The entire process is very social—that is, highly dependent on personal interactions. One of the first things that a child learns in school is that the individual must make accommodations to the group. Within this cultural and social milieu, behaviors are changed, learning takes place, and individuals change. Schools provide a social resource that individuals learning on their own might lack.

> School as group orientation, complex social network

Embedded within the social context of the school is the concept of *social capital*. **Social capital** is the sum of interpersonal relationships that provide support or encouragement. Sources of social capital include families, communities, public institutions, and ethnic relationships. Emanating from these sources come social trust, norms, communication, and collaborative networks, to list only a few outcomes. (See Carnevale 2001; Israel, Beaulieu, and Hartless 2001; Putnam 2000.)

The school is an especially critical source of social capital for its clientele. It provides the physical and social framework for teachers, students, and parents/caregivers to work toward a common good, or to extend the **acculturation** process of children or adolescents. **Norms**, those unwritten rules of behavior for specific groups, and normative pressures are all part of the school's culture and its vast resource of social capital.

Schooling provides social capital to all.
© Joel Gordon.

As a teacher, you help to create social capital for all students, especially those whose social capital, for whatever reason, has a near-zero balance. These include children growing up in poverty and new arrivals to the United States. You provide information that helps students become a part of social networks. By knowing your students personally, you help them gain experiences with things they don't know. You show the students how to employ all the school's resources—counselors, coaches, sponsors of extracurricular or club activities, the music director, the school newspaper advisor. By your own actions, you demonstrate that you are in your students' corner. These methods of supporting students socially are all aspects of meeting our professional obligation. Collectively, these social elements of schooling aid in the acculturation processes of preparing students to be successful in our society.

Teachers create social capital.

Key Ideas

Elements of Social Capital

- Families
- Personal relationships
- Public institutions
- Churches
- Communities
- Clubs
- Ethnic relationships

Now add to these interactions the phenomenon we call *pluralism,* and you can appreciate the social interactions and conflicts that can be predicted to take place in the schools. The term **pluralism** refers to the fact that our society and our schools are composed of many different types of people, creating a mixture of nationalities, races, classes, religions, occupational groupings, philosophies, value systems, and economic beliefs. Given this broad social spectrum, it is inevitable that you will observe contradictory points of view as a teacher (see Livingston and Wirt 2004). You will observe **intrapersonal** conflicts, in which an individual tries to reconcile conflicts within his or her own value structure. You will also observe **interpersonal** conflicts, in which the values of different individuals or groups openly clash. These kinds of conflicts generate considerable energy. Sometimes the energy is positive and leads to common problem solving and beneficial activities. In other cases, the energy leads to disharmony. As a teacher, one of your major roles will be to foster positive social interactions and relationships.

The Emotional Context   As we said before, the educational enterprise is a helping profession. People who enter teaching tend to do so for altruistic, moral, or ethical reasons. If education is to help all persons achieve their maximum potential, then those in it must develop an organization that cares about all individuals in it. That quality of *caringness* adds the human element

Emphasize caring and values.

to impersonal buildings and institutionalized delivery systems. The close interactions among teachers and students forge bonds of trust and mutual support, especially for children who have trouble meeting expectations for achievement (see Noddings 2002).

Additionally, caringness is a part of the social capital of the school organization. This trait, then, makes it a bit easier to help students at all ages to develop moral and ethical values. Do not be alarmed about the last sentence. Yes, the schools have an obligation to teach those values, and virtually all parents or guardians will strongly endorse them because they fall under the umbrella of becoming a good or virtuous citizen (see Comte-Sponville 2001).

The Educational Context   Just what composes the educational context of our schools? This is a tough question to answer, for it depends on your own educational philosophy. Over the years, the schools have either inherited or subtly adopted a social philosophy aimed at accommodating many social, emotional, and familial needs in addition to educational ones. Yes, the schools still teach the basics. But "the basics" now extend to many topics that were once considered extras. To be sure, reading and writing, communicating, mathematics, science, history, and geography still form the core academic disciplines, but the schools now also teach health and life skills, HIV/AIDS prevention, driving, and a host of other skills, both social and behavioral. This is the complicated montage we call the curriculum today. We will return to the topic of the curriculum in Chapters 3, 4, and 5, when we discuss lesson designs.

Redefining the basics

The Collegial Context   Over the academic year, principals or supervisors might spend a total of one or two hours observing and evaluating a teacher, with greater time for a novice and less for a veteran; but the vast amount of service that any teacher performs goes uncritiqued or unnoticed by fellow professionals. When teachers develop personal teaching styles that are not especially beneficial to student learning, it is often as the result of working in seclusion.

Working in isolation is one aspect of many school cultures that tends to perpetuate the "batch processing" of students—that is, using large classes and large-class techniques. This is especially noticeable in self-contained elementary school classrooms and subject-centered high schools. The physical isolation keeps new ideas from spreading. If you do not have opportunities to observe your colleagues, you may miss out on some great ideas (see Woolfolk-Hoy and Hoy 2003).

Even though you may often work in seclusion, you can use the Internet to facilitate participation in the professional community by linking with professional associations' websites. All state departments of education also have extensive websites. We highlight some useful tips to expand your learning in the Technology Insight boxes found throughout the book, and conclude each chapter with a few select sites for your consideration.

However, you might be fortunate enough to be working in a school where the culture maintains a **learning community**. In these instances, you will seldom be alone, as there is greater teacher-student-administrator collaboration and planning. You will also find teachers conducting research and self-reflecting on their practices. The learning community culture encourages

VIDEO CASE   ◀◀ ▶ ▶▶

View the Video Case "Teaching as a Profession:Collaboration with Colleagues" on our website to listen in as a group of teachers develop recommendations for their math reporting system and present their ideas at a faculty meeting. How do these teachers define collaboration?

Importance of finding a teacher learning community

continued studies or professional staff development, and even encourages teaching professionals to seek a National Board Certification. (For details, see the website at **http://www.nbpts.org.**) Further, there appears to be an attempt afoot to make schools into smaller, cohesive units. This includes "schools within a school," "core groupings," and even discrete learning groups. The goal of these techniques is to improve professional interactions and provide an environment conducive to student achievement.

Schools tend to develop their own independent **school culture**, apart from other schools in the same district. Their norms and values may be generated from the inside. As a result, subtle or even intentional pressures may be placed on teachers to conform. The outcome can be positive if the school culture includes healthy values, innovative teaching styles, and respectful communication patterns. If, however, the school culture includes less desirable qualities, this unfortunate tendency to encourage teachers to conform may undermine the profession. Education, like all professions, is rooted in the development of its practitioners' individual expertise. And, indeed, novice teachers have at their disposal a broad range of teaching strategies. This book is designed to help develop the best teachers possible. Study this and the following chapters with the goal of influencing your environment in a positive way instead of becoming a victim to its negative characteristics. In that way, your school ethos can evolve; you can establish new norms that stress problem solving, active teaching, and positive student expectations. We advocate entering into professional discussions and collaborating with other teachers in your school. Share books and journals with one another. This is one way of helping to shape the intellectual and instructional dimensions of your school's culture.

Each school has its own culture.

Contexts of Schooling

- Social
- Emotional
- Educational
- Collegial (professional)

Incentives of the Teaching Culture

Why do teachers continue to do what they do? Teachers bask in the success of their students, and students' success reflects on their teachers' effectiveness. It is great to be with winners. That statement is true whether you are a second-grade teacher whose pupils have mastered addition or a high school French teacher whose students have grasped the concept of the subjunctive. A teacher's level of functioning is largely determined by the attitude displayed toward the students—whether inviting or disinviting interaction. (See the box on page 12; Purkey and Novak 1996). The highest-level teacher, the one who is intentionally inviting, strives most for student success. These teachers reinforce their own most powerful incentive. (See Stanley and Purkey 2001 for a series of studies on invitational learning.)

One job incentive is recognition as an excellent teacher (Williams 2003). This recognition is reflected in your students' warmth, enthusiasm, and appreciation. This provides a strong internal motivation for teachers. Remember how you felt when your teacher helped you complete a tough assignment, or when you accomplished something and shared that feat with the responsible teacher? Yes, that's a real glow in a teacher's eyes!

The respect of colleagues is another incentive. Phi Delta Kappa, the educational honor society, once had the motto. "The esteem of our colleagues is the foundation of power." Such esteem helps make teachers feel a sense of **efficacy**, a feeling that they can get the job done. Effective teachers demonstrate a sense of efficacy. They believe that they control their own classroom destinies, and they show behaviors related to self-actualization and transcendence, which are the very highest of human needs (Maslow, 1970; see Margolis and McCabe 2003 for an excellent discussion of self-efficacy).

You gain respect from your colleagues when your students achieve better than expected, when they are successful in your classes, and when the tough cases are not too tough for you. These accomplishments will result if you use the broad spectrum of teaching strategies we illustrate in the ensuing chapters. Efficacy, in the last analysis, is being able to see yourself doing the job, no matter how difficult or demanding it is. (See Brouwers and Tomie 2000.)

Another incentive is working with other professionals. As we pointed out earlier, most teachers are isolated from other professionals for most of a typical working day. Part of being a teaching professional is working on school problems, curriculum projects, or instructional designs with your colleagues. These activities allow you to participate in the decision-making processes of the school. Working in a collegial manner with your fellow professionals to improve the environment for learning is one aspect of teacher empowerment, in which the concept of efficacy is moved up one level to collective action rather than referring only to individual excellence.

The school is a most complex institution, and the school culture has a profound impact on your teaching. We know of a high school where a large sign in the teachers' lounge proclaims, "School Business Is Not Discussed Here." Do you want to guess what kind of teaching culture has evolved there? (Maybe you'd rather not.) But you immediately become a part of any school's culture, and you can have a positive impact on it. Being efficacious is the quickest way to influence that culture. Use this book to develop a variety of instructional skills that make you the best teacher that you can be, and inspire others to do their best.

Don't be afraid to improve your school's teaching culture.

Teachers' Levels of Functioning

- Intentionally disinviting
- Unintentionally disinviting
- Unintentionally inviting
- Intentionally inviting

reflect

- How did your schooling enhance your social capital?
- What evidence would you seek to determine the level of caringness in a school?
- Choose two of the four contexts of schooling discussed here—social, emotional, educational, and collegial or professional. Compare the two. How might the forces and influences of these two contexts create conflict in your teaching environment? How might they agree or reinforce each other?

Professionalism and Diversity

As educators, we realize that the United States is an amalgam of a broad spectrum of individuals. Schools reflect a diverse range of ethnic, language, racial, and religious groups. Further diversity results from regional influences and the physical characteristics in the school-age population: gender, disabilities, physical dimensions, and other observable personal traits. Our national diversity makes if difficult to define a single U.S. culture. While the people of the United States have a common root language and many shared values, we are a culturally plural society.

It's our professional obligation to be aware of commonalities and differences in the many cultures represented in schools. Students and their teachers are similar in many ways and yet different in others. A major question you will face as a teachers is this: Should the selection of instructional objectives and teaching strategies promote unity or exalt differences? Or should it do both? What resources does your school provide to make necessary accommodations to instruct all students at an optimal level?

For professionals, diversity also means providing a wide range of instructional options. There are age-related considerations to the instructional options that you offer, but middle school classes can be equally diverse, as can an Advanced Placement high school course. We hope you will give your students the broadest possible view of the subjects or areas that you teach. In so doing, you provide a global view of history, art, or science rather than a narrow parochial perspective. The transmission of our culture is a key element to teaching. Thinking about diversity in all dimensions makes for a richer educational environment.

key ideas

Professionalism and Diversity

- Recognize different cultures in your classrooms.
- Respect all who show up in your classes.
- Be cognizant of similarities and differences in groups.
- Offer an enriched curriculum.

SECTION 2: THE CHALLENGE OF REFLECTIVE TEACHING AND DECISION MAKING

Teaching as Art and Science

Professional-level teaching is both an art and a science (see Eisner 2003). Like an artist, a good teacher makes decisions from both a technical and a creative perspective. Great artists display a mastery of technical skills—painting, glass blowing, sculpting—that involves the science behind how these techniques work. They also know when and in what way to apply those technical skills. They make decisions. That part is the art. Similarly, teachers develop their science by using carefully planned, fine-tuned lessons that reflect an understanding of many different teaching techniques. They apply each technique skillfully to gain the desired intellectual, social, affective, or kinesthetic result. They develop artistry by being aware of what they are doing and how what they do affects their learners. They are constantly aware that the choices they make affect the intellectual, attitudinal, and psychomotor skills of their students. Above all, they make decisions.

Nearly all of the instructional techniques that are presented in this book have an extensive body of research supporting them. You will be consumers of research and may even contribute to that literature; as you progress through your teacher education program, you may encounter advocates of some golden technique. Ask for empirically derived data, that is, longitudinal experimental and control group results that have been replicated. The educational fads that abound usually have no such data. Understanding and interpreting research is part of teaching's science. Using that knowledge appropriately, making the right decisions, is the artistry.

Decisions and judgment put the art in teaching.

Decision Making and Responsibility

VIDEO CASE

The Video Case "Teacher Accountability: A Student Teacher's Perspective" explains a national movement that holds teachers responsible for student performance. To what extent do you agree that student performance is your responsibility? How much responsibility rests with administrators, school boards, or the students themselves?

Implicit within the concept of decision making is the notion of *responsibility*. Teachers cannot pass the buck. If you make a decision, you must be willing to take responsibility for both the implementation and the outcome. As we mentioned previously, some decisions are made for you—class sizes, time schedules, curriculum guides, lunch schedules. But you make the instructional decisions (see Lashway 2002 for an interesting statement).

In our opinion, many teachers do not recognize their responsibility for making decisions. They tend to blame the administration or the school board. To be sure, administrative regulations and school board policies do govern some instructional procedures and content. But most classroom instructional decisions are, in fact, the teacher's. It is you who will answer such questions as "Should I spend one period on the map-making activity, or two?" "Shall I have the students prepare poster sessions for small group presentations?" "How many periods can I allot for a class activity?" On the surface, these are not monumental decisions, but they all have an impact on your students. Take responsibility for making such decisions, and make them logically and deliberately rather than according to impulse.

The buck stops with you.

Teachers choosing materials. © Michael Zide

Teachers who take responsibility for decision making obtain as much information as possible about both students and subject matter and then develop an instructional plan geared for success. This plan is based on their conclusions about the interaction between the subject matter, the students, and the teacher. One way to begin acting more deliberately is to use "if-then" logic in your thinking. Think about causes and effects. For example, *if* you desire to encourage students to learn through inquiry techniques, *then* you must provide them with the initial learning skills they need to make inquiries. This technique helps raise your level of cognitive awareness; it provides a cognitive map for you to use in generating rules and principles, and in thinking about relationships between classroom activities and students.

> Act deliberately, thinking cause + effect.

If there is one indisputable statement about teaching, it is that there is no one "right" way to teach anything or anyone. With alarming frequency, educational authorities and critics announce that they have discovered the answer to the nation's teaching problems. In this book, we will never say that we have discovered *the* teaching method to use in a given situation. Instead, we will present a series of options, all of them practical and all able to provide results. This is our way of showing diversity. If teaching is a decision-making activity based on individual teachers' skills, knowledge, and artistry, then there ought to be a variety of means for accomplishing any instructional objective.

REFLECT

- What topics in your teaching specialty can be used to illustrate teaching as artistry?

- How can you determine how well a teaching episode has integrated the technical skills into the art of teaching?

Selecting Developmentally Appropriate Content and Processes

As you plan to teach a subject, you must remember that the processes that students use to master the content of a lesson are just as important as the content itself. Cunard Steamship Lines once advertised that "Getting there is half the fun!" The same idea applies to teaching. Students must know how to accomplish what you want them to learn. And, once they know how to get there, they'll enjoy the journey.

For example, a middle school math teacher wants to teach the students how to use ratios. Before they can use ratios, however, the students must be able to understand the meaning of division, to comprehend the concept of whole numbers, to conceptualize the notion of proportions, and to perform basic arithmetic operations. These different kinds of knowledge are typically divided into two categories—**declarative** or **content knowledge** (knowing *what*) and **procedural** or **process knowledge** (knowing *how*).

Table 1.1 shows this distinction. In the teaching of ratios to middle school students, there are at least four specific concepts to master, listed on the left. Mastering these concepts involves both declarative knowledge (rules, facts, information), and procedural knowledge. (Division, for example, entails both declarative and procedural knowledge.) We use this example because many of the academic concepts taught in school are a mix of some content base (poetry, art, history, geography, science) and processes (writing, drawing, analyzing, experimenting). The table illustrates how learning one concept—ratios—calls for a carefully integrated approach that requires students to know and understand both content and processes, when applicable.

You can make your instructional decision-making process more deliberate by being aware of content and process implications.

Grade-Level Considerations: Subject Orientation vs. Child Orientation When prospective teachers are asked what concerns them most as they anticipate beginning their career, many secondary education majors identify knowledge of subject matter as their chief concern. Thus prospective secondary school teachers tend to be *subject oriented*. In contrast, prospective elementary school teachers tend to be *child oriented*. Their primary objective is to help children grow and mature mentally and physically, not just to teach mathematics, science, or writing. Accordingly, the activities of elementary school teachers will be oriented toward processes, such as helping children

Content = declarative knowledge
Process = procedural knowledge

TABLE 1.1

Declarative Versus Procedural Knowledge		
Specific Concept	Declarative Knowledge (Content/Information)	Procedural Knowledge (Thinking Skills and Processes)
Division	Yes	Yes
Whole numbers	Yes	No
Dividing whole numbers	Yes	Yes
Stating ratio (interpretation)	Yes	Yes

Transition from child to
subject orientation

adjust from their home environment to the institutional dimensions of school, rather than content.

Middle school provides the transition from a human-growth orientation to a content orientation. It is critically important for middle school educators to understand that young adolescents are just beginning to emerge cognitively from Jean Piaget's concrete operational stage and are entering the initial formal stage (refer to Orlich 2000). To teach this group effectively, teachers must combine hands-on activities with thinking activities for all major concepts. Techniques such as preparing time lines, conducting experiments, designing charts and graphs, classifying, and sequencing are useful to learners at this age. High school teachers tend to focus on content, a focus endorsed by our society at large.

More than half a century ago, anthropologist Clyde Kluckhohn (1949) concluded that the schools of any society mirror that society. The wishes and beliefs of a society are subtly translated into the values, curricula, and instructions of its schools. In the late 1960s and early 1970s, many secondary school educators wanted to "humanize" secondary schools by making them more process oriented (see Read and Simon 1975). But when journalists, school board members, legislators, and parents began to pressure high school teachers to improve test scores and raise academic standards, those same teachers refocused their efforts on content.

To some extent, processes must be taught along with content, with an eye toward the needs of each student. Occasionally a teacher will say, "Well, if they didn't have the knowledge or techniques before they got into my class, that's too bad!" (This is an example of being intentionally disinviting.) But if students do not have the **prerequisite skills**, then you as a teacher must provide them. If you provide the basics, then your students will be successful. If you do not, then your students will fail. This important decision is yours, and it reflects being intentionally inviting.

Equity Considerations   So far our discussion has focused on decision making based on students' cognitive levels, but your decisions should also be affected by equity considerations. What do we mean by *equity*? In our view, the term means that *every* student in your class has an equal opportunity to learn. It means that you consciously decide to include all members of the class in all activities. This means fairness in asking questions, in delegating student work assignments, and in providing access to resources, such as computer time. In short, it means that you give every student the same opportunity to excel.

Give each child a chance
to excel.

We are bothered, quite frankly, by curriculum frameworks designed around a single standard that every child must attain regardless of aptitude. Instead, curriculum frameworks should stress individual excellence. And this is where you come into the process: If you decide to hold every student responsible for doing his or her very best, your students will rise to the occasion.

reflect

- Think about your elementary, middle school, and secondary education. What are some of the processes you learned at each stage of your education? What were some of the content areas?

- Were there points at which one, process or content, was clearly emphasized over the other?

- Were there points at which process and content were inseparable?

VIDEO CASE

Discover the benefits of a student-run school store in the Video Case "Motivating Adolescent Learners: Curriculum Based on Real Life." What are the intrinsic motivations of working in the store? What are the extrinsic ones?

Intrinsic vs. extrinsic motivation.

Motivation and Learning

The vast majority of school-age children can master most topics, assuming the content is appropriate and learning is paced appropriately (see Bloom 1984). You, as the teacher, will be responsible for making decisions that will help every student in your class. A particularly important one is to encourage each child to take responsibility for learning. This is an important attitude. Teachers can teach only if the learner has some desire to learn. We call that desire **motivation**.

Motivation is the inner drive to do something—to finish a book, complete a tough assignment, make the cross-country track team. Motivation is an abstract concept, but it will become very much a part of your vocabulary. Winning coaches have more going for them than good players—they are also great motivators. They can get their players to perform better than the players think they are capable of performing. The same principle applies to great teachers. In the classroom, you try to motivate students to do their best work. You may appeal to their inner selves, hoping that they will do an assignment to please themselves, because they enjoy it, or to meet a challenge. In other words, you appeal to students' **intrinsic motivations**. However, not all students are intrinsically motivated, so we also use a range of **extrinsic motivations**. These include stars on a paper, letter grades, special treatment (a party or time off to do something a student wants to do on his or her own), and even prizes. Part of the artistry of teaching is in knowing when to use intrinsic motivators and when to use extrinsic motivators. Part of the science of teaching is in determining which ones to use on specific students. (See Cretu 2003 for an interesting treatment on the topic.)

Choosing Technology Wisely

It may surprise you, but we consider the use of high-tech equipment in the classroom an extrinsic motivator. Why? Children and adolescents view the use of personal computers and other peripheral equipment as a game or challenge. That qualifies technology as an external motivator. Because students enjoy computer use so much, it's important to make sure the time spent on computers is truly worthwhile. Our concern is that you be aware of the role that your decisions will play in using technology to enhance student learning and excitement in the classroom.

Our main concern is that you analyze each technology for its potential to help your students achieve their maximum potential. You will make decisions for your students and perhaps others as you plan for the appropriate integration of any technology as an *instructional tool*. All the modern and not-so-modern technologies are simply tools that make the process of learning a bit more efficient. This book offers references available on the World Wide Web and suggests Web-based reflective activities. To learn more about using technology in your classes, consult resources such as Mark and Cindy Grabe's *Integrating Technology for Meaningful Learning* (2007).

Obviously, the full potential of the available technological resources has yet to be reached in the schools. We predict that school reform will focus on expanding learning opportunities through electronic media. And, just think, you are on stage as the excitement commences.

TECHNOLOGY INSIGHT

Internet Safety and Security: Acceptable Use Policies

Many schools and other public institutions have developed guidelines for the appropriate use of Internet resources for their constituents. The guidelines are most often referred to as Acceptable Use Policies, or AUPs.

A school's AUP describes the legal rights and responsibilities of the school itself, as well as a description of the responsibilities of those who make use of Internet resources through the school's computers and Internet connections. The document often also describes the penalties associated with violating the school's AUP.

The World Wide Web has some great AUP resources (try searching Google or Yahoo! using the term "Acceptable Use Policy"). A particularly good resource on the subject of AUPs and Internet safety is WWW4Teachers, supported by the University of Kansas, at **http://www.4teachers.org/4teachers/intech/AUP.shtml**.

Regardless of any local AUPs, keep in mind that the World Wide Web is a public forum; much of the information available is not reviewed or edited and may be of questionable use to you professionally.

Teaching as Reflection and Problem Solving

Reflective teaching stems from John Dewey's concept of "reflective inquiry" (Dewey 1998). Dewey viewed the student as an inquirer and an active participant in learning. He assumed that the interaction of subject matter and method of inquiry could not be ignored in schooling. Following this line of thinking, the reflective teacher makes decisions based on a problem-solving paradigm. In other words, problems are not viewed as obstacles to overcome, but as opportunities to be met. Teachers reflect on problems, and as part of a learning community, they call on others to reflect on identified problems. In such cases, the staff collectively lists a series of alternatives that they can take. Ultimately, they narrow such lists to sets of actions that are ethical, just, and educationally sound.

Now you might be thinking, "Isn't a lot of problem solving a matter of using intuition?" Actually, it is not. Intuition is subjective and spontaneous. Although reflective teachers may rely on past experiences to solve problems, they tend to make decisions on what they know about the learner and the content to be mastered. The reflective teacher is deliberate, rational, and organized (see Distad and Brownstein 2004).

Reflective teachers incorporate social aspects in their instructional planning. They cognitively make the necessary adjustments in their instruction so that all students have an opportunity for success. The reflective teacher also questions others' decisions that may have negative social impact. For example, in 2001 the parents of students attending a middle school in Palo Alto, California, were asked to purchase their sixth-graders $2,000 laptop computers ("Calif. School" 2001). Such a policy would not have been implemented if the teachers and administrators of that school had been the least reflective on the negative economic impact it would have on family budgets. Even Palo Alto, a generally prosperous community, has a significant number of families at the poverty line. (See Ancess 2000 for an interesting case study along these lines.) The box on page 21 sums up the major characteristics of reflective teachers.

Do you think of air traffic controller as a challenging, fast-paced job? As a classroom teacher, you'll be exceeding air traffic controllers in the number of decisions made per day. As we stress in Chapter 6, a large number of decisions will be made as a consequence of your personal observations of the class—who is doing what, what is being done, what you can anticipate. You are the primary decision maker on how your classroom is organized and managed for instruction.

As you develop the artistry and science of teaching, you will become more aware of how your decisions affect the intellectual and attitudinal development of your students. You alone make the decision to plan, to be organized and well prepared. As national and state standards become more broadly incorporated into curriculum designs, you will find that some of your control over content will be modified. But effective teaching will always involve dynamic interactions between and among teachers and administrators, teachers and teachers, teachers and parents, teachers and learners, and learners and learners, in which all participants are continuously making decisions—including the all-important decision, made by your student, to embrace learning.

SECTION 3: MEETING MANDATED PROFESSIONAL STANDARDS

Today's schools and teachers are subject to increasing public scrutiny and criticism. One criticism that you will undoubtedly hear is "Teachers are

key ideas

- Care about students.
- Understand the social context of schooling.
- Question assumptions.
- Know content.
- Identify problems or issues.
- Collect relevant data.
- Construct a plan of operation.
- Use many instructional strategies.
- Practice problem-solving strategies.
- Think prospectively and retrospectively.
- Realize that reflection is cyclical.
- Evaluate the results and processes used.

VIDEO case

Sit in on the roundtable discussion "Foundations: Aligning Instruction with Federal Legislation" with school principal Joseph Petner. What pros and cons do faculty members present about recent legislation? How can you maximize the pros and minimize the cons in your own teaching?

not prepared to teach." Sometimes those expressing this opinion are uninformed persons with hidden political agendas or advocates of some magic educational elixir. At this point in your educational career, however, you can feel confident that you are constructing a very firm knowledge base that has been soundly validated through empirical studies. The material in this book gives you prerequisite knowledge about instructional techniques and issues from which you will be able to make reasoned and reflective choices. Additionally, you will gain the background to expand your basic understandings by enrolling in graduate courses that are curriculum or instruction related. We hope to give you some prerequisite knowledge on how to incorporate content standards that have been legislated into use.

In 2001, P.L. 107-110, the No Child Left Behind Act (or NCLB), was passed by the U.S. Congress and signed into law by President George W. Bush. In it, a new element—*highly qualified teacher*—was mandated. The term is a semantic triumph, for who would be against highly qualified teachers? States have long had teacher education programs that required teachers to hold BAs, MAs, or completion of fifth-year programs as the academic basis for entering a classroom.

With NCLB in effect, teacher tests will be a new norm. Let us quickly look at five new or established organizations or governing bodies that will have some impact on your entry-level preparation and subsequent professional development.

State Teacher Education Standards As a consequence of NCLB, each state has generated its own set of criteria to meet the national mandate. Michigan has a fourteen-page document specifying criteria for teacher education programs. Arizona has a multiple-choice teacher test called the Arizona Educator Proficiency Assessment. Nearly all states have checklists of behaviors that are deemed appropriate for new teachers. Suffice it to say that teacher testing is a way of life as of this writing.

National Council for Accreditation of Teacher Education (NCATE)

The NCATE establishes criteria for accrediting teacher education programs. Each institution completes a very detailed report showing how it meets the various conditions. The five points below affect your program of studies, as you must show evidence of meeting these criteria.

1. You must pass a state licensure examination of content knowledge.
2. You must pass at least one additional assessment of content knowledge.
3. You will be assessed for your ability to plan instruction.
4. Your clinical practice will be thoroughly evaluated.
5. You must demonstrate that your teaching has a positive effect on student learning.

The Praxis Series   Education Testing Services (ETS) now generates a series of education-related tests called Praxis. Over forty states require these assessments, which are used to determine your worthiness to obtain a teaching credential. Both content and instructional strategies are tested.

American Association of Colleges of Teacher Education (AACTE)

The AACTE has developed its own Standards-Based Teacher Education Project (STEP). This project is based on the following three principles.

1. Teachers must know the subjects they are teaching.
2. Teachers must know how to teach students to learn at high levels.
3. Teachers must know how to monitor and assess how well students are learning.

National Board for Professional Teaching Standards (NBPTS)   There

is yet one more hurdle to gain top-level professional recognition. The NBPTS came into being as a consequence of the Carnegie Task Force on Teaching as a Profession in 1989. The NBPTS has established both content and instructional standards for the profession, which are based on the following five "core propositions."

1. Teachers are committed to students and their learning.
2. Teachers know the subjects they teach and how to teach those subjects to students.
3. Teachers are responsible for managing and monitoring student learning.
4. Teachers think systematically about their practice and learn from experience.
5. Teachers are members of learning communities.

Obtaining NBPTS certification is a rigorous endeavor, and most states add a handsome bonus to teachers' salaries for those who pass muster. At least one research study shows that teachers in grades 3 through 6 in Arizona who were NBPTS certified tended to be more effective in terms of student achievement (Vandervoort, Amrein-Beardsley, and Berliner 2004).

As you can see, much is expected of professional teachers, both from within the occupation and outside it. In keeping with our goal of providing you with a basic core of technical aspects of teaching to make your entry into the classroom an informed one, the inside cover of this textbook lists a set of generic standards and where in this textbook you will gain the entry-level knowledge to meet them.

reflect | **A Closing Reflection**

- "Harm no one." How does this motto apply to teacher decision making?
- Plan a short study to determine how many decisions a teacher makes in a day.
- What motivational techniques are espoused in your teacher education program?
- How would being a reflective teacher affect your plans to teach?
- How does your teacher education meet the various professional standards?
- Examine the full Code of Ethics (at http://www.nea.org/code.html) and compare those statements to the enabling clauses of your state teacher standards.
- To what extent do mandated state teaching standards advance or inhibit teacher professionalism?

summary

1. Teaching is a profession with its own body of knowledge, techniques, internal organization, and code of ethics.
2. Schooling takes place within many contexts, including social, emotional, educational, and collegial or professional.
3. Teaching is a science because it requires knowledge of technique. It is also an art because it requires decision making.
4. Effective teachers take responsibility for their decisions.
5. Teachers should select content and processes on the basis of developmental appropriateness and educational equity.
6. For both teachers and students, intrinsic motivation comes from within, and extrinsic motivation comes from outside sources.
7. Teachers should employ careful decision making in evaluating and using technology.
8. Teacher education standards are in a state of flux.

print resources

Benninga, J. S. *Moral and Ethical Issues in Teacher Education. ERIC Digest.* ERIC Clearinghouse on Teaching and Teacher Education. Washington, DC: EDO-SP-2003-03, 4 pp.

This short document is a must-read statement on the general topic of moral and ethical issues in teaching.

Danielson, C. *Enhancing Professional Practice: A Framework for Teaching.* Alexandria, VA: Association for Supervision and Curriculum Development, 1996, 140 pp.

Charlotte Danielson describes twenty-two broad components for successful teaching. In one sense, this book summarizes the spectrum of teacher education standards.

Michie, G. *See You When We Get There: Teaching for Change in Urban Schools.* New York: Teachers College Press, 2005, 224 pp.

An essential book for those who will teach in inner-city schools. The author weaves personal experience with relevant vignettes.

Purkey, W. W., and J. M. Novak. *Inviting School Success: A Self-Concept Approach to Teaching Learning, and Democratic Practice* (3rd edition). Belmont, CA: Wadsworth, 1996, 222 pp.

This little book might be the most important statement about positive school interactions that you ever read. We invite every middle school and high school teacher to read it.

Stronge, J. H., P. D. Tucker, and J. L. Hindman. *Handbook for Qualities of Effective Teachers.* Alexandria, VA: Association for Supervision and Curriculum Development, 2005, 233 pp.

If you are seeking a set of checklists for classroom observations, planning, management, organizational skills, and more, then this is your resource.

Thomas, D. B., editor. *Reflective Teaching: A Bridge to Learning.* Ann Arbor, MI: Pierian, 2004, 176 pp.

This book has a collection of papers that expands the concept of reflective teaching.

INTERNET RESOURCES

Go to the website for this book to find live links to resources related to this chapter.

> The U.S. Department of Education provides an enormous listing of education-related Internet resources.
> **http://www.ed.gov/**

> The two major teachers' organizations in the United States, the American Federation of Teachers and the National Education Association, each maintains a website devoted to a variety of issues of interest to K–12 teachers.
> **http://www.aft.org**
> **http://www.nea.org**

> Teachers.net is a commercial resource for teachers. The site includes a wide variety of professional development opportunities and resources from preschool to adult education.
> **http://www.teachers.net/**

References

Ancess, A. "The Reciprocal Influence of Teacher Learning, Teaching Practice, School Restructuring, and Student Learning." *Teachers College Record* 102(3) (2000): 590–619.

Bloom, B. S. "The 2 Sigma Problem: The Search for Methods of Group Instruction as Effective as One-to-One Tutoring." *Educational Researcher* 13(6) (1984): 4–16.

Brouwers, A., and W. Tomie. "A Longitudinal Study of Teacher Burnout and Perceived Self-Efficacy in Classroom Management." *Teaching and Teacher Education* 16(2) (2000): 239–253

"Calif. School Rethinks Mandatory Laptops." *USA Today*, November 5, 2001, p. 11A.

Carnevale, A. P. "Investing in Human Capital." *School Administrator* 58(3) (2001): 32–35.

Comte-Sponville, A. *A Small Treatise on the Great Virtues* (translated by Catherine Temerson). New York: Metropolitan, 2001.

Cretu, D. "Students' Motivation in Class." *Thinking Classroom* 4(2) (April 2003): 21–28.

Dewey, J. *How We Think* (revised and expanded edition). Boston: Houghton Mifflin, 1998. (Originally published in 1910 and republished in 1933 as *How We Think, A Restatement of the Relation of Reflective Thinking to the Educative Process*, by D. C. Heath, Boston.)

Distad, L. S., and J. C. Brownstein. *Talking Teaching: Implementing Reflective Practice in Groups*. Lanham, MD: Scarecrow Education, 2004.

Eisner, E. W. "Artistry in Education." *Scandinavian Journal of Educational Research* 47(3) (July 2003): 373–384.

Grabe, M., and C. Grabe. *Integrating Technology for Meaningful Learning* (5th edition). Boston: Houghton Mifflin, 2007.

Israel, G. D., L. J. Beaulieu, and G. Hartless. "The Influence of Family and Community Social Capital on Educational Achievement." *Rural Sociology* 66(1) (2001): 43–68.

Kluckhohn, C. *Mirror for Man: The Relation of Anthropology to Modern Life*. New York: Whittlesey House, 1949.

Lashway, L. *Trends in School Leadership. ERIC Digest*. ERIC Clearinghouse on Educational Management, Eugene, OR: EDO-EA-02-09, 2002.

Livingston, A., and J. Wirt. *The Condition of Education 2004 in Brief* (NCES 2004-076). U.S. Department of Education, National Center for Education Statistics. Washington, DC: U.S. Government Printing Office, 2004.

Margolis, H., and P. P. McCabe. "Self-Efficacy: A Key to Improving the Motivation of Struggling Learners." *Preventing School Failure* 47(4) (Summer 2003): 162–169.

Maslow, A. *Motivation and Personality* (2nd edition). New York: Harper and Row, 1970.

National Commission on Excellence in Education. *A Nation at Risk: The Imperative for Educational Reform*. Washington, DC: Author, 1983.

National Education Association, *Code of Ethics of the Education Profession*. Washington, DC: Author, 1964, 1975. http://www.nea.org/code.html. (Adopted by the NEA 1975 Representative Assembly.)

Noddings, N. *Educating Moral People: A Caring Alternative to Character Education*. New York: Teachers College Press, 2002.

Orlich, D. C. "Education Reform and Limits to Student Achievement." *Phi Delta Kappan* 81(6) (2000): 468–472.

P.L. 107-110, "No Child Left Behind Act of 2001." Washington, DC: 107th Congress, 1st Session, January 8, 2002.

Purkey, W. W., and J. M. Novak. *Inviting School Success: A Self-Concept Approach to Teaching, Learning and Democratic Practice* (3rd edition). Belmont, CA: Wadsworth, 1996.

Putnam, R. D. *Bowling Alone: The Collapse and Revival of American Community*. New York: Simon and Schuster, 2000.

Read, D. A., and S. B. Simon, editors. *Humanistic Education Sourcebook*. Englewood Cliffs, NJ: Prentice Hall, 1975.

Stanley, P. H., and W. W. Purkey. *Abstracts of Published Research Articles, Dissertations, and Master Theses Concerning Invitational Theory and Practice*, 2001. ED 450 329

U.S. Department of Education. *Mini Digest of Education Statistics 1997*. http://nces.gov. See Table 6.

U.S. Department of Education. *Mini Digest of Education Statistics 1999*. http://nces.gov. See Figure 3.

U.S. Department of Education. *Projections of Education Statistics to 2008*. http://nces.ed.gov/pubs98/. See Tables 1, B8, 34, 37, and chap. 6.

U.S. Department of Education. National Center for Education Statistics. *The Condition of Education 1997*. NCES 97-388. Washington, DC: U.S. Government Printing Office, 1997.

Vandevoort, L. G., A. Amrein-Beardsley, and D. C. Berliner. "National Board Certified Teachers and Their Students' Achievement." *Education Policy Analysis Archives* 12(46) (September 8, 2004). Retrieved July 13, 2005, from http://epaa.asu.edu/epaa/v12n46/.

Williams, J. S. "Why Great Teachers Stay." *Educational Leadership* 60(8) (May 2003): 71–74.

Woolfolk-Hoy, A., and W. K. Hoy. *Instructional Leadership: A Learning-Centered Guide*. Needham Heights, MA: Allyn and Bacon/Longman, 2003.

The Big Picture in Your Classroom: Focusing the Instruction in a Social Kaleidoscope

1

A HOLISTIC VIEW OF INSTRUCTION

The Holistic Instructional Cycle

Bases for Instructional Decision Making

2

THREE PERSPECTIVES ON INSTRUCTIONAL DECISION MAKING

Developmental Perspective

Behavioral Perspective

Cognitive Perspective

Active Learning

3

EDUCATIONAL EQUITY AS THE BIG PICTURE

Ethnic Diversity

Racial and Socioeconomic Diversity

Physical Diversity

Multicultural Perspectives

Language Diversity

Ability Diversity: Who Is Exceptional?

Encouraging Equity in the Classroom
    Environment

Gender Equity: Awareness of Bias

Jim completed a degree in business administration, worked a few years in the private sector, and then concluded that his calling was teaching. As he sat in his final education class, he wondered why he was being exposed to so many different instructional and learning perspectives. Then, while observing a classroom prior to student teaching, a *gestalt*-type event took place. It became very clear to him why teachers needed to know several different learning models. The master teacher was applying multiple instructional models and making use of a variety of psychological theories as the lessons were taught.

When Jim assumed his initial teaching position and was assigned to his own class, he had some experience, professional knowledge, and educational theory on which to base his instructional decisions. More important, as Jim planned for various lessons, he considered the "big picture" in the planning, with details unfolding in the process. As he gained more professional skills and confidence, his teaching subtly changed to incorporate newly learned ideas and practices.

In Chapter 1, you got an overview of the teaching profession and some of the external forces at work on the classroom. Now let's go inside the classroom and explore the learning frameworks and other considerations that directly influence your instructional decision making. As you read, think about how you would respond to the following questions.

- How do I envision a dynamic instructional cycle?
- How might learning perspectives affect my instructional decisions?
- How do I ensure instructional equity for every student?

SECTION 1: A HOLISTIC VIEW OF INSTRUCTION

The Holistic Instructional Cycle

As Jim realized, dynamic instruction must be viewed as a *grand picture*, as well as a collection of details. This is the notion of a **holistic instructional view**. As a teacher, you simultaneously shift back and forth from the big picture that you have for your students to the specific parts that you want mastered. This thinking begins on the first day of school.

By thinking about several instructional aspects at once, you complete the holistic picture. That is, you are considering variables that can affect both your teaching and the students' learning. Your vision helps you to be more organized and systematic. As this chapter unfolds, you'll realize how the interaction of theory and practice are complementary to all teaching acts. For example, this textbook emphasizes the procedural, or technical, aspects of instruction. Taken collectively, all ten chapters interact with the attitudinal and psychological components of teaching plus that all-important learner. Figure 2.1 illustrates this phenomenon, as does the Key Ideas box on page 30.

Holistic teaching: big picture + detailed implementation

Bases for Instructional Decision Making

Observe the dynamic interaction that takes place between the four elements in Figure 2.1. Each element informs the others.

FIGURE 2.1

A Holistic Model of Instruction

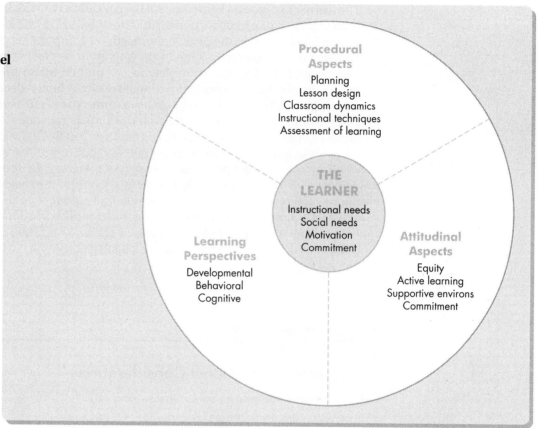

The main point is that you try to envision the entire teaching scenario before you ever begin teaching it. For example, when you begin a new unit of instruction, you want to establish some common experience for the entire class. Establishing common experiences is going to be a very important part of your instructional planning as uniform and mandatory educational standards are fully implemented. We will revisit this issue later in Chapter 3.

You might decide to show a video or take the class to the computer center to "surf the Web." Then, after making this decision, you ask yourself, "What purpose does this introductory activity have to do with the lesson as a whole?" You also ask yourself what big ideas you are trying to stress in this unit. Or you might be working with a team of teachers, and as a group you'll brainstorm ideas. In addition, you need to consider the learning perspective from which you might approach either the entire class or subgroups within the class. You also need to consider the content to be learned. The easy part of teaching is to cover content. The hard part is deciding what is to be covered (or deleted), how fast, by whom, and to what degree of depth. In the Key Ideas box on page 30, we list some of the big-picture considerations that you must make to be an effective instructor.

Obviously, the learner and the learner's needs are always at the center of this model. It is for the learner that you use different instructional techniques.

The learner's successes help to create the conditions by which all the elements coalesce. As you progress through this textbook, you will be provided with in-depth coverage on the principal procedural components of Figure 2.1.

Even though you are systematic in your approach to instruction, you must still respond flexibly and effectively to the numerous on-the-spot decisions that you make during every instructional activity. A final reflection before leaving the holistic model: Most schools have some type of curriculum guide. They range from specific, scripted daily guides to general statements about standards or state-required academic content. During the holistic phase of planning, these guides need to be examined and addressed because the students will be assessed at set points in their school lives. Yes, the tests do affect what is taught. Of course, we firmly believe it should be the reverse—that what is taught affects what is tested. But that policy is not for us to decide just yet.

The manner in which you approach a specific concept or standard will have some social-psychological basis. Let's look at three such theoretical perspectives that profoundly influence instruction.

key ideas

Holistic Instructional Considerations

- What is my instructional purpose or goal?
- Who are the learners?
- How will I cover the content?
- What management decisions must I make?
- What techniques or processes do I use?
- How will I share responsibilities with others?
- What instructional resources do we have?
- What special student considerations must I take into account?
- How can I ensure instructional equity?
- How will I assess learning?

reflect

- Describe a time in your teacher education when you suddenly saw the big picture of what you were learning. How did the big picture and the smaller elements fit together?

- Think about an area in which you anticipate teaching. What would be the big picture for one unit? What are some smaller ways to achieve the holistic goal?

SECTION 2: THREE PERSPECTIVES ON INSTRUCTIONAL DECISION MAKING

From your study of educational psychology, you know that there are several learning theories or perspectives that can guide teaching and learning. Three perspectives in particular tend to have a great impact on what is taught and how it is presented: the *developmental, behavioral,* and *cognitive* perspectives. The specific teaching strategies that you use probably will be based on one of these three or on an **eclectic** model—one that borrows or mixes approaches. Let's briefly explore how learning theories apply to instructional strategies. You can refer to a standard educational psychology text for more detailed information about each theory.

Developmental Perspective

Piaget's Developmental Stages   A very popular teaching and learning model is the *developmental* approach, most often associated with Jean Piaget (1896–1980). This model assumes that humans develop intellectually in various overlapping stages. In Piaget's model (1969), there are four stages or periods of development—the **sensorimotor stage**, from birth to two years; the **preoperational stage**, from two to eight years; the **concrete operational stage**, from eight to eleven years; and the **formal operations stage**, from eleven to fifteen years and up. The last stage is what schools attempt to reach, what we loosely call the "thinking and analyzing stage." However, the bulk of students in middle and high school are still at the concrete operational stage, and thus they require many illustrations, models, pictures, and activities. The developmental stages in Piaget's model are not fixed for any one individual or group; instead, they tend to overlap. In the middle school grades, for example, you will find a wide range of developmental levels, from students who are not yet in the early concrete operational stage to students who have already reached the formal stage. High school students also show a range of intellectual development. Additionally, the developmental stages are not uniformly attained for individuals within different academic disciplines: An individual might be at the formal stage in the social sciences, but only at the concrete stage in mathematics.

Piaget: Age-based, but possibly overlapping, thinking stages

For intellectual growth to occur, teachers must provide students with key experiences or activities.

Vygotsky's Socially Mediated Learning   Another well-respected learning theory is one proposed by Lev Vygotsky (1896–1934). (You'll see his name spelled "Vygotskii" sometimes.) His **schema**, or model, of intellectual growth centers not on developmental stages but on what he terms the zone of proximal development and on patterns of social interaction (Vygotsky 1962).

The **zone of proximal development** is the difference between the intellectual level a child can reach on his or her own and the level he or she can potentially reach if aided by an expert peer or adult. How do you know where a given child's zone falls? You find out somewhat by trial and error. When your instruction is appropriate for the child's zone, learning occurs rather rapidly. Instruction outside the zone is not effective.

In Vygotsky's theory, there are no maturation levels such as those implied by Piaget's stages of growth. If a child does not learn some concept, according to Piaget's theory, the child was not developmentally ready. For a Vygotskian, the instruction was outside the child's zone of proximal development. (See Shayer and Adey 2002 for an excellent discussion.)

Vygotsky: what the child can learn with adult's help

The second aspect of Vygotsky's theory is that learning has a social quality. As a child listens to a discussion, the child can think along. Eventually, the child will **internalize** the ideas and can then work individually. Social interaction is a key to learning. Piaget and Albert Bandura (1977, 1997) also observed this quality (see Becker and Varelas 2001).

Social interaction is key.

Implications for Instructional Decision Making In Piaget's theory, two concepts for instructional effectiveness are critical: age and individual appropriateness (see Adey and Shayer 1994; Bredekamp 1997; Shayer and Adey 2002). If you subscribe to Piaget's stages of growth, then you will attempt to find age-appropriate materials. That means for grade 3 you need materials that can be mastered by nine- or ten-year-olds. The same idea would apply to instructing sixteen-year-old high school sophomores.

As a Piagetian, you would first introduce some activity that has learning value. After the children experience the activity, you would label the concept being taught so that your students could understand the experience and the formal term together. For example, if you were teaching the concept of time zones, you might show students a map of the United States and tell them what time it is in various cities. Then you would have the children come to some conclusion about what happens to times as you move from east to west or vice versa. Once students had gained some more experience with this exercise, you would label the zones Eastern, Central, Rocky Mountain, and Pacific.

How would you approach the time zone lesson using Vygotsky's model? First, you would assess your students' zone of proximal development to determine whether introducing the concept would be worthwhile or futile. In the early primary grades, for example, you can teach children how to tell time, but the concept of time zones is simply beyond their zone of proximal development. No matter how hard you might try to teach the concept, the children would not understand it.

But if the children were ready, say by the sixth or seventh grade, you probably would divide the class into small discussion groups and provide each team with maps, markers, and time information for various cities. The groups would be actively and socially involved in trying to visualize some pattern related to times. Finally, with your help, one group would come to the conclusion that there are four distinct time zones in the continental United States. Each group would share this finding. Finally, each learner would understand the concept on an individual basis.

But suppose two students still could not solve time zone problems alone. What would you do then? You would continue the social interaction aspect by assigning peer tutors to the students who had not mastered the time zone concept and hope that further social interaction would complete the learning cycle.

Table 2.1 shows an array of ages, grades, and developmental levels. Let us assume that you want to introduce a concept that is clearly at a formal level of thinking. The data in Table 2.1 show that, even at the junior and senior years of high school, a large percentage of the students are not yet at that cognitive level. In Chapter 5, we illustrate some techniques that will help you teach difficult concepts.

But at this point we simply want you to be aware of planning for instruction. We also encourage you to use reflective thought about providing instruction and experiences at the appropriate cognitive levels where the bulk of your students may reside. (See also Shayer and Adey 1981.)

Providing experiences essential in both theories

TABLE 2.1

Age	Grade	Intuition (a)	Entry Concrete (b)	Advanced Concrete (a)	Entry Formal (b)	Middle Formal (b)
5.5	P	78	22			
6	K	68	27	5		
7	1	35	55	10		
8	2	25	55	20		
9	3	15	55	30		
10	4	12	52	35	1	
11	5	6	49	40	5	
12	6–7	5	32	51	12	
13	7–8	2	34	44	14	6
14	8–9	1	32	43	15	9
15	9–10	1	15	53	18	13
16	10–11	1	13	50	17	19
16–17	11–12	3	19	47	19	12
17–18	12	1	15	50	15	19
Adult	—	20	22	26	17	15

Percentage of Students at Piaget's Cognitive Levels

1. Level a in each category is composed of children who have just begun to manifest one or two of that level's reasoning schemes, whereas level b refers to children manifesting half a dozen or more reasoning schemes.
SOURCE: Table derived by Herman T. Epstein, personal communication, June 8, 1999. Sources used are J. Smedslund, *Concrete Reasoning: A Study of Intellectual Development* (Lafayette, IN: Child Development Publications of the Society for Research in Child Development, 1964); P. Arlin, personal communication with H. T. Epstein; T. D. Wei et al. "Piaget's Concept of Classification: A Comparative Study of Socially Disadvantaged and Middle-Class Young Children," *Child Development* 42 (1971): 919–924; J. W. Renner, D. G. Stafford, A. E. Lawson, J. W. McKinnon, F. E. Friot, and D. H. Kellogg, *Research, Teaching and Learning with the Piaget Model* (Norman: University of Oklahoma Press, 1976); M. Shayer and P. Adey, *Towards a Science of Science Teaching* (London: Heinemann, 1981). Permission to reprint granted by Dr. Herman T. Epstein. (For a detailed discussion, see Herman T. Epstein, "Biopsychological Aspects of Memory and Education," in *Advances in Psychology Research*, Volume 11, S. P. Shohov, editor, New York: Nova, pp. 181–186.)

reFLeCT
- Prepare a chart that illustrates the key elements of Piaget's and Vygotsky's theories. Where are they different? Where are they similar?
- Examine a school district curriculum guide for some selected grade level. Do you find terms such as *developmental* or *age appropriate* in the guide? If so, how are they used?

Behavioral Perspective

Overview   According to the **behavioral perspective**, learning can be defined as an observable change in behavior. The modern behavioral movement was initiated by B. F. Skinner (1938). However, Ralph W. Tyler (1949), with his use of behavioral objectives to guide lesson design, instituted a major educational application of behaviorism. One might even be so bold as to suggest that the twenty-first century's enthusiasm for standards and accountability is simply an extension of Tyler's behavioral objectives. Behaviorism is usually aimed at students who display some inappropriate behavior or who have emotional disorders. Behaviorism is a very complex model, with many ramifications and applications to life outside of education. One element of the theory is **transfer of learning**. This term refers to the act of **applying** something learned in some specific situation to a novel or new setting. For example, you have just completed instruction on ratios. One of your students comes up to you and says, "Do you realize it is cheaper per ounce to buy a twenty-ounce bottle of soda pop than a ten-ounce bottle?" You ask the student to tell you more. The student then shows how, by setting up ratios to determine per-ounce costs, the relative unit values can be computed. You smile! (We will discuss this technique in detail, as it relates to behavioral management, in Chapter 6.)

Direct Instruction   When you apply behavioral theory to instruction, you will find yourself establishing specific learning objectives and building a sequence of learning activities that proceed from simple to more complex. More than likely, you will adopt a teaching model that is called **direct instruction** (see Carnine 2000). This model has its foundations embedded in behavioral principles. It is a popular technique, and we illustrate it here as an application of the behavioral perspective. (Also do realize that many "constructivist" strategies, such as cooperative learning groups, are based on behavioral assumptions and implications.)

Direct instruction is often called "whole-group" or "teacher-led" instruction. Basically, the technique involves academic focus, provides few optional choices for student-initiated activities, tends to be large-group oriented, and tends to emphasize factual knowledge. In response to those who have criticized direct instruction as being oriented toward rote learning, one study showed that elementary school pupils taught via direct instruction showed progress in the higher-order intellectual areas associated with problem solving (Elliott, Busse and Shapiro 1999). A review of the research indicates that direct instruction does transfer skills across a broad range of learners and

Direct instruction relies on the application of behavioral principles.

Not a rigid, low-level instructional model

subject areas (Adams and Engelmann 1996). The technique is used to increase on-task learning time, thinking skills, problem solving, computer literacy, writing skills, and science learning. Sara G. Tarver (2003) and others provide a rather comprehensive review of issues relating to direct instruction that is worth your time to examine.

Martin A. Kozloff et al. (2001) summarize steps for using the technique effectively. These steps and the strengths of the system are listed in the Key Ideas box and the box on this page.

Key Ideas

Strengths of Direct Instruction

- Content is delivered to entire class.
- Teacher controls focus of attention.
- Process maximizes available time.
- Feedback assesses class understanding of learning.
- Teacher focuses on class objectives.
- Teacher provides clarity through explanations.
- Less teacher preparation is required.
- All students work on same task.

Steps for Direct Instruction

1. Review and check previous work.
2. Present new material in small units.
3. Provide for guided practice.
4. Provide for feedback and correctives.
5. Supervise independent seat-work.
6. Review concepts every week and every month.

Programmed Instruction   When you use computer-assisted instruction, the basic learning theory supporting the technique is grounded in the behaviorist concept of **programmed instruction**. That technique provides for small, discrete increments of instruction plus immediate reinforcement for correct responses. When you use lessons that are subdivided into achievable components or modules, you use behavioral principles. We will expand on these topics in Chapters 3 and 4.

Cognitive Perspective

Cognitive Psychology   We want to provide you with a framework for analyzing any instructional model or curriculum to discover its theoretical basis.

You can then align your teaching methods with the content, thereby helping your students be more successful learners. So far we have briefly explored selected aspects of the developmental and behavioral theoretical perspectives that will affect your instructional decision making.

Over the past several years, a school of thought known as **cognitive psychology** has emerged. The goal of this model is to develop student academic and thinking skills from a novice level to a more expert level. Obviously, it takes maturity and time for this transition to occur. One way to help it along is to teach students how to think about thinking and how to make plans to learn new information more efficiently.

A second major goal of cognitive psychology advocates is to provide adequate experiences in which students structure the learning and teaching themselves. Obviously, students will need to have access to knowledge, know how to organize it, and be self-motivated to learn. The box below gives a quick overview of the cognitive model (from Ashman and Conway 1993).

Move students to expert level; teach students about thinking.

Some Principles of the Cognitive Model of Instruction

- Students engage in active learning and problem solving.
- Students use a wide range of learning strategies.
- Time is allocated for students to apply new skills.
- Responsibility for learning and problem solving is transferred from teacher to student.
- Strategies to be learned by students are clearly specified.
- Rate of student learning is determined by the teacher.
- Teacher is responsible for instructional decisions.

Tips for Cognitive Instruction   As you examine the list in the box above, you will undoubtedly note that some of these principles overlap with those of other learning theories. Further, you might even infer that school environments play a major role in motivating students to become active learners. Yes, they do, and there are some interactive elements in all learning theories. But what strategies should you use to incorporate cognitive ideas into your teaching? Let's just list a few that are used in **information processing**.

The first process is one called **mnemonics**—the use of some memory-aiding device. A mnemonic device commonly used in mathematics is "Please Excuse My Dear Aunt Sally," which reminds students that in algebraic operations the correct order is Parentheses, Exponents, Multiply, Divide, Add, Subtract. Surely you have used mnemonic devices to remember a series or chain of events.

A second strategy is to create visual or graphic organizers such as charts or time lines. Enter a middle school history class, and you will probably see a time line skirting the entire perimeter of the classroom. This helps students visually place historical events into order. Or look back at the beginning of each chapter in this book, where we provide a concept map. This tool is an information-processing device to help you learn and remember what each chapter covers.

Visualizing is a method often used in physical education as well. Participants try to understand just how they will dance, run a course, take a turn on a ski hill, or complete some game strategy. Visualization techniques are also very helpful when a student is setting up laboratory equipment or solving a multistep problem. Remember, it is your responsibility to teach your students how to use these cognitive devices. Linda Campbell (2003) provides over 100 instructional tips relating to cognitive science strategies.

Learner-Activated Instruction   One of the more difficult tasks you will face as a teacher is how to structure your classroom in a way that will let your students initiate learning. A major set of decisions that you will continuously make during your teaching career is how much instructional control to maintain. At one end of the instructional spectrum (see the box below) is **student-initiated learning** (or self-directed learning), where students determine how to reach the desired learning outcomes. A classroom that uses student-initiated learning will be a maze of activity: small groups, working groups, and individuals working on projects or activities simultaneously. There is little sequencing of instruction, and the teacher can be observed moving about the room acting as a prompter, question asker, clarifier—in short, a facilitator of learning. (See Agran et al. 2003 for details.)

How much control?

The Spectrum of Instructional Control

Student-Initiated Learning ◄ - - - - - - - - - ► Direct Instruction (Teacher Initiated)

At the other end is teacher-initiated instruction, or direct instruction, which we have already introduced. In this mode you will find an academic focus, little choice of activity for individual students, large-group instruction, and teacher domination over most curricular and instructional decisions. Table 2.2 contrasts these two approaches. The table is included for comparison purposes only; actual practice may be quite different.

In addition to student-initiated learning, there is also the practice of **independent study**. Independent study as described by John Marlowe (2000) is neither home-schooling nor in-class work. A successful independent study program allows students to work alone on a project or problem. The teacher helps the student plan, but the student has multiple options by which to accomplish the purposes prescribed. (See Alvarado & Herr (2003) and Tate (2003) for strategies associated with student-based learning.)

However, we must add a word of caution. With the advent of state and national standards that prescribe the curriculum, the perspective of student-initiated learning can be expected to decline precipitously. The highly prescriptive nature of state and national standards and high-stakes tests means that teachers will have little time to allow students to pursue their own interests. (See Amrein and Berliner 2002 for compelling evidence.) The use of independent learning outside of the classroom may be a possible solution for the coming dilemma.

TABLE 2.2

Student-Initiated Instruction Versus Direct Instruction	
Student-Initiated Instruction	Direct Instruction
Flexibly arranged furniture	Somewhat fixed arrangements
Emphasis on individual or small-group work	Delivery to entire class
Teacher as facilitator	Teacher as controller
Little concern about time	Time used efficiently
Varied assessments	Prompt delivery of feedback
Emphasis on exploration	Emphasis on fundamentals
Flexible classroom structure	Tight classroom structure
Simultaneous activities	All students on same task
Time-consuming preparation	Preparation time minimal

SOURCE: Adapted from Kohn 1996.

Obviously, there are many more facets to these two models of instructional control. That is where you come in. You make the decisions, for the most part, concerning how to structure the content and the processes by which it is delivered. Clearly, you need to examine several models of instruction. You need to identify the key features and relative strength of each model. We strongly support using as many different instructional techniques or methods as possible. Why? Because it helps you make decisions deliberately about the best instructional practice for any given content or student need, it helps you involve students actively, and it helps you choose the best level of instructional control for the situation at hand (see Cunningham et al. 2000 and Wells 2001).

Constructivist Theory and Practice   Constructivist philosophy, which has evolved over the last half of the twentieth century, is a subset of the cognitive perspective. As educators and others begin to seek a more student-centered instructional model, they tend to be drawn toward the *social-constructivist* camp summarized in the box on page 40. Views of that camp are summarized in the box also on page 40 (Anderson et al. 1994).

Constructivism is not a monolithic philosophy or methodology—it encompasses a range of beliefs and pedagogical approaches (see Bandura 1977, 1997; Gagnon and Collay 2001; Phillips 2000; Shapiro 2000). Our discussion here is of pure or theoretical constructivism; what you find in actual practice will cover an entire spectrum, including limited use, selected use, mixed use, and even inappropriate use of the concept. Here are some of its hallmarks.

1. Emphasis on Prior Experience   The foundation of the constructivist model is the idea that learners bring with them prior knowledge and beliefs. Learning builds on what learners have already constructed in other contexts.

VIDEO CASE

In the video "Constructivist Teaching in Action," you will see high school teacher Sarabinh Levy-Brightman prepare her students for a debate on Jeffersonian democracy. How would you describe her role in the process and the way she uses authority?

2. *Personal Construction of Meaning* Another hallmark of the model is that learners must construct what they learn. For example, just giving students vocabulary exercises in science and social studies may not result in their assimilating those concepts. The model calls for learners to be active. Rote memorization is antagonistic to the constructivist. However, learners can construct and use memorization strategies on their own. For example, constructivists hold that children can understand multiplication tables at once if they see them as arrays.

3. *Contextual and Shared Learning* The constructivist model requires concrete experiences rather than abstract presentations. In addition, learners deepen their knowledge by shared experiences. Cooperative learning and discussions are key strategies (see Chapter 8).

4. *Changing Roles for Teachers and Learners* In the constructivist model, learners and teachers learn from one another. Teachers look for signals from learners so that they may facilitate understanding. The teacher is not perceived as the sole authority; rather, the teacher facilitates learning, guiding and supporting learners' own construction of knowledge.

---

professional voices from the field

Véronique Paquette, Kenroy Elementary School, East Wenatchee, Washington

Integrating Curriculum/Active Teaching

When I began teaching, I would plan my curriculum on a daily basis. However, it became apparent that if I used a theme as a planning guide, my second-grade students would be immersed in not only reading and writing, but in observing how some many different topics are interrelated. This type of integration is not unusual; what makes my curriculum stand out is the choice of themes. All the themes studied during the school year are science based. Each unit builds upon the first unit, developing prior knowledge that encapsulates the entire year. The units focus on the various habitats and environments of the earth. We begin with the smallest environment, using insects and their life cycles as the basic theme. As the year progresses, we expand to the vastness of space.

Each unit is closely related and connects to the unit that follows. All of my students use reading, writing, mathematics, art, social studies, and computer technology to help reach an inquiry level of learning. Students' project-based units incorporate the critical areas of learning into their knowledge base, and we use graphic organizers aplenty. As the last months wane, we all discuss the connections that have occurred during the school year. My students do the summarizing, and they realize how important each piece of learning is to every life cycle.

Key Ideas

Tenets of Modern Social Constructivism

- Learning is dependent on the prior conceptions the learner brings to the experience.
- The learner must construct his or her own meaning.
- Learning is contextual.
- Learning is dependent on the shared understandings learners negotiate with others.
- Effective teaching involves understanding students' existing cognitive structures and providing appropriate learning activities to assist them.
- Teachers can use one or more key strategies to facilitate conceptual change, depending on the congruence of the concepts with student understanding and conceptualization.
- The key elements of conceptual change can be addressed by specific teaching methods.
- Greater emphasis is placed on "learning how to learn" than on accumulating facts. In terms of content, less is more.
- Students are motivated through modeling.

Reflect

- Are you leaning toward a particular perspective (developmental, behavioral, or cognitive) in your own teaching philosophy? If so, why? How will this inform your teaching?

Active Learning

Active learning encompasses a wide range of teaching strategies, all of which engage the learner in the actual instruction that takes place. Seat-work is passive. Students working on problems in small groups is active.

Regardless of your theoretical orientation, you probably will structure your classroom to enhance interaction between you and your students. You likely will set up a cheerful, inviting classroom, covering the walls with student work and posters appropriate for your class. Think of your classroom as a pleasant environment for work. School is the work of youth. And if you stress that students take pride in their work, you will get it. An active learning classroom is a learning community where all participate, including the teacher.

Active learning engages the learner and increases participation.

A Baker's Dozen Activities for the Active Learning Classroom

- Cooperative learning groups
- Inquiry-oriented activities
- Teacher demonstrations
- Teacher–student joint planning
- Use of hands-on, minds-on activities
- Use of Internet resources
- Use of instructional manipulatives
- Small-group discussions
- Student-conducted demonstrations
- Student-initiated projects
- Student portfolios
- Student presentations of work
- Student self-evaluations

reflect

- Compare direct instruction and active learning. How might you use them? How and when can each be effective?

section 3: educational equity as the big picture

The past two decades have seen a rise in the volume and rhetoric of arguments, pro and con, concerning diversity, multiculturalism, and other emerging social issues. No one is arguing that the racial and ethnic makeup of the United States and its schools is not diverse. However, the proper educational approach to take in light of this diversity is subject to debate. As a future teacher, you will need to consider various viewpoints before you weigh in on this debate. Awareness of student diversity is an important element of responsive instructional decision making. In this section, we spotlight some aspects of diversity and equity that will affect your instructional planning. In subsequent courses, your teacher education program will cover the topics in great detail.

As Arthur M. Schlesinger, Jr., so ably stated, "Our public schools in particular have been the great instruments of assimilation and the great means of forming an American identity. What students are taught in schools affects the way they will thereafter see and treat other Americans, the way they will thereafter conceive the purposes of the republic. The debate about the curriculum is a debate about what it means to be an American" (Schlesinger 1993, p. 17).

The diversity of our students is our most compelling strength and also our greatest challenge. Until our educational institutions evolve a strategy for maximizing the potential of all our youth, regardless of gender, race, ethnicity, or disabilities, we will have a country of haves and have-nots. This is an institutional challenge; in the meantime, teachers can make a difference on a personal level.

First you must understand clearly the many factors that will contribute to diversity in your classroom. During the 1995–1996 school year, for example, 33 percent of the students in U.S. central-city schools (grades K–12) were African American, and 25 percent were Hispanic (Wirt et al 1998). Of all children aged five to seventeen in U.S. schools, almost 19 percent speak a language other than English at home (NCES 2005-094). And, the children who speak a language other than English at home score below their classmates on standardized tests (NCES 97-472, p. 1).

The United States is an amalgam of many diverse ethnic, language, racial, and religious groups. Further diversity results from the broad spectrum of physical characteristics in the population (physical characteristics include gender, disabilities, physical dimensions, and traits). This diversity makes it difficult to define "a U.S. culture." Although the people of the United States may have a common root language and many shared values, we are truly a culturally plural society. As a society, we have both commonalities and differences; we are similar in some ways and different in many others. The question you will have to face as a teacher is this: Should the selection of instructional objectives and teaching strategies promote unity or exalt differences? Or should it do both?

Emphasize commonalities or differences?

Lest you conclude that diversity is a concern only for central-city schools, let's examine a bit of data from a small rural community in Washington State with a K–12 student enrollment of 529. There are Russian-Ukrainian students, Hispanic students, Native American students, and Asian students, accounting for almost one-half of the district's students. With the exception of the Native American students, English is not the language any of these students speaks at home.

One of our goals in this section is to broaden the scope of discussion on diversity. Accordingly, we address not just ethnicity and race, but also language diversity and physical diversity. Although we address these different facets of diversity as distinct topics, it is important to recognize their overlapping nature. Note that we focus on the concept of *equity* as being all encompassing. **Equity** means that all students are treated equally well and that school resources are shared equally. We realize that each topic in Section 3 has several books devoted to it, full courses taught in schools of education, and even areas of graduate specialization. We present these topics only to establish an overview. (See Corley 2003 for an interesting treatment of the topic.)

Equity: all students treated equally

Ethnic Diversity

Challenge—to balance diversity with achievement, norms

An ethnic population is a group of people classed according to common traits, customs, or social views (Cashmore 2004). Common ethnic traits include heritage, values, and rituals. *Heritage* refers to inherited cultural models for hous-

Inclusive classrooms welcome all learners.
© Evan Johnson/Jeroboam.

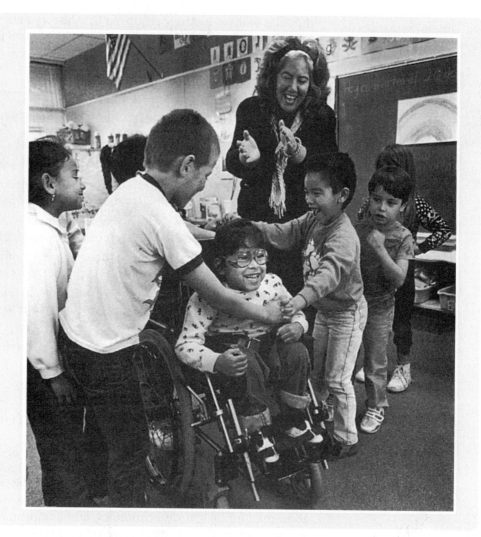

VIDEO CASE ◀◀ ▶ ▶▶

Watch second-grade students from diverse ethnic backgrounds collaborate on Japanese Kamishibai books in the Video Case "Diversity: Teaching in a Multiethnic Classroom." What impact do you think the activity has on the Japanese students in the class? What impact does it have on the non-Japanese students?

ing, foods, clothing, music, family structure, and education. Values include group behavioral norms, ethics, religious beliefs, and commonly held attitudes. An ethnic group's rituals frequently include aspects of festivals, dance, sports, medicine, and religion.

The challenge you face is to join a concern for ethnic diversity on the one hand with an equal concern for academic and social norms on the other. The educator's task is to provide a developmentally appropriate instructional program that values diversity while fostering achievement. The box on page 44 provides a few ideas for incorporating students' ethnic heritage into your instructional plans.

The essence of ethnic inclusion is to stress that the United States is built on a foundation of diverse participation and contributions. Examinations of the roles of diverse ethnic groups in U.S. history and culture should provide a critical review of both positive and negative impacts (Banks 2002).

INSTRUCTIONAL
STRATEGIES

Incorporating Students' Ethnic Heritage into Instruction

Discuss diverse ethnic groups' heritage, values, and rituals.

Use local representatives of ethnic groups as resources and role models for achievement, demonstration, and explanation.

Incorporate activities and materials that reflect local traditions and appropriately augment the more traditional curriculum.

Acknowledge and affirm each student's unique ethnic background and show how it adds to our national character and unity.

Discuss different ethnic groups' participation in historic events and provide literature that illustrates different ethnic groups' heritage, values, and rituals.

Racial and Socioeconomic Diversity

Although race is the most recognizable element of diversity, it is frequently the most misunderstood. Members of specific racial groups have distinct experiences in society and common perceptions of it, and this is where racial difference has an impact on the schools. Much of this difference can be accounted for by history, economics, and environment. John U. Ogbu (2003) also shows how the role models that students emulate can have both positive and negative consequences on school behaviors. Research has demonstrated that educational achievement is influenced by economic and social factors: A stable family, educated parents, and a higher household income are clear predictors of educational success (see Knapp and Woolverton 2004; Orlich and Gifford 2005). In the United States, racial minorities have often been denied these advantages.

Minorities sometimes affected by socioeconomic disparity

As indicated by the evolving categories of race used by the U.S. Census Bureau, the exact definition of race may face continued debate. But the implications of race for our classrooms is clear: Educators have an obligation to find the best methods and materials to achieve the best result for *all* students. You can suggest adaptations to the school curriculum that reflect the racial identity of all your students and the historical and literary contributions that have been made by members of all races. To create a positive educational environment that promotes racial unity, consider the points in the Instructional Strategies box titled "Working Toward Racial Unity in the Schools." (For detailed examinations, see Banks and Banks 2004; Greene and Abt-Perkins 2003.)

INSTRUCTIONAL
STRATEGIES

> ### Working Toward Racial Unity in the Schools
>
> Encourage parental participation and responsibility within the institutional framework of the schools.
>
> Open channels of communication among schools, communities, and parents that encourage the use of programs aimed at improving family stability and achievement for all racial groups.
>
> Help all students to participate in class activities.
>
> Discuss with students the economic risks of dropping out of school.
>
> Provide short- and long-term instructional plans that stress academic success for all students.

Physical Diversity

Whereas great attention has been paid to gender and racial discrimination in recent years, relatively little attention has been given to the **physical diversity** of the population and to discrimination based on physical characteristics. People do lose jobs, find career and social opportunities limited, and feel a general lack of societal acceptance due to various physical attributes. The elements of physical diversity include age, sex, physical condition, physical attributes, and physical impairments and disabilities.

Includes age, sex, appearance, ability

Your job is to ensure that all students have equal access to instruction and essential services, and that discrimination based on physical attributes and other characteristics is not tolerated. Raymond Orkwis (2003) shows how using "universal design" for instruction, you can accommodate all types of differences in abilities. Being organized and flexible are but two concepts that he develops.

> ### Aspects of Universal Design
>
> - All students have equal access to resources, especially those with diverse abilities.
> - A wide range of individual preferences and abilities are accommodated.
> - Instructional strategies are uncomplicated and simple to understand.
> - Instruction must be perceptible to all learners.
> - There is a high tolerance for error or unintended actions.
> - Assessment is flexible.

Multicultural Perspectives

A quote from James A. Banks is a good starting point for our discussion of multiculturalism. Banks asserts that multiculturalism will promote the sharing of power by encouraging students to "participate in social change so that the marginalized and excluded racial, ethnic and cultural groups can become full participants in U. S. society and the nation will move closer to attaining its democratic ideals." (2005, p. 253).

It is within this context of prior exclusion and future participation that educators like you must seek to balance multiculturalism with academic goals and norms. William Sierichs, Jr., underscores the balance educators must achieve when he states: "There is much the world can learn from the West. Rejecting Western culture is a form of intellectual self-mutilation as severe as rejecting multiculturalism" (Sierichs 1994, p. 114). In other words, it is self-defeating to exclude Western culture and literature in favor of another brand of ethnocentrism. Our educational policy should be inclusion, not exclusion. Clearly, we can all agree that minority groups have contributed mightily to the country we have become, and thus schools at all levels can and should be doing more about teaching minority group history and culture. Most educators will grant that having pride in one's people plays a vital role in building self-respect, and this can translate into academic achievement. *Include all, exclude none!*

It is not difficult to include multicultural education in your classroom. It takes nothing away from Shakespeare or Emily Dickinson to include the dramas of August Wilson and the poetry of Langston Hughes in the school curriculum. (For details refer to Banks and Banks, 2004).

Language Diversity

Language is the vehicle for most learning and communication in a classroom. Therefore, if the educator fails to understand and respond appropriately to the language of the student (and vice versa), academic achievement will suffer. Language barriers are the greatest impediment to social and economic advancement in our country. If obtaining an advanced education in the United States depends on the individual's success with standard English, then failure to master standard English dooms the individual to the economic underclass (Ogbu 1990) because personal income tends to rise with education (see Table 2.3). Mastery of this country's common or standard language is thus essential for its inhabitants' economic and social progress. Over 3 million children in our schools are classified as having limited English proficiency (National Center for Education Statistics August 2004, NCES 2004-035).

However, as the twenty-first century progresses, a critical set of decisions is being made, primarily at the state level, to shift from a **bilingual education** model, in which students are taught their first and second languages simultaneously, to immersion. The immersion approach is to prepare non–English-speaking students in a "crash course" of English and integrate the students into the English-speaking classrooms as quickly as possible. The decision on which model will be followed is being made state by state (Rossell 2003).

As a new teacher, you may not be familiar with the first languages or cultures of many of your students. We suggest that you consult with your principal and district English-language learner (ELL) specialist for helpful learning techniques for your charges. The Instructional Strategies box on page 47 lists several of our suggestions.

Draw from European, North and South American, and other cultures in your teaching.

Learning English is key to social and economic advancement in the United States.

Learning in two languages at once

TABLE 2.3

Actual 2003 Median Income of Year-Round, Full-Time Workers, 25 Years or Older, by Years of School

| | Median Income ($) | |
Years of Education	Male	Female
Less than 9th grade	21,217	12,978
9 through 12, with no diploma	26,468	13,695
High school graduate	35,412	20,759
Some college, but no degree	41,348	24,018
Associate degree	42,871	26,872
Bachelor's degree	56,502	35,109
Master's degree	70,640	42,466
Doctoral degree	87,131	56,182
Professional degree	100,000	56,143

SOURCE: U.S. Bureau of the Census 2001, Current Population Survey, June 25, 2004, Table PINC-03, Charts 137 and 253.

INSTRUCTIONAL
STRATEGIES

Integrating ELL Students into Your Classroom

1. Provide a warm, encouraging environment by using techniques such as the buddy system and group work, which allow students to practice language skills and receive assistance from peers.
2. If possible, use satisfactory/unsatisfactory grading until students can successfully complete assignments.
3. Avoid forcing students to speak up immediately. Students may need a long wait time, especially when being introduced to new concepts.
4. Have meaningful, relevant print material available in your classroom. Many ELL students read better than they speak.
5. Record important lessons or lectures on tape for use by students.
6. Start classroom interaction with questions that can be answered with a simple yes or no.
7. Try to talk individually with students.
8. Encourage students to use their bilingual dictionaries.
9. Become informed about students' culture.
10. Incorporate and recognize students' culture whenever appropriate.

reflect

- A culturally pluralistic curriculum is a necessity in an ethnically diverse society. How can you balance the need for incorporating other cultures with the teaching of U.S. and European cultures? How will you as a teacher know if you've gone too far in one direction or another?

- How can various cultures and languages be incorporated specifically into some of your lessons? What specific problems might your students have with the subject matter due to cultural factors? What will you do to help them overcome their difficulties?

---

video case ⏮ ▶ ⏭

Observe a third-grade inclusion classroom through the Video Case "Inclusion: Classroom Implications for the General and Special Educator." What categories of exceptionality exist in this classroom? What adaptive tools and strategies are being used on behalf of these students?

IDEA: free, appropriate learning for students with disabilities

---

Twenty-seven categories of exceptionality

Ability Diversity: Who Is Exceptional?

On December 3, 2004, H.R. 1350, the Individuals with Disabilities Education Act of 2004 (IDEA), was signed into law. This law renews a federal act for five years. The essence of the act is that all children with disabilities have available to them a free and appropriate public education. Now we would like to expand that definition to include gifted students and students with learning disabilities. Our focus is on how you can adapt your instruction to meet the learning needs of a diverse school population.

There are many definitions of **exceptionality**—up to twenty-seven different categories of it (Ysseldyke, Algozzine, and Thurlow 2000). In the box that follows, we explain six generally agreed-on categories that can be used to describe the range of students that may be present in your classroom (Kirk, Gallagher, and Anastasiow 2005). You can teach to all these groups by adapting your basic instructional strategies.

You are not alone when helping any child with disabilities or giftedness. The inclusion principle has caused a shift in the deployment of school personnel from individual teachers to collaborative efforts. For help with exceptional children in your classes, turn to such specialists as speech therapists, social workers, school nurses, resource room specialists, and school psychologists. In special cases for hearing-impaired or visually impaired students, you may request a *signer* or a *reader*. Your collaborating team members will help you adapt your curriculum for selected students. A large number of options are available to you for adapting your instruction. Today's teaching professionals recognize the need to build on students' strengths and learning preferences as a way of remedying their weaknesses. Happily, there are many approaches and curricula available to support your goals for all learners (see Hammrich, Price, and Nourse 2002). The box on page 49 lists a few sample strategies and tools. You will be required to enroll in classes or seminars that cover the IDEA and state regulations in depth.

Categories of Exceptionality

- *Intellectual*. Includes both students who have superior intelligence as well as those who are slow to learn
- *Communicative*. Students with specific learning disabilities or speech or language impairments
- *Sensory*. Students with auditory or visual disabilities
- *Behavioral*. Students who are emotionally disturbed or socially maladjusted
- *Physical*. Students with orthopedic or mobility disabilities
- *Multiple*. Students with a combination of conditions, such as cerebral palsy and dyslexia

Strategies and Tools for Adapting Instruction to Meet Special Needs

- Mastery learning
- Study/strategy skills training
- Tutoring
- Cooperative learning
- Computer-assisted programs
- Listening labs
- High-interest books
- Large print or Braille materials
- Task groups
- Buddy systems
- Special teachers

VIDEO CASE

Join a fourth- and fifth-grade inclusion classroom in studying the maps, food, music, and flags of the Caribbean in the Video Case, "Inclusion: Grouping Strategies for Inclusive Classrooms." How does teacher Sheryl Cebula 1) observe her students, 2) set the tone, and 3) involve others?

Encouraging Equity in the Classroom Environment

To create an **inclusionary classroom**, you must strive to create an inclusive, interactive classroom environment (see also Ciaccio 2004; Rex 2003). Three important skills will help you to be successful.

1. *Observe carefully.* An inclusionary classroom is a volatile social milieu. One emotionally disturbed child, in one explosive outburst, might ruin the entire day for you and all the other students. We acknowledge that potential problem. But, by continuously observing students and paying attention to their behavioral clues, you can avoid, perhaps even predict, unwanted interruptions (refer to Chapter 6). You can counter this by sharpening your observation skills.
2. *Set the tone.* You must set the tone for the classroom so that inclusion is not undermined. Under your direction, teamwork, cooperation, independence, autonomy, and competition are all brought into action. You make the decision to adapt instruction to help every child. The

Teachers use interactive instructional methods in an inclusionary classroom. © Jean-Claude Lejeune.

Instructional Strategies box below lists several specific ways you can install and maintain a diverse and inclusionary classroom. (We will cover these in more detail in subsequent chapters.) Be prepared to adapt your instruction to individual needs every day, all day long.

3. *Involve others.* Discuss your plans with the principal, the school counselor, the school nurse, the social worker, and other support personnel. You are not alone. There is a wide range of specialists who can provide that extra effort—just when the load seems too heavy to lift. Master teachers develop a collaborative network of assistants who can make the environment positive, caring, productive, and equitable (see Sergiovani and Starratt 2002).

For successful inclusive classroom: observe, set tone, involve

INSTRUCTIONAL STRATEGIES

Adapting Instruction to Promote Success for All

Promote autonomy.

Promote student-initiated learning.

Organize support groups.

Use multimethodology.

Illustrate a caring attitude.

Celebrate learning.

Instill pride in workmanship.

Rearrange the room for positive interactions.

Stress student responsibility.

INSTRUCTIONAL
STRATEGIES

Adapting Instruction to Promote Success for All—Cont'd

Accommodate students with special needs.

Vary the pace of instruction.

Collaborate with colleagues.

VIDEO CASE

Watch the Video Case "Gender Equity in the Classroom: Girls and Science," to learn how middle-school teacher Robert Cho provides role models and mentors to prevent girls from losing interest in science. What do you think turns girls off science in the middle-school years?

Gender Equity: Awareness of Bias

Bias against women needs to be openly discussed in a book such as this because such bias affects one-half of the student population. Myra Sadker, David Sadker, and Susan Klein (1991) summarized findings from dozens of studies of subtle and not-so-subtle ways women and girls are shortchanged by educational materials, as listed in the following box.

Signs of Gender Bias in Educational Materials

- Women and girls tend to be vastly underrepresented in textbooks, and that tendency grows worse at higher grade levels.
- Males outnumber females by as much as six to one in stories and folktales commonly used in schools.
- In history texts, traditionally male activities (hunting, for example) are discussed in depth, whereas traditional women's activities receive a scant sentence or two.
- Newbery and Caldecott medals are awarded far more frequently to boy-oriented books than to girl-oriented books.
- Boys or men are usually portrayed as heroes, whereas women or girls are shown as selfish or dependent.

The list of bias could be expanded (see *The Jossey-Bass Reader on Gender in Education* 2002), but what are the implications for classroom instruction? The Jossey-Bass authors cited study after study showing that in elementary schools boys received more praise, criticism, and rewards from teachers than did girls. Young girls tended to receive "neutral" teacher reactions. In general, teachers expect less from girls, and therefore girls develop a **learned helplessness**. That condition is notably described by David Bartz and Gary Mathews (2000–2001).

Girls overlooked in textbooks and by teachers

Gender bias is perhaps most serious in mathematics and the sciences, fields in which women are vastly underrepresented (Linn and Hyde 1989). The National Science Foundation is currently making an all-out effort to recruit women and minorities into math, science, and engineering programs, so perhaps this will change. Girls need to be encouraged to complete science and mathematics courses in high school in order to assume leadership roles in the nation's best jobs. The important question, the one that will affect your teaching career, is how do you ensure that every boy and every girl in your classes receives **instructional equity**? The answer should be familiar by now: You must make your classes intentionally inviting—for everyone.

Misinformation and Low Expectations   Socialization and cultural mores have a powerful effect on girls in school, and gender stereotypes and the media tend to perpetuate misinformation regarding girls' abilities (Coley 2001). People assume that girls will suffer from math anxiety, so the girls oblige. Thus it is extremely important for teachers to communicate high expectations to girls and to be intentionally inviting to improve girls' motivation and success in mathematics and science classes.

Classroom social interactions can contribute to the development of dependent behaviors and a lack of confidence in young girls. By grade 6, young girls report less confidence in their mathematical ability than boys, even when the girls achieve at the same level as boys (Fennema 1987). This research should send up a red flag for any teacher who works with girls, minority students, or non–English-speaking children. If you show preferences or lowered expectations for any group or individual, you are reinforcing learned helplessness. **Sex-role stereotyping** can be reduced or eliminated in classrooms by talking about it openly, stressing the value of learning, and communicating high expectations for everyone. All students must be given an equal opportunity to succeed because research has shown that interest in a subject is a by-product of success (Bloom 1968). For too long, educators have operated on the erroneous belief that success is a by-product of interest.

Instructional Implications of Gender Equity   As a teacher, you must provide leadership opportunities for both girls and boys. If boys are always asked to lead or to set up apparatus in science classes, then girls will simply assume dependent roles. Obviously, complex social and emotional processes take place in classrooms. The manner in which a teacher engages every student has potential learning overtones. This means that you must be consciously aware of your verbal and nonverbal actions and reactions to every class member, every day! Use the suggestions in the Instructional Strategies box on page 53 to promote gender equity in your classroom.

Technology has an impact on the ways we teach. Yet, with the advent of new teaching technologies, we must not forget that teaching and learning are very human dimensions. The humanness of schooling is one of the messages we have woven into this chapter. The more humanely we treat those who enter the classroom, the more positive our impact will be on those individuals with whom we come into contact.

When addressing any diversity issue, values and value systems come into play. The messages in this chapter are all affectively oriented; that is, they challenge our basic value structure and the attitudes we express through our words, actions, and deeds. Our job is to instill a love of learning in every student. If our teaching is biased, we may unintentionally alienate some of our students from the disciplines we teach. This, in turn, may adversely affect their desire to learn. Perhaps the observation made by Robert F. Mager (1968), the person who popularized behavioral objectives, is appropriate to end this section. He wrote, "If I do little else, I want to send my students away with at least as much interest in the subjects I teach as they had when they arrived" (p. i).

Don't let your attitudes turn students off learning.

TECHNOLOGY INSIGHT

Technology and Gender Bias

The effect of gender bias on classroom behavior, learning and achievement is a cultural construction. In Western societies, girls and boys are expected to behave differently. Boys are supposed to be active and curious, and aggressive and competitive behavior from boys is widely tolerated. Girls are expected to be more collaborative and supportive. Boys are encouraged to pursue studies in disciplines like engineering and computer science, while girls are encouraged to study disciplines that focus on personal aesthetics—for example, fashion (see Bray, Brown, and Green 2004).

These differences cause males and females to look at technology differently. Margaret Honey and her colleagues (1991) suggest that males see technology as a way to gain power and control over the physical world. Females, on the other hand, see technology as a way to improve communication and collaboration. In the classroom, boys typically use computing tools more often than girls. Boys often receive encouragement to use computers as toys as well as accomplish specific tasks, while girls are more often expected to use the computer just to accomplish specific tasks. Regardless of the roles boys and girls are expected to play, research indicates that girls and boys are equally capable of developing computing skills (Bray, Brown, and Green 2004).

INSTRUCTIONAL STRATEGIES

Promoting Gender Equity in Your Classroom

Call on girls as often as you call on boys.

Rotate classroom responsibilities and leadership roles between girls and boys.

Use wait time in your questioning (see Chapter 7).

Make no distinctions between boys and girls in assigning problems. (Some teachers assign easy problems to girls and difficult ones to boys.)

Add to reading lists stories or books about women prominent in the subject area being studied.

Assign research reports on women's contributions to the topics being studied.

Place equal numbers of girls and boys in small discussion and cooperative learning groups (see Chapter 8).

Organize a brainstorming session to answer this question: How are girls treated in our school compared to boys

reFLeCT

- List the elements of instruction that you can control that will ensure instructional equity-among the races represented in your classes.

- Examine a middle-school curriculum guide for American literature. What evidence do you find that an attempt is being made to provide a multicultural perspective?

- Do you agree with the research that shows that girls are shortchanged in schools? In your experience in elementary, middle, and high school, were girls shortchanged? Were boys? What steps can you take to avoid subjecting your future students to gender bias?

- How can you plan for an inclusive classroom environment that meets the intent of IDEA?

TeCHNOLOGY INSIGHT

Not All Information Is Created Equal: Validity and Reliability of Information

A great many Web-based resources exist for teachers. It is important to keep in mind, however, that information found on the World Wide Web may or may not be appropriate for every setting. Much of the information available on the Web is personal opinion that is unedited and not reviewed. For example, many of the lesson plans available on the Web are simply ideas that education students have had and have not been tested in a real classroom, or they may be valid only for very specific classroom settings. The best websites for valid and reliable information are those that are organized and controlled by professional organizations or edited by groups of people known and respected in their field. For teachers, Web-based information should include some evidence of a positive impact on student achievement.

As you search the Web for information that will help you become a better teacher, ask yourself this question: What is the evidence, or how good is the evidence that this is valid and reliable information? Keep in mind the time-honored warning, "*Caveat emptor*" ("Let the buyer beware"). It is all too easy to trust information that is printed or appears publicly as a webpage, but you have to make the information earn your trust.

reFLecT | **A Closing Reflection**

- How much and what type of background would a teacher need to use holistic planning? Discuss with a group of peers.

- Picture an active learning model that reflects in some way all three educational perspectives—developmental, behavioral, and cognitive. What does it consist of?

- What types of attitudes would a teacher and his or her class need to effectively embrace the concept of instructional equity and make it work in the classroom?

- Think of three films, books, museum exhibits, or other works of art that you've experienced in the past year and that express a different culture. Are any of them developmentally appropriate for the grade you expect to teach? How might they be incorporated into a multicultural teaching activity?

summary

1. Instructional decisions have two components: holistic vision and detailed implementation.

2. Instructional decisions are predicated on the learner's needs.

3. Piagetian theory assumes that learners develop in stages and that instruction should be developmentally appropriate.

4. Vygotskian theory asserts that there is a right time to teach any concept and that learning requires social interaction.

5. Behavioral perspectives emphasize that learning causes a change in behavior.

6. The cognitive model of instruction assumes that students can learn how to learn.

7. Social constructivism posits that prior experience and shared learning are part of the instructional context.

8. For a significant number of students, educational success depends on their school's sensitivity to and respect for equity, defined in terms of diversity, ethnicity, race, language, disability, or gender.

9. The skillful and deliberate inclusion of multicultural activities in the classroom promotes appreciation of all cultures, as well as pride, self-respect, and dignity for all students.

10. In the United States, proficiency in English is a prerequisite for success in school and beyond. Therefore, the schools have a responsibility to increase students' proficiency in English.

11. Gender biases have been found in textbooks, educational activities, and classroom interactions. Gender equity is an important goal of the inclusionary classroom. Teachers must be aware of the danger of placing low expectations on girls.

print Resources

Thousands of papers and books have been written on the topics discussed in this chapter. The following sources are of particular value.

Banks, J. A. "The Canon Debate, Knowledge Construction and Multicultural Education." *Educational Researcher* 22(5) (1993): 4–14.

A national debate is raging over the role of diversity and multicultural education in the school curriculum. In our opinion, Banks presents the single best analysis of the entire conflict. He skillfully shows the interrelationships of four types of knowledge—personal, popular, mainstream academic, and transformative academic. A case example using the Westward Movement is used to show how multicultural concepts can be incorporated into the curriculum.

Glasgow, N. A., and C. D. Hicks. *What Successful Teachers Do: 91 Research-Based Classroom Strategies for New and Veteran Teachers.* Thousand Oaks, CA: Corwin, 2003, 210 pp.

The authors provide a very worthwhile list of tricks of the trade for structuring an inclusive classroom environment.

Good, T. L., and J. E. Brophy. *Looking in Classrooms* (9th edition). Boston: Allyn and Bacon, 2003, 590 pp.

Two prominent educational researchers provide firsthand observations of what transpires in classrooms.

Howard, G. R. *We Can't Teach What We Don't Know: White Teachers, Multiracial Schools.* New York: Teachers College Press, 1999, 141 pp.

Howard presents a journal of his several years of teaching in racially diverse schools. His work stresses the need to create caring and humane schools—a major thesis of this book.

internet Resources

Go to the Web site for this book to find live links to resources related to this chapter.

> The University of Washington sponsors Project DO-IT (disabilities, opportunities, Internetworking, and technology). The goal is to increase representation of individuals with disabilities in science, mathematics, and technology academic programs and careers. Dr. Sheryl Burgstahler is the project director.
> **http://www.washington.edu/doit**

> Columbia University's Institute for Learning Technologies maintains a Web site that features documents and projects on increasing student motivation.
> **http://www.ilt.columbia.edu/**

> The Jean Piaget Society database is an on-line source of information and publications on Piagetian developmental ideas.
> **http://www.piaget.org/**

> The National Clearinghouse for Bilingual Education provides assistance for issues dealing with linguistically and culturally diverse students.
> **http://www.ncela.gwu.edu/**

> The American Psychological Association maintains a site containing databases, information, abstracts, news, and other related information.
> **http://www.apa.org**

References

Adams, G. L., and S. Engelmann. *Research on Direct Instruction: 25 Years Beyond DISTAR.* Seattle: Educational Achievement Systems, 1996.

Adey, P., and M. Shayer. *Really Raising Standards: Cognitive Intervention and Academic Achievement.* New York: Routledge, 1994.

Agran, M., M. E. King-Sears, M. L.Wehmeyer, and S. R. Copeland. *Student-Directed Learning. Teachers' Guides to Inclusive Practices.* Baltimore: Brookes, 2003.

Alvarado, A. E., and P. R. Herr. *Inquiry-Based Learning Using Everyday Objects: Hands-On Instructional Strategies That Promote Active Learning in Grades 3–8.* Thousand Oaks, CA: Corwin, 2003.

Amrein, A. L., and D. C. Berliner. "High-Stakes Testing, Uncertainty, and Student Learning." *Education Policy Analysis Archives* 10(18) (March 28, 2002): 1–52. http://epaa.asu.edu/epaa/v10n18.

Anderson, R. D., et al. *Issues of Curriculum Reform in Science, Mathematics and Higher Order Thinking Across the Disciplines,* OR 94-3408. Washington, DC: U.S. Department of Education, Office of Research, 1994.

Ashman, A. F., and R. M. F. Conway. *Using Cognitive Methods in the Classroom.* New York: Routledge, 1993.

Bandura, A. *Social Learning Theory.* New York: General Learning, 1977.

Bandura, A. *Self-Efficacy: The Exercise of Control.* New York: Freeman, 1997.

Banks, J. A. "The Canon Debate, Knowledge Construction and Multicultural Education." *Educational Researcher* 22(5) (1993): 4–14.

Banks, J. A. "Approaches to Multicultural Curriculum Reform." In *Multicultural Education: Issues and Perspectives* (5th edition). J. A. Banks and C. A. M. Banks, editors. Wiley: Hoboken, NJ: 242–264.

Banks, J. A. "Race, Knowledge Construction, and Education in the U.S.A.: Lessons from History." *Race Ethnicity and Education* 5(1) (2002): 7–27.

Banks, J. A. "Multicultural Education: Historical Development, Dimensions, and Practice." In *Handbook of Research on Multicultural Education* (2nd edition). J. A. Banks, editor, and C. A. M. Banks, associate editor. San Francisco: Jossey-Bass, 2004, pp. 3–29.

Bartz, D., and G. Mathews. "Enhancing Students' Social and Psychological Development." *Here's How* 19(2) (2000–2001): 1–5.

Becker, J., and M. Varelas. "Piaget's Early Theory of the Role of Language in Intellectual Development: A Comment on DeVrie's Account of Piaget's

Social Theory." *Educational Researcher* 30(6) (August–September 2001): 22–23.

Bloom, B. S. "Learning for Mastery." *Evaluation Comment* 1(2) (1968): 2.

Bray, M., A. Brown, and T. Green. *Technology and the Diverse Learner: A Guide to Classroom Practice.* Thousand Oaks, CA: Corwin, 2004.

Bredekamp, S., editor. *Developmentally Appropriate Practice in Early Childhood Programs Serving Children from Birth Through Age 8* (revised edition). Washington, DC: National Association for the Education of Young Children, 1997.

Campbell, L. *Mindful Learning: 101 Proven Strategies for Student and Teacher Success.* Thousand Oaks, CA: Corwin, 2003.

Carnine, D. *Why Education Exerts Resist-Effective Practices.* Washington, DC: The Thomas B. Fordham Foundation, 2000.

Cashmore, E. *Encyclopedia of Race and Ethnic Studies.* New York: Routledge, 2004.

Ciaccio, J. *Totally Positive Teaching: A Five-Stage Approach to Energizing Students and Teachers.* Alexandria, VA: Association for Supervision and Curriculum Development, 2004.

Coley, R. J. *Differences in the Gender Gap: Comparisons Across Racial/Ethnic Groups in Education and Work.* Princeton, NJ: Educational Testing Service, 2001.

Corley, M. A. *Poverty, Racism and Literacy. ERIC Digest.* ERIC Clearinghouse on Adult, Career, and Vocational Education, Columbus, OH: ED 475392, 2003.

Cunningham, J., C. Kroll, N. Land, and S. Russell. "Motivating Students to Be Self-Reflective Learners Through Goal-Setting and Self-Evaluation." Chicago: Master of Arts Action Research Project, St. Xavier University, ED 446 872, 2000.

Elliott, S. M., R. T. Busse, and E. S. Shapiro. "Intervention Techniques for Academic Performance Problems." In *The Handbook of School Psychology* (3rd edition). C. R. Reynolds and T. B. Guthin, editors. New York: Wiley & Sons, 1999, pp. 664–685.

Fennema, E. "Sex-Related Differences in Education: Myths, Realities and Interventions." In *Educator's Handbook.* V. Richardson-Koehler, senior editor. New York: Longman, 1987, pp. 329–347.

Gagnon, G. W., Jr., and M. Collay. *Designing for Learning: Six Elements in Constructivist Classrooms.* Thousand Oaks, CA: Corwin, 2001.

Good, T. L., and J. E. Brophy. *Looking in Classrooms* (9th edition). Boston: Allyn and Bacon, 2003.

Greene, S., and D. Abt-Perkins, editors. *Making Race Visible: Literacy Research for Cultural Understanding.* New York: Teachers College Press, 2003.

Hammrich, P. L., L. Price, and S. Nourse. *Daughters with Disabilities: Reframing Science, Math, and Technology for Girls with Disabilities.* Arlington, VA: National Science Foundation, ED 466 868, 2002.

Honey, M., B. Moeller, C. Brunner, D. Bennett, P. Clements, and J. Hawkins. *Girls and Design: Exploring the Question of Technological Imagination.* New York: Bank Street College of Education, Center for Technology in Education. Technical Report No. 17, August 1991.

Howard, G. R. *We Can't Teach What We Don't Know: White Teachers, Multiracial Schools.* New York: Teachers College Press, 1999.

H.R. 1350, "The Individuals with Disabilities Education Act (IDEA)." Washington, DC: 108th Congress, 2nd Session, December 3, 2004.

The Jossey-Bass Reader on Gender in Education. San Francisco: Jossey-Bass, 2002.

Kirk, S. A., J. J. Gallagher, and N. J. Anastasiow. *Educating Exceptional Children* (11th edition). Boston: Houghton Mifflin, 2005.

Knapp, M. S., and S. Woolverton. "Social Class and Schooling." In *Handbook of Research on Multicultural Education* (2nd edition). J. B. Banks, editor, and C. A. M. Banks, associate editor. San Francisco: Jossey-Bass, 2004, pp. 656–681.

Kohn, A. "What to Look for in a Classroom." *Educational Leadership* 54(1) (1996): 54–55.

Kozloff, M. A., L. LaNunziata, J. Cowardin, and F. B. Bessellieu. "Direct Instruction: Its Contributions to High School Achievement." *The High School Journal* 84(2) (2001): 36–54.

Linn, M. S., and J. S. Hyde. "Gender, Mathematics and Science." *Educational Researcher* 18(8) (1989): 17–27.

Mager, R. F. *Developing Attitude Toward Learning.* Palo Alto, CA: Fearon, 1968.

Marlowe, J. "Learning Alone." *American School Board Journal* 187(12) (2000): 56–57, 62.

Ogbu, J. "Understanding Diversity: Summary Comments." *Education and Urban Society* 22(4) (1990): 425–429.

Ogbu, J. U. *Black American Students in an Affluent Suburb: A Study of Academic Disengagement.* Mahwah, NJ: Lawrence Erlbaum Associates, 2003. Orkwis, R. *Universally Designed Instruction. ERIC/OSEP Digest.* ERIC Clearinghouse on Disabilities and Gifted Education. Arlington, VA: ED 475 386, 2003.

Orlich, D. C., and G. Gifford. "The Relationship of Poverty to Test Scores." *Leadership Information. In Press.*

Piaget, J. *Psychologie et Pedagogie.* Paris: Denoel/Garnier, 1969.

Phillips, D. C., editor. *Constructivism in Education: Opinions and Second Opinions on Controversial*

Issues. National Society for the Study of Education, Part I. Chicago: University of Chicago Press, 2000.

Rex L. A. "Loss of the Creature: The Obscuring of Inclusivity in Classroom Discourse." *Communication Education* 52(1)(2003): 30–46.

Rossell, C. H. *Policy Matters in Teaching English Language Learners: New York and California.* ERIC Clearinghouse on Urban Education. New York: ED482 922, 2003.

Sadker, M., D. Sadker, and S. Klein. "The Issue of Gender in Elementary and Secondary Education." In *Review of Research in Education,* Vol. 17. C. Grant, editor. Washington, DC: American Educational Research Association, 1991, pp. 269–334.

Schlesinger, A. M. *The Disuniting of America: Reflections on a Multicultural Society.* New York: Norton, 1993.

Sergiovanni, T. J., and R. J. Starratt. *Supervision: A Redefinition* (7th edition). Boston: McGraw-Hill, 2002.

Shapiro, A. S. *Leadership for Constructivist Schools.* Lanham, MD: Scarecrow, 2000.

Shayer, M., and P. Adey. *Towards a Science of Science Teaching: Cognitive Development and Curriculum Demand.* London: Heinemann Educational, 1981.

Shayer, M., and P. Adey, editors. *Learning Intelligences: Cognitive Acceleration Across the Curriculum from 5 to 15 years.* Buckingham, England: Open University Press, 2002.

Sierichs, W., Jr. "Multicultural Education Is Helpful." In *Culture Wars: Opposing Viewpoints.* F. Whitehead, editor. San Diego: Greenhaven, 1994, pp. 109–115

Skinner, B. F. *The Behavior of Organisms.* New York: Appleton-Century-Crofts, 1938.

Tarver, S. G., editor. "Direct Instruction News: Effective School Practices, 2003." *Direct Instruction News* 3(1–2) (2003): 1–78.

Tate, M. L. *Worksheets Don't Grow Dendrites: 20 Instructional Strategies That Engage the Brain.* Thousand Oaks, CA: Corwin, 2003.

Tyler, R. W. *Basic Principles of Curriculum and Instruction.* Chicago: University of Chicago Press, 1949.

NCES 2004-035. *Issue Brief: English Language Learner Students in U. S. Public Schools: 1994-2000.* U. S. Department of Education, Washington, DC: Institute of Education Sciences, August 2004, (NCES 2004-035).

NCES 2005-094. U. S. Department of Education, National Center for Education Statistics. (2005). *The Condition of Education 2005.* Washington, DC: U.S. G. P. O. (NCES 2005-094).

Wirt, J., T. Snyder, J. Sable, S. P. Choy, Y. Gae, J. Stennett, A. Gruner, and M. Perie, NCES 98-013, Indicator 43, p. 135.["STET, keep this as edited. DCO'] Vygotsky, L. S. *Thought and Language.* Cambridge, MA: MIT Press, 1962.

Wells, G., editor. *Action, Talk, and Text: Learning and Teaching Through Inquiry.* New York: Teachers College Press, 2001.

Ysseldyke, J. E., B. Algozzine, and M. L. Thurlow. *Critical Issues in Special Education* (3rd edition). Boston: Houghton Mifflin, 2000.

Fundamental Tools for Instructional Planning

Part 2 presents you with the basic tools for instructional planning. Objectives, taxonomies, lesson and unit planning, and sequencing are the most static elements of teaching. We also illustrate how much teacher planning and work it takes to convert standards to teachable objectives. But as Michelangelo's *David* illustrates as he stands poised to throw a rock at Goliath, thought and contemplation precede action, and they may have a brilliance in their own right. Planning provides the basis for the dynamic, interactive phases of teaching. We also introduce the concept of *effect size* as a gauge by which to measure the worthiness of any instructional strategy on student achievement.

In Part 2 you will be introduced to instructional planning models, all oriented toward effective lesson design. This section gives you the entry-level skills you will need to plan successful lessons and to discuss instructional planning with any experienced teacher or would-be educational reformer.

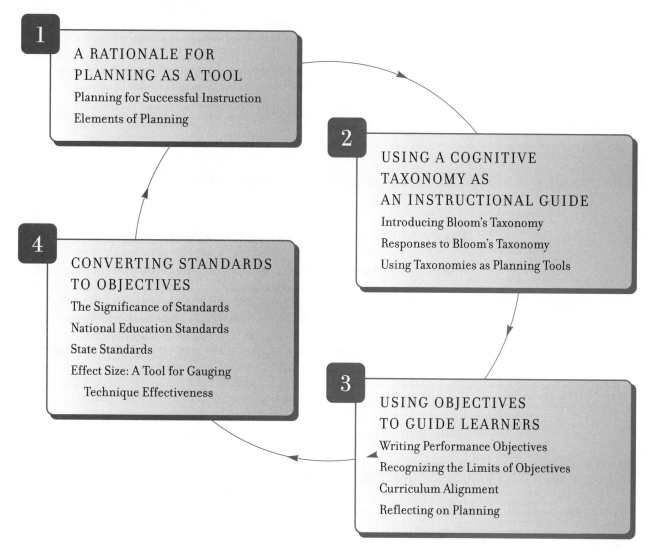

3

Objectives, Taxonomies, and Standards for Instruction

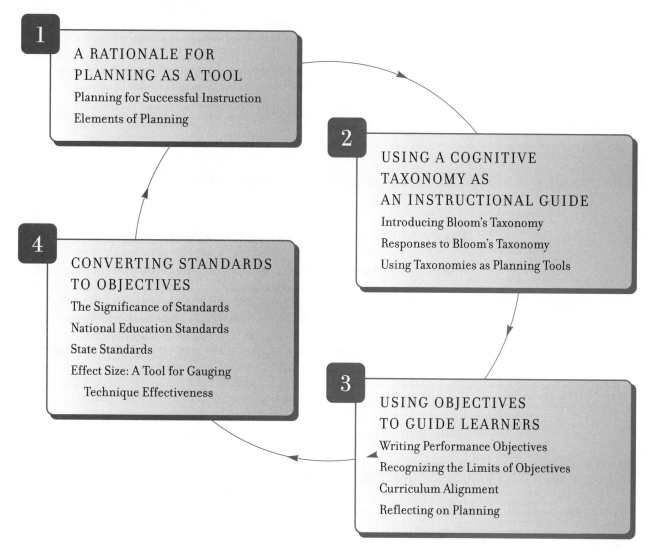

1

A RATIONALE FOR PLANNING AS A TOOL

Planning for Successful Instruction

Elements of Planning

2

USING A COGNITIVE TAXONOMY AS AN INSTRUCTIONAL GUIDE

Introducing Bloom's Taxonomy

Responses to Bloom's Taxonomy

Using Taxonomies as Planning Tools

4

CONVERTING STANDARDS TO OBJECTIVES

The Significance of Standards

National Education Standards

State Standards

Effect Size: A Tool for Gauging
    Technique Effectiveness

3

USING OBJECTIVES TO GUIDE LEARNERS

Writing Performance Objectives

Recognizing the Limits of Objectives

Curriculum Alignment

Reflecting on Planning

As a high school and college student, Carlos had been critical of teachers who did not clearly communicate their instructional goals to their students. He remembers thinking, "Why don't teachers tell us what they expect from us? Why don't they present material in a more systematic manner?"

Now, as a new high school history teacher with an assignment of two basic courses, an advanced course, and an elective course, Carlos is overwhelmed with the task of organizing the first week's lessons. Here are just a few of the questions buzzing in his head: "How much material can I cover in one period? How is what is taught in my courses related to other courses? How do I use the curriculum guides, textbooks, and all the information I learned in college? How do I plan for survival? How do I teach to the newly adopted standards?"

This chapter, together with Chapter 4, will help you find out how to solve problems similar to those raised by Carlos. We provide basic information that will help you put instructional planning in perspective. In Chapters 4 and 5, we go into the specifics of instructional design. As you read this chapter, think about how you would address the following questions.

- What processes do teachers use to plan successful instruction?
- What are my goals for my students?
- How can I use a cognitive taxonomy of objectives as an instructional guide?
- How can I write clear objectives for my learners that will guide them to success?
- How can standards be converted into appropriate and learnable objectives?
- How can I determine whether the teaching strategies I want to use are really effective?

SECTION 1: A RATIONALE FOR PLANNING AS A TOOL

Planning for Successful Instruction

One hallmark of teaching as an organized activity is the process of planning. If you wish to instruct in a systematic manner, then you will need to devote a substantial proportion of your time and activity to **planning**—deciding what and how you want your students to learn. Master teachers exhibit three common traits: They are well organized in their planning, they communicate their instructional objectives effectively to their students, and they have high expectations for their students.

The more systematic your instructional planning, the greater the probability that you will succeed. Planning instruction or lessons means establishing priorities, goals, and objectives for students. **Goals** are really statements of intent, stated in broad and general terms. For example, one commonly stated goal of education is "to produce a literate citizenry." This is a noble goal, and it shows intent. But to achieve a goal, a series of specific action steps is needed, which we'll call **objectives**. One such objective, to meet the goal of producing a literate citizenry, would be that "formal reading instruction will be delivered in grades 1 through 6." Written **lesson plans** set out in advance illustrate your priorities concerning time, learning materials, objectives, and

Goals state intent; objectives lay out the steps.

types of instruction. They are tools for success, both for you and for your students. Let's look more closely at lesson plans.

Time—we have only so much of it. Even master teachers cannot create a single extra second in the day, but master teachers do *control* time by systematically and carefully planning its productive use for instruction. The lesson plans teachers prepare help them organize and deliver their daily lessons efficiently. Numerous studies have shown that, for teachers, being well organized correlates highly with effectiveness (see Stronge and Hindman 2003).

The types of lesson plans used by teachers vary widely due to the teacher's experience, the grade level, and the subjects being taught. Writing lesson plans is similar to learning to ride a bicycle. Beginners concentrate on balance, feet on the pedals, and hands on the bars. They complete only short trips. With experience, however, pedaling and balance become automatic, and the focus is on safety, comfort, and fun, not to mention on getting somewhere. Similarly, new teachers tend to overplan—that is, to prepare very elaborate plans, being careful not to omit any point they will make in the lesson. To be effective and systematic in your planning, you must become aware of the decision areas and techniques of lesson preparation. The goal of this chapter is to provide the basic information you will need to make instructional plans as well as a rationale for using a wide variety of teaching techniques and models. In Chapter 4, we build on this foundation with more specific information and present an instructional planning model that will help you format actual written lesson plans.

As a new classroom teacher, you probably will begin making detailed plans by imitating a favorite teacher. Later, after further study and experience, you will expand or adapt the basic planning skills you have acquired to your students' specific needs. Classroom innovations will come to you once you are in your own classroom with your own set of learners, have developed your own instructional resources, and have experimented with various strategies. Although the fundamental steps in lesson planning remain the same, the basic formula is always modified to suit individual teachers' objectives and style.

Planning is more than thinking about what you want accomplished. You think about the details, such as who does what, when, for what length of time, and what opportunities will be created for effective student learning. Note that we said *opportunities*. This is a good spot to introduce you to Louis E. Raths's classic dictum (1967, pp. ix–xi). As a teacher, you are responsible for providing opportunities for changing behavior. Students may or may not change. If they don't, that's not the teacher's responsibility. Teachers do not manipulate children to change. Teachers model, demonstrate, and encourage. Any changes are up to the student! The responsibility is a two-way commitment.

The main goal of lesson planning is to ensure that all activities and processes provide a supportive educational environment for the learner. Teachers sometimes forget about the learner and concentrate on the teaching process or on what is being taught. If lesson planning is to be a useful task, it must always focus on the interaction between what is to be learned and the learner.

Like the cyclist who knows where he or she is going, teachers who develop highly structured and detailed plans rarely adhere to them in lock-step

Experienced teachers adjust plans as they go.

fashion. Indeed, such rigidity probably would hinder rather than help the teaching and learning process. For example, you may plan for a twenty-minute student activity, only to discover it requires sixty minutes to complete. You would then make the appropriate adjustment in your plan to ensure student success. The planning tools described in this chapter should be thought of as guiding principles, as aids rather than blueprints to systematic instruction. Although you have prepared carefully (perhaps precisely) to teach a lesson effectively, you must allow for flexible delivery. During the actual classroom interaction, you need to make adaptations and add artistry to each day's plan.

Team planning is commonplace in effective schools.
© Michael Zide.

Elements of Planning

In Chapter 1, you learned that the process of planning is a reflective experience. As a teacher, you will spend a great deal of time reflecting on what and how you will teach. You will also find yourself planning with your students for various student-led activities. And you will find yourself planning with your colleagues. Look back at the Key Ideas box on page 30 of Chapter 2 that summarizes "Holistic Instructional Considerations." Those ten items are really the questions that one asks as the planning process is initiated. The box on page 67 illustrates an overview of additional process components.

Planning Process Components

- Student characteristics
- Standards being met
- Goals
- Theme or unit
- Time allotted
- Specific objectives
- Cognitive level check
- Assignments
- Special needs
- Assessment
- Reteaching as needed

reflect

- Interview a few select teachers with varying years of experience to learn how they plan. Do you observe any trends or differences?

- Interview a school principal to determine what procedures are required for teacher planning in that school.

SECTION 2: USING A COGNITIVE TAXONOMY AS AN INSTRUCTIONAL GUIDE

Introducing Bloom's Taxonomy

Identifying and developing instructional objectives takes time and planning. One way to begin is to start with broad goals and then work toward specific objectives. This is a deductive process: You proceed from general statements to specific ones. Most objectives fit into three broad instructional areas: the cognitive, affective, and psychomotor domains. Tables 3.1, 3.2, and 3.3 outline the general categories and levels of the three domains.

The **cognitive domain** encompasses objectives that deal with the recall or recognition of knowledge and the development of intellectual abilities and skills. Most curriculum development focuses on the cognitive domain. Objectives within this domain are most clearly defined using descriptions of student behavior (Bloom et al. 1956).

The **affective domain** is the area that concerns attitudes, beliefs, and the entire spectrum of values and value systems. For example, committing to follow ethical or moral behavior is an affective value. This is an exciting area that curriculum developers are now reexploring (Krathwohl, Bloom, and Masia 1964).

TABLE 3.1

General Categories of the Cognitive Domain

Category	Cognitive Implication
Knowledge	Knows facts, concepts, symbols, principles
Comprehension	Understands meanings
Application	Transfers knowledge to new settings
Analysis	Reduces complex issues to components
Synthesis	Blends older ideas into novel or creative uses
Evaluation	Generates criteria for judging

SOURCE: From Benjamin S. Bloom et al. *Taxonomy of Educational Objectives.* © 1984. Published by Allyn and Bacon, Boston, MA. Copyright © 2000 by Pearson Education. Adapted by permission of the publisher.

TABLE 3.2

General Levels of the Affective Domain

Level	Characteristics
Receiving (attending)	Willing to listen to some message and point
Responding	Willing to make choices about issues
Valuing	Willing to exhibit a behavior that shows a commitment to a principle
Organization	Willing to defend values
Characterization by a value or value complex	Willing to allow values to drive behavior

SOURCE: From David R. Krathwohl, Benjamin S. Bloom, and Bertrand B. Masia *Taxonomy of Educational Objectives, Book 2: Affective Domain.* Published by Allyn and Bacon, Boston, MA. Copyright © 2000 by Pearson Education. Adapted by permission of the publisher.

TABLE 3.3

Levels of the Psychomotor Domain

Level	Performance
Imitation	Models skill development
Manipulation	Performs skill independently
Precision	Exhibits skills effortlessly and automatically

SOURCE: K. D. Moore and C. Quinn, *Classroom Teaching Skills*, McGraw-Hill Companies, © 1998.

The **psychomotor domain** involves aspects of physical movement and coordination. It integrates cognitive and affective events with bodily actions (Moore and Quinn 1994). For example, developmental physical education programs have objectives drawn from the psychomotor domain of instruction.

In this book, we emphasize the cognitive domain because most of what teachers explicitly do fits into this category. State and national standards are also cognitively driven.

A **taxonomy** is a cumulative, hierarchical system for describing, classifying, and sequencing learning activities. Although a taxonomy is basically a classification system—a way of categorizing selected items into naturally related groups, such as plants, animals, performance objectives, or questions—it is more than just that. What differentiates a taxonomy from a simple classification system is that a taxonomy is *hierarchical*; that is, the items in a taxonomy are grouped by level or rank. The method by which the items in a taxonomy are ranked depends on the organizing principle and on the type of taxonomy.

Bloom's taxonomy is a system that classifies cognitive behaviors into six categories, ranging from fairly simple to more complex. These categories are briefly described in Table 3.4. Like other taxonomies, Bloom's is hierarchical, in that learning at higher levels is dependent on having attained prerequisite knowledge and skills at lower levels. We begin our discussion of the taxonomy with a description of the first level—knowledge.

Knowledge   The **knowledge** category emphasizes remembering—either by recall or by recognition. An example of a recall operation is a fill-in-the-blank exercise; an example of a recognition operation is a multiple-choice exercise requiring the recognition of information previously encountered. Both processes involve the retrieval of information stored in the mind. The

Three instructional areas: intellectual, values, physical

TABLE 3.4

Characteristic Behaviors of the Cognitive Domain

Level	Characteristic Student Behaviors
Evaluation	Making value decisions about issues, resolving controversies or differences of opinion
Synthesis	Creating a unique, original product that may be in verbal form or may be a physical object
Analysis	Subdividing something to show how it is put together, finding the underlying structure of a communication, identifying motives
Application	Problem solving, applying information to produce some result
Comprehension	Interpreting, translating from one medium to another, describing in one's own words
Knowledge	Remembering, memorizing, recognizing, recalling

SOURCE: From Benjamin S. Bloom et al. *Taxonomy of Educational Objectives.* © 1984. Published by Allyn and Bacon, Boston, MA. Copyright © 2000 by Pearson Education. Adapted by permission of the publisher.

information is retrieved in basically the same form as it was stored. For example, if an elementary school social studies teacher teaches his or her students on one day that Washington, D.C., is the capital of the United States, then an appropriate knowledge-level question to ask on the next day would be, "Name the capital city of the United States." In answering this question, the student would be retrieving the knowledge in the same form as it was received.

The primary focus of knowledge-level objectives is the storage and retrieval of information. In answering a knowledge-level question, the student must find the appropriate signals in the problem, those that most effectively match the relevant knowledge stores. The student is not expected to transform or manipulate knowledge, but merely to remember it in the same form as it was presented. Knowledge-level activities may consist of

1. Recalling specific *facts* or *bits of information* (for example, "Who was the first president of the United States?")
2. Recalling *terminology* or *definitions* (for example, "What is a noun?")

Although the knowledge level forms the factual foundation for the rest of the categories, its overuse in the classroom causes a number of problems.

1. Simply recalling information does not actively involve the learner. Students are often poorly motivated when much of their work consists of memorizing facts.
2. Because knowledge-level questions usually have only one right answer, they do not lend themselves to classroom sessions in which students work together to discuss and solve a problem. Consequently, students' interpersonal and problem-solving skills are not adequately developed.

Knowledge-level objectives do have their place since they provide background knowledge. Effective-schooling studies provide evidence that attention to background knowledge skills helps students learn higher-order skills more effectively (see Marzano 2004). A general rule of thumb to use in judging which knowledge-level objectives should be included in the curriculum is to ask yourself, "Will this knowledge be useful to the student at a later time in one of the higher categories?" If the answer is no, you should possibly redesign the lesson.

Comprehension   The basic idea behind the comprehension category is for students to understand the material, not just memorize it. For example, memorizing the Pledge of Allegiance falls into the knowledge category, but understanding what the words mean falls under comprehension. However, unlike some of the higher categories, the comprehension level does not ask students to extend information but merely to integrate it into their own frame of reference. In other words, if students rephrase material into their own words, or if they organize it to make sense to themselves personally, they probably will learn the material more quickly and retain it longer (see Fisk and Hurst 2003).

The comprehension category is an essential gateway to higher levels; if students don't understand something, they can't use it to engage in the higher-level processes of analyzing and solving problems (L. W. Anderson et al. 2001; Wenglinsky 2000). It is worth your time and effort to ensure that all students understand an idea before you ask them to use it in more complex activities.

Knowledge focuses on memory.

Comprehension: understanding, not memorizing

In Bloom's taxonomy, the comprehension category is divided into four components: interpretation, translation, examples, and definitions. In this section, we describe each component and provide examples of questions for each one.

Interpretation   **Interpretation** involves the student's ability to identify and comprehend the major ideas in a communication and to understand the relationship between them. For example, a student who is asked to relate one idea in an essay to another must go through the process of interpretation: giving meaning to a response by showing its relationship to other facts. This relationship may be shown by comparing and contrasting or by demonstrating similarity. "How" and "why" questions often call for some type of interpretation. In answering these questions, the student relates major points and, by so doing, shows an understanding of them. Following are some examples of **interpretive exercises**. Note that the italicized key words may be used in a variety of disciplines to frame comprehension objectives or questions.

- *What are some similarities between* French and German sentence structure?
- *What differences exist between* the high school curricula of today and those of the 1980s?

Interpretation: show meaning, relationships

Translation   **Translation** involves changing ideas from one form of communication into a parallel form, retaining the meaning. Reading a graph or describing the main point of a pictorial cartoon are examples of translation. Another example of translation is summarization. In summarization, the student translates a large passage into a shorter, more personal form. Translation questions require the student to construct or change the material into a different form.

- Describe in your own words the first paragraph of the Declaration of Independence.
- Record the results of your laboratory findings in tabular form and summarize your findings.

Examples   One of the best ways a person can demonstrate comprehension of an idea is to give an **example** of it.

- Give an example of a quadratic equation.
- Name two countries that are constitutional monarchies.

In asking students to provide examples of an abstraction, the teacher should require that those examples be new or previously undiscussed. Otherwise, the student will be operating only at the knowledge level, remembering examples from previous classes.

Definitions   A **definition** requires students to describe a term or concept in their own words. This involves more than just repeating verbatim a textbook or dictionary definition. The teacher expects students to formulate the definition with words that are familiar and meaningful to them; for example:

- Define in your own words the knowledge category.
- Explain in your own words the meaning of the term *photosynthesis*.

Note that these examples call on the student to do more than just open the dictionary and copy meaningless words or synonyms.

Application   The **application** category involves using information to arrive at a solution to a situation. In operating at the application level, the student typically is given an unfamiliar problem and must apply the appropriate principle or method to it without being told to do so. The student must therefore choose the correct method and use that method correctly. When evaluating an answer to an application problem, you should check both the solution and the process because how a student solves a problem may be more important than the answer he or she obtains. To be sure that a question reaches the application level, you must make the problem unique or novel. If the class went over the same problem the day before, the task for the student would involve mere recall, not application.

The two-step application process can be visualized as shown in Figure 3.1. In the first step of the process, the student encounters a new problem and recognizes it as a type of problem solved before. During the second step of solving an application-level problem, the student selects an appropriate solution and applies it to the data at hand. This solution can consist of an algorithm, a formula, an equation, a recipe, or a standardized set of procedures for handling a specific type of problem.

If you view application problems as a two-step process, you can analyze students' responses and diagnose problems on the basis of error patterns (see Dickie 2003; Sprenger 2003). If students are having difficulty recognizing certain equations, then you need to give them a wide variety of these types of problems to recognize and prescribe solutions for. However, if students can recognize equations but cannot plug the values in the problem into the correct formula or equation, give them practice in the computational aspects of the problem. This is another instance of how the taxonomy keeps teachers adapting instruction to meet diverse student needs.

Typically, an application problem has one solution, but there may be alternative ways to solve the problem. These usually involve the use of formulas or principles that have been learned previously, with the student selecting the appropriate application to solve the problem.

For instance, students encounter a problem in which the formula $a^2 + b^2 = c^2$ should be used. To evaluate performance at the application level optimally, wait a few weeks after the original presentation of the content and then introduce a new problem dealing with right triangles. This will ensure that

Application: use the information in a situation or process

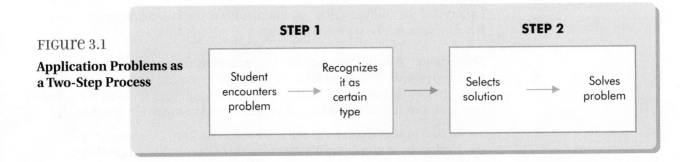

FIGURE 3.1

Application Problems as a Two-Step Process

STEP 1 — Student encounters problem → Recognizes it as certain type

STEP 2 — Selects solution → Solves problem

students can demonstrate the knowledge in a unique and novel situation. They are doing more than using a formula on a math test because it was the only topic covered for the previous three weeks.

Analysis   Application involves bringing together separate components to arrive at a solution. **Analysis** is the reverse of that process; it involves taking apart complex items—such as speeches, written communications, organizations, or machines—and explaining their underlying organization. The emphasis in analysis-level operations is on explaining how the various parts of a complex process or object are arranged or work together to achieve a certain effect.

Analysis can be differentiated from comprehension by means of the depth of processing involved. Comprehension involves finding similarities and differences in making comparisons. Basically, the task at that level is to show relationships that can be discovered by understanding the communication itself. Analysis, however, involves looking beneath the surface and discovering how different parts interact. In this sense, analysis involves working backward, taking a situation or event, and explaining how all the parts fit together to produce a total effect. Comprehension, on the other hand, involves primarily describing what that effect is.

We can divide the analysis category into two subcategories: *identifying issues* and *identifying implications*.

Analysis: explain function of parts

Identifying Issues   In this type of analysis operation, students subdivide a broad communication into its constituent parts. This entails discovering the "skeleton" of a communication because the issues involved are sometimes not explicitly stated in the communication. In this sense, identifying the issues means going beyond the information in the message to show the relationship between assumptions and key points, stated or otherwise.

Following are examples of questions that ask students to identify issues.

- Using the six campaign speeches of the presidential candidates, point out the major differences between the candidates, relating the differences to specific sections of the speeches.
- Explain the main points of the Bill of Rights in terms of current injustices.

Identifying Implications   Stating implications requires students to identify the relationship between two propositions. The relationship may be expressed in terms of influence, association, or necessary consequences, and it need not be stated directly. It should be noted that inferring an implication does not necessarily mean cause and effect. Following are examples of questions that ask students to state implications.

- What were some of the motives behind the NATO interventions in Bosnia?
- Why do many organizations keep lobbyists in Washington, D.C.?

Synthesis   **Synthesis** entails the creative meshing of elements to form a new and unique entity. Because its key is creativity, the synthesis category may be the most distinctive and one of the easiest to recognize—but it may also be the most difficult to teach. Synthesis is the process of combining parts in such a way as to constitute a pattern or structure that did not exist before. A research paper can belong to either the application or the synthesis category, depending on the level of originality it displays. If the paper is comprehensive and thorough, but does not add new knowledge to the topic, we would consider the writer to be operating at the application level. If, however, the writer puts ideas together in new or unique patterns or creates new idea configurations, then we would consider the writer to be engaging in a synthesis-level activity.

Because of the stress on creativity, operations at the synthesis level are usually difficult to grade objectively. You need to use more subjective judgment in evaluating synthesis operations than in evaluating operations at other levels. However, be sure your judgments are based on appropriate criteria; otherwise, your comments may stifle creativity. To encourage creativity, give your students ample leeway in their creative expression.

Like the other levels, synthesis can be subdivided in terms of the type of processing involved and the products of those operations—*unique or original communication, plans for operations,* and *creating abstractions.*

Unique or Original Communication   In one type of synthesis, the product or performance is a unique type of communication. Examples are an essay, a speech, or an original art form, such as a poem, a painting, or a musical composition. Students' originality and creativeness are among the criteria used in evaluating these products (see also Ennis 1985; McAlpine et al. 1987; Paul 1985).

Plans for Operations   The second subcategory of the synthesis level involves developing a plan or a proposed set of operations to be performed. These operations result in the creation of a tangible product. This tangible product and the creativity displayed in creating it are the two distinguishing characteristics of the synthesis level.

Creating Abstractions   The third type of synthesis involves creating a set of abstract relations. This typically involves working with observed phenomena or data and forming patterns that did not exist before. For example, you might ask students to experiment with liquids of different densities and then formulate hypotheses about what they observed. In social studies, after students have studied the constitutions of a number of different nations, you might ask them to formulate principles for drawing up a workable constitution.

Evaluation   **Evaluation** requires making decisions on controversial topics and substantiating these decisions with sound reasons. Judgment is to evaluation what creativity is to synthesis. Evaluation questions ask students to state their judgments and to give the criteria on which they are based. To function at the evaluation level, the student must (1) set up appropriate standards or values by which to make a judgment and (2) determine how closely the idea or object meets the standards or values.

The evaluation category projects the analysis category into another dimension. An evaluation question requires the student to make a judgment in addition to analyzing. The criteria for judgment must be clearly identified,

Synthesis: create something new from existing elements

Evaluation: making and substantiating decisions

and the quality of the evaluation response should be graded according to how well the student has met the criteria.

An evaluation response should consist of two parts:

1. The student should establish criteria on which to base his or her judgment.
2. Using the prescribed criteria, the student should state his or her own judgment.

For example, if you ask the question, "To what extent should the federal government regulate health care?" you are asking the student first to decide what regulatory role the federal government should play and then to determine to what extent that role should apply to health care. There will be some difference of opinion about the role of the federal government. This brings out the subjective and creative component of evaluation. The student must exercise judgment in matching these criteria with the subject being evaluated.

Criteria are formed usually from one of three sources:

1. Cultural or social values
2. Religious or historical absolutes
3. Individual justifications

Examples of each follow:

1. "The expectations for the twenty-first-century public schools are excessive." This statement could be answered in several ways, depending on which social or cultural values the person answering it believes to be important.
2. "Should abortion be legal?" To some people, this is a religious question and is couched in absolute values; to others, it is a personal moral decision; and to still others, it is a medical decision.
3. "To what extent are educational standards useful or useless?" Different people probably would arrive at different answers based on their different value systems.

Did you notice how the evaluation category of the cognitive domain tends to overlap with the lower levels of the affective domain? There is a **correlation** among feelings, attitudes, values, and the way we select criteria by which to judge or evaluate.

Because different students have different values, you will receive different responses to the same evaluation question. You can use evaluation questions to help students learn to live with and accept the different views of others, thus preparing them for a life in a pluralistic society. You can also prepare students for taking a stand on issues with evaluation questions such as "What do you think is best/worst or more/most important?" But, caution: Always require a *rationale*. Opinions, for the most part, are irrational.

---

reflect

- When should you use knowledge or comprehension-type questions?
- Generate at least three comprehension-type questions appropriate to your students' grade level.

reflect
- Give an example of an application problem from your own field of study.
- Under what circumstances would you use analysis questions that ask students to identify examples? To state implications? Give examples of both.

reflect
- The last three items in the cognitive taxonomy—analysis, synthesis, and evaluation—are often called "higher-order skills." What makes them "higher order"?
- How could you encourage your students to use these skills when you teach controversial subjects?
- Examine Table 2.1 and categorize the various benchmarks via Bloom's taxonomy.
- Of all the skills listed in Bloom's taxonomy, which have you been most successful using in your own schooling? Which have come most naturally to you? Which are more challenging?

Responses to Bloom's Taxonomy

In the fifty years that Bloom's taxonomy has existed, it has been widely used and accepted by educators at all levels. Research on the taxonomy, as well as research in cognitive psychology, has generally supported the ideas behind the taxonomy but has also raised some questions about its internal structure. This section focuses on that research.

Questions and Concerns   Despite its widespread acceptance and use, Bloom's taxonomy has raised some persistent questions. One question is about its comprehensiveness. Some critics state that the taxonomy is too narrow and does not include all the important goals taught in our schools (Furst 1994). When you think about the broad range of goals existing in such diverse areas as home economics, art, music, and physical education, you can see that this concern is probably valid. As this chapter points out, teachers in these diverse areas can still use the taxonomy, but they will have to adapt it to their own classroom. In fact, all teachers seem to do this—they customize an

Concerns: not broad enough, sometimes overlap

educational idea to make it their own (see A. Anderson 2001).

A second concern centers on whether the levels in the hierarchy are discrete or overlapping. You may have encountered this problem yourself as you tried to keep the levels separate. For example, is application of a formula knowledge, comprehension, or application? Though a problem for researchers, this concern is not as great for individual teachers using the taxonomy to guide their teaching (see L. W. Anderson et al. 2001).

Uses of the Taxonomy   The taxonomy has been much used in curriculum and test construction. It has been used in general curriculum design and alignment (Aviles 2001; Pratt 1994), to provide stimulating experiences for preschoolers through technology (Morgan 1996), and in test construction (McLaughlin and Phillips 1991; van der Wal and van der Wal 2003).

Instructors at all levels have used the taxonomy to determine the cognitive levels for classroom activities (McCormack and Whittington 2000), to categorize question-asking (Schurr 2001; Shaunessy 2000), and to assist in differentiating instruction (Distad and Heacox 2000). It has been used to assess the cognitive levels of test bank questions (Masters et al. 2001) plus the test questions asked in textbooks (Risner, Nicholson, and Webb 2000), and to classify the levels of classroom questions (Magner 2000). Another novel use has been to encourage greater cognitive complexity in counselors in training (Granello 2000). Researchers have found Bloom's taxonomy to be a useful analytic tool as well. For example, the six conceptual levels in the taxonomy were used to relate data obtained from a satellite remote sensing exercise. Concepts and principles associated with the satellite images were arranged in hierarchical order that ranged from simple data (knowledge) to interpretations and evaluations of data (Marks, Vitek, and Allen 1996). Other researchers have made use of the taxonomy for analyzing verbal interactions in a classroom (Fisher and Hiebert 1990).

Perhaps the taxonomy's greatest contribution has been in the development of a professional language. Teachers and administrators who describe and analyze instruction know that terms such as *knowledge level* and *higher levels of learning* will be understood by educators everywhere. This universal vocabulary, reflecting a specialized body of knowledge, was an essential step in the professionalization of teaching (Danielson 1996).

The importance of the comprehension category as a gateway to the other levels is also becoming clear. In a retrospective review of this area of cognitive psychology, Raymond Nickerson (1985) argued convincingly that comprehending an idea or a concept is an essential prerequisite to applying it, analyzing it, or using it creatively or evaluatively. Thus teachers need to make a special effort to determine that students understand an idea before asking them to use it. Don Orlich (1991) has raised some questions about the sequence of the levels. Though he supports the general idea of increasing cognitive complexity, he questions whether progress through the taxonomy occurs in six uniform steps. His observations led to the conclusion that comprehension was the key to upper categories. This is a practical problem that you can test by making observations and collecting data in your own classes (see Sagor 2000). The overriding message is clear. If your students are to learn effectively, you need to plan and implement strategies that require internal processing of information. Establish goals, lay a knowledge base, and teach actively toward higher cognitive levels.

> Broad applications within and inside of teaching

Using Taxonomies as Planning Tools

Teaching can be envisioned as a triad of strategies, outcomes, and evaluations, as illustrated in Figure 3.2. In this model, the formulated outcomes, or objectives, determine both the teaching strategies and the evaluation procedures—all the elements affect all the others. A taxonomy can be used in each of these activities: in formulating outcomes or objectives at an appropriate level, in developing classroom questions and learning exercises, and in constructing evaluation instruments congruent with the outcomes and strategies to be employed. In other words, you can use taxonomies to decide what to teach, how to teach, and how to evaluate the effectiveness of your teaching (see Marzano, Pickering, and Pollock 2001).

You can make a broad array of adaptations with the taxonomy. However, for our immediate purpose, we focus only on planning uses because other topics are amplified in subsequent chapters. Effective teaching requires that teachers think strategically about the taxonomic level of objectives, questions, and test items when they plan. Five different ways that a taxonomy can help in the planning process are listed below. (You may want to add your own after reading ours.)

1. *Provides a range of objectives.* A taxonomy provides a range of possible outcomes or objectives for any subject. Closely examining the categories may prevent you from overemphasizing one dimension of learning, such as knowledge, in your teaching. In this respect a taxonomy not only adds variety to your repertoire, but also gives greater breadth to your objectives.
2. *Sequences objectives.* An analysis of learning tasks suggests the learning experiences necessary for the student to obtain the intended outcomes. A taxonomy provides one means of sequencing learning from simple to complex outcomes.
3. *Provides a cognitive structure.* Research has shown that students learn and retain information better if it is organized into some type of cognitive structure rather than presented as isolated items (Hohn 1995). Taxonomies can provide cognitive structure to students by showing them how facts can be used in the application, analysis, synthesis, and evaluation of other ideas.

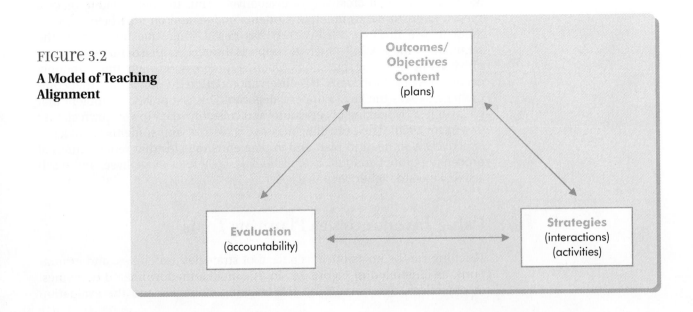

FIGURE 3.2

A Model of Teaching Alignment

4. *Provides a learning model.* By experiencing a series of learning activities sequenced based on a taxonomy, students are able to perceive that learning is logical and sequential, thus obtaining a model of learning that they can use even after they leave the classroom (see Dyment and O'Connell 2003).

5. *Reinforces learning.* Because each lower category of the taxonomy is subsumed by the next-higher category, reinforcement of previous learning occurs if learning experiences are sequenced in terms of a taxonomy. Further, activities can be focused on a specific level.

INSTRUCTIONAL
STRATEGIES

Using the Taxonomy as a Planning Tool

Provide a range of objectives.

Sequence objectives from simple to complex.

Show the relationship of objectives.

Plan for logical and sequential activities.

Build on previous learnings.

Plan for appropriate levels of instruction and assessment.

SECTION 3: USING OBJECTIVES TO GUIDE LEARNERS

Objectives tell students
where they are going

So far we have considered two sources teachers can draw on in writing objectives and planning instruction: (1) goals and standards and (2) cognitive taxonomies. We turn now to a third major resource teachers need in planning: knowledge of how to write appropriate educational objectives. The value of creating objectives, both long and short term, is to provide intent and direction to your instruction. Students need to know where they are going and why. In this section, we provide guidelines for writing and evaluating objectives.

You can use several techniques to state objectives. We demonstrate first the most specific formats because they add the greatest clarity and structure. This type of objective, called a *performance objective*, was popularized by Robert F. Mager. Throughout our entire objectives discussion, keep in mind that there is no right way or wrong way to state outcomes or objectives. The key point is that you must alert the students to what they are to learn. Instructional fairness is the essential prerequisite in specifying learning outcomes, objectives, or whatever.

Writing Performance Objectives

Performance objectives are very precise statements of what you expect the student to do (Mager 1962, 1997). Although performance objectives are written in a wide variety of styles, three elements are generally included (see Figure 3.3).

1. The statement of an observable behavior, or performance, on the part of the learner
2. A description of the conditions under which learner behavior or performance is to occur
3. The prescription of a minimally acceptable level of performance, or criterion, on the part of the learner

Performance Statement   The first element of a performance objective is an **outcome**, generally a verb that indicates what the learner is to perform, do, or produce. Verbs such as *match, name, compute, list, assemble, write, circle,* and *classify* describe observable learner behaviors or outcomes, which will help you evaluate student achievement of performance objectives. For example, if you state that the student must name the capital cities of ten states listed, the student's behavior is manifested when this performance takes place; everyone will know that the student has attained the stated objective or outcome.

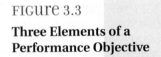
Outcome stated with action verb

The specifications of the performance come from the general goals, of course. If you teach social studies in the United States, one goal always will be to provide instruction about the U.S. system of government and the Constitution. An intermediate goal surely will be to study the Bill of Rights. Specific performance objectives may be as follows. The learner will

1. Paraphrase the first ten amendments to the U.S. Constitution
2. Distinguish between statements that are from the Bill of Rights and those that are not
3. Conduct a survey to determine how many students in the high school can identify the Fifth Amendment

Words such as *know, understand, analyze, evaluate, appreciate, comprehend,* and *realize* are not action verbs. Although such terms are important in describing the processes of learning and behaving, they are not observable actions and thus cannot be used when writing performance objectives. However, these terms are used plentifully in state and national standards

FIGURE 3.3

Three Elements of a Performance Objective

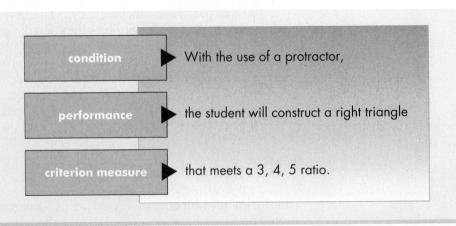
condition ▶ With the use of a protractor,
performance ▶ the student will construct a right triangle
criterion measure ▶ that meets a 3, 4, 5 ratio.

documents. Such terms may be used when you specify goals, as noted in our discussion of taxonomies. Remember that you make the decisions about the kind of performance you think is most appropriate or relevant. Thus the first and most important element of any performance objective is selecting the action verb and its direct object.

Elaboration of Conditions   The second element in prescribing a performance objective is elaboration, or description, of the conditions under which the learner is to perform the behavior. The **conditions** refer to the circumstances under which the learner must perform. Generally, conditional elements refer to

1. How the performance may be accomplished—for example, using memory, a textbook, or a computer program
2. Time elements (although time may also be used in evaluation)
3. Location of the performance (for example, in the classroom, in a gymnasium, or in the library)
4. What materials may be used to perform the tasks

For example, in "With the aid of the periodic table, the student will list the atomic weights of the first ten elements," the conditional statement is "with the aid of the periodic table." This tells students that they need not memorize the atomic weights; they should simply identify them from the periodic table. We often refer to the conditional component of a performance objective as a "statement of givens": "given this" or "given that," the learner will accomplish something.

The conditional element of a performance objective is the "fair-play" part of the instruction. As a student, did you ever arrive in class to find that, when the teacher said to "study" a poem, what he or she really intended you to do was to "memorize" the poem? Such imprecision can be confusing, if not demoralizing. We recommend that you always present this element of instruction to students explicitly, whether you use performance objectives or not.

The list below contains a list of a few conditional statements that could be included in the appropriate performance objectives.

Sample Conditional Statements

- "From memory, . . ."
- "Using a map, a compass, a ruler, and a protractor, . . ."
- "On a computer disk, which describes, . . ."
- "Given six different material samples with labels, . . ."
- "From the notes taken while viewing, . . ."
- "Within a ten-minute time span and from memory, . . ."
- "Using IRS Form 1040A, . . ."

These are some examples of the conditions under which a student can achieve a desired performance objective. The teacher sets the conditional statement in advance and gives it to the student. We recommend that the condition be the first component of the performance objective. For instance, if you were to assign a short essay, a reasonable conditional element would be: "With the use of a dictionary, . . ." We believe it has a significant impact on instructional planning and teacher behavior, so it should never be omitted.

Conditions: how, when, where, with what

Conditions must be realistic. Even though feasible, "reciting the Declaration of Independence from memory in five minutes" would be an inappropriate condition. One must always ask, "What is my main priority for the objective?" If memorizing is the priority, then that condition will define the attainment of the objective. If identifying the key ideas in the Declaration of Independence is the priority, then a condition less rigorous than memorization would be more compatible with the objective.

An integrated social studies and language arts outcome might be written as follows:

> Students will read the two essays [specify essays] found on the Internet. Orally, they will analyze the main points, showing how figures of speech and metaphors enrich the meanings. Each student must prepare a one-page, written summary of the historical and social events that affected each author, using the reference books reserved for this unit. Students will prepare their reports during class time on the computers scheduled exclusively for class use. Before final drafts are prepared, each paper must be critiqued by two members of the working group for grammar, spelling, and punctuation.

Criterion Measure   The third element of a performance objective—the definition of an acceptable standard of performance—is perhaps the most difficult to write. This standard may be referred to as the **criterion measure**, level of performance, minimum criterion, or minimum acceptable performance. Whatever term is used, the designated level is the minimum or lowest level of acceptable performance. When this is specified, students know in advance exactly what the standards are by which their work will be judged.

Following is a list of clearly written criterion measures (the condition and the performance verb are missing from the statements):

1. ". . . 70 percent of a given list of problems."
2. ". . . within 2 mm. . . . "
3. ". . . nine out of ten of the elements. . . . "
4. ". . . within five minutes, with no more than two errors of any kind."
5. ". . . the project will be compared to the two models completed by the instructor."
6. ". . . without any grammatical or spelling errors."
7. ". . . containing one dependent and one independent clause."

Each of these criterion elements states a well-defined standard for which the student can strive. These standards are always devised so that students have a high probability of achieving them and will thus be encouraged to continue to strive toward meeting the established criterion. A word of caution: Many teachers expect far too much from their students and set standards that are too high or impossible to reach. You must know at what level your students are working so that you can establish reasonable minimum standards—a skill that is part of the artistry of teaching.

Frequently an instructor will require 100 percent of the class to attain 100 percent of the objective—that is, for everyone to demonstrate complete mastery. This is called a *100/100 criterion measure*. There are many areas in which an instructor will require mastery, such as basic reading skills, math facts,

Criterion measure defines level of acceptable performance.

using equipment, or learning safety procedures. In these cases, mastery is the minimum acceptable level of performance. The mastery criterion is most appropriate when completing prerequisite or entry-level tasks because later skills are contingent on successfully performing the initial ones.

Although carefully defined standards of student performance are essential to a well-written performance objective, we recognize that much of what is taught in the classroom focuses on activities or experiences. Providing meaningful criterion measures for instruction of this type will be easier if you keep two things in mind. First, remember that activity, experience, or competency learning experiences are made up of previous learning that can be given clear standards of student performance. For example, the activity of playing volleyball is made up of a number of specific behaviors that can be isolated and given clear criterion measures. Competence in building a multimedia presentation is preceded by many skills that more easily provide clear standards of student performance. Performance objectives that focus on activities, experiences, or competencies are often more global in scope, and criterion measures for them can be difficult to write. However, they are always preceded by smaller increments of learning, for which clear standards of performance can be written. In effect, the totality of all the objectives that precede an activity, experience, or competency objective make up the criterion measure for that objective.

Second, to write only narrow, skill-based performance objectives would destroy much of the richness that should be a part of every classroom. Many times, it is the activity—the interdisciplinary or experientially focused instruction—that gives a classroom spice and interest. Do not avoid writing objectives because the criterion measure is not as precise and tight as you might like. Broadly stated objectives in which the criterion measure is less well defined can be desirable as long as they flow from a sequence of clearly articulated objectives. For example: "Describe at least four conditions of the Great Depression of the 1930s that were missing in the recessions of the 1980s and 1990s." As you will learn, much of the most exciting, high-level learning comes from mastering the lower-level material and the skills that precede it (see Rohwer and Sloane 1994). The box below summarizes the approach to use for complex tasks.

Objectives for Complex Tasks

- Focus on prerequisite knowledge and skills.
- Use broadly focused objectives for complex tasks.
- Proceed from simple to complex.

Criterion Grading   A word of caution about criterion levels: Far too frequently, the teacher prescribes a percentage or a time as the evaluation element of the performance objective. For example, if time is a critical factor in the real world—as in CPR, braking actions (that is, in a car), or manipulating machinery—then a timed criterion is appropriate. But to set a time for student learning experiences that is identical to that of professionals in the field is inappropriate. Skills can be built or improved by using variable criterion measures, just as they can with any systematic method. Thus a criterion measure of thirty seconds for a skill in the first experience may be reduced systematically as learners improve. When providing keyboarding skills, teachers have observed this principle in action many times. As time goes by, students are allowed fewer mistakes per time period. In short, the standards for an A or even a C grade are shifted to higher levels of achievement as the course progresses.

Use increasing criterion measures for skills development

Some educators have criticized performance objectives for seemingly forcing them into giving A grades for minimal student performance. This need not be the case. As a teacher, you may write performance objectives with clear criterion measures and make the meeting of those objectives worth any letter grade you choose. For example, you may state that meeting the criterion measures in your objectives will earn your students a C grade. Not meeting the criterion measures in your objectives will earn students a grade of less than C, and performing beyond your objectives will earn a grade higher than C. We provide a detailed discussion about grading in Chapter 10.

Tying criterion measure to grade

Several alternative methods are available for using performance objectives and grades. You may choose to write several performance objectives for a single sequence of instruction. Each objective can be progressively more difficult, with each worth a higher letter grade. Thus meeting performance objective 1 earns a grade of D, meeting objective 2 earns a grade of C, and so on. Rather than pressuring the teacher into giving a high grade for mediocre performance, carefully phrased performance objectives enable the teacher to prescribe a precise value and meaning to grades in terms of overt learner performance.

KEY IDEAS

Performance Objectives

- Performance statements are precise.
- Conditional elements are the givens.
- Criterion measures alert students to expectations for success.
- Assignment of grades can be based on objective criteria.

Recognizing the Limits of Objectives

Even well-written objectives are not an educational panacea that will resolve all learning problems. Objectives have limited purposes; they are only a means to an end, not an end per se. The purpose of the objective is to communicate the exact intent of the lesson. The objective is one component of the lesson plan. The teacher can construct technically correct objectives but can fail completely in the classroom because of a lack of teaching skills and interpersonal competencies or strategies.

When developing lessons that use objectives, the teacher must accept the following four assumptions.

1. Learning is defined as a change in the learner's observable performance.
2. Behavioral changes are observable in some form and may be measured by *appropriate* measuring devices over a specified period of time.
3. Observed learner outcome is directly linked to the teaching strategies, the content, or the media used.
4. The majority of children at all ages can master appropriate subjects at some acceptable developmental level if they are given enough time and adequate, appropriate learning experiences.

reflect

- As you think about writing objectives for your own lessons, what kinds of objectives do you believe will prove more useful to you as a teacher? Would your response change if you focus instead on which would prove more helpful to your students? Why or why not?

Curriculum Alignment

Another rationale for performance objectives centers around the concept of **curriculum alignment** (Cohen 1987, 1995; Steinbrink and Jones 1991). In its simplest form, a curriculum is all the subject matter that is taught and is composed of objectives, instruction, and assessment, which you saw in Figure 3.2. When all three elements match—that is, when instruction and assessment focus on stated objectives—the curriculum is in alignment. Curriculum alignment is much more difficult to attain than it seems. Teachers emphasize different learning experiences based on their skills and interests. Students have different talents and have mastered different skills at different levels. Teachers have a variety of materials to use for instruction. Performance objectives do provide a key, however, that teachers can use to align the instruction in their own classrooms. For that matter, performance objectives are essential for alignment at the district and building level, as well as aligning with any set of standards.

Objectives, instruction, assessment all in line

    The basis for successful curriculum alignment is in the process of carefully analyzing the skills, competencies, and other measures of student learning that you want to result from instruction. You test what you teach, and you teach what is in your objectives—this is an idea that is simple to state but difficult to carry out without carefully planned and written performance objectives. Curriculum can be aligned from either end of the process—the objective end or the assessment end. Too often, what teachers teach is influenced by what they know or anticipate will be on the tests. To make instructional decisions based on what is to be tested is to pervert the process. Done correctly, assessment flows from the decisions you made about what is best for your students to learn. Start from the objectives and make the rest of the process fit. If your objectives are clear and sharp, instruction and assessment will be aligned. The box on page 86 summarizes curriculum alignment.

    When all parts of the curriculum—performance objectives, activities, instruction, and assessment—are congruent (in alignment), student learning improves dramatically. Curriculum alignment has been identified as a principal sign of effective schools (see Kelly 1991). Curriculum alignment has been proven as a major tool in changing less successful schools into successful ones.

All in all, curriculum alignment is a powerful concept—one that begins with identifying your objectives.

Curriculum Alignment

- Start from your objectives, not from assessment.
- If your objectives are clear, instruction and assessment will be aligned.
- Curriculum alignment is a recurring cycle.

Reflecting on Planning

Effective planning has a positive impact on student achievement. Planning is a time-consuming process for the beginning teacher. Although you have spent many hours in the classroom as a student, you probably have never been responsible for student learning. As you gain experience, you will begin to know which activities take detailed planning and which do not.

Knowing when to abandon plans to take advantage of that unintended learning opportunity is a master teacher's skill. A good plan provides you with the context for this decision. Does this new opportunity (teachable moment) contribute more positively to the objectives of the lesson? Are you meeting a student's important need with a lesson detour? A teacher must exhibit a balance between preparation and flexibility in executing the plan. That, of course, is the artistry of teaching.

Addressing individual differences is extremely difficult. Even experienced teachers struggle to meet the learning needs of all their students. Initially, students in your class will need to adapt to your teaching style. As you gain experience and confidence in the teaching and learning processes, you will begin planning for and addressing individual student needs, and eventually accommodate your teaching style to match the students' needs.

Planning is a dynamic process. It often seems downright chaotic. The United States is unique in that responsibility for planning and teaching at the classroom level rests with you, the teacher. In most countries, teachers are told what to teach and often even how to teach. With this in mind, you should be even more aware that—if state standards shift from general statements to specific learner objectives—you might be responsible only for the "how" part.

In this chapter we have described the basic planning tools of goals, taxonomies, and objectives, and provided examples of how to use these tools to develop instructional plans. Don't be afraid to refine, modify, or experiment with these tools. You are the technicians; the tools are there to serve you and those all-important students.

Plans are dynamic, not set in stone.

SECTION 4: CONVERTING STANDARDS TO OBJECTIVES

The Significance of Standards

With the advent of federal legislation enacted in 2001/2002, the No Child Left Behind Act (PL 107-110), all states must establish "challenging academic standards." One component of the standards movement has been the *high-stakes test* phenomenon. Such tests are called "high stakes" because teachers, students, and schools are rewarded or penalized if the scores are not adequate. National and state standards have a huge effect on what is being taught in the schools and how it is being taught.

National Education Standards

Momentum for contemporary U.S. school reform and the subsequent academic standards movement can be traced to the 1983 report *A Nation at Risk: The Imperative for Educational Reform,* sponsored by the National Commission on Excellence in Education (1983). One of its most often-quoted line states, "If an unfriendly foreign power had attempted to impose on America the mediocre instructional performance that exists today, we might well have viewed it as an act of war." By using a war metaphor, the national commission intentionally created a crisis of confidence, which is amply documented by David C. Berliner and Bruce Biddle (1995) in their book, *The Manufactured Crisis: Myths, Fraud, and the Attack on America's Public Schools.* Gerald W. Bracey's (2003) *What You Should Know About the War Against America's Public Schools* amplifies the debate.

A crisis of confidence?

Background and Perspective   During the 1980s, educational reform had at least eight additional factors driving it.

Factors Driving Educational Reform and Standards

- Global economic competition
- Disparities between socioeconomic groups
- Declining wages
- Exporting of jobs overseas
- New technologies
- Renewed business-sector interest in education
- Perceived decline in student achievement
- Demographic changes in the schools

None of these factors alone could provide impetus for reform, but collectively they caused public education to become a focal point for social and economic changes. As early as 1986, Bill Chance reported that there were more than 275 educational task forces organized in the United States, generating scores of reports to "fix the schools" (1986). The current enthusiasm for educational reform and standards is politically motivated; that is, the drive and energy come from two nonschool sources: (1) policymakers and (2) professional associations desiring to enhance academic rigor. Forty-nine states have adopted their own standards. The broad subject areas for which standards have been adopted tend to be in civics, English, fine arts, geography, history, language arts, mathematics, performing arts, science, work skills, and world languages.

Professional groups and associations are involved in establishing educational goals (see Table 3.5). The National Science Education Standards, by the National Research Council (1996), and *Atlas of Science Literacy*, by the American Association for the Advancement of Science (2001), are two attempts by science education professional groups to provide guidance through educational standards—that is, to provide criteria against which performance may be judged. The goals of these national education standards are to produce students who are able to

- Use scientific principles and processes appropriately in making personal decisions.
- Experience the richness and excitement of knowing about and understanding the natural world.

49 states have standards.

TaBLe 3.5

A Sampling of National Education Standards	
Report Title and Author	**Brief Description**
National Standards for Arts Education: What Every Young American Should Know and Be Able to Do in the Arts (National Consortium of National Arts Education Associations 1994)	Creates criteria for fine arts and music instruction.
National Standards for Civics and Government (Center for Civic Education 1994)	Establishes standards for instruction in civics and government classes.
National Standards for History: Basic Edition (National Center for History in the Schools 1996)	The NCHS provides a series of topics for U.S. and world history K–12.
Moving into the Future: National Standards for Physical Education: A Guide to Content and Assessment (National Association for Sport and Physical Education 1995)	Establishes curriculum requirements for physical education.
National Science Education Standards (National Research Council 1996)	These standards set the agenda for science education K–12.
Atlas of Science Literacy (American Association for the Advancement of Sciences 2001)	The *Benchmarks* set the framework for science reform under "Project 2061."
Principles and Standards for School Mathematics (National Council of Teachers of Mathematics 2000)	The NCTM standards are widely used as a model for K–12 programs.
Curriculum and Evaluation Standards for School Mathematics (National Council of Teachers of Mathematics 1993)	Curriculum standards for Grades K–12 are presented.

TABLE 3.5

A Sampling of National Education Standards—(cont.)	
Report Title and Author	Brief Description
Standards for the English Language Arts (National Council of Teachers of English 1996)	The NCTE presents its standards for language arts instruction.
Foreign Language Standards: Linking Research, Theories, and Practices (Phillips 1999)	The American Council on the Teaching of Foreign Languages makes a detailed statement.
Standards for Technology Literacy: Content for the Study of Technology (International Technology Education Association 2000)	The ITEA standards relate to computer and other high-tech programs.

- Increase their economic productivity.
- Engage intelligently in public discourse and debate about matters of scientific and technological concern.

The push for standards is inspired by many factors, but most importantly by increased global competition in an increasingly technological world. (See also Jennings's 1998 discussion about the politics involved and how political and business leaders, not educators, advocated national standards and high-stakes tests.)

What exactly are standards? The term **standards** has multiple meanings and applications. For example, no distinction is made between the standards and educational objectives. Standards can be criteria by which to judge the quality of what students know and are able to do, the quality of the science programs available to them, the quality of the science teaching they receive, the quality of the system that supports their science teachers and programs, and the quality of their school's assessment practices and policies. Unless carefully designated, these five aspects of schooling are lumped together. In these cases, the same data—usually test scores—are used as the only yard-sticks for the success of five distinct and independent activities, at which point we must ask, "How can one measure on a test be valid to evaluate five very disparate phenomena?"

Standards also refer to a vision of learning and, as you saw in Chapter 1, teaching. In both capacities, as performance criteria and as an educational vision, standards tend to provide conflicting expressions. (See Bracey 2004 for a thought-provoking critique.)

State Standards

A Sampling of State Standards   With 49 states now having standards for instruction, let us examine just a tiny sample of them—keeping mind that, in total, thousands of pages are on file.

Mathematics **Arizona.** The Grand Canyon State spells out in detail the mathematics standards by grade level. At the high school level, the "strands" relate to "number sense and operations"; "data analysis, probability and discrete mathematics"; "geometry"; and "logic." Below are three examples.

1. Apply subscripts to represent ordinal positions.
2. Interpret the relationship between data suggested by tables/matrices, equations or graphs.
3. Create inductive and deductive arguments concerning geometric ideas and relationships, such as congruence, similarity and the Pythagorean relationship.

Ohio. The Buckeye State standards include the following.

Grades 5–7

1. Relate mathematical ideas to one another and to other content areas; e.g., use area models for adding fractions; interpret graphs in reading, science, and social studies.
2. Explain how inverse operations are used to solve linear equations.

Grade 8

Demonstrate an understanding that the probability of either of two disjoint events occurring can be found by adding the probabilities for each and that the probability of one independent event following another can be found by multiplying the probabilities.

Grade 9

1. Define the basic trigonometric ratios in right triangles: sine, cosine and tangent.
2. Use theoretical and experimental probability, including simulations or random numbers, to estimate probabilities and to solve problems dealing with uncertainty; e.g., compound events, independent events and simple dependent events.

By the end of grades 11–12

Use descriptive statistics to analyze and summarize data, including measures of center, dispersion, correlation and variability.

Social Science **California.** The following are from the Golden State's History-Social Science Content Standards.

Grade 5

1. Describe the competition among the English, French, Spanish, Dutch and Indian nations for control of North America.
2. Identify the significance and leaders of the First Great Awakening, which marked a shift in religious ideas, practices and allegiances in the colonial period, the growth of religious toleration and free exercise of religion.
3. Understand how the British colonial period created the basis for the development of political self-government and a free-market economic system and the differences between the British, Spanish, and French colonial systems.

Colorado. The Centennial State has a Model Content Standards: Economics.

Grades K–4

Identify the three basic economic questions all economic systems must answer: What goods and services will be produced? How will they be produced? For whom will they be produced?

Grades 5–8

Describe how different economic systems affect the allocation of resources (for example, steel production in the former Soviet Union was determined by economic planners. This affected the allocation of many resources: coal, labor, etc. In the United States, all of these resources are allocated by the market).

Grades 9–12

1. Compare and contrast economic systems in terms of their ability to achieve economic goals.
2. Explain the benefits of the United States economic system.

English/Language Arts   Published standards in this arena are copious. Here's a random sampling.

Florida: Grades 6–8

Determine main concept, supporting details, stereotypes, bias and persuasion techniques in a non-print message.

Massachusetts: Grade 7

1. Students will identify, analyze and apply knowledge of the themes, structure and elements of myths, traditional narratives and classical literature and provide evidence from the text to support their understanding.
2. Identify and analyze similarities and differences in mythologies from different cultures (for example, ideas of the afterlife, roles and characteristics of deities, types and purposes of myths).

North Carolina: Grade 10

Demonstrate an understanding of conventional written and spoken expression by employing varying sentence structures (e.g., inversion, introductory phrases) and sentence types (e.g., simple, compound, complex, compound-complex).

Grade 12

1. Recognize common themes that run through works, using evidence from the texts to substantiate ideas.
2. Relate the cultural and historical contexts to the literature, identifying perceived ambiguities, prejudices and complexities.

Texas. In the Lone Star State, the standards are included in the Texas Administrative Code, giving them a legal status. This excerpt from the Introduction to English I (Grade 9) provides an excellent summary of the subsequent standards that are spelled out for high school freshmen.

(1) Students enrolled in English I continue to increase and refine their communications skills. High school students are expected to plan, draft and complete written compositions on a regular basis. Students edit their papers for clarity, engaging language, and the correct use of the conventions and mechanics of written English and produce final error-free drafts. In English I, students practice all forms of writing. An emphasis is placed on organizing logical arguments with clearly expressed related definitions, theses and evidence. Students write to persuade and to report and describe. English I students read extensively in multiple genres from world literature, such as reading selected stories, dramas, novels and poetry originally written in English or translated to English from oriental, classical Greek, European, African, South American and North American cultures. Students learn literary forms and terms associated with selections being read. Students interpret the possible influences of the historical context on a literary work.

(2) For students enrolled in English I whose first language is not English, the students' native language serves as a foundation for English language acquisition.

Teaching to Standards   Here is a list of steps you can take to convert a standard into teachable lessons. Visit our website for a more detailed example of this process.

1. Create a series of specific and discrete objectives from the general standards statement.
2. To visualize relationships, sketch flow charts showing connectedness between objectives and standards.
3. Identify appropriate print, nonprint, and Internet-based materials.
4. Plan appropriate lessons, including a variety of teaching strategies and accommodations for special education students or ESL learners.
5. Integrate assessments into the lesson design.
6. Draft a calendar showing time commitments.
7. Evaluate the entire process to optimize student achievement.

This sequence is obviously labor intensive. There will be few short cuts. And no state has prepared a series of print materials such as textbooks that align with the adopted standards. We encourage you to discuss the implications of state standards for instruction in your education classes.

Looking Critically at State Standards   State standards cover a wide range of topics, concepts, and subjects. Most appear to be arbitrarily generated, even though several states note in their documents that they are modeled after the many nationally published sets. Reading them, one wonders if any of the standards were field-tested to determine developmental appropriateness (refer to Table 2.1). In most cases, the lengthy lists are not arranged in any meaningful sequence or any hierarchical order. The standards collectively do not have flow charts or illustrate how a student or teacher progresses for one standard to another. In numerous instances, the standards do not set a standard that teachers would find adequate; rather, they tend to be performance objectives without a statement of the conditions. Most disturbingly, there is often a 100/100 criterion for the standards: Every child in every state must meet every standard. (NCLB dictates that every child must pass a state test by 2013/2014.)

Standards are one of two aspects of educational reform. The second one is **accountability**, which is defined by testing the children at grades 3–12. Arizona has developed an Arizona Instrument to Measure Standards (AIMS) to use in assessing math skills. When first given in late 1999 and early 2000, at grade 10, the AIMS failure rate was extremely high, approaching 90 percent for all takers and 97 percent for students of color. As late as 2002, more than 80% of the minority students failed and 66% of all takers failed (Arizona Dept. of Ed. 2002). So Gene V. Glass and Cheryl A. Edholm (2002) conducted a survey to test the validity of the math skills being assessed in the AIMS tests. They wished to determine how relevant the tests and test results were to a student's future success in the workplace.

Glass and Edholm sent questionnaires to fifty-four managers in ten different categories of industries in the greater Phoenix area. Forty-three completed their questionnaires (a respectable 80 percent return rate). The results were not encouraging for those who assert that tests and standards lead unequivocally to school improvement. The range of "mathematics used in daily work" ranged from a high of 26 percent to a low of 7 percent. Although politicians support standards as necessary for developing forward-looking job skills, employers in Arizona suggested that the tested skills were irrelevant to their work forces. Concluded Glass and Edholm, "The overall conclusion is undeniably one in which these managers regard the mathematics tested by Grade 10-AIMS mathematics test as irrelevant to the functioning of their employees" (2002, p. 3).

A Final Word About Standards   In January 2005, the very conservative Thomas B. Fordham Foundation issued letter grades for all the published sets of state standards in mathematics and English. The Fordham group established a set of criteria by which they judged the various state standards. They looked at qualities such as clarity, content, reason, teachability, and consistency. "Scathing" would be the best description of this critique (see Finn 2005). The average grade given for math was a D, with a C being the average

reFLecT

- How do the National Science Education Standards seek to address the increasingly competitive nature of the world economy?

- Are there common elements or themes in the collective set of goals that have been recently published?

- What issues do your state's education goals or standards address? How are they related to national standards? Examine your state standards in your area of specialization. How general or specific are they?

- To what extent have state standards been fully analyzed for developmental appropriateness in your education classes?

- If every child must pass a state test, what are the implications for Individuals with Disabilities Education Act (IDEA) and English Language Learners (ELL) students? Discuss with your colleagues and instructors.

- In your view, is the purpose of education to train students for future employment? If not, then what is it? What standards might you devise to suit this goal?

grade for English standards. We cannot overemphasize that you must critically examine all standards to determine their validity and developmental appropriateness before applying them in your classroom.

Effect Size: A Tool for Gauging Technique Effectiveness

Intuitively, we know that certain instructional treatments have a positive effect on student learning. But how can you find evidence that a specific teaching strategy has a positive impact on student achievement? One useful gauge is **effect size**. Effect size (Cohen 1988) tests results by applying a formula to before-and-after test scores once a teaching strategy has been used.

1. To determine effect size, you need a control group (pretest) and an experimental group (posttest), the test scores yield averages (means), and standard deviations. (The formula for computing a standard deviation is located in any statistics book, or search for "standard deviation" on the Internet.)
2. To calculate the effect size, subtract the mean score of the pretest from the mean score of the posttest, and then divide the difference by the standard deviation of the pretest.
   Example:
   90 posttest mean score
   <u>– 80 pretest mean score</u>
   = 10 difference
   <u>÷ 8.0 standard deviation</u>
   = 1.25 effect size
3. An effect size of 1.0 means a gain of 1 standard deviation based on a normal curve for the treatment group. Effect sizes less than 0.2 are usually not important. An effect size of 0.25 begins to show importance. At 0.3, an effect size becomes useful or important. An effect size of 2.0 would be phenomenal. In the example above, the effect size was 1.25. If you get a result like that from one of your teaching techniques, stick with it—it's a winner!
4. Effect sizes are cumulative but not additive. You can use several teaching strategies and expect a total effect to be greater than any single one. A combination of techniques will seldom go beyond an effect of 2.0. However, that effect size is large enough that a child who is classified as learning disabled would be achieving at an above-average level after being provided with several tested techniques.

For each major technique that we discuss in this book, we provide the published effect size on our website at **http://education.college.hmco.com/students**. We generally use the effect sizes reported by Benjamin S. Bloom (1984) in his classic paper; those computed by Herbert J. Walberg (1999), for which he and his collaborators reviewed thousands of studies with relevant student data from elementary and secondary schools; and the work of Robert J. Marzano et al. (2001). We encourage you to examine these studies, especially Marzano's. By knowing where to find effect size data, you have access to information far beyond that held by the vast majority of practicing educators.

TECHNOLOGY INSIGHT

Using Computers in the Classroom: Good News and Bad News

Planning instructional activities that make use of computers or computing networks (the Internet) can add a great deal to a learning environment. However, these additions may be considered both positive and negative.

Computing tools can be highly motivating: Students can produce reports and presentations that look exceptionally good. The computer will perform tasks such as formatting text and images, and adding color, movement, and sound with ease. Problems may sometimes arise from students' spending too much time on form and too little time on content (for example, making the video about triangulation may become much more engrossing than learning the concepts of triangulation). It is important to strike a balance between learning new concepts and ideas, and formatting the report that indicates learning has occurred. The computer is very good at helping with the formatting—sometimes *too* good.

Using the Internet as a resource has advantages and disadvantages as well. Research indicates that teachers who encourage their students to make use of the Internet develop their own abilities to teach in a constructivist manner. Instructional activities that make use of the Internet often result in students' choosing to perform more research for longer periods of time. The problem with this is that more time is needed to participate in constructivist-oriented learning activities. This includes the extra time it takes to discuss how best to conduct research using the Internet and avoid abuses of Internet privileges. Teachers must find ways to adjust schedules to better fit the activity.

Many teachers feel it is worth the extra time and effort to plan for the use of computers and the Internet in their instruction. However, most teachers also agree that planning for this use requires extra time and effort.

SOURCE: Becker and Ravitz 1999.

reflect A Closing Reflection

- How does planning allow you to become more or less spontaneous?

- List the pitfalls and advantages of using a planning device such as a cognitive taxonomy.

- With all the thinking you've done about standards so far, how will you use them to aid in your planning? What would you do if you found a state standard that was impossible to teach?

- How can you be sure that your planning reflects what your students should really learn?

summary

1. Instructional planning requires a careful consideration of student needs, content goals, and instructional techniques.
2. Goals are broadly stated intentions; objectives or outcomes are specific expectations.
3. Instructional planning follows a cycle ranging from prelesson planning to postlesson reflection.
4. National standards are in vogue and guide state and local efforts to plan instruction.
5. Instruction can be planned around the cognitive, affective, and psychomotor domains.
6. The cognitive domain tends to be the focus of school curricula.
7. Performance objectives show learners what is expected, how the work will be done, and what the minimum standards are.
8. Curriculum or instructional alignment ensures that objectives, content, activities, teaching techniques, and assessment are congruent.
9. Standards must be converted into student objectives.
10. Effect size is a useful means of gauging effectiveness of a teaching strategy.

Print Resources

Anderson, L. W., and D. R. Krathwohl, editors. *A Taxonomy for Learning, Teaching, and Assessing: A Revision of Bloom's Taxonomy of Educational Objectives.* New York: Longman, 2001, 352 pp.

This book provides a historical treatment about the development of the cognitive taxonomy and illustrates in great depth a new and complete cognitive psychological perspective for classifying school learning.

Brown, J. L. *Making the Most of Understanding by Design.* Alexandria, VA: Association for Supervision and Curriculum Development, 2004, 205 pp.

The author provides a model of applying instructional design principles as a framework to improve student achievement and teacher efficacy. Two chapters relate directly to teaching to standards and promoting student understanding.

Carr, J. F., and D. E. Harris. *Succeeding with Standards: Linking Curriculum, Assessment, and Action Planning.* Alexandria, VA: Association for Supervision and Curriculum Development, 2001, 204 pp.

The authors illustrate in great detail techniques by which a classroom teacher can address standards.

Internet Resources

Go to the Web site for this book to find live links to resources related to this chapter.

> The URL below will provide information and a list of several other Internet sites, all relating to Bloom's taxonomy.
> **http://www.uct.ac.za/projects/cbe/mcqman/mcqappc.html**

> The current status of Goals 2000 and related educational issues are provided via an on-line database managed by the U.S. Department of Education.
> **http://www.ed.gov/pubs/EPTW/eptwgoal.html**

References

American Association for the Advancement of Sciences, *Benchmarks for Science Literacy: Project 2061*. New York: Oxford University Press, 1993.

Anderson, A. "In the Process." *Clearing House* 74(5) (2001): 285–286.

Anderson, L. W., et al. *Taxonomy for Learning, Teaching, and Assessing: A Revision of Bloom's Taxonomy of Educational Objectives* (complete edition). New York: Addison Wesley Longman, 2001.

Aviles, C. B. *Curriculum Alignment: Matching What We Teach and Test Versus Teaching to the Test*. Buffalo: Buffalo State College, 2001. ED 448 402.

Becker, H. J., and J. Ravitz. "The Influence of Computer and Internet Use or Teachers' Pedagogical Practices and Perceptions." *Journal of Research on Computing in Education* 31(4) (1999): 356–384.

Berliner, D. C., and B. J. Biddle. *The Manufactured Crisis: Myths, Fraud, and the Attack on America's Public Schools*. Reading, MA: Addison-Wesley, 1995.

Bloom, B. S. "The 2 Sigma Problem: The Search for Methods of Group Instruction as Effective as One-To-One Tutoring." *Educational Researcher* 13(6) (1984): 4–16.

Bloom, B. S., M. D. Engelhart, E. J. Furst, W. H. Hill, and D. R. Krathwohl. *Taxonomy of Educational Objectives: The Classification of Educational Goals. Handbook I: Cognitive Domain*. New York: McKay, 1956.

Bracey, G. W. *What You Should Know About the War Against America's Public Schools*. Boston: Allyn and Bacon, 2003.

Bracey, G. W. *Setting the Record Straight: Responses to Misconceptions About Public Education in the U.S.* (2nd edition). Portsmouth, NH: Heinemann, 2004.

Chance, W. . . . *The best of educations*. Chicago: The John D. and Catherine T. MacArthur Foundation, 1986. (Released in 1988 by the Education Commission of the States, Denver.)

Cohen, J. *Statistical Power Analysis for the Behavioral Sciences* (2nd edition). Hillsdale, NJ: Erlbaum, 1988.

Cohen, S. A. "Instructional Alignment: Searching for a Magic Bullet." *Educational Researcher* 16(8) (1987): 16–19.

Cohen, S. A. "Instructional Alignment." In *International Encyclopedia of Teaching and Teacher Education* (2nd edition). L. W. Anderson, editor. Tarrytown, NY: Elsevier Science, 1995, pp. 200–204.

Danielson, C. *Enhancing Professional Practice: A Framework for Teaching*. Alexandria, VA: Association for Supervision and Curriculum Development, 1996.

Dickie, L. O. "Approach to Learning, the Cognitive Demands of Assessment, and Achievement in Physics." *Canadian Journal of Higher Education* 33(1) (2003): 87–111.

Distad, L., and D. Heacox. "Differentiating Instruction Using a Matrix Plan." *Southern Social Studies Journal* 25(2) (2000): 70–76.

Dyment, J. E., and T. S. O'Connell. "Getting the Most Out of Journaling: Strategies for Outdoor Educators. *Pathways: The Ontario Journal of Outdoor Education* 15(2) (2003): 31–34.

Ennis, R. H. "A Logical Basis for Measuring Critical Thinking Skills." *Educational Leadership* 43(2) (1985): 44–48.

Finn, C. E., Jr., et al. *The State of English Standards 2005. The State of Mathematics Standards 2005*. Washington, DC: Thomas B. Fordham Foundation,

2005. Retrieved at http://www.edexcellence.net/foundation

Fisher, C. W., and E. W. Hiebert. "Characteristics of Tasks in Two Approaches to Literacy Instruction." *Elementary School Journal* 91(1) (1990): 3–18.

Fisk, C., and B. Hurst. "Paraphrasing for Comprehension." *Reading Teacher* 57(2) (2003): 182–185.

Furst, E. J. "Bloom's Taxonomy: Philosophical and Educational Issues." In *Bloom's Taxonomy: A Forty-Year Retrospective*. L. W. Anderson and L. A. Sosniak, editors. Chicago: University of Chicago Press, 1994, pp. 28–40.

Glass, G. V., and C. A. Edholm. "The AIMS test and the Mathematics Actually Used by Arizona Employers." Education Policy Studies Laboratory, Arizona State University, Tempe, Education Policy unit. EPSL-0209-119 EPRU, October 2002. Retrieved at http://edpolicylab.org

Granello, D. H. "Encouraging the Cognitive Development of Supervisees: Using Bloom's Taxonomy in Supervision." *Counselor Education and Supervision* 40(1) (2000): 31–46.

Hohn, R. L. *Classroom Learning and Teaching*. White Plains, NY: Longman, 1995.

Jennings, J. F. *Why National Standards and Tests? Politics and Quest for Better Schools*. Thousand Oaks, CA: Sage, 1998.

Kelly, T. F. *Practical Strategies for School Improvement*. Wheeling, IL: National School Services, 1991.

Krathwohl, D. R., B. S. Bloom, and B. B. Masia. *Taxonomy of Educational Objectives. The Classification of Educational Goals. Handbook II: Affective Domain*. New York: McKay, 1964.

Mager, R. F. *Preparing Instructional Objectives*. Belmont, CA: Fearon, 1962.

Mager, R. F. *Preparing Instructional Objectives: A Critical Tool in the Development of Effective Instruction* (3rd edition). Atlanta: Center for Effective Performance, 1997.

Magner, L. "Reaching All Children Through Differentiated Assessment: The 2-5-8 Plan." *Gifted Child Today Magazine* 23(3) (2000): 48–50.

Marks, S. K., J. D. Vitek, and K. P. Allen. "Remote Sensing: Analyzing Satellite Images to Create Higher Order Thinking Skills." *The Science Teacher* 63(3) (1996): 28–31.

Marzano, R. J. *Building Background Knowledge for Academic Achievement*. Alexandria, VA: Association for Supervision and Curriculum Development, 2004.

Marzano, R. J., D. J. Pickering, and J. E. Pollock. *Classroom Instruction That Works: Research-Based Strategies for Increasing Student Achievement*. Alexandria, VA: Association for Supervision and Curriculum Development, 2001.

Masters, J. C., et al. "Assessment of Multiple-Choice Questions in Selected Test Banks Accompanying Text Books Used in Nursing Education." *Journal of Nursing Education* 40(1) (2001): 25–31.

McAlpine, J., S. Jeweler, B. Weincek, and M. Findbiner. "Creative Problem Solving and Bloom: The Thinking Connection." *Gifted Child Today* 10 (1987): 11–14.

McCormick, D. F., and S. M. Whittington. "Assessing Academic Challenges for Their Contribution to Cognitive Development." *Journal of Agricultural Education* 41(3) (2000): 114–122.

McLaughlin, M. W., and D. C. Phillips, editors. *Evaluation and Education at Quarter Century*. Nineteenth Yearbook of the National Society for the Study of Education, Part II. Chicago: University of Chicago Press, 1991.

Morgan, T. "Using Technology to Enhance Learning: Changing the Chunks." *Learning and Leading with Technology* 23(5) (1996):49-51.

Moore, K. D., and C. Quinn. *Secondary Instructional Methods*, Madison, WI: WCB Brown & Benchmark, 1994.

National Commission on Excellence in Education. *A Nation at Risk: The Imperative for Educational Reform*. Washington, DC: Author, 1983.

National Research Council. *National Science Education Standards*. Washington, DC: National Academy Press, 1996.

Nickerson, R. "Understanding Understanding." *American Journal of Education* 93 (1985): 201–239.

Orlich, D. C. "An New Analogue for the Cognitive Taxonomy." *The Clearing House* 64(3) (1991): 159–161.

Paul, R. "Bloom's Taxonomy and Critical Thinking Instruction." *Educational Leadership* 42(8) (1985): 36–39.

P. L. 107-110, "No Child Left Behind Act of 2001." Washington, DC: 107th Congress, 1st Session, January 8, 2002.

Pratt, D. *Curriculum Planning: A Handbook for Professionals*. New York: Harcourt Brace, 1994.

Raths, L. E. *Teaching for Thinking: Theory and Application*. Columbus, OH: Merrill, 1967.

Risner, G. P., J. I. Nicholson, and B. Webb. "Cognitive Levels of Questioning Demonstrated by New Social Studies Textbooks: What the Future Holds for Elementary Students." Paper presented at the Annual Meeting of the Mid-South Educational Research Association, Bowling Green, KY, November 15–17, 2000. ED 448 108.

Rohwer, W. D., Jr., and K. Sloane. "Psychological Perspectives." In *Bloom's Taxonomy: A Forty-Year Perspective*, L. W. Anderson and L. A. Sosniak, editors. Ninety-Third Yearbook of the National Society for the Study of Education, Part III. Chicago: University of Chicago Press, 1994, pp. 41–63.

Sagor, R. *Guiding School Improvement with Action Research*. Alexandria, VA: Association for Supervision and Curriculum Development, 2000.

Schurr, S. *How to Improve Discussion and Questioning Practices: Tools and Techniques. Staff Development Kit #2*. Westerville, OH: National Middle Schools Association, 2001. ED 453 196.

Shaunessy, E. "Questioning Technique in the Gifted Classroom." *Gifted Child Today Magazine* 25(5) (2000): 14–21.

Sprenger, M. *Differentiation Through Learning Styles and Memory*. Thousand Oaks, CA: Corwin, 2003.

Steinbrink, J. E., and R. M. Jones. "Focused Test Review Items: Improving Textbook-Test Alignment in Social Studies." *The Social Studies* 82(2) (1991): 72–76.

Stronge, J. H., and J. L. Hindman. "Hiring the Best Teachers." *Educational Leadership* 60(8) (2003): 48–52.

van der Wal, R. J., and R. van der Wal. "Assessing Life Skills in Young Working Adults—Part 1: The Development of an Alternative Instrument." *Education + Training* 45(3) (2003): 139–151.

Walberg, H. J. "Productive Teaching." In *New Directions for Teaching Practice and Research*. H. C. Waxman and H. J. Walberg, editors. Berkeley, CA: McCutchan, 1999, pp.75-104.

Wenglinsky, H. *How Teaching Matters: Bringing the Classroom Back into Discussions of Teacher Quality*. Princeton, NJ: The Milken Family Foundation and Educational Testing Service, 2000.

4 Instructional Design

1 OVERALL CONSIDERATIONS FOR INSTRUCTIONAL PLANNING

Factors Affecting Planning

Planning Resources

2 INSTRUCTIONAL PLANNING PROCEDURES

Preplanning

Unit Planning

Lesson Planning

Postlesson Activities

3 HOW EXPERT TEACHERS PLAN

Planning Routines

Reflective Practice

Treasury of Teaching Materials

What the Research Shows

Having reflected on her own experiences as a student and her new knowledge about state standards, instructional and performance objectives, and the several domains of learning and their taxonomies, Chaka feels more comfortable about planning instruction. She's confident in her understanding of these concepts, at least at a basic level, and she recognizes their importance in planning and implementing instruction.

Now, though, Chaka begins to consider some implications of her new knowledge. She wonders, for instance, about how to specifically arrange instructional time; how to be sure to include all that's important; how to arrange facts, concepts, and generalizations into manageable pieces for teaching and learning—in short, how to plan as master teachers do.

What Chaka is reflecting on, of course, is the *reality* of instructional planning. Our purpose for this chapter is to provide you with practical guidelines for systematic planning, to help you create effective long-range plans, unit plans, and lesson plans. The chapter continues the discussion begun in Chapter 3, covering three main topics: preparation, planning procedures, and the planning practices of expert teachers.

New concepts and techniques introduced in this chapter will help you answer the following questions.

- What factors must I consider for instructional planning?
- What are planning levels, and how do I connect them?
- How can I create an effective unit plan?
- How can I devise lesson plans to implement my unit plans?
- What can I learn from the planning techniques of master teachers?

SECTION 1: OVERALL CONSIDERATIONS FOR INSTRUCTIONAL PLANNING

As Chapter 3 notes, teachers have a primary responsibility to design and implement instruction. They prepare plans that aid in the organization and delivery of their daily lessons. These plans vary widely in style and degree of specificity. Just as there are many ways to teach and learn, there are many ways to plan—there is no single "best" way. Some instructors prefer to construct elaborately detailed, impeccably typed outlines; others rely on brief notes in the weekly lesson plan book. Probably most teachers fall somewhere between these extremes. But regardless of the format they choose, master teachers use planning to help them select the content and methods that will most help their students achieve predefined learning goals. Without effective planning, students are less likely to achieve those goals. As one Washington State high school teacher put it, "Less planning leads to less learning" (Walsh 1992, p. 114).

Planning: content + methods to achieve goals

Planning for a lesson is like planning for an automobile trip. Most drivers, before leaving on a trip to a new area, carefully study a road map and, while driving, continue to check the map. The driver who has taken the same trip many times needs to consult the map less often. Similarly, the first time you teach a lesson, you develop a detailed lesson plan, and you continue to consult the lesson plan while teaching the lesson. After you gain experience, you depend less on the written plan.

Factors Affecting Planning

As you can well imagine, you have much to consider when you plan instruction. Summarized below are some of the initial areas you need to think about. These are not listed in any order of importance because each is equally important. You will find it useful, especially at the beginning of your planning, to write down your thoughts for each consideration. This will help you focus your thinking and confirm that you are considering your situation thoroughly. An excellent source to help with these steps is Amy Baylor, Anastasia Kitsantas, and Hyunmi Chung (2001).

Use these questions to begin planning.

- *Student considerations.* Students are the reason for and focus of your instruction. What do you know about them, individually and as a group? Are they easy or difficult to motivate? What do they already know about the subject you're planning? How might they best learn? What accommodations will be needed for special students?
- *Content and process considerations.* What main ideas and concepts are involved? Will you need to teach skills as well? In what order should the instruction be arranged? Can you devise a variety of learning activities and instructional methods to teach the material?
- *Time Considerations.* How much time is available for this part of the instruction? Are other school functions—assemblies, plays, extracurricular activities—or holidays and vacations likely to interfere? Do you need more than one day or one period?
- *School Considerations.* Are there district or state learning outcomes or standards to be considered? Graduation requirements? Legal requirements for special students?
- *Available Resources.* In addition to school textbooks and supplementary materials, are other resources available in the community, such as historical sites, museums, art galleries, or other special places? Are there people within the community who might provide a perspective?
- *Teacher Considerations.* How knowledgeable are you about the material you're planning? Can you arrange what you know in terms that students will understand?

reflect
- How might you incorporate the goal "reads different materials for a variety of purposes" into your subject?
- How do lesson plans vary by area of discipline or grade level?

Planning Resources

Numerous resources are available to help you with instructional planning, and we discuss several of the major ones later. Keep in mind, however, that effective teachers do not limit themselves to resources specifically designed for planning or for the education professional. They fill file drawers, cabinets, and computer files with materials that they have found useful or that simply look as if they might be useful in planning a lesson or unit. One secondary school history teacher has a large collection of pictures of wooden sailing ships, showing the masts and rigging in detail and describing how the ships were operated. Together with other materials, these help students visualize and understand the reality of Columbus's journey and other "voyages of discovery." A middle school art teacher stores photos of her previous students' artwork on a compact disc. She uses these examples in lesson demonstrations and makes them available for students to view and study on their own.

Effective teachers collect materials long term.

Curriculum Guides   Most schools have **curriculum guides**—statements detailing what should be taught in each grade and in each content area. These guides are created by the state, and sometimes by the district as standards or "essential student learnings," but they are almost always written by teams of teachers after careful consideration of the aims and goals of local schools. Curriculum guides should be the first place to look when you are considering what to teach and how to plan instruction. They provide a framework—in terms of both time and subject matter—for organizing instruction. Guides spell out, often in great detail, the specific knowledge and skills students are expected to attain and the attitudes they should exhibit. They tend to be arranged by grade level for elementary schools and by content area for middle and secondary schools. Of particular benefit to new teachers, they identify

Effective teachers share planning resources.
© Michael Zide.

Try curriculum guides first.

what instruction your students have already had as well as what will be expected of them after your grade or course. (See also Tyler 1949 for a rationale on instructional planning that has stood the test of more than half a century.)

The example goal statements below were written by several groups of teachers in Washington State to meet local needs. Curriculum guides are often phrased in broad terms such as these, thus giving individual teachers freedom to develop appropriate unit and lesson plans. (See criticism of curriculum guides in English 1987.)

Essential Academic Learnings in Reading, #3

The student reads different materials for a variety of purposes. To meet this standard, the student will:

- Read to learn new information, such as reading in science, mathematics, technical documents and for personal need.
- Locate and use information to perform tasks such as using schedules, following directions, filling out job applications and solving problems.
- Read for literary experience in a variety of forms such as novels, short stories, poems, plays and essays to understand self and others.
  (Washington State Commission on Student Learning, 1996, pp. 2–3)

Notice in the above example that "reads different materials for a variety of purposes" is a goal statement, as explained in Chapter 3. Each bulleted statement above shows what students can do to reach the goal. This very desirable goal applies to all levels and subjects in the curriculum. It is as relevant to first-graders as it is to high school physics students, and it can be approached at a variety of levels, from simple to complex, in all grades. Each goal statement would be converted into an age-appropriate instructional objective. The bulleted statements could then state specific or performance objectives of how students will demonstrate evidence of mastery, just as is described in Chapter 3

Standards and Goals   As noted in Chapter 3, Section 4, you will find that national and state standards, available in most subject areas, are an excellent source of goals to aid or direct you in your planning. The federal "No Child Left Behind Act" legislation that requires benchmark testing in reading and math at third though eighth grades will undoubtedly influence the curriculum because of possible sanctions for poor test scores. This legislation may be expanded through the eleventh grade (Tarron Lively and Gary Emerling, *Washington Times*, January 13, 2005, M-1).

Sources of useful standards: federal government, states, academic associations

National academic centers and associations also have developed useful standards and goals for most subject areas. For example, in 1995 the Center for History in the Schools specified this standard: "Students should be able to demonstrate understanding of the Americas by describing the social composition of early settlers and comparing their motives for exploration and colonization."

Every state has standards and goals for most subject areas, with testing at selected grade levels. These standards and goals provide a context for benchmarking testing. Many states are also proposing graduation requirement testing.

National and state standard and goal statements can be a significant help in organizing instruction. But even though you find yourself implementing society goals and standards, don't be reluctant to include other goals that are particularly relevant to your students, your district, or your school, and what your believe is important in the subject you teach.

Textbooks   Another source for planning is the text or texts adopted by the school. Especially for elementary teachers, these can offer useful insights into the curriculum and how to plan for and teach it. School districts often buy a series of elementary school texts from a single publisher—a set of materials to teach math, for instance, from kindergarten through grade 6. Teachers often say, "We're using FOSS Science," or "We've had much success with Houghton Mifflin's literacy program."

These textbook series generally provide a structured sequence of lessons. They specify instructional objectives, provide a variety of teaching suggestions, offer supplementary readings and practice aids, and include an evaluation program. Many also provide lessons designed specifically to help with cooperative learning, thinking processes, decision-making skills, and a variety of problem-solving techniques. Assuming that the materials meet your objectives, they can be an extremely useful resource, helping you make the best use of your planning time. Publishers' aids deserve much study and consideration.

Publishers' materials can help save time.

To illustrate our point, below are selected resources that come with the textbook adoption of *Houghton Mifflin Mathematics,* an elementary program. Some are found in the program's components; others are located on the company's website: **http://www.eduplace.com**.

- *Student texts* feature a variety of lessons in different formats so that students can gain experiences ranging from concrete to abstract.
- The *teacher's edition* is an annotated version of the student text with various planning guides, objectives to be taught, and assessment tools with diagnosis and prescription.
- *Family Letters* are included so that teachers can then send them home to students' families explaining each major topic in a chapter. The letters are available in English, Spanish, Chinese, Hmong, Khmer, Korean, Tagalog, and Vietnamese.
- *The Test Prep Practice* feature provides interactive quizzes that complement those in the student texts and that are located on their websites.
- *Test Quest* is an interactive feature that allows students to choose strategies by which to better understand a math problem.
- *Brain Teasers* contain math puzzles for each chapter and may be solved on-line or photocopied.
- *What Is It?* This feature provides teachers with a detailed description of the mathematics operation or content so that they may teach the material more effectively.
- *Tips and Tricks* show teachers some methods of instruction that can help their students master the specific content or process.
- *When Students Ask* is a set of questions that students most often ask about some operation or concept. The teacher is given a convenient scripted response. A second feature is an on-line page where the teacher may share suggestions with the publisher and subsequently, via the Web, with other teachers.

- *Graphic Organizers* is a set of thirty-seven different graphic organizers made available as teacher instructional aids. These range from Word Webs, Idea Wheels, and Time Lines to Venn Diagrams.
- *Overhead Teaching Activities* provide complete developmental activities that can be used to teach a lesson with transparencies and scripted support for the teachers. These activities may also be used with small groups for preteaching or reteaching.
- *Problem Solving for Success* is an intervention program that builds on using representations to visualize word problems in which models for problem-solving strategies and skills are illustrated for the teacher.
- *English Language Learners Handbook* provides strategies for teaching mathematics concepts, vocabulary, and problem solving to students who are nonnative English speakers or for native speakers needing additional language support.
- *Combination Classroom Guide* has instructional strategies and management ideas for teachers who have combined grade levels in their classrooms.
- *Assessment, Performance Assessment, Spiral Review, Practice, Reteach, Challenge, Problem of the Day, Problem Solving for Advanced Learners, Math Centers, Big Books, Trade Libraries,* and *Skills Tutorial* are available as books in a kit or on CD-ROM.

Much valuable assistance is available from publishers; just be sure that the materials match your objectives, and don't be overwhelmed by the quantity—nobody uses all of the materials for a particular subject. Decide which items are most appropriate for your objectives, your students, and the time available.

Other Resources   Beyond formal school curriculum guides and the supplementary materials associated with textbooks, there are myriad sources of materials that successful teachers use to bring life to their lessons. The following list is suggestive, not comprehensive. Your imagination and the experience of one year of teaching and thoughtful planning should double its length.

- *Colleagues.* Most other teachers will be more than willing to help you find resources and to discuss what works well for them. School librarians can be especially helpful, not only in suggesting resources but also in helping you determine how to include them into instruction (see especially Wolcott 1994).
- *The Internet.* A tremendous amount of educational material is found on the Internet and the World Wide Web, including unit and lesson ideas for all subjects and grades. If you are selective and can adapt the materials you find to fit your students and objectives, then cyberspace can be a positive force in your planning. We provide suggested sites at the end of each chapter.
- *Local libraries, museums, and historical sites.* Each of these can offer considerable aid in structuring a lesson.
- *Government agencies.* From local police departments to county agencies to the Library of Congress—the thoughtful teacher uses all of these and more to make learning a hands-on and stimulating activity.

SECTION 2: INSTRUCTIONAL PLANNING PROCEDURES

From a consideration of planning materials, we now turn to a detailed description of useful planning steps. Experienced, successful teachers do not follow a standard planning procedure. All teachers, however, wrestle with common factors that determine the success of their instruction. Refer to Figure 4.1, which illustrates planning steps in the form of a cycle. We discuss these steps in the order they appear on the chart, but remember that teachers do not necessarily consider each factor in that order. Planning is more a recursive than a linear process: Teachers consider instructional objectives in terms of learning activities and then reconsider each in terms of time and student abilities. All parts are interdependent; a change here likely requires a correction there.

A recursive process with interdependent parts

As stated earlier, much instructional planning is done mentally and may never appear on paper. Effective teachers, especially after several years of experience, rehearse much of their instruction in their heads or by talking to themselves. Plans are never far from their minds, and more than one unit or lesson plan has been worked out in the shower or at the shopping mall (Kagan and Tippins 1992; Sardo-Brown 1988). One outstanding high school teacher notes, "Planning is not just when I am sitting at my desk and writing. Planning includes plenty of think time when I am considering possibilities" (Walsh

FIGURE 4.1

The Instructional Planning Cycle

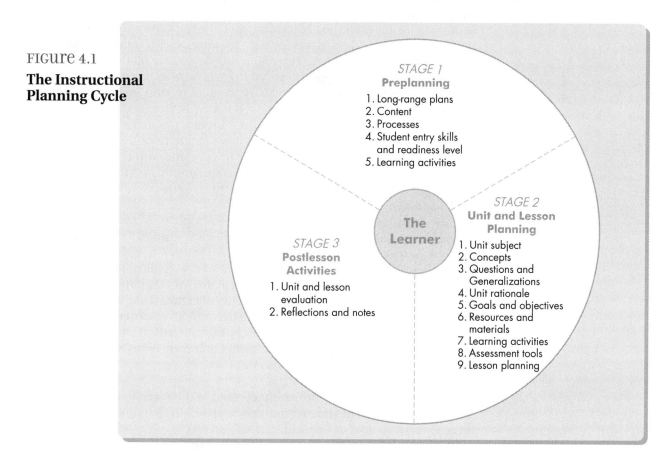

Mental rehearsal as well as
written planning

1992, p. 198). We noted earlier that, as a beginning teacher, you are well advised to write out your plans in some detail. The writing process itself helps you focus your thinking and detect confusion or inconsistency that otherwise inevitably would come out during instruction.

Preplanning

As Figure 4.1 shows, it is useful to consider several general concerns before focusing on unit and lesson planning.

- *Long-range plans.* In this grading period, semester, or year, what days are available for instruction, and which are taken for other purposes?
- *Content.* What is the content to be taught?
- *Processes.* What processes will most effectively reinforce the content?
- *Student entry skills and readiness level.* What must your students know to be successful in the planned course of instruction? Do they need prerequisite instruction?
- *Learning activities.* What learning activities seem most relevant to the content and your instructional goals?

Developing Long-Range Plans   A useful beginning, before school starts, is to create a long-range planning calendar, using a large sheet of paper for each month. (This is a planning technique borne out by the research of Sardo-Brown [1988], for example.) Mark what you already know on your calendar—holidays, in-service days, dates for each grading period, semester end dates, and any other pertinent data. The remaining days make up the time available for instruction. How can you fit everything you want to teach or must accomplish into those remaining squares? Try to fit all of your instructional major topics into the calendar. Do you have too many? Is there not enough time for all? You have just faced one of teaching's biggest problems—there just isn't time for all we need to do. You now begin assigning priorities, deciding what topics to include, which to deemphasize or combine with others, and which to omit. This is one of your most important responsibilities as a teacher, so consider the choices carefully. We will return to the calendar idea when we consider unit and lesson planning.

Start with a big calendar and
then break it down.

The importance and design of long-range plans is amplified by Heidi Hayes Jacobs (2004). She suggests using *big ideas* around which to structure content and *curriculum mapping*, which requires a collaborative effort among teachers to integrate various topics where applicable. We might add that the mapping technique requires a great deal of planning time and effort. The process begins with a system of data collection. Data are collected on your students, their background knowledge and all resources that you have for instruction. The key idea behind mapping is to utilize all the talent in the school and align your instruction with what is known about the students with the curriculum and finally the assessment.

Deciding on Content   Providing content is the essence of most lessons. Textbooks are content rich, sometimes maybe too rich, and require you to be selective about what you will stress. Consider text material carefully. The only content you need is what is relevant to the theme or concept you are developing. You probably have endured classes that were overloaded with content; they had more facts and details than anyone could ever remember. Don't let yours be one of those classes. Delete content that is irrelevant to your major idea. But work hard to find and include activities and examples that make clear to your students the main ideas of your focus topic.

Choose content that focuses the topic.

Deciding on Processes   As we note in Chapter 1, processes are as important to teach as content. Thinking processes—imagining, problem solving, comparing and contrasting, analyzing, organizing, classifying, and numerous others (can you think of some others?)—are critical to almost any subject or topic you are teaching. As you identify content for your units and lessons, note also what thinking processes your students might reasonably need to understand the material. Then make it a point to identify these processes during instruction, helping students to become more aware of deliberate uses of their own thought processes. Consider the following example.

Help students make their thinking explicit

In planning a social studies unit on the U.S. Civil War, you want to include material on the several causes. One way to approach this material is to ask students to consider this question: "What reasons would *you* need to justify killing an acquaintance, a friend, or even a family member (as happened in the Civil War)?" In discussing the question, students can respond by analyzing reasons, classifying and categorizing ideas and arguments, determining importance, and justifying decisions. By planning ahead for this attention to process, you can be sure to include it.

Identifying Students' Entry Skills and Readiness Levels   Another important task, at the early planning stage as well as at all subsequent ones, is to identify your students' **entry skills** and **readiness** levels. (Refer to Table 2.1

Students and Teachers Share in the Excitement of Learning.

on page 33.) What will students need to know to understand what you will be teaching? Are their basic skills adequate for the planned activities, or must you also teach these? As much as 50 percent of the variability in achievement among students can be attributed to insufficient knowledge or skills (Bloom 1976, p. 167; House, Hurst, and Keely 1996).

Are students ready for your unit or lesson?

The sixth principle of the Coalition of Essential Schools (founded in 1984 by Theodore R. Sizer to create a consortium of collaborating schools that would model effective and humane learning communities) requires all students entering high school to have sufficient skills or to receive remediation to gain the necessary skills to be successful (Sizer 1996, p. 154). It is possible that the widespread adoption of constructivist learning theory, with its emphasis on prior knowledge and teaching for understanding, has the potential to reduce the problems related to insufficient entry skills and knowledge. (See Wiggins and McTighe 2005.)

In general, elementary and middle school teachers and schools accept a student's promotion as confirmation that he or she is ready for the next grade, although emergent literacy is often assessed each year at the primary levels. For high school students, whose instruction is arranged by subjects rather than grade level, placement testing is sometimes done, especially in math and English. In most cases, however, placement within a grade or class is assumed to indicate readiness until evidence to the contrary accumulates.

An effective way to identify entry levels is to give a pretest. Ask yourself what knowledge and skills a student would need, beyond reading level, to understand the proposed instruction. If you can identify several skills or pieces of information, write a short quiz and administer it to see if most students are ready. Remember, you are determining the skills students need to *begin* the new unit—not the skills they should learn from it!

Gauges: placement, promotion, pretest

Experience will soon show you which entry skills should be assessed. In the meantime, you will find that most current standard instructional materials provide a range of grade-appropriate options, although you will need to make some changes for some students.

Incorporating Learning Activities   **Learning activities** are hands-on, interactive experiences such as experiments and role playing. These should be considered in your long-term planning, although they will play a larger part in your unit planning. As a beginning teacher, you have to find or create such activities; after a few years' experience, you should have several file drawers full of activities that have worked with past students. As you construct your long-term calendar and consider the goals you need to work toward, try to block out time for those activities that were (or are expected to be) particularly useful in helping students succeed, or note the activities that were not successful and need to be changed (see Brophy and Alleman 1991; Pressman and Dublin 1995; Price and Nelson 2003.

Unit Planning

As teachers, we divide instructional time and topics into pieces to make learning manageable. Because we can't teach everything all at once, we sort content into blocks called **units**, and we arrange these across time using our long-range planning calendar. However, having subdivided our instruction into pieces to make it *manageable,* we must also be careful to allow time to pull the pieces together again to make the content *understandable.* "Unit planning is the most important as well as the most time-consuming level of planning for each teacher" (Walsh 1992, p. 178).

An eighth-grade social studies teacher planning a year's course in U.S. history serves as a convenient example. To make learning the subject manageable, the teacher divides it chronologically: the pre-Columbian era, colonial times, the revolutionary period, and the present. (Note that chronology is neither the only nor necessarily the preferred way to organize history classes; it is simply used as a familiar example to illustrate a point about instructional planning.) Teachers of other grades and subjects might use **topics** as an organizer. In science, topics such as matter, sound, electricity, leaves, and waste disposal can all serve as organizers. Language arts teachers might organize their ideas around topics such as love, friendship, or heroes to integrate literature and composition. Primary and lower elementary grades do much the same with seasons, holidays, or special events.

After identifying units, the teacher makes a subjective judgment—on the basis of his or her content knowledge, student readiness levels, and the desired outcomes—about the relative importance of each topic. Those deemed more important will need relatively more class time. Working with the planning calendar and topic list, the teacher then arranges the topics in the desired order (sequences them), leaving time within each unit to analyze the topic and combine it with other material as needed.

This method of planning seems reasonable and logical, yet in practice it can become messy and frustrating. The basic problem, as we noted previously, is that you will inevitably want to cover more material than you can fit into the available time. The big questions, then, become "What must be included?" and "What must I omit to make enough room?" All teachers, at all levels, face this dilemma—and no one answers it easily. The penalty for teachers not answering these questions at the planning stage, though, is that they may inadvertently omit some important material or dwell too long on less important matters.

Having identified major topics and worked them into your planning calendar, you are now in a position to make detailed plans to provide instruction for each topic. Most teachers call these **unit plans**.

Unit planning is the mainstay, the bread and butter, of teachers at all levels—both teachers of self-contained elementary school classes and teachers of content-specific middle and secondary school classes such as science and history. And although teachers plan in a variety of ways, the unit plans they develop contain a number of common elements.

Although we will discuss these elements separately, in practice you are more likely to move back and forth among them recursively rather than to proceed in a straight line through them.

Defining the Unit Subject   Unit subjects or topics vary across both grade levels and content areas. Often, as in the example of history, the subject seems apparent—the Civil War, the Great Depression. Mathematics also seems self-explanatory—fractions, division, polynomials. These are reasonable topics, and effective units certainly can be built around them. You can create many similar examples within your own subject field

---

Organize the year by unit or topic.

reflect

- Think of activities that would help a student link each of the following to his or her affective experiences: discrimination, friendship, and democratic processes.

- Within each of the following content areas, identify several topics around which you could build a unit: Euclidean geometry, the conflict in Iraq, Columbus's impact on the Western Hemisphere, and presidential elections.

Possible unit topics: a chronological period, an interdisciplinary concept, a question

Concepts   Teachers at all levels find they can often tie content to student interests by building units around concepts. We explore this term more deeply in Chapter 5, but for now think of **concepts** as "category" words, enabling us to group many individual objects or ideas under a common label. For example, *desk* is a word (concept) that stands for all the objects we see that have "desky" characteristics. (Can you name some characteristics?) Because a desk is a concrete object, it's easy to get agreement on most of its characteristics. As concepts become more abstract, however (love, democracy, friendship), people often have vague and different ideas about their characteristics. These abstract concepts are ones that students often are confused by or simply find interesting. Thus concepts almost automatically become useful unit topics.

For instance, a language arts teacher might select "friendship" as a unit concept or topic. Students could then read and write short stories, plays, poems, biographies, and other works that would help them better understand the topic, themselves, and others. Alternatively, teachers might have students suggest concepts that interest them, perhaps with different small groups or individuals making explorations and reporting to the class. Notice, by the way, that this approach works on students' interests and builds knowledge from their present level—which is one basis of constructivist learning theory (see Hurst 2001). The box below lists some possible themes or concepts for U.S. history units. Note that the themes focus on people, ideas, and trends rather than chronology.

Examples of Historical Concepts

- Elections
- Economic depressions
- Immigration and emigration
- Changing laws for changing times

Elementary school teachers, particularly those in self-contained classrooms, often include ideas from several content areas in their thematic units, thus developing an **interdisciplinary thematic unit**. For instance, in the "friendship" unit, in addition to the language arts activities, the teacher might include social studies by helping the children develop questionnaires and make a survey of what other students in the school consider to be characteristics of friends.

During art time, students might create pictures illustrating types of friendship—people with animals or animals with animals, for instance, as well as the varieties of friendship among people. Math might be included by making charts and graphs of the results from the questionnaires. The concept could even be integrated into lunchtime. Only the teacher's and students' imaginations limit the possibilities (see Castanos 1997; Martin 1995; Martinello and Cook 2000; McDonald and Czerniak 1994). Patricia L. Roberts and Richard D. Kellough (2004) have published a very practical source for developing thematic or interdisciplinary units. Refer to their work for lesson plans, ideas, and models.

Interdisciplinary teaching involves a conscious effort to apply knowledge, principles, and values to more than one academic discipline simultaneously. The disciplines may be related through a central theme, issue, problem, process, topic, or experience. The framework for such instruction is the creation of themes, thematic units, or units framework that specify what students are expected to learn as a result of the experiences and lessons that are a part of the unit (from Houghton Mifflin, eduplace.com, 2005).

Language arts tends to be a major area for interdisciplinary teaching. Integrated through a common theme—for example, television advertisements—are listening, speaking, reading, writing, and critical thinking. A broader kind of integration attempts to encompass several curricular areas.

Interdisciplinary teaching provides one technique in which students can use knowledge learned in one context as a knowledge base in other contexts in and out of school. Student motivation for independent learning is a spin-off from this model.

PROFESSIONAL VOICES FROM THE FIELD

))))

Jack C. Horne, North Central Educational Service District, Wenatchee, Washington

Using Technology to Improve Reading and Writing

The Endangered Species Project (ESP) was a project of nine rural school districts for children in grades 3 to 8 in central Washington. The program integrated technology, literacy skills, and science as an interdisciplinary means of helping those children improve their reading and writing skills. The project was driven by the question "How can technology be utilized to improve basic skills?"

Over the course of the one-year project, teachers participated in a very intensive set of staff development activities. Writing was based on the "Six Traits of Writing" rubric. Hands-on science was implemented in the schools, and each school had a weather station built for student daily use. In addition, native plants, animals, and birds were mapped and flights of birds recorded and shared via an ESP website. Students who had the self-motivation wrote about various aspects of science and school life and shared those thoughts on-line with students from other schools.

A pre- and posttest third-party evaluation using the Iowa Test of Basic Skills showed improvement on 35 of 36 possible tested traits.

Students can be involved at all levels—selecting the concept and determining what content areas might be involved, what activities are appropriate, and even what instruction (or instructional methods) might be most useful (see Johns 2003; O'Connor-Petruso 2003). Student participation in preplanning requires teachers to account for these activities in their long-range plans. Having the students help preplan instruction is not a spontaneous act.

Consider involving students in planning.

Questions and Generalizations   Although concepts make excellent unit organizers and planning tools, they are not your only choices. A well-worded question can also effectively focus your unit (or lesson). Consider the following question: "In what ways was the participation of the United States in the War of 1812 and the Vietnam War similar?" What information would be useful in a response? A detailed description of each war is not necessarily relevant, nor is a lengthy discussion of causes and results—unless such information is relevant to the question. Notice how focus and content of the unit are almost dictated by the wording of the question.

Here's another example that could organize biology or ecology by examining evolution and extinction: "Who will survive?" Again, notice how usefully the question focuses and organizes content. Such a unit allows plenty of room for investigation of both historical evolution and current threats to species. (See Hanifi, Kelly, and Zeegers 2003 for a model that incorporates student questions.)

In addition to questions, generalizations (a full discussion is presented in Chapter 5) can be useful for organizing unit content. **Generalizations** are inferential statements that express a relationship between two or more concepts, can be verified, and have a predictive value. Here are two examples: "As you shorten or lengthen a vibrating string, the sound increases or decreases, respectively." "Cold fronts cause a temperature drop in the affected geographic areas." Notice how instruction is almost automatically selected and organized by making clear the concepts involved and exploring the relationships. Notice also that both questions and generalizations provide built-in motivation because both present students with a question to be answered or a problem to be solved rather than just a statement of "learn this." Using generalizations often stimulates thinking and problem solving. The Instructional Strategies box below gives two examples of generalizations that could be used as unit topics.

INSTRUCTIONAL
STRATEGIES

Generalizations Used as Unit Topics

The development of the personal automobile revolutionized social and family behavior.

Waterways, as paths of transportation, determined much of the course of colonization.

As you consider organizing units, try to consider what you hope the students will remember long after they leave your class. Certainly, much information will be soon forgotten, but if you have helped them organize knowledge in ways that clarify concepts, answer questions, and explain relationships in terms they understand, they will have truly learned. (See Jacobs [2004] for examples of *big ideas*.)

> **reflect**
>
> • What are some useful focusing questions or big ideas in your subject area?

Defining the Rationale   An educational **rationale** answers the question "Why is it important to your students to learn this material?" The response should be a reasoned one, not just "It's good for them," "It's required at this grade," or "They have to have it to get into another class." These reasons might be true, but you need to identify a more substantial one, and you need to be intellectually honest with yourself, your students, and your profession. If a parent asks why you are teaching certain material, he or she deserves a thoughtful response based on the importance of the content to the student. So do your students. (And they, at least in high school, are apt to be more blunt in their request: "Hey! How come we gotta learn this stuff?") In the Instructional Strategies box below, we provide two example rationales.

instructional strategies

Example Rationales for Units

Primary Science Unit

   Understanding scientific principles and processes is important for every student. Helping students become interested in science at an early age will increase their motivation to want more science as they get older. Additionally, doing science at an early age is an excellent introduction to such higher thinking processes as observing, classifying, making inferences, and withholding judgment until sufficient data have been gathered. Thus this unit on water, besides having many informative, interesting activities, will help prepare students mentally for enjoying the observation of the world around them.

Ninth-Grade Literature Unit

Through a study of Greek mythology, this unit helps students build a foundation for understanding imagery and symbolism in literature. Additionally, students should gain appreciation for differing worldviews and human diversity as they examine ancient peoples' perspectives on life and nature. Mythology lies at the source of many themes, images, and symbols in both classical and modern literature. Learning to understand and enjoy these ancient tales will help students understand and interpret all literature.

Why learn this?

Define unit objectives in terms of content, skills/processes, and attitudes.

Defining Goals and Objectives   In planning units and lessons, teachers need to develop learning outcomes in the three areas of *content understanding* (as opposed to simply memorizing facts), *skills/processes*, and *attitudes*. These three areas drive instruction at all levels, although the emphasis among them may shift across the grade levels and for content areas. The focus in elementary school may be on skills/processes with content being stressed more in middle school; by high school, most of the focus is in the content realm. At all levels, however, instruction must integrate skills and processes with content understanding.

Attitudes—such as willingness to share or cooperate, to enjoy reading or music or dance, to suspend judgment until sufficient facts are known, and to tolerate ambiguity in decision making—are not specified as objectives as often as content and process. Nonetheless, they are important for students to recognize and deserve more teacher attention than they seem to receive.

At the risk of repetition, we emphasize that these three areas of content understanding, skills/processes (especially thinking processes), and attitudes are interrelated. We probably don't teach or learn purely in any one of them without involving at least one of the others. "Thinking" obviously requires something to think about (content) as well as a willingness to do so (attitude). It is simply convenient for planning and instruction to separate these and emphasize one part or another. Students (and teachers) need to be reminded frequently, however, that learning and understanding are integrated, holistic acts.

What should unit outcomes be? They are best stated as general instructional objectives. (You might want to check back through our full discussion of objectives writing in Chapter 3.) Try to include objectives from each of the areas: content, skills/processes, and attitudes. These objectives should be attainable (not necessarily mastered) in perhaps as little as a week or as much as three or four weeks. A unit lasting longer than this should have logical dividing points, for both understanding and manageability. The example outcomes in the box below are typical.

INSTRUCTIONAL
STRATEGIES

Example Unit Outcomes

Examples of Subject Matter/Content Outcomes

- The student understands the relationships among current, resistance, and voltage in a simple series electrical circuit.
- The student knows the significance of Presidents Kennedy, Johnson, and Nixon in involving the U.S. people in the war in Vietnam.
- Students understand how developments in naval architecture prior to 1500 made possible the "discovery" and colonization of Africa below the Sahara and of both the Americas.

Examples of Skill/Process Outcomes

- The student demonstrates satisfactory competence in using the Internet as a research resource.
- Each student uses appropriate skill in gathering and classifying data to make inferences for a history project.

INSTRUCTIONAL
STRATEGIES

> ## Example Unit Outcomes—Cont'd
>
> - The student states an appropriate series of steps in diagnosing and repairing an automobile that won't start.
>
> Examples of Attitude Outcomes
>
> - Students show progress (indicated by the teacher's anecdotal records) in delaying a decision until sufficient data have been assembled.
> - Students achieve a level of personal satisfaction (indicated in self-reports) from completing the history project.
> - Students apply a "decision tree" (evidenced by student journals and self-reports) in making several personal decisions.

The example outcomes imply that at least several lessons will be required to achieve the level of competence indicated. Notice also that, from the wording, both the necessary instruction and the proper evidence of achievement (for evaluation) are implied. For attitudinal outcomes, evaluation tools are indicated because these outcome goals are less frequently seen in unit plans (and, in some locales, might be subject to citizen criticism for encroaching on personal thoughts or feelings).

In summary, your unit objectives will target specific contents, skills/processes, and attitudes. It is useful to state content objectives as concepts, questions, or generalizations. Skills/processes should include those related to learning, communicating, thinking, decision making, and relationships with other people. Attitudinal objectives, particularly concerning self-esteem and relating oneself to others, need to be deliberately built into unit plans so students can be "set up" for success. Finally, objectives are statements of *student outcomes,* not teacher behaviors. "In this unit I will teach about time zones" is a statement of teacher intent, not a student learning outcome (see Yelon 1996; Zemelman, Daniels, and Hyde 1998).

Selecting Resources and Materials   We discuss resources in Section 1 of this chapter as part of the preparation stage, but remember their importance. Each unit you create should have as many appropriate resources as you can find to support your instruction and to provide as many ways as possible for students to connect their experiences to the unit. Keep an index of the resources you use; as you gain teaching experience, you can save yourself many hours of searching by having a handy record of sources and items you have used in the past. Resources are entered into the unit plan most conveniently as a list, with perhaps a note about location or intended use.

By the fall of 2003, nearly 100 percent of U.S. public schools had access to the Internet (Parsad and Jones 2005). Teachers are reporting that computers and Internet connectivity are readily available to them in their classrooms, and teachers are generally expected to have at least basic computer literacy to effectively integrate computing tools into their lesson plans. Computers are powerful tools that can be used for communication, creation, and administration (Hansen and Brown 1997). Using the computer as part of an instructional plan is not a spur-of-the-moment decision. You plan for computer use just as you plan the use of textbooks, crayons and paper, or videotaped programs.

As with any instructional tool, some teachers are more likely to incorporate computers into their instructional plans than are others, for a variety of reasons. (See Smerdon et al. 2000 for insight.) Teachers with an active learning orientation are more likely to make use of computers for instruction. Whether hardware and software are readily available in sufficient number and whether the teacher feels that he or she is a competent user will also affect how and if computers are included in instructional activities (Becker 2000).

Computer usage should be planned, not impulsive

TECHNOLOGY INSIGHT

Finding Lesson Plan Resources on the World Wide Web

A great many Web-based resources exist for teachers. Using a search engine and combinations of Boolean terms such as "lesson plan" and "multiplication + grade 4," it is possible to locate many suggestions for specific instructional activities. As mentioned previously (see the Technology Insight box entitled "Not All Information Is Created Equal: Validity and Reliability of Information," in Chapter 2), a good teaching resource should include some evidence of a positive impact on student achievement.

The best websites for teaching resources tend to be those that are organized and controlled by professional educational organizations or edited by groups of educators. Two of the most respected teaching resources on the Web include the Eisenhower National Clearinghouse for Mathematics and Social Education (**http://www.enc.org**) and the Gateway to Educational Materials (**http://www.thegateway.org**). Both of these sites are funded at least in part by the U.S. Department of Education. The Eisenhower National Clearinghouse states that part of its mission is to "identify *effective* curriculum resources." The Gateway to Educational Materials states that it is dedicated to providing a *comprehensive* collection of resources. Making the sponsoring agencies known and stating the organizations' intentions make it easier to decide how best to make use of these resources.

Creating Your Own Learning Activities   Learning activities were introduced briefly in the discussion on preplanning. Like resources, however, they also play an important part in the unit-planning process. This section will give you some specific aids in creating and finding activities beyond the textbook that will reinforce your instruction.

As much as possible, learning activities should reach students through the several intelligences that Howard Gardner (1999) has brought to our attention, among them linguistic, musical, spatial, and interpersonal (see also

Lazear 1999). Gardner and other researchers have made it clear that students learn in a variety of ways; they have also provided us with useful tools and techniques to plan instruction that recognizes this variety.

> ## Gardner's Eight Intelligences
>
> Bodily/kinesthetic
> Intrapersonal
> Interpersonal
> Logical/mathematical
> Musical/rhythmic
> Naturalist
> Verbal/linguistic
> Visual/spatial

One of the most useful aids in planning unit and lesson activities is the **Kaplan matrix**, created by Sandra Kaplan (1979). The matrix is used to plan outcomes and activities at the several levels of Bloom's cognitive taxonomy; it is illustrated in Table 4.1. Such planning is extremely important if you are to avoid presenting most instruction and assessing at the knowledge level. Use of this matrix forces you at least to consider the other taxonomic levels; if you then choose to remain at the knowledge level, it will be an intentional decision rather than an oversight.

The matrix idea can be used in many ways. Table 4.2 shows it in use as a work plan, indicating objective levels, teacher activities, learning experiences, and student products. Again, the act of making such a planning document is itself a positive planning activity—it forces you to think about student outcomes and the types and levels of activities that will most likely help students achieve those outcomes.

Learning activities are what you use to get your students involved—in as many ways and through as many senses as possible. Your imagination (right hemisphere) is the key, but a planning matrix (left hemisphere) will help you organize and sequence this important piece of your teaching.

Formulating Assessment Tools   The final portion of your unit plan is assessment of student progress. Because planning is a recursive activity, you need to consider assessment throughout the planning process. Indeed, some teachers find it useful to consider it first—How will I measure what my students can do?—and then create appropriate instruction and activities. In other words, they create a test and teach to it. We urge you to consider assessment throughout your planning. Good instruction entails appropriate assessment.

Because Chapter 10 focuses in detail on assessment, we provide only some general guidelines here. First, and perhaps most important, is to remember that the purpose of assessment is to provide evidence of the degree of achievement *each* student has made toward *each* objective. Whatever your system, it must provide that type of individual data.

Correlate new activities to Bloom's taxonomy.

TABLE 4.1

The Kaplan Matrix for Extending the Curriculum

	Performance Objectives and Related Student Activities					
Content or Concepts	Knowledge	Comprehension	Application	Analysis	Synthesis
Volcanoes	List facts about the Mt. Saint Helens devastation.	Compare Mt. Saint Helens to the volcanoes of Hawaii.	How could we use the piles of volcanic ash?	What do the people near Mt. Saint Helens feel?	Make a volcano model for our class.
Minerals and gems	List the important gems found in the Northeast.	Contrast the hardness of the minerals found in the Northeast.	Field-test the hardness of ten minerals.	What would happen if the government imposed tougher mining regulations?	Grow crystals of various shapes and colors.
Space travel	Name all the people who have gone to the moon.	Compare the Russian space program to the U.S. space program.	If you were an astronaut, what would you study about space?	What do you think would happen if we found life elsewhere?	Make a rocket and fly it.
Weather and climate	Name the different types of clouds.	Contrast the climates of the Southwest and the Southeast.	Chart the amount of rainfall for the next week.	What effect did El Niño have on the world's weather?	Create a wind generator.

SOURCE: Adapted from Kaplan 1979, with permission of the author.

TABLE 4.2

Teacher-Student Work Plan

Content	Level of Objective	Teaching Activity	Learning Experiences	Student Product
Places of origin	K	Lecture/ recitation Reading assignment Worksheet	Note taking Reading	Completed worksheet
Places of origin	C	Demonstration of how to construct graphs	Note taking Constructing a graph	Graph
Places of origin	AP	Small-group presentation	Each group makes a prediction and presents to the class.	Presentation by small groups to whole class
Places of origin	AN	Presentation of assignment Discussion of resources Description of final product Breaking class into groups	Each group focuses on one immigrant group and is responsible for explaining its motives for coming to the United States, using references, filmstrips, and other resources.	Report to class

SOURCE: Adapted from Kaplan 1979, with permission of the author.

Second, it is important to think of assessment as occurring throughout your units—it is not simply "a big test at the end." If your units include some skills/processes as objectives (and they should), you can assess these as students complete them, using rating scales or checklists. Attitudes can be assessed with your own anecdotal records throughout the unit and periodically by student self-report forms. Particularly for a unit that includes many concepts or much complex information, understanding of content should be assessed with short quizzes at several points during the unit rather than all at once at the end.

Finally, explain your assessment methods to your students—they want and need to know how their performance will be judged. Knowing the ground rules helps them clarify their efforts and probably will result in higher achievement. If your state uses high-stakes assessments, then model some of your test questions after the state required items.

Assess frequently, not just at the end.

KEY IDEAS

Parts of a Unit Plan

- Subject or topic
- Rationale
- Instructional objectives
- Content
- Processes
- Resources
- Learning activities
- Evaluation

REFLECT

- We usually think of assessment as tests of subject matter knowledge. What other areas of student progress are important for you to monitor?
- For the eight areas identified by Gardner, what types of assessment tools, other than subject matter tests, would be useful?

INSTRUCTIONAL STRATEGIES

A Model Lesson Plan

Teacher
Course Title

1. Unit
2. General Instructional Objectives
3. Specific Learning Outcomes
4. Rationale
5. Content and Skills/Processes
6. Instructional Procedures
   (a) Focusing Event
   (b) Teaching Procedures
   (c) Student Participation and Activities
   (d) Formative Check
   (e) Closure
7. Assessment
8. Materials, Aids, and Computer Needs
9. Notes/File Comments

INSTRUCTIONAL STRATEGIES

A Model Lesson Plan—Cont'd

(The intent of each part is probably clear to you, but some amplification of several parts may help and is provided below.)

1. *Unit:* Record your unit title here.

2. *General Instructional Objectives:* As discussed earlier, these are the *unit* outcomes that this lesson is meant to reinforce. A general instructional objective might be "Each student will understand the relationships among voltage, resistance, and current in an electrical circuit." A lesson typically will reinforce several objectives. Thus this lesson might focus on content but could also reinforce skills and attitudes.

3. *Specific Learning Outcomes:* These are the specific objectives of this *lesson.* You might have several in a lesson. An example might be "Using Ohm's Law for calculations, the student will correctly determine the needed values in each of the following circuits: (a) Current is 3.0 amps; resistance is 5,000 ohms. (b) Voltage is 9 volts; current is 0.3 amps. (c) Resistance is 10k ohms; voltage is 6 volts."

4. *Rationale:* This is the same as the rationale for the unit plan but stated in a way that relates this lesson to the unit. In other words, a rationale for a lesson would explain why this particular lesson is important in achieving the unit goals: "To use electricity safely in the home, shop, and business, it is necessary to understand how current, voltage, and resistance are related. The physical relationship can in part be understood mathematically. This lesson will help the student achieve this understanding."

5. *Content and Skills/Processes:* It is important to separate in your mind (and on paper) the content and skills you want students to learn and the procedures or techniques you will use to teach them that content and those skills. This lesson plan format helps you do that. Under "Content" you list the specific concepts or ideas you want students to learn in the lesson. Content for the above lesson in electrical circuits might include working with the following:

Circuits	Ohm's Law	Resistance
EMF	Currents	Amperage
Volts	Inverse ratios	Ohms

6. *Instructional Procedures:* In this section, you list the specific methods you will use to teach each part of the lesson. For our lesson on electrical circuits, for example, some parts might be done by questioning to review an earlier lesson and establish focus on this one. Other parts might have students experiment with a circuit in small groups or view a video and take notes. Your efforts to find activities for the several intelligences should appear here.

7. *Assessment Procedures:* Include a brief explanation of what you will do to determine whether students have reached the objectives. For our sample lesson, students' answers to the computations and explanations of how the problems were solved would be sufficient for assessment.

Lesson Planning

General Plans   Although it is often considered as a separate topic, lesson planning is simply an extension of unit planning. Individual lessons are one means we use to help students achieve desired unit learning outcomes (objectives). We will show you what elements a lesson plan should include and some ways to arrange those elements, but you must be the one to determine what methods work best for you.

Think of a **lesson** as a piece of a unit, not as a block of time (see Bryant and Bryant 2000). Lesson plans are not the same as activity schedules for the school day. Student teachers are often confused when they see their cooperating teacher's "lesson plan" book and find that it contains mostly notes like the following:

Think of lessons in terms of meaning, not time.

Tuesday, 8th-grade English, 1st period
1. Review spelling words.
2. Dictate test—be sure students make answer sheet first.
3. Introduce Poe's "Tell-Tale Heart." Discuss mental aspects first.
4. Silent reading, Poe
5. Announce preparations for dismissal at 9:55.

This example is not a lesson plan; it is a schedule of what the teacher intends to do during a class. Lesson plans, like unit plans, are statements of what *students* will do. A good lesson plan contains most of the elements of a unit plan, just on a reduced scale. See the Instructional Strategies box on pages 124–125.

Experienced teachers frequently do not write comprehensive lesson plans, although they may expect you, as a student teacher or novice, to do so. An experienced teacher probably spent several years writing similar plans but now has them largely in his or her head, jotted down in margin notes in textbooks, and summarized in brief notes the several activities a lesson might contain. Also, an experienced teacher's unit plan or outline may contain much of what a novice would put into lesson plans. Thus, even if an individual teacher's lesson plan book looks much like the above example, he or she probably did do the planning.

There are many different lesson plan formats from which to choose; the best one to use is determined by your specific instructional goals and teaching strategies. The authors of this text, and many of their students, have found the lesson plan format shown in the box to be useful. The importance of lesson plans and the unit plans they support cannot be overstated for professional instruction. As one high school teacher puts it, "The better the teacher plans, the better the teacher" (Walsh 1992, p. 97). (Excellent examples of lesson plan formats and other considerations are found in Johns 2003; Little 2003; O'Connor-Petruso 2003; Pappas 2003; and Price and Nelson2003.)

Constructing IEPs   All children with disabilities, by federal law, must have **individual education plans** (IEPs) *written* for them. The IEP is a special and extended adaptation of a lesson plan. We have seen them typed in as few as four pages and as many as twenty! Your employing school district will provide the specified format for you to follow. However, just to illustrate their complexity and attention to detail, we present the box on page 127, which simply lists all the key descriptors or key elements mandated by Washington State's

Office of the State Superintendent of Public Instruction. As you examine the box, keep in mind that, for each item listed, a complete justification or detailed description is required for a total of 39 separate points. Did we mention that IEPs are labor intensive? And, most likely, at least 12 percent of your students will be legally classified as disabled.

Basic Elements of an IEP Required in Washington State

- General characteristics and demographics
- Services to be rendered
- Placement where services will be done
- Recommendations for placement or sites
- Levels of expected performance

But don't give up in despair! You aren't alone. There will be specialists available to help with the planning and delivery of services. (See Bateman and Linden 1998–2000 and Ysseldyke, Algozzine, and Thurlow 2000 for detailed models of IEPs.) You *will* be able to do IEPs.

Postlesson Activities

Evaluating Unit and Lesson Plans   Up to this point in this chapter, we have used the term *assessment* several times to indicate monitoring of student progress. However, we also wish to monitor our own progress as teachers. In this section, we use the term *evaluation* for this process.

What worked and what didn't?

At the conclusion of every class session, ask yourself a series of questions about the effectiveness of your lesson and unit plans: Were the objectives realistic and appropriate? Did the instructional methods work? For which learners and to what degree? What components of the lesson succeeded? What aspects could be improved? Write your thoughts in a journal or in your textbook's margins to help you identify difficulties experienced by learners and to relate these problems to specific elements of the lesson and unit.

Keeping Planning Notes and Reflecting on Future Planning Needs
Also jot down any notes or comments about the lesson or unit that will help you the next time you teach it. Master teachers refer to the previous year's notes and resource files as they plan their lessons (Walsh 1992). In fact, one of the greatest distinctions between novice and expert teachers is that the experts have large quantities of previously gathered material to draw on—*and they use it continually.*

An emerging document that you can continually improve

Lesson and unit plans should be thought of as *emerging documents*; the first ones you construct will be at only the earliest stage of development. After your initial use of these plans, the actual classroom conditions (learner entry skills, teaching procedures, and learner outcomes) need to be compared to the planned situation. The resulting data will allow for refinement and recycling, making the unit and lesson plans more effective instructional tools. You will continually evaluate your instructional plans each time you use them, always attempting to improve content, activities, and methods.

reflect

Instructional planning can be envisioned as a grid with a series of principles and strategies. This grid includes deciding what to teach, how to teach, and how to communicate realistic expectations as key principles for instructional planning (Ysseldyke and Elliott 1999).

Under the component of managing instruction, the grid highlights instructional preparations, productive use of time, and the establishment of a positive classroom environment. Obviously, we concur. Do you? List several specific classroom management benefits you believe might flow from good instructional planning.

section 3: how expert teachers plan

We close this chapter by describing some planning behaviors that separate expert and novice teachers, and what the research shows. If you are aware of good planning practices and research when you begin to teach, you will have less to learn through experience to become an efficient and effective classroom planner and teacher.

Differences in planning between novice and expert

In general, three areas separate the novice and expert planner: (1) planning routines and interdependent planning levels (McBer 2000; Ornstein and Lasley 2004), (2) reflective practice, and (3) a treasury of teaching materials (Walsh 1992, pp. 12–24). We will consider each of these in some detail.

Planning Routines

Many repetitive tasks will confront you each day as a teacher. These **routines** include activities such as gathering and dispensing papers, recording tardiness and absences, recording participation in activities, checking assignments, and giving all students an equal chance to respond to questions. Expert teachers devise and revise plans to simplify and systematize the accomplishment of such tasks. For instance, students can be assigned on a rotating schedule to distribute papers and to take roll. A student can be assigned to mark on a class roster which students you call on to help you avoid missing any or calling on some too often (see Clement 2000).

Use student workers to save time.

Expert teachers work out many aids like these, frequently involving student help when appropriate, and thus save a few (or perhaps quite a few) minutes of instructional time each day. Consider: Five minutes saved daily is twenty-five minutes a week, or nine hundred minutes in a 180-day school year. Your students deserve an extra fifteen hours of instructional time.

Expert teachers consistently implement several distinct planning levels—long range, unit, and daily—as an interdependent set of routines (Walsh 1992). These routines help convert long-range plans into daily and weekly schedules, and keep short-term instruction aligned with long-range goals and the overall school calendar (McBer 2000; Ornstein and Lasley 2004.

Reflective Practice

Donald A. Schön (1995) examined how various professionals—architects, physicians, engineers, and educators—actually practice. He discovered that competent professionals usually know a great deal more than they verbalize. In other words, they have a depth of knowledge; in their professional lives, they reflect on that knowledge and then apply it to new or unusual problems. Schön encourages professionals to think, ponder, and reflect about past, present, and future actions as a means of designing productive problem-solving strategies.

Applying Schön's postulates to education has encouraged many educators and educational researchers to promote reflection as a key element in stimulating professional growth and improving professional practice. **Reflection** is an active mental process that master teachers use consistently as they interact with students and the curriculum (see Panasuk and Sullivan 1998; Strong, Silver, and Perini 2001).

Walsh (1992) observed evidence of "reflective dialogue" in the planning behaviors of award-winning teachers. The ones he interviewed stated that they consistently rehearsed classroom scenarios before teaching, frequently talking to themselves about what they wanted to have happen in class. These rehearsals included consideration of the best instructional options and methods for handling anticipated classroom dilemmas, such as a class that doesn't respond as expected to a lesson. Furthermore, these teachers followed each lesson, as soon as possible, with a period of reflection, taking quick notes on what worked well and what didn't.

PROFESSIONAL VOICES FROM THE FIELD

Jack Guske, Washtucna High School, Washtucna, Washington

A Well-Planned Student-Teacher Collaboration

The State Parks Department of Washington State decided to close thirty-two parks around the state to save money. One of them was the scenic and beautiful Lyons Ferry State Park in central eastern Washington.

The students in social studies classes asked if they could solve the problem of closing Lyons Ferry. By using student-teacher collaboration, the problem was jointly analyzed, culminating with a list of the benefits of the park—camping, swimming, fishing, the only boat launch for thirty miles, picnicking, tourism, and general aesthetics.

The solution was to make the general public aware of the problem. Students conducted hearings, initiated a letter-writing campaign, and undertook other forms of activism to save Lyons Ferry. Letter writing even extended to the elementary schools, where pupils colored sad faces with no place to swim. The results of these efforts were sent to the state legislature.

A public hearing was held with managers from the State Park Service. Teams of students prepared research analyses of each of the benefits and generated questions or comments for the park personnel to address during that hearing. In the end, the decision to close Lyons Ferry was rescinded, and we celebrated a victory for ourselves and a very successful project.

Treasury of Teaching Materials

Planning is the heart of
instruction.

Much of planning confidence and expertise stems from two sources that all master teachers possess: (1) file cabinets or computer files full of valuable resources collected over the years and (2) last year's plan book. These two sources constitute part of an experienced teacher's planning edge over new teachers.

Novice teachers cannot compensate for the full file cabinets. Novices who want to become excellent teachers simply have to become savers and collectors (and develop a retrieval system that allows them to find what they have). What do you save? Virtually anything that relates to your instruction, but especially successful learning activities, tests, quizzes, magazine articles and pictures, bulletin board materials, computer and Internet resources, assignments, study guides—the list is almost endless.

Having last year's plans obviously simplifies this year's planning—much of the groundwork has been done. This is one part of teaching the student teacher usually doesn't see. However, don't be misled into believing that master teachers just reuse their old plans each year. Those plans are only the starting points for current lessons. True professionals are always thinking about and planning how to update content, find more effective instructional methods, and devise better activities to help their students succeed. As three recognized classroom observers stress, it is the lesson that transforms youngsters into students (Mitchell, Ortiz, and Mitchell 1987). Learning is the primary goal of the schools. Your job is to make planning decisions that ensure learning is always intentionally inviting.

An old unit plan is only the
starting point; keep
improving, updating.

Planning is the heart of teaching. To the degree that you can become a successful planner, you will become a successful teacher. Refer to our webpage at **http://education.college.hmco.com/students** to examine the effect sizes associated with planning per se, as well as various specific planning elements.

What the Research Shows

Lest you come away from this chapter unconvinced of the value of planning, let's take a look at some research. Studies of the actual processes that teachers use in planning were conducted primarily in the early 1970s through the 1980s. Christopher M. Clark and Penelope L. Peterson (1986) prepared the high-water mark for the genre. Although it is now dated, their work and that of others led to the set of research-based findings described below. These findings will be useful to you as you begin instructional planning.

1. *Researchers have neither identified nor validated any widely accepted or consistently practical planning model* (see McBer 2000). Plans, planning efforts, and planning methods vary widely among teachers. Planning seems to be influenced most by the selection of learning activities, instructional objectives, content, students' age, available time, and teaching strategies. Of these, *time* and *proven activities* appear to have the greatest influence on the way that teachers plan.

Variability in planning

2. *Teachers use a variety of lesson plan formats.* Time is a critical teaching constraint, and all teachers organize blocks of instructional time in les-

sons for years, semesters, months, weeks, and a day. Content is also a major consideration, and teachers generally agree in organizing content into coherent segments (unit plans) and subsequently into manageable parts (lesson plans). (See Clark and Peterson 1986; Hawbecker et al. 2001; Kagan and Tippins 1992; Price and Nelson 2003)Richardson 2000; Sardo-Brown 1988; Sawyer 2001; and Wiggins and McTighe 2005.)

3. *Planning serves as a guide to action.* Plans are written to act as a guide during the instructional interactions. In this regard, plans provide and maintain a sense of direction and instill confidence in your teaching. Of course, weekly or daily lesson plans are typically an administrative requirement in most schools (Johnson 2000).

4. *Teachers tend to carry much of their planning in their minds rather than on paper.* Particularly as they gain experience, teachers may make notes about main ideas, yet they base much of their daily teaching on mental images of how the instruction should best proceed. Thus, in your observations of teachers, you may note large differences in the amount of planning that appears on paper. Until you have several years' experience, we urge you to make written plans; the more you work out your plans on paper, the more effective you will become (Sardo-Brown 1988; Wolcott 1994).

Transition from paper to mental notes.

5. *Teachers rarely plan in the linear model often encouraged in textbooks.* Many years ago, Ralph W. Tyler (1949) suggested a sequential planning process of several steps: (1) specify an objective, (2) select appropriate learning activities, (3) organize the activities, and (4) specify an assessment process. The method has been taught frequently in teacher education programs, but practicing teachers seem to use it infrequently. Instead, teachers mostly use a recursive process that focuses on previous successful activities, perceived student needs, and ongoing curriculum programs (Fisher 2000).

Planning's recursiveness

6. *The best teachers apply planning flexibly.* In their review, "Excellence in Teaching," Maribeth Gettinger and Karen Callan Stoiber (1999) illustrate the point that planning for instruction is the key to excellence. In every model they present, a teacher must first plan, but that plan must be flexible so that it can be adapted to fit the actual teaching moment. We encourage you to exercise flexibility in your delivery of instruction.

Planning's flexibility

Summary of Teacher Planning

- Planning is based on a plethora of models and a variety of lesson plan formats.
- Planning serves a wide array of purposes.
- Planning is a continuous process.
- Planning is seldom linear.
- Planning must be flexible.

reflect   **A Closing Reflection**

- Which of your strengths will make you a successful planner? What limitations must you work around?

- How can you build a resource file when you haven't yet been hired?

- To what extent have you had to justify your content selection by specifying a written rationale?

- What criteria would you generate to critique your lesson plans in the postlesson evaluation?

- Ask your instructor for models of IEPs. Do you observe any commonalities?

summary

1. The preplanning phase is essentially one of teacher reflection.
2. Planning decisions are often influenced by what content is *not* included since there is so much.
3. National and state agencies, textbook publishers, and state education agencies supply more than adequate instructional guides and resources.
4. Long-range planning is simplified by use of a school day activity calendar.
5. Student readiness is critical for content mastery.
6. Unit planning makes learning manageable.
7. Each lesson is designed and executed to achieve desired learning outcomes and instructional objectives.
8. Learning activities provide students with hands-on experiences.
9. Assessment is essential to determine students' levels of achievement.
10. Expert teachers and novices take different approaches to planning.

print resources

Bruer, J. T. "In Search of . . . Brain-Based Education." *Phi Delta Kappan* 80(9) (1999): 648–654.

The author critiques brain-based education literature and research. He cautions that the area lacks empirical testing.

Irvine, J. J., B. M. Armento, A. E. Causey, J. C. Jones, R. S. Frasher, and M. H. Weinburgh. *Culturally Responsive Teaching Lesson Planning for Elementary and Middle Grades.* Boston: McGraw-Hill, 2001, 224 pp.

This team provides content-related lesson plans that are multiculturally oriented.

Skowron, J. *Powerful Lesson Planning Models: The Art of 1,000 Decisions.* Arlington Heights, IL: Skylight, 2001, 163 pp.

Ideas, examples, and models are illustrated to aid in developing useful lesson plans.

Tinnesand, M. *Kids and Chemistry: Large Event Guide.* Washington, DC: American Chemical Society, 2003, 156pp.

Demonstrations are an effective form of interactive learning activity. Here is a guide on how to conduct appropriate and safe demonstrations in science.

Woodward, T. *Planning Lessons and Courses.* New York: Cambridge University Press, 2002, 266 pp.

This book is aimed at language instruction, but the author makes a critical point—lesson plans are just that, plans. She differentiates the quantity and the quality of planning needed by inexperienced and master teachers.

Internet Resources

Go to the website for this book to find live links to resources related to this chapter.

The following will direct you to many of the best lesson-planning sites:

> "The Educator's Reference Desk," maintained by the Information Institute of Syracuse contains more than 2000 lesson plans written by teachers of all grades and subjects.
>   **http://www.eduref.org/Virtual/Lessons/index.shtml**

> Yahoo!—an index of World Wide Web sites—has an Education section, which contains a large listing of sites that sell or supply free of charge a wide variety of instructional materials.
>   **http://www.yahoo.com/education/K_12/teaching/lesson_plans**

References

Bateman, B. D., and M. A. Linden. *Better IEPs* (3rd edition). Longmont, CO: Sopris West, 1998–2000.

Baylor, A., A. Kitsantas, and H. Chung. "The Instructional Planning Self-Reflective Tool: A Method for Promoting Effective Lesson Planning." *Educational Technology* 41(2) (2001): 56–59.

Becker, H. J. (July 2000). *Findings from the Teaching, Learning and Computing Survey: Is Larry Cuban Right?* Revision of a paper written for the January 2000 School Technology Leadership Conference of the Council of the Chief State School Officers, Washington, DC.

Bloom, B. S. *Human Characteristics and School Learning.* New York: McGraw-Hill, 1976.

Brophy, J., and J. Alleman. "Activities as Instructional Tools: A Framework for Analysis and Evaluation." *Educational Researcher* 20(4) (1991): 9–23.

Bryant, C., and R. Bryant. "Social Studies in the Block Schedule: A Model for Effective Lesson Design." *Social Studies* 91(1) (2000): 9–16.

Castanos, J. "Interdisciplinary Instruction." *Thrust for Educational Leadership* 26(6) (1997): 33–38.

Clark, C. M., and P. L. Peterson. "Teachers' Thought Processes." In *Handbook of Research on Teaching* (3rd edition). M. C. Wittrock, editor. New York: Macmillan, 1986.

Clement, M. C. "Just How Do You Teach Someone to Be a Teacher?" *Phi Delta Kappan* 82(4) (2000): 308–309.

English, F. W. "It's Time to Abolish Conventional Curriculum Guides." *Educational Leadership* 44(4) (1986/1987): 50–52.

Fisher, D. "Curriculum and Instruction for All Abilities and Intelligences." *High School Magazine* 7(7) (2000): 21–25, 52.

Gardner, H. "Who Owns Intelligence?" *The Atlantic Monthly* 283(2) (1999): 67–76.

Gettinger, M., and K. C. Stoiber. "Excellence in Teaching. Review of Instructional and Environmental Variables." In *The Handbook of School Psychology* (3rd edition). Cecil R. Reynolds and Terry B. Gutkin, editors. New York: Wiley, 1999, pp. 933–958.

Hanifi, H., D. Kelly, and Y. Zeegers. "Planning a Unit of Work: Incorporating Students' Questions." *Investigating* 19(1) (2003): 24–29.

Hansen, L., and A. Brown. *The Benchmarks Project.* Bloomington: Center for Excellence in Education and Indiana University, 1997. Retrieved at http://www.logicalcreativity.com/projects/benchmarks.

Hawbecker, B. W., M. Balong, S. Buckwalter, and S. Runyon. "Building a Strong BASE of Support for All Students Through Coplanning." *TEACHING Exceptional Children* 33(4) (2001): 24–30.

Houghton Mifflin Eduplace. The Web site for this service is: http://www.eduplace.com

House, J. D., R. S. Hurst, and E. J. Keely: "Relationship Between Learner Attitudes, Prior Achievement, and Performance in a General Education Course: A Multi-Institutional Study." *International Journal of Instructional Media* 23(3) (1996): 257–271.

Hurst, B. "ABCs of Content Area Lesson Planning: Attention, Basics, and Comprehension." *Journal of Adolescent and Adult Literacy* 44(8) (2001): 692–693.

Jacobs, H. H., editor. *Getting Results with Curriculum Mapping.* Alexandria, VA: Association for Supervision and Curriculum Development, 2004.

Johns, P. "Horizontal and Vertical Line Designs." *Arts & Activities* 133(5) (2003): 37.

Johnson, A. P. "It's Time for Madeline Hunter to Go: A New Look at Lesson Plan Design." *Action in Teacher Education* 22(1) (2000): 72–78.

Kagan, D. M., and D. J. Tippins. "The Evolution of Functional Lesson Plans Among Twelve Elementary and Secondary Student Teachers." *Elementary School Journal* 92(4) (1992): 477–489.

Kaplan, S. M. *Inservice Training Manual: Activities for Development Curriculum for the Gifted/Talented.* Ventura, CA: Ventura County Schools, 1979.

Lazear, D. G. *The Intelligent Curriculum: Using Multiple Intelligences to Develop Your Student's Full Potential.* Tucson: Zephyr, 1999.

Little, M. E. "Successfully Teaching Mathematics: Planning Is the Key." *Educational Forum* 67(3) (2003): 276–282.

Lively, T., and G. Emerling. "Students Like Bush, Not His Proposal." *The Washington Times,* January 13, 2005, M-1. Retrieved at: http://www.washtimes.com/metro/20050112-101258-9433r.htm

Martin, P. L. "Creating Lesson Blocks: A Multi-Discipline Team Effort." *Schools in the Middle* 5(11) (1995): 22–24.

Martinello, M. L., and G. E. Cook. *Interdisciplinary Inquiry in Teaching and Learning* (3rd edition). Upper Saddle River, NJ: Merrill, 2000.

McBer, H. *Research into Teacher Effectiveness.* London: Report by Hay McBer to the Department for Education and Employment, June 2000.

McDonald, J., and C. Czerniak. "Developing Interdisciplinary Units: Strategies and Examples." *School Science and Mathematics* 94(1) (1994): 5–10.

Mitchell, D. E., F. I. Ortiz, and T. K. Mitchell. *Work Orientations and Job Performance: The Cultural Basis of Teaching Rewards and Incentives.* Albany: State University of New York Press, 1987.

National Center for History in the Schools. *National Standards for United States History: Exploring the American Experience, Grades 5–12.* Los Angeles: University of California at Los Angeles, 1995.

O'Connor-Petruso, S. A. "A Model for Implementation." *Learning & Leading with Technology* 30(8) (2003): 32–35, 38–41.

Ornstein, A. C., and T. J. Lasley II. *Strategies for Effective Teaching* (3rd edition). Boston: McGraw-Hill, 2004.

Panasuk, R. M., and M. M. Sullivan. "Need for Lesson Analysis in Effective Lesson Planning." *Education* 118(3) (1998): 330–345.

Pappas, M. L. "My America in Poetry and Pictures." *School Library Media Activities Monthly* 19(8) (2003): 21–24, 26.

Parasad, B., and J. Jones. *Internet Access in U. S. Public Schools and Classrooms: 1994-2003.* (NCES 2005-

015). U. S. Department of Education. Washington, DC: National Center for Education Statistics, February, 2005.

Pressman, H., and P. Dublin. *Accommodating Learning Style Differences in Elementary Classrooms.* New York: Harcourt Brace, 1995.

Price, K. M., and K. L. Nelson. *Daily Planning for Today's Classroom, 2nd Edition.* Belmont, CA: Wadsworth, 2003.

Richardson, J. "Learning Benefits Everyone." *Journal of Staff Development* 21(1) (2000): 54–59.

Roberts, P. L., and R. D. Kellough. *A Guide for Developing Interdisciplinary Thematic Units* (3rd edition). Upper Saddle River, NJ: Merrill, 2004.

Sardo-Brown, D. S. "Twelve Middle-School Teachers' Planning." *The Elementary School Journal* 89(1) (1988): 69–87.

Sawyer, L. "Revamping a Teacher Evaluation System." *Educational Leadership* 58(5) (2001): 44–47.

Schön, D. A. *The Reflective Practitioner: How Professionals Think in Action.* Aldershot, England: Arena, 1995.

Sizer, T. R. *Horace's Hope: What Works for the American High School.* Boston: Houghton Mifflin, 1996.

Smerdon, B., S. Cronen, L. Lanahan, J. Anderson, N. Iannotti, and J. Angeles. *Teachers' Tools for the 21st Century: A Report on Teachers' Use of Technology* (NCES 2000–102). Washington, DC: U.S. Department of Education, 2000.

Strong, R. W., H. F. Silver, and M. J. Perini. *Teaching What Matters Most: Standards and Strategies for Raising Student Achievement.* Alexandria, VA: Association for Supervision and Curriculum Development, 2001.

Tyler, R. W. *Basic Principles of Curriculum and Instruction.* Chicago: University of Chicago Press, 1949.

Walsh, F. M. *Planning Behaviors of Distinguished and Award-Winning High School Teachers.* Unpublished doctoral dissertation, Washington State University, Pullman, 1992. Various ideas and materials reprinted by permission of the author.

Washington State Commission on Student Learning. *Revised Essential Learnings: Reading, Writing, Communication, Mathematics.* Olympia, WA: Commission on Student Learning, 1996.

Wiggins, G., and J. McTighe. *Understanding by Design* (expanded 2nd ed.). Alexandria, VA: Association for Supervision and Curriculum Development, 2005.

Wolcott, L. L. "Understanding How Teachers Plan: Strategies for Successful Instructional Partnerships." *School Library Media Quarterly* 22(3) (1994): 161–165.

Yelon, S. L. *Powerful Principles of Instruction.* White Plains, NY: Longman, 1996.

Ysseldyke, J. E., B. Algozzine, and M. L. Thurlow. *Critical Issues in Special Education* (3rd edition). Boston: Houghton Mifflin, 2000.

Ysseldyke, J. E., and J. Elliott. "Effective Instructional Practices: Implications for Assessing Educational Environments." In *The Handbook of School Psychology* (3rd edition). Cecil R. Reynolds and Terry B. Gutkin, editors. New York: Wiley, 1999, pp. 497–518.

Zemelman, S., H. Daniels, and A. Hyde. *Best Practice: New Standards for Teaching and Learning in America's Schools* (2nd edition). Portsmouth, NH: Heinemann, 1998.

Sequencing and Organizing Instruction

1

BASIC CONCEPTS

What Is Sequencing?

Content Forms

Modes of Presentations: Deductive and
   Inductive Reasoning

2

MODELS OF LESSON ORGANIZATION

Task Analysis Model

Concept Analysis Model

Advance Organizer Model

3

MULTIMETHODOLOGY AS AN INSTRUCTIONAL PROCESS

Hemisphericity: Functions of the
   Right and Left Brains

Diversity and Learning Styles

Multiple Intelligences

Varying Your Teaching Techniques

Jeff, a new English teacher at West Central High School, had just finished his first month of school. It had been emotionally and physically exhausting. Tired, he slumps in his chair, reflecting on the highlights and difficulties of the first month. Ms. Chan, an experienced teacher from the room next door, enters.

"Welcome to the world of teaching. You seem exhausted," says Ms. Chan.

"I am beat," replies Jeff. "How do you stay so calm? You have everything under control; you're so organized." He couldn't understand why students always seemed to know what Ms. Chan expected of them, completed their assignments on time, and took pride in their work.

"Jeff," she answers, "teaching is both an art form and a science. The science of successful teaching is planning and organizing a sequence of steps. You plan so the students have opportunities to learn. As you take things one step at a time, you add activities that make learning understandable and meaningful. And that is the art that makes it enjoyable for the students."

Ms. Chan's point is that you have to plan instruction in a logical order so that each instructional activity is purposeful and related to the overall goal of the course. In Chapters 3 and 4, you learned how to use goals and standards as guideposts for planning, how to use a cognitive taxonomy when translating goals into objectives, and how to use procedures and skills for instructional planning.

In this chapter, we continue our discussions of planning and begin to address the transition from planning to teaching. This chapter addresses the following three questions.

- How can I select the most appropriate sequencing techniques for my course?
- Which model of organization provides the greatest assistance to students in mastering lesson goals and objectives?
- How can I ensure that my teaching is enriched by multimethodology?

SECTION 1: BASIC CONCEPTS

What is Sequencing?

Sequencing is the art of developing a logical plan for instructional activities that will help your students effectively master a body of knowledge or discipline in an organized way. Presenting knowledge in a series of carefully interrelated steps not only helps students to master content but also develops their information-processing skills—that is, their ability to think.

Sequencing has two basic purposes. The first is to isolate either a piece of knowledge (a fact, concept, generalization, or principle) so that students learn and understand its unique characteristics or a thinking process to help students master it under varying conditions. The second is to relate the knowledge or process being taught to a larger organized body of knowledge. The first function—isolating what is being taught—helps make learning more manageable. The second function—relating the information to the bigger picture—makes learning more meaningful.

Isolate one piece of knowledge; relate it to the big picture.

For example, to teach the concept of a metaphor, you would first teach the characteristics of a metaphor by providing examples of one. This provides students with a manageable amount of information and a focus for their study. You can then teach a second figure of speech—a simile—in the same way. After the students have mastered both concepts, you can show that similes and metaphors have common characteristics; that is, they are both figures of speech. In this way you relate the lesson content to a larger body of knowledge. This example shows the relationship between instructional sequencing and hierarchies of knowledge. A sequence is an instructionally related process because it establishes a schedule for learning the various parts of the related content. In a subject area such as mathematics, in which there is an accepted hierarchy of knowledge, the sequence and hierarchy are very similar because the relationships among the content components usually dictate a sequence of learning activities. Students learn to add before learning to multiply. In a subject such as social studies, on the other hand, in which it is difficult to agree on an established hierarchy of information, the sequencing of learning is usually established by either the interest or the experience of the teacher or a curriculum committee. If a **content hierarchy** exists, it influences the instructional sequence. If a content hierarchy does not exist, the sequence of instruction establishes a hierarchy for the student.

The type of hierarchy can vary with subject area.

To teach effectively, you must sequence learning objectives in a way that reflects the relationships between the various components of the curriculum, a practice that is referred to as "bridging." This allows you to identify and teach prerequisite or entry-level skills and competencies at the appropriate stage. For meaningful learning to take place, the sequenced objectives should be communicated to students so they will understand the relationships among the various components of the unit or the overall curriculum.

General Principles of Sequencing   Four general principles apply to all kinds of sequencing. The first principle is that you always *begin with a simple step*. This does not mean that you "talk down" to your students. Rather, it means that you structure your lessons so that learners can understand easily identified characteristics of the content. At this step you should provide numerous examples. Using analogies often helps. In a biology class, you could start by stating, "The circulatory system is similar to a river system, in that it carries both food and waste and can be overused and misused." Because your students studied river systems in a previous year, you have provided them with a simple beginning to understanding the circulatory system through an analogy.

The second principle is to *use concrete examples*. This means that you use materials, simulations, models, or artifacts that illustrate the fact, concept, or generalization being taught. Let's stay with the biology class example. You call your students' attention to the circulatory system on the life-size plastic model of the human body at the front of the classroom. You point out major arteries and discuss their similarity to major rivers such as the Mississippi and the Columbia. Then you proceed to identify and name the major arteries and veins, discussing the primary functions of each one.

Analogies can help.

The third principle is to *add complexity to the lesson*. Sequence the learning experience so that it becomes more and more complex as you progress. You can do this by introducing additional variables, generating new sets of criteria, or establishing relationships between the content of the lesson and other content. For example, you may add the functions of the heart, liver, and other organs of the circulatory system to the discussion. The topic now becomes significantly more complex; as you add the organs one at a time, explaining the function of each, you may need to go back to the first step (the river–circulatory system analogy) or the second (the plastic human model)— bridging.

Finally, the fourth principle is to *introduce abstractions*. You might want to do this with a question: "When you are sick, why does the doctor start an examination by checking your blood pressure and listening to your heartbeat?"

Add complexity and abstractions.

кеу ıpeas

Four Principles of Sequencing

1. Begin with a simple step.
2. Use concrete examples.
3. Add complexity to the lesson.
4. Introduce abstractions.

Again, you may need to go back to previous steps. For example, you might point out that blocking a river tributary produces pressure on the banks and that this is similar to what happens when a vein or artery becomes blocked. Or you might note that, by testing water systems for contaminants, you can determine the health of an ecosystem, which is similar to what blood testing does.

The four steps or principles of sequencing are useful in that they provide a logical progression of learning. They are interactive, though, in that you may need to go back to a previous step to help explain the idea currently under discussion.

Although we have divided sequencing into four steps, don't be fooled into thinking too literally that on Monday your lesson should be "simple," on Tuesday it should be "concrete," on Wednesday you should address "complex" issues, on Thursday you should deal with the "abstract" issues, and on Friday you should test. It may take years to apply all four principles in the teaching of certain complex topics—for example, the basic concept of democracy is never completely taught and mastered. The process of teaching the concept of democracy begins at the preschool level and is continued throughout the entire educational system, becoming more complex and abstract at each successive level. Or you may use all four principles in a single lesson such as the circulatory system. Each discipline or area of the study has similar core facts, concepts, and generalizations that permeate the entire curriculum. What we wish to stress is that understanding the interrelationships of these four principles helps teachers teach. Using this instructional technique will remind you of the sequential nature of learning and thus help you incorporate appropriate learning experiences for each instructional objective. Figure 5.1 provides a visual model of the technique.

Not a lockstep process

FIGURE 5.1

A Hierarchy for Student Success

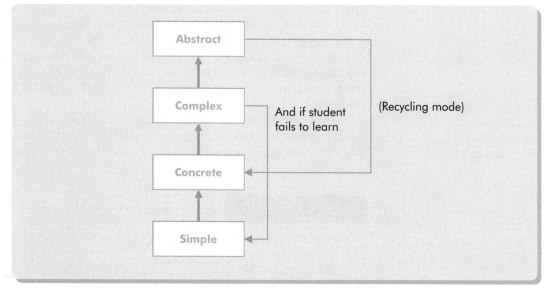

One concept can grow throughout the child's school career.

Example: Graphing   To illustrate the long-term nature of sequencing, let's examine a concrete example. In the first grade, teachers introduce the concept of graphing. The overall goal is to provide a series of experiences through which the idea of graphing will emerge. The complete sequence of instruction, which includes all types and levels of difficulty of graphs, may take ten years or more.

The sequence begins with a first-grade science lesson. The children plant bean seeds to study plant growth. The teacher raises the idea of regularly measuring the growth of the plants (say, every Friday). All plants are watered as uniformly as possible. As the seeds germinate, the teacher gives each child a strip of paper. The child places the paper next to the seedling and tears the strip to equal the height of the plant on the prescribed day. (This measuring technique uses a 1:1 scale, or one-to-one correspondence.)

Each child glues his or her strip to a large piece of paper, with a date label. This process continues each week until the unit has been completed. The teacher asks the children to observe the changes in plant height, which are discussed. Everyone has a concrete graph of the changes over time—a simple histogram. The teacher encourages the class to discuss how they made the histograms and then introduces the concept of one-to-one correspondence.

Next year the second-grade teacher also uses histograms but makes them more complex. The teacher shows that, if a dot is placed at the top of the piece of paper and scales are made (labeling the axes), all the information will be available in a form that is easier to use. This is reinforced with many examples during the second grade or maybe the third grade.

At the next grade level, the teacher provides other data, such as daily maximum temperatures and, later, minimum temperatures. The graphing concepts thus become more complex and abstract; yet these activities provide a concrete experience that the class shares. A possible culmination of this set of experiences would be to have the children obtain data of their own choosing and make graphs of them, providing foundational knowledge for research projects.

Obviously, not all concepts take that amount of time to teach. In high school, it often takes only a few days to complete a unit. Still, it is often helpful to sequence lessons from simpler to more complex concepts, even in very short units. Each unit should illustrate the use of the principles described previously. Our main point is that you, the teacher, control the learning environment.

---

reflect

- How does sequencing help relate isolated pieces of information to an organized body of knowledge?

- Why can you sequence the same content in more than one way?

- How has sequencing helped your learning processes? Do you remember teachers who were good at sequencing course activities?

- What is a concept from your own schooling that you continued to explore over many years? Think of one in any subject area. Make a list of the different ways you learned this concept over the years.

Content Forms

You want your students to understand both content and processes as well as the relationship between the two. **Content** is the information you want them to learn; *processes* are the thinking skills you want them to acquire (see Marzano 2004). For example, in a geography course, you want students to understand that there are different kinds of land forms, such as mountains, plateaus, and valleys, and to recognize the characteristics of each. The processes you want them to acquire will involve map-reading skills, reference skills, and information-gathering and organizing techniques. We focus on your instruction of skills and processes in Part 3, especially in Chapters 7, 8, and 9. In this section, we concentrate on content.

Content = information

Although terms may differ occasionally, educators agree that content exists in three primary forms: facts, concepts, and generalizations (see Figure 5.2).

Facts   The most fundamental piece of information is called a *fact*. A **fact** is a type of content that is singular in occurrence, occurs or exists in the present time, does not help you predict other facts, and is acquired solely through the process of observation. The following are examples of facts.

1. Olympia is the capital city of the state of Washington.
2. President George W. Bush was governor of the state of Texas.
3. The sun set at 4:15 P.M. today.

FIGURE 5.2

Hierarchy of Content Forms

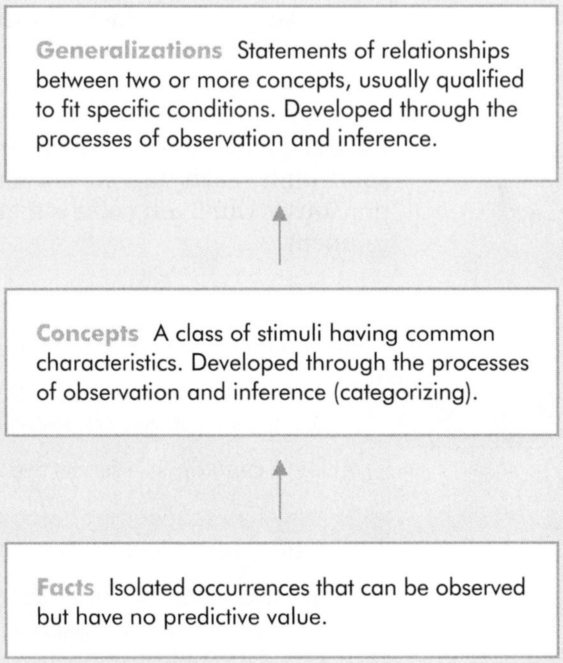

> **Generalizations** Statements of relationships between two or more concepts, usually qualified to fit specific conditions. Developed through the processes of observation and inference.

↑

> **Concepts** A class of stimuli having common characteristics. Developed through the processes of observation and inference (categorizing).

↑

> **Facts** Isolated occurrences that can be observed but have no predictive value.

Because facts do not lead to predicting other facts, the primary means of learning facts is through memorization and recall. One of the most effective ways of learning facts is verbal repetition. It is also easier to remember facts that are related to other content. A program of studies built on facts is at the lowest level of Bloom's taxonomy, knowledge (see Chapter 3). Facts are fundamental to learning, but learning is limited if teaching does not go beyond facts.

Facts are individual and specific.

Concepts   **Concepts** are expressions, usually consisting of one or two words, or ideas having common characteristics. We define them in Chapter 4 as category words that we use to group objects as ideas. They are the result of the categorization of a number of observations. Forming concepts seems to be a natural process in the human brain. For example, young children form concepts of what cats and dogs are like based on their observations of these familiar animals. Children learn to differentiate dogs and cats because of the distinctive behavior of each species, the sound each produces, the distinctive shape of their heads, and perhaps some other characteristics. They do not rely on a single characteristic, such as size. Thus, for example, even though a particular cat may be larger than a particular dog, a child is able to tell the difference between them.

Concepts group and categorize.

Much of schooling consists of learning concepts. For example, in a beginning class on parts of speech, students learn that a noun is a "person, place, or thing." All concepts have the following five components.

1. **Name.** For example, *noun* is the name, or label, of a concept. When it is used, people who have learned the concept understand what is being communicated. The name is more efficient than a lengthy definition.
2. **Definition.** A definition is a statement about the concept's characteristics. For example, "a noun is a person, place, or thing."
3. **Characteristics.** Characteristics are qualities that must be present for the concept to apply. For example, the characteristics of a noun are "person, place, or thing." Only one of these must apply to a word for it to be considered a noun. For other concepts—for example, democracy—a number of characteristics must be present for the concept to apply.
4. **Examples.** Examples are members of a class of things that show a concept's essential characteristics. *Tom* is an example of a noun; so are *car* and *Iceland*.
5. **Place in a hierarchy.** Most concepts are part of a content hierarchy that gives meaning to the concept and makes it easier to learn. The content hierarchy for *noun* is parts of speech. Related, or coordinate, concepts to *noun* are *verb, adverb,* and *adjective*. Subordinate concepts are *common noun, proper noun,* and *pronoun*. In Section 2 of this chapter, you will learn about concept analysis, an approach for the sequencing of concepts. This approach will teach you to use all five components to develop lessons that will help your students learn and remember concepts.

Generalizations   As Chapter 4 explains, a **generalization** is an inferential statement that expresses a relationship between two or more concepts. It applies to more than one event and has predictive and explanatory value. For example, "People who smoke have a higher incidence of lung cancer than those who don't" is a generalization. It states a relationship between smoking (a concept) and lung cancer (another concept). The statement is predictive and applies to anyone who smokes. A good example of the use of generalizations in teaching is given in James A. Banks's book *Teaching Strategies for Ethnic Studies* (2003). Banks presents the following generalizations about immigration and migration: "In all cultures, individuals and groups have moved to different regions in order to seek better economic, political and social opportunities. However, movements of individuals and groups have been both voluntary and forced" (p. 112).

Given this general statement, students would expect evidence of both forced and voluntary migration, regardless of the country being studied. Therefore, Banks's statement has predictive value and applies to more than one event. The statement also contains many concepts—*cultures; individuals and groups; economic, political, and social opportunities;* and *voluntary and forced*. The statement suggests relationships among these many concepts.

As students proceed from facts to concepts and then to generalizations, the amount of information increases and becomes more complex. Using Bloom's taxonomy, which Chapter 3 explains, facts are at the knowledge level, concepts are at the comprehension level, and generalizations are at the application and analysis levels. Students can recall facts, concepts, and generalizations, but facts and concepts are not adequate for application

Generalizations have
predictive value.

and analysis because neither has predictive nor explanatory value (Vasilyev 2003).

Facts are often confused with generalizations, but there are three important differences between them.

1. Generalizations are inferences that condense a large amount of data; facts are statements that are singular in occurrence. For example, the statement "Sunset occurs earlier every day between June 21 and December 21 in the Northern Hemisphere" is a generalization. "The sun set at 4:15 P.M. today" is a fact.
2. Facts are statements of events that occurred in the past or exist in the present, whereas generalizations are statements about general trends or patterns. For example, "Governors often choose to run for the U.S. presidency" is a generalization; "Ronald Reagan was governor of California before becoming president of the United States" is a fact.
3. Generalizations can be used to make predictions, whereas facts, because they are singular in occurrence, do not have predictive value. For example, "Studying enhances learning" is a generalization because it makes a prediction. By contrast, "Liza is studying for her calculus test" is a statement of fact because it does not predict Liza's performance.

Now let's look at two modes of presenting cognitive information that influence sequencing of activities within a lesson.

Modes of Presentation: Deductive and Inductive Reasoning

There are two basic modes of thinking: deductive reasoning and inductive reasoning. **Deductive reasoning** moves from the general to the specific; **inductive reasoning** proceeds from the specific to the general.

The primary modes of presentation are based on these modes of thinking. As a teacher, you have options: You can teach students a concept or a generalization by providing them with a definition followed by examples, or you can help students form the concepts or generalizations themselves based on observation or examples you provide. The type of reasoning you select will determine the sequence of lesson activities. The scenarios in the Instructional Strategies box on page 146 illustrate the different approaches.

Mr. Jones and Ms. Shamison were teaching the same content, and both wanted their students to learn the same generalization: "Magnets attract objects made of metal." Additional similarities in their approaches are using magnets and examples and asking questions.

However, there were major differences. Mr. Jones initiated the activity with a generalization, whereas Ms. Shamison started the activity by asking students to make observations. The two examples illustrate the essential difference between inductive and deductive reasoning and how this difference influences sequencing within a lesson. They also illustrate that sequencing is

Deductive: concept first, inductive: examples first

Exciting modes of instruction can captivate your students. © Suzie Fitzhugh.

influenced by things other than content because the content was the same in both cases.

If a music teacher has an objective that students understand that the length of the string determines the sound, he or she can share the generalization with students and then have them hear strings of different lengths or play strings of different lengths and have students observe the pattern. In teaching the color wheel in an art class, the teacher can provide the concepts followed by a demonstration with paints or provide paints to let the students experiment and see if they develop the concepts. In both the inductive and deductive mode, the teacher uses examples as part of the instruction.

Your choice of mode of presentation is often determined by the lesson objectives. If you want your students to understand the process by which a generalization is formed, you may want to use the inductive approach. If your primary concern is only that your students know a particular concept or generalization, you may want to use the deductive approach. The next section provides more examples of inductive and deductive teaching.

Which to use? Determined by learning objective

INSTRUCTIONAL STRATEGIES

Modes of Lesson Presentation

Mode 1: Deductive Reasoning

Mr. Jones began a lesson on magnetism by giving each student a handout. On the handout was this statement: "Magnets are attracted to some objects and not to others, and the things magnets are attracted to are called 'metals.'"

After a brief discussion regarding the concepts in the statement (such as *attraction*), Mr. Jones asked, "Will a magnet pick up your textbook?"

"No," responded the class.

"Why?"

"Because it is not a metal."

Mr. Jones gave each student a magnet and asked the class to use their magnets on objects on their desks. The discussion continued.

Mode 2: Inductive Reasoning

Ms. Shamison wanted her students to understand magnetism. She began the lesson by handing out a magnet and an envelope to each student. In each envelope were objects—paper clips, plastic buttons, an iron nail, a penny, a plastic chip, an aluminum nail, a pencil. She asked the students to observe what happened when the magnet was applied to each object or other objects on their desks. After allowing a brief time of exploring, she called the class to order by saying, "Let's describe some observations you made about the magnet."

After a brief discussion that ranged from color and size of magnets to objects that were picked up by magnets, one of the students said, "It seems that magnets pick up some things but not others."

"Fine," said Ms. Shamison. "Let's organize what we have observed into lists. One list is for the objects that magnets pick up, and one list is of those objects that the magnet does not pick up."

After students made lists and discussed the characteristics of each object, Ms. Shamison asked, "Would someone summarize in statements what we have discovered?"

Angelica raised her hand and said, "We found that magnets pick up things that are called 'metals' and do not pick up things like plastic and wood."

Both Mr. Jones and Ms. Shamison would use graphic organizers or visuals, such as pictures, drawings, Venn diagrams and student summaries. This technique keeps the topic in clear focus for the students.

REFLECT

- What topics that you teach would be best taught by the modes of instruction?

- Think about a movie, TV show, or book that you have seen or read involving detectives or investigators. What mental processes did these professionals use to solve the cases? Was their reasoning inductive or deductive?

SECTION 2: MODELS OF LESSON ORGANIZATION

Each model of lesson organization has intrinsic strengths.

Section 1 of this chapter discusses the following components of instructional planning: sequencing, content forms, and modes of presentation. In this section, we describe how these components are integrated into three models of lesson or unit organization: the *task analysis, concept analysis,* and *advance organizer* models.

Each model presents a guideline for sequencing objectives and activities and establishes a hierarchy or relationship of knowledge. Each model has unique characteristics that assist the teacher in selecting a planning model. (See Table 5.1.) Although each model has intrinsic strengths, no model is inherently superior. The teacher as a decision maker should choose the one that provides the greatest assistance in lesson planning, organizing, and implementing.

Task Analysis Model

VIDEO CASE

In the Video Case "Academic Diversity: Differentiated Instruction," third-grade teacher Chris Colbath-Hess uses graphic organizers and task analysis in her writer's workshop for a heterogeneous classroom. What makes these approaches suitable for such a wide range of learners?

Consider the following common scenario: You have taught a lesson, and you assume that your students will be able to answer nearly all the questions you plan to ask on an examination covering that lesson. From all indications, your students enjoyed the lesson, and you anticipate no problems at assessment time. To your dismay, the class performs poorly on the examination. Was the test poorly conducted, or was the instruction lacking? An incident similar to this happened to one of America's foremost learning theorists, Robert M. Gagné (Gagné, Wager, Golas, and Keller 2005). The lesson was in subtraction, but the content could have been high school chemistry, college calculus, English, physical education, or any subject at any level. What is important is that Gagné was not satisfied with the results and wanted to determine why.

Task Analysis and Sequencing   Gagné began to study the sequence in which his learning activities were planned. He concluded that some instructional elements should have preceded others and that some concepts he had omitted should have been introduced. This initial study led Gagné to rearrange some of the learning sequences and try the lesson again. The result was a dramatic change in student success as measured by test results.

Task analysis breaks learning into steps

TABLE 5.1

Models of Lesson or Unit Organization	
Model	Primary Characteristics
Task analysis	Careful sequencing of intermediate and terminal objectives
Concept analysis	Sequencing of concept characteristics or examples that relate to the concept or to a concept hierarchy
Advance organizer	Use of an "identical scaffold" to teach the interrelationships within an organized body of knowledge

Gagné arranged the concomitant learning experiences in his lesson in a chart (see Figure 5.3). The top of the chart contained the end of the instructional sequence, usually called the *terminal objective*. The terminal objective is what students should achieve after a series of planned instructional encounters (in this case, "subtract whole numbers of any size"). Below the terminal objective he listed the *intermediate objectives*. Until students master the basic skills (the bottom half of the chart), they probably will not be able to reach the learning objectives at the higher levels (the top half of the chart). In Figure 5.3, the roman numerals refer to the order of presentation, and the lines illustrate the relationships between each cell.

FIGURE 5.3

A Learning Hierarchy for Subtracting Whole Numbers SOURCE: From *Principles of Instructional Design*, 4th edition, by Robert M. Gagné, Leslie J. Briggs, and Walter W. Wager. Copyright © 1992. Reprinted with permission of Wadsworth, a division of Thomson Learning: www.thomsonrights.com. Fax 800-730-2215.

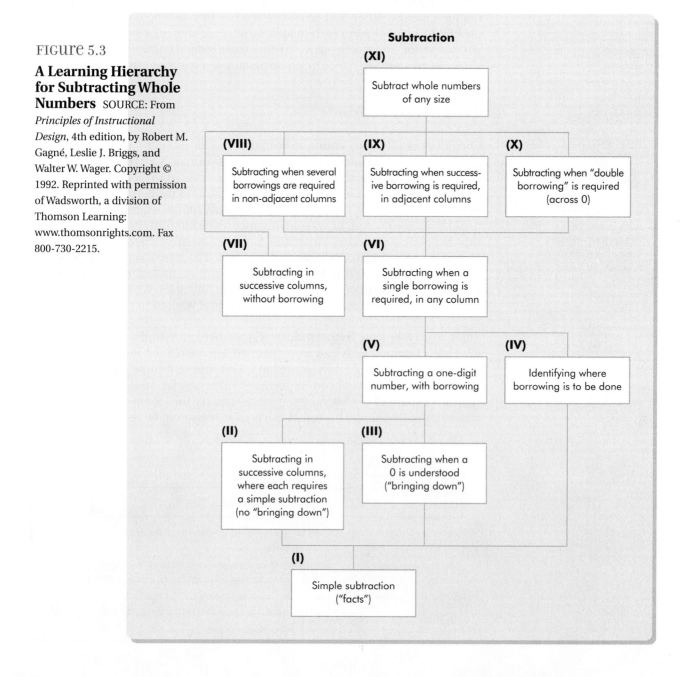

Typically, a lesson on subtraction begins with "simple subtraction" (facts). As a teacher, you have two options. You can prepare activities that teach "simple subtraction," or, as we discussed in Chapter 4, you can first identify your students' entry skills with a brief test. The benefit of using a concept hierarchy chart is that, through testing, you can ensure that students have the requisite necessary skills to be successful learners.

To study the effects of a hierarchical structure on learning, Gagné employed the **task analysis model**, which subdivides a lesson's content, concepts, or processes into smaller, sequential steps, beginning with the least complex and progressing to the most complex. This model has long proved valuable in business and industry. Careful sequencing of tasks has been and continues to be a critical element of efficient production in education, as it is in the industrial and technological sectors. You can imagine how chaotic and costly education would be if there were no grade levels and no methods for identifying the difficulty level of university courses. If you think your program of studies seems disorganized, think of the problems you would have if each piece of information you learned were taught in isolation and not as part of a course or if your courses had no titles or identifying numbers. You can arrange almost any set of facts, concepts, or generalizations into the Gagné system.

Procedures for Task Analysis   The major purpose of task analysis is to discover the interrelationships among subskills and to use this information to plan for effective instruction. **Enabling skills** are the facts, concepts, and processes that students must be taught before they can move on to the most complex skills or the target objectives. It may be unrealistic to assume that you, as a classroom teacher, will have the time or methodological expertise to identify and validate enabling skills empirically with the perception of Gagné's investigations, but you can effectively and efficiently use task analysis in your own teaching. The following procedures need to be accomplished to analyze learning tasks successfully.

1. **Select an instructional objective that is at the appropriate level of difficulty.** To make this initial determination, the teacher must know the structure of the content area (such as physics, health, education, mathematics, or social studies) and what the learner has already achieved.

    This step may seem obvious, but its importance is often overlooked. For example, teachers sometimes make statements such as "When students are in the ninth grade, they should read *Julius Caesar*" or "Seventh-graders should master percentages." Such curriculum decisions fail to identify where learners are located in the curriculum plan. For example, it makes little sense to teach students how to figure percentages if they do not first understand decimals—regardless of their grade level.

    Therefore, in selecting appropriate learning objectives, you need to identify the general area where your students' knowledge ends. This process is referred to as *diagnostic vigilance*. This is the point at which you should formulate new learning objectives and analyze the subskills that lead to the attainment of these objectives. The technique of diagnostic vigilance allows the teacher to check on whether the original objective is, in fact, at the right level of difficulty.

Test first to measure entry skills.

Organize learning tasks from simplest (subskills) to most complex (terminal objective).

2. **Identify the enabling skills students need to attain the objective.** For example, in a physical education class, students are to be taught the golf skill of putting. Without regard to sequencing, the teacher lists the skills necessary for putting: gripping the club, maintaining the proper stance, positioning the club face correctly, using the appropriate amount of force, executing the backswing, following through, and mentally visualizing the ball's path.

3. **Subdivide independent and dependent enabling skills and learning sequences.** For any given objective, there are two basic types of enabling skills: independent and dependent. (Sometimes an objective requires both.) Learning these skills can be thought of in terms of sequencing: In an independent sequence, the enabling skills are not incremental. For example, when you learned to tie your shoes, it did not matter whether you started with the right or the left shoe. These activities are independent of each other. In the dependent sequence, on the other hand, accomplishment of one skill is essential before attainment of the next skill in the series. For example, when first learning to hit a baseball in T-ball, the coach demonstrates to the players how to hold the bat. The players learn how to swing followed by learning how to stand while swinging the bat. This practice allows the players to actually hit the ball off the tee. The successful hitting of the ball is dependent on the sequence of skills.

4. **Arrange the independent and dependent sequences in order.** Use this sequence to construct a lesson that will systematically facilitate the learning of the terminal objective. Once you have analyzed the objective and discovered its component parts (independent and dependent enabling skills or learning sequences), these parts will provide an entry point of learning for all students. The enabling skills themselves become objectives that you use to help students learn the terminal objective. As an example, let's return to the putting lesson. The teacher determines that the grip and stance are **independent skills** that can be learned in any order, but they should be mastered before the backswing and follow through because you need to know how to grip the club and how to stand in order to practice these **dependent skills**. Because the grip and the stance are independent skills, the teacher may decide to teach the grip first because it may be easier to teach the stance when students are holding a golf club.

   It is doubtful that you will be able to identify all the prerequisite enabling skills before implementing a lesson and consistently emphasize the most important ones. As you teach, your judgment will allow you to adjust, to add other skills to the list, and to emphasize certain skills with particular students. Keep notes about such skills in your daily lesson plan book. These notes will be a handy reference for your next class.

5. **Sequence specific tasks for students.** Before you do this step, you must first plan the sequence in which you will conduct the class. As Chapters 3 and 4 explain, there are some tasks that you must accomplish every time you prepare and implement a lesson. You must (1) identify the instructional objectives; (2) plan the appropriate educational activities or experiences; (3) obtain the materials; (4) plan the strategies that you

will employ in the teaching act; (5) evaluate the students; and (6) develop a student assessment—that is, decide how you would improve the lesson. But now you need to establish the sequence or order in which specific dependent tasks will be taught. This sequencing plan ensures student success.

Task analysis is an especially useful tool for planning instruction for children with special needs (Reigeluth and Beatty 2003), integrating topics in a multidisciplinary unit, and designing multicultural activities. As you identify each task, you can analyze it for content that is culturally biased, skills that are difficult for students with special physical or learning needs to accomplish, and skills and knowledge that were not covered previously. You might even be surprised to learn that a task analysis approach can be used to help students write better papers (Bailey 2001). In the same vein, task analysis principles are used for creating lesson plans (see Baylor et al. 2001).

Susan Black (2001) uses an adaptation of task analysis in describing her "backward design" for key curriculum concepts, instructional activities, and planning. When introducing new material, you may find such an analysis beneficial for student understanding.

Example: Density   One of the authors of this text, a science teacher, has observed that teachers often have difficulty teaching the concept of density. By observing student errors, he inferred that if the tasks associated with learning the concept of density were identified and structured, some of the problems could be reduced. Table 5.2 lists the various tasks or elements that are prerequisites to mastering the concept of density.

On examining Table 5.2 carefully, are you surprised at the number of operations and prerequisite skills that are needed to learn about density? Several teachers were, and so were we.

Once this table was created, it became apparent that it is inappropriate to teach this concept before the seventh grade. Students simply do not have the

Task analysis ideal for special needs

TABLE 5.2

Task Analysis for Teaching the Concept of Density
I. Using the metric system A. Weight B. Linear measurements
II. Understanding two-dimensional measurements: computing the area of a rectangle and a circle
III. Computing volumes A. Rectangular objects B. Cylindrical objects C. Irregularly shaped objects 1. Those that float in water 2. Those that sink in water
IV. Defining and using a "unit standard" A. Linear B. Volumetric
V. Using mathematics skills A. Division B. Multiplication C. Linear equations ($a = b/c$)
VI. Knowing that the mass of water in grams approximates the volume of water in cubic centimeters (cc)
VII. Deriving that density is mass per unit of volume.

necessary intellectual background until that time—and some may not until one year later.

As researchers and teachers, we often wonder why students cannot learn certain concepts or principles. The truth is that, in many cases, teachers have to revise even the order of the text pages students read so that the material is understandable. To maximize the benefits to the learner, you may have to sketch rough hierarchy charts for every chapter, unit, or module you teach. Thus it is beneficial to set aside a few minutes to prepare a task analysis chart for each new unit you plan.

When you observe student **learning deficits**, you can construct your own hierarchy chart to determine whether key elements of instruction are missing. No doubt other charting modifications can be devised using three techniques. Try your hand at creating such a chart for, say, a concept in English grammar, biology, mathematics, or social studies. We believe that, if more teachers used this technique, teaching would improve immeasurably. Both teachers and students would be happier in school—and more successful!

When students can't learn, sequencing may be faulty.

---

key ideas

Analyzing Learning Tasks

1. Select an appropriately difficult instructional objective.
2. Identify enabling skills.
3. Subdivide independent and dependent skills and sequences.
4. Arrange independent and dependent sequences in order.
5. Sequence specific tasks for students.

---

reflect

- Examine some complex textbook in your area. To what extent is the content structured hierarchically?

- Why would you make the effort to use task analysis? What benefits would you expect to derive from it?

- Prepare a chart showing the relationships of various facts, concepts, and generalizations you have learned in previous education courses. Use the concept of dependent and independent sequencing.

Concept Analysis Model

Teaching Concepts   The teaching of concepts encompasses a substantial portion of all instruction. For example, science requires students to understand the concepts of systems, energy, plants, and animals; language arts applies the concepts of communication, paragraphs, parts of speech, and punctuation; mathematics requires students to apply the concepts of sets, commutative property, and inverse operations. A lengthy list could be compiled for every subject area.

When you teach concepts, you must use both sequencing and task analysis. As the example of the magnetism lesson illustrated, you have two sequencing options: (1) start the lesson by describing the concept and follow this with an analysis of characteristics (facts) and a series of illustrations or examples (facts) so that the students gain a thorough understanding of the concept, or (2) provide examples (facts) related to the concept and allow students to discover the concept themselves. As we observed earlier, when you start the lesson by defining the concept, you are teaching deductively; when you begin with examples and expect students to discover the concept, you are teaching inductively. In either instance, a procedure called "concept analysis" is helpful.

Example: Proper Nouns   For example, if you were teaching the concept *proper noun,* it would be helpful to develop a conceptual hierarchy of the content to illustrate the characteristics of the concept (show its uniqueness) and its relationship to the larger body of content covered by the course. An example of this kind of chart is shown in Figure 5.4.

A concept hierarchy provides the teacher with a sequencing technique. To teach the concept *proper noun,* for example, the teacher must demonstrate the characteristics that make a proper noun both "proper" and a "noun." Thus the teacher provides examples that illustrate the characteristics of a proper noun—in this case, the names of two *persons,* Jim and Mary.

One way to describe the relationship of concepts formed using a concept hierarchy is in terms of *superordinate, coordinate,* and *subordinate* concepts. These terms refer not only to the scope of inclusiveness of a concept but also to its relationship to other concepts. For example, the concept of *parts of speech* is inclusive and subsumes the concept of *noun,* which in turn subsumes

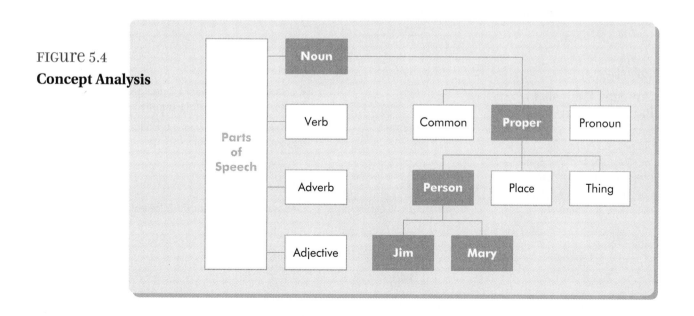

FIGURE 5.4
Concept Analysis

How concepts relate to one another

the concept of *proper*. In this respect, *proper* is a type of *noun*, which is a part of speech. Related concepts such as these form a hierarchy, or ordered arrangement.

In Figure 5.4, the concept *parts of speech* is superordinate to the concepts *noun, verb, adverb,* and *adjective*. The concepts *common, proper,* and *pronoun* are subordinate to the concept *noun*. The connection among the concepts *noun, verb, adverb,* and *adjective* is called a "coordinate relationship."

Analyzing Seven Dimensions   In preparing to teach a concept, the teacher must have a thorough understanding of that concept. A **concept analysis** is a thorough examination of the different aspects of a concept, which is described earlier in this chapter, plus the concept hierarchy. A concept analysis includes the following components: (1) concept name, (2) definition, (3) characteristics, (4) exemplars, (5) superordinate concepts, (6) subordinate concepts, and (7) coordinate concepts. Concept analysis is a planning tool that has proved valuable to teachers in structuring their concept-learning activities. Each dimension of concept learning describes a different and unique aspect of the concept. This process not only provides teachers with a thorough understanding of the concept to be taught but also can serve as a plan for instruction. An example of concept analysis for the concept "parallelogram" is provided in Figure 5.5, which shows each step.

In the second phase of teaching a concept, the teacher determines whether the lesson should be taught inductively or deductively. Should the students be given the concept and then be provided with examples of its characteristics, or should they be given examples from which to induce the concept? Whether the lesson is taught inductively or deductively, a thorough analysis of concept characteristics and examples is necessary. The concept analysis hierarchy is an excellent procedure for accomplishing this task.

Select inductive or deductive approach.

The teaching of concepts is often a prerequisite for the teaching of generalizations. For example, a civics teacher might want to use the generalization

FIGURE 5.5

Concept Analysis for Parallelogram SOURCE: From *Strategies for Teachers: Information Processing Modes in the Classroom* by P. D. Eggen, D. P. Kauchak, and R. J. Harder. Copyright © 1979 by Prentice Hall. Used with permission.

Concept Name:	Parallelogram
Definition:	A parallelogram is a four-sided geometric figure whose opposite sides are parallel.
Characteristics:	Four-sided, opposite sides parallel, opposite angles equal
Exemplars:	
Superordinate Concept:	Geometric shapes or quadrilaterals
Subordinate Concept:	Rhombus, Square
Coordinate Concept:	Trapezoid

"Incumbents usually win elections" in a unit on politics. For students to understand this generalization, they must understand the concept *incumbent*. Although incumbents may be older or wealthier or even more experienced than challengers, these are not characteristics of the *concept* of incumbency. If the students don't correctly understand the concept, they will not correctly understand the generalization; they may think incumbents usually win because they are older rather than simply because they are incumbents.

One of the most effective methods for teaching concepts is the use of examples. In planning a lesson, the teacher must come up with enough examples to illustrate all the dominant characteristics adequately. For concrete concepts such as *dog* or *verb*, it is easy to find good examples. For concepts such as *anger, justice,* or *poetic,* the teacher must spend considerable time developing good exemplars. Providing examples of coordinate concepts often helps students understand the characteristics of the concept being taught. For example, you might give the examples of *hostility, indignation,* and *wrath* to help students understand the concept *anger.* Negative examples (opposites) can also be used.

Advance Organizer Model

Teaching abstract and complex concepts such as *hate, bigotry, ecosystem, diversity,* and *democracy* can be a great challenge. Often students confuse such concepts. For example, many students believe that *democracy* and *capitalism* are the same concept, not realizing that one is a political concept and the other is an economic concept. The advance organizer model is an effective tool for teaching such concepts. This model is based on an **advance organizer**, which is a statement of those elements that the learner will be required to master in the lesson. It is designed to introduce the material that follows and it must be broad enough to encompass the information. You can use this model to compare *capitalism* to the coordinate concepts *socialism* and *communism,* for example. One of the model's primary purposes is to teach the relationships among such concepts by presenting the "big picture." Sometimes the advance organizer is a study guide, syllabus, or list. Often, it is a visual representation such as a chart.

The advance organizer model is based on Ausubel's (1968) explication of deductive learning. The deductive mode of inquiry includes three basic components: advance organizers, content differentiation, and integration. It requires a body of knowledge that can be organized hierarchically. The purpose of the advance organizer model is to provide students with a structure so that they understand each part of the hierarchy of knowledge in the lesson as well as the relationships among the parts. The model consists of three phases: presenting the advance organizer, content differentiation, and integration.

Presenting the Advance Organizer   As an example of an advance organizer, let's use an English teacher who is starting a unit on metaphors, similes, and personification. This teacher would start the lesson with a *definition of* or *generalization about* figures of speech. The teacher might follow a simple hierarchy chart like the one shown in Figure 5.6.

Begin lessons with the big picture of what students will learn.

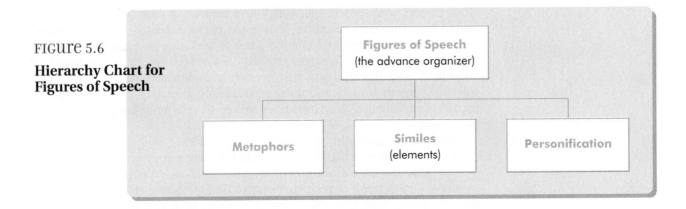

FIGURE 5.6

Hierarchy Chart for Figures of Speech

If each student understands the advance organizer, it will provide a frame of reference for the lesson so that each part of the lesson can be more easily understood. The organizer enables the learner to relate the lesson materials to previous knowledge. The teacher's task is to develop an abstract statement that encompasses all aspects of the lesson and that the student can relate to previously learned material.

The teacher then has considerable latitude in organizing and developing the lesson. Therefore, two teachers using the same advance organizer may develop and teach the lesson differently. A practical note is helpful here: Record the advance organizer and brief hierarchy chart on a transparency or large sheet of paper. This allows students to refer to it throughout the lesson and thus provides direction and focus (see Forsten, Grant, and Hollas 2003; Lenz and Schumaker 2003).

Content Differentiation   After you have presented the advance organizer and are sure your students understand it, the second phase of the model begins. This phase, content differentiation, is the process by which the content is subdivided into narrower, less inclusive ideas. The English teacher can start a lesson on metaphors with the statement "A metaphor is one kind of figure of speech. The primary characteristics of a metaphor are . . ." The teacher has used a broad, abstract concept *(figure of speech)* and taken from it a narrower, more concrete concept *(metaphor)*. **Content differentiation** is the process of isolating each fact, concept, or generalization within a hierarchy of knowledge so that it can be learned independently. Highlighting the unique and discrete characteristics of an element of information makes it easier to understand.

Content differentiation isolates each piece of knowledge.

Integration   The third component of the advance organizer model is **integration**, which is the process of teaching students how main concepts and underlying facts are related or how underlying facts are different or similar. In this phase, you make a deliberate attempt to help students understand similarities and differences among the components of the hierarchy of knowledge and to reconcile real or apparent inconsistencies between the ideas presented. In our English lesson example, the teacher makes certain that students understand the relationship between figures of speech and metaphors (one is a broad category to which the other belongs) and that they comprehend the differences and similarities between metaphors and similes (they are both in the same category). In most hierarchy charts (such as Figure 5.6), broader, more abstract, more inclusive concepts (in this instance, *figures of speech*) are placed above less inclusive, narrower concepts (*metaphors*). *Metaphors, similes,* and *personification* are on the same horizontal level. The terms *vertical integration* and *horizontal integration* describe the way students learn these relationships.

Integration shows relationships.

In summary, the advance organizer model is designed to teach organized bodies of content deductively (based on Ausubel's conception of deductive learning). The advance organizer provides the students with an overview and focus, content differentiation provides items of information that can be more easily understood, and integration provides meaningful learning by helping students understand the relationships among the elements of the content being taught. Ausubel gives you a tool that helps the learner connect the known with the unknown (see Gil-Garcia and Villegas 2003).

key ideas

Steps in the Advance Organizer Model

1. *Advance organizer.* Abstract introductory statement related to previously learned material that encompasses all aspects of the lesson. It defines and/or generalizes the information to be learned.
2. *Content differentiation.* Process of subdividing broad ideas into narrower, less inclusive ones
3. *Integration.* Process of examining similarities and differences among related concepts

The Steps in Interaction   Although the three components are presented as sequential, in reality they interact with one another (especially content differentiation and integration). If the comparison and differentiation discussion develops students' understanding of a specific concept or generalization, then the teacher should not hesitate to use the two steps concurrently. As with any teaching model, the teacher should use the model and its components in the way that most effectively helps his or her students learn. The model should be applied with flexibility and not become a straitjacket: Really it is a scaffold for learning, bridging the known with that to be learned.

The three steps can be used flexibly, recursively.

Be careful not to confuse deductive teaching with lecturing. Often, lectures are neither deductive nor inductive. A deductive lesson can contain as much teacher-student or student-student interaction as an inductive lesson does. After presenting the advance organizer, the teacher can hold students responsible for content differentiation and integration by having them provide characteristics and examples and explain relationships (Ausubel 1968). In this instance, the teacher becomes the facilitator of the learning process, in much the same manner as in an inductive lesson. The box on page 158 provides a few suggestions for teaching deductive lessons.

> ## Tips for Deductive Lessons
>
> 1. Have students verify an understanding of the advance organizer by providing examples, definitions, and characteristics of it.
> 2. Whenever appropriate, students should help with content differentiation by providing definitions, characteristics, or examples.
> 3. Develop a chart that illustrates both the relationship among ideas and their uniqueness.

For the advance organizer model to work effectively, the teacher must prepare an advance organizer that provides students with an understandable focus for the lesson and a visual representation that illustrates the relationships among the information to be taught. When you bridge previous knowledge and materials to new learning, there are important achievement gains (see Marzano, Pickering, and Pollock 2001, p. 117). If you use advance organizers systematically, along with continuous reviews and student summaries, your students will outperform others. Thus this model is a valuable addition to your knowledge base of teaching.

Benefits of Graphic Organizers   Look back at the beginning of each chapter in this book. We use a graphic organizer called a "concept map" or "concept web." In this chapter alone, we use a variety of **graphic organizers** or, as they are often called, "nonlinguistic representations" to illustrate learning hierarchies, principles of sequencing, the list of items in a task analysis for density, and the concept analysis for parts of speech. As you read the text, you will observe others that we incorporate with the written text. The box below lists several common graphic organizers. Graphic organizers can be extremely helpful at the beginning of the advance organizer process, when you define the material to be learned.

Graphic organizers go beyond words: shapes, pictures, structures.

> ## Examples of Graphic Organizers
>
> - Historical time lines
> - Flow charts
> - Bar graphs
> - Pie graphs
> - Networks
> - Taxonomic keys
> - Tables
> - Continuum scales
> - Family trees
> - Venn diagrams
> - Cyclic diagrams
> - Content outlines

Many researchers have verified the effectiveness of graphic organizers for students at all grade levels. The use of concept maps shows promise in determining whether students relate prior knowledge more efficiently and thus expedite current learning (Dochy and Alexander 1995). Concept maps have a long history of helping students absorb content at higher levels, from kindergarten to the university (see Chang, Sung, and Chen 2001; Chase, Franson, and An 2001; Sungur, Tekkaya, and Geban 2001).

They expedite and focus student learning.

Other types of graphic organizers, such as pictures, have enhanced student learning in geography (Fitzhugh 1995) and in science (Tippett 2003). Explicit graphic organizers facilitated information retrieval processes (Dennis 2003).The use of graphic organizers in elementary classrooms helped students to make significant writing progress. Significant student improvements were reported in fourth-grade writing test scores when different forms of concept maps were used when presenting instruction (Hyerle 1995–1996). Using nonlinguistic representations is a must when teaching an inclusive classroom (Baxendell 2003). By using graphic organizers in your teaching, you may help your students reach a level of understanding they would not reach without the organizers (see Calhoun and Haley 2003; Capretz, Ricker, and Sasak 2003).

Each group of students, because its members have different experiences and levels of maturity, provides a different challenge to the teacher. Every discipline has different types of learning problems. Mathematics is very different from social studies or English.

Graphic organizers are *right-brain hemisphere–related,* a topic that is discussed in Section 3 of this chapter. Thus, while you stress left-brain hemisphere content or processes, you reinforce the learning by using techniques that incorporate right-brain hemisphere learning. Graphic organizers provide an instructional double whammy.

Teach students to use graphic organizers too.

Teach your students how to use graphic organizers as they study for your lessons. You can use them as advance organizers, or students can make their own as they work. Their use provides another way to enrich the classroom environment, especially for disabled learners (Eden, Wood, and Stein 2003).

Because graphic organizers have a positive impact on student achievement, we stress their use. For example, using them along with other interactive teaching methods helps increase reading comprehension (Bowman, Carpenter, and Paone 1998). Likewise, teachers report increased comprehension in K–8 schools when graphic organizers are appropriately used (Culbert et al. 1998). Leticia Ekhaml (1998) describes a wide variety of graphic organizers that aid both teaching and learning.

Adapt the instructional planning models presented in this chapter for specific teaching situations. Perhaps the one valid generalization that can be made about planning is that, more often than not, teachers assume students have the prerequisite knowledge when in fact they do not. Some students may have already mastered the intended lesson, whereas other students in the same class do not have the requisite experiences and academic background for success.

INSTRUCTIONAL
STRATEGIES

Teaching the Concepts of Government

This is a lesson on government and the concepts associated with it. The class has already studied basic forms of government; the current topic is the functions of government. To understand how government functions, the students need to understand the relationship of government to other societal institutions. The teacher might introduce the lesson with the following advance organizer.

> Government is but one of the institutions serving society. The state or government is essential to civilization, yet it cannot do the whole job by itself. Many human needs are met by the home, the church, the press, and private business.

With the presentation of the advance organizer, the teacher is ready to proceed with the content differentiation component of the lesson. He or she makes materials available to students so that they may begin their investigations into human needs that are met by different institutions. First, the teacher and the class prepare a list of different problems that can be studied. As an alternative, they might list steps they could take to identify areas in which various institutions serve society and in which institutional functions overlap. Functions that are not covered by any institution would also be listed. As the students gather material and present it to the class, the teacher leads them in the content differentiation and integration processes. The result is an interactive, deductive lesson.

TECHNOLOGY INSIGHT

The Role of Cognitive and Psychomotor Skills in Computer Use

Because computing tools were originally designed by people with certain abilities (mathematicians and engineers), people with similar abilities tend to use computers more easily. In *The Trouble with Computers*, Thomas Landauer points out that people with certain cognitive skills find computers particularly appealing and easy to use. These cognitive skills are the ability to understand and apply formal logic and the ability to visualize imaginary spaces (spatial relations). Landauer also observes that people who type quickly and accurately (a psychomotor skill) find computers easier to use because almost all software requires the use of a keyboard to input information.

When planning learning activities that include the use of computing tools, it may be helpful to focus on developing students' cognitive abilities with logic and spatial relations, and supporting the improvement of keyboarding skills.

SOURCE: T. K. Landauer, *The Trouble with Computers: Usefulness, Usability, and Productivity.* (Cambridge, MA: MIT Press, 1995).

reflect

- How is the relationship between ideas illustrated by content differentiation and integration?

- Think about a time you taught something to a child, either within or apart from your teacher training. Did you teach it inductively or deductively? Would it be possible to teach the same thing the opposite way? Is there any way to change the experience so that the child is more involved?

- What graphic organizers from the list could you use to instruct concepts in your teaching field?

SECTION 3: MULTIMETHODOLOGY AS AN INSTRUCTIONAL PROCESS

We begin this section on instructional **multimethodology** by briefly introducing three theories that support our thesis of providing an instructionally rich teaching repertoire. The first topic relates to the functions of the right- and left-brain hemispheres in information processing; the second, to learning preferences; and the third, to multiple intelligences. With those points as your advance organizer, we'll fully develop the idea of multimethodology.

Hemisphericity: Functions of the Right and Left Brains

Over the past several decades, a major theory about how the brain works, called *hemisphericity*, has given teachers another tool to use in planning instructional experiences. **Hemisphericity** is the study of where in the brain—in the left hemisphere or the right hemisphere—different types of mental functions occur. Research suggests that the right cerebral hemisphere is involved in visual, non-verbal, spatial, divergent, and intuitive thinking. The left cerebral hemisphere is involved in verbal, logical, categorical, detail-oriented, and convergent thinking. The right brain works more with approximations and creativity, whereas the left brain works more with specifics and analysis. For example, the right side of the brain processes the visual information that allows you to recognize a face, but the left side provides the name to go with the face.

Implications for Teaching   The facts that allow us to understand the kinds of functions that occur on each side of the brain are important because they help educators understand that instruction must be planned to enhance both hemispheres. Research conducted over many years has demonstrated that teachers persistently emphasize objectives and instruction that focus on the left side of the brain. The vast majority of objectives focus on the cognitive, analytical, and convergent (i.e., focusing in) functions dominated by the left side of the brain (Caine and Caine 1997; Given 2002; Jensen 2005; Sylwester 1995).

Research also tells us that, although each side of the brain tends to emphasize a specific kind of function, the most productive intellectual functioning

Left = logical, right = creative

occurs when both sides of the brain cooperate. Learning exercises that are focused on the left side of the brain (the majority of the learning objectives and instructional experiences we plan for students) are enhanced when the right side of the brain is included in the experience. So, not only have we largely ignored the right-side functions of the brain in devising instructional experiences, we have also limited the effectiveness of left-side functions in students' learning. To teach most effectively to either side of the brain, we must balance outcomes and learning experiences to involve *both* sides whenever possible (Baker and Martin 1998; Eden, Wood, and Stein 2003).

Including Creativity in Instructional Plans   It is important to plan learning experiences that use the right side of the brain, but a brief caution applies. Because objectives or outcomes for the right side of the brain emphasize creative functions, the criterion of any outcome for the right side of the brain can be difficult to write. By their nature, the more creative functions of the brain are less measurable in terms of quantity and quality. For example, suppose you assign your students the problem of designing a novel use for plastic soda pop bottles. How do you define an objective for such an assignment? How do you quantify or define creativity? Remember that effective instruction includes a balance between left- and right-brain emphasis, and you will have taken care of most of your problem. A musically inclined student may use the bottles to develop an instrument by filling the bottles with different levels of water or some other material. An art student could construct a sculpture to look like an animal, or a student interested in insects could develop a collection display. One of the benefits to this activity is that fellow students are able to observe creativity in action. Objectives are not presented in isolation; rather, as this chapter shows, they are presented as sequences of expectations that lead to a general outcome. If you write carefully constructed objectives that allow students to master left-brain activities, you can also construct a framework to define and assess right-brain objectives so that they are part of the whole sequence of learning. Such a framework could resemble the Kaplan matrix (see Chapter 4). We offer in the box below a brief sample of objectives that emphasize right-brain functions.

Incorporate both left- and right-brain activities in objectives.

> ## Right-Hemisphere Objectives
>
> 1. Using only a pencil and a blank sheet of paper, draw a sketch of a fellow class member that is recognizable by the majority of the class.
> 2. Presented with ten objects of different sizes, shapes, and textures, develop a scheme that will enable another person to classify all ten objects, using only the senses.
> 3. Given a story starter, create a short story in which all the physical elements of the story starter are incorporated into the plot.
> 4. Using only the three primary colors, create a painting that includes all the elements of the modern style.
> 5. Using the computer simulation "The Oregon Trail" as a model, construct a simulation for travel from an earth-orbit space station to the moon that adheres to the physical principles regulating movement in an airless and weightless environment.

Do not assume that stressing right-hemisphere activities automatically enhances creativity. No clear evidence supports that a close relationship between creativity and brain hemispheres exists (Hines 1991). Hemispheric differences tend to be relative rather than absolute, and implications for schooling may yet be speculative (Hellige 1988). We strongly suggest that you study Robert Sylwester's *A Celebration of Neurons: An Educator's Guide to the Human Brain* (1995). He provides an excellent overview of how the brain functions.

There is considerable interest in and controversy about brain-based education (Bruer 1999; Weiss 2000; Winters 2001). Experimentation with brain-based strategies shows promise (Erlauer 2003; Myrah and Erlauer 1999). Although neuroscience has much to offer teaching and learning conceptualization, it is rather new, and educators must be cautious about applying lab research prematurely (Jensen 2000). Further, application of these findings takes considerable study and practice, so the topic is an excellent one for your lifelong learning.

reflect

- Prepare a lesson plan that includes right-brain student activities.

- Examine a set of textbooks or computer programs for your intended grade level. What hemisphericity traits do you recognize?

- Obtain a set of your state's standards for any curricular area. Apply the test of hemisphericity to those standards.

professional voices from the field

Lisa K. Cartwright, Franklin Elementary School, Pullman, Washington

Employing Multimethodology

As a fifteen-year veteran of the classroom, I find it surprising that good teaching practice is still difficult to come by. With experience, lesson design becomes easier—more creative and flexible. Focus and effort shifts to learning equity; that is, is every child in my classroom able to access the learning and show me that they've done so?

True child-centered teaching creates a learning environment in which each student in a classroom *will* learn and develop, moving, in a sense, from her or his individual Point A to Point B. As the teacher, I provide the learning objectives, and I work toward helping each student attain those Point Bs. Many students will work beyond expectations, but it is my duty to see that all students reach the basic objectives for each and every lesson.

Creating a context within which such learning can take place is more difficult than one would think. Good teaching includes multiple avenues through which children can learn. Multimethodology, therefore, is critical to the success of a child-centered classroom. I plan lessons with learning preferences, multiple intelligences, and right- and left-brain hemispheres

PROFESSIONAL
VOICES
FROM THE
FIELD

Lisa K. Cartwright,
Franklin Elementary
School, Pullman,
Washington

Employing Multimethodology—Cont'd

in mind. I want students to be able to show me what they're learning in multiple ways; learning avenues are active, process-oriented, and often technological.

It follows, then, that I also assess using multiple methods. This is the most important component of true child-centered teaching, and the hardest to accomplish. It often means augmenting traditional pencil/paper assessment techniques and allowing children to show what they know in a variety of ways. I use a combination of assessment tools, feeling that this gives me a good snapshot of what each student has learned. In the end, I feel satisfied that, for every child, I have taught and assessed to the best of my ability.

Diversity and Learning Styles

No two people think exactly alike, and it is safe to say that no two people learn in exactly the same way either. Teachers respond to this diversity in a number of ways, one of the most prevalent being grouping (Slavin 2003). At the elementary level, grouping often means dividing classes into subgroups on the basis of students' skills and abilities, particularly in math and reading. At the high school level, grouping often results in tracks, with the curriculum in each track aimed at different educational and vocational goals. But students differ in other, more subtle ways than aptitude and ability. In this section, we consider some factors that may have a positive or negative effect on student learning; then we present a few techniques you can use to accommodate individual learning styles.

Students' cultural and background experiences influence how they understand new material and how they respond to, and benefit from, instruction. Differences in background, experience, socioeconomic status, culture, and language all influence learning (Banks and Banks 2004,). For example, teachers who move from a rural setting to a big-city school will find that they need to adapt how they teach. A question to first-graders about where milk comes from may elicit one response from rural kids (cows) and a completely different one from suburban or inner-city kids (the store).

Educators have recognized the impact of experiential and cultural differences on student success for some time (Cushner, McClelland, and Safford 2003), and most teacher education programs contain courses or units on multiculturalism to help teachers become sensitive to the powerful effect of background experiences (see Knapp and Woolverton 2004 for a detailed discussion). But, more recently, considerable attention has been focused on other, less apparent dimensions of individual differences.

Researchers in this area have termed this dimension "learning style" and have developed instructional programs to meet the needs of different groups

Societal differences affect learning.

of students. **Learning style** or **preference** is usually defined as the cognitive, affective, and physiological traits that learners exhibit as they interact in the classroom environment. Students with different learning styles understand problems in different ways, and they tend to try to solve them in different ways.

At this point you might be saying to yourself, "Hey, this is very close to schema theory, which we studied in psychology." In one sense it is. As students of any age or learning style study something, they fit what they learn into a meaningful pattern, or schema. When students are introduced to a new concept, their schema for it might be disorganized, irrational, or just plain wrong. Such a schema obviously will hinder learning. Similarly, in terms of learning styles, students' individual and environmental attributes can help or hinder learning (see Wilson 1996).

Researchers and advocates in the area of learning styles think of these styles as being on the borderline between mental abilities and personality. Learning styles fall between these two areas and are the individual's preferred way to learn new skills, knowledge, or techniques (see Sternberg 1997) The remainder of this chapter illustrates how to accommodate all students by using a diverse array of teaching styles.

Multiple Intelligences

There are at least three key findings about human intelligence that relate to our current discussion. First, intelligence is a dynamic quality not fixed at birth. Second, through appropriate learning experiences, intelligence can be enhanced. Third, intelligence has many different attributes (Gardner 1993). The latter finding is the key element for instructional planning and sequencing; that is, intelligence is a multiple facet, not a singular one associated only with verbal or quantitative aptitudes. This notion has led to an idea called **multiple intelligences**. The chief proponent of the concept of multiple intelligences is Howard Gardner (1985, 1991, 1999a, 1999b). Gardner's work is applicable in the school setting because of its ease of use for planning. He identifies eight basic intelligences. These are listed in the box below.

> ## Gardner's Eight Intelligences
>
> - Verbal/linguistic • Logical/mathematical • Visual/spatial
> - Body/kinesthetic • Musical/rhythmic • Interpersonal
> - Intrapersonal • Naturalist

Gardner asserts that we all possess these eight intelligences, but schools tend to develop only the first two to any extent. As a consequence, six areas of intelligence are consciously depressed (discriminated against) by schooling. The notion of treating these multiple intelligences as learning styles may cause educational psychologists to shudder because there are so many different variables to control. We believe it is helpful for teachers to at least make themselves aware of these different intelligences and structure class activities to accommodate the eight intelligences as appropriate (Stanford 2003).

Different ways of problem solving

Intelligence can take eight forms.

As you begin planning for student outcomes, you need to be cognizant of how many ways school learning can be approached. Verbal/linguistic learning undoubtedly will remain the area that receives the most attention in schools. There are many more cognitive and affective dimensions of the brain (see Guilford 1967), but in a classroom environment, you can have only so many balls in the air at once! Nevertheless, by being aware of the other seven intelligences, verbal/linguistic learning can be greatly enhanced, and you can plan to provide multimethodological experiences for all your students (see Marzano et al. 2001).

Plan for more than
verbal/linguistic

Varying Your Teaching Techniques

As you know, effective teachers use a wide variety of teaching methods and techniques. For example, if you want to use an inductive presentation mode, then your lesson will include at least the following elements (which we greatly expand in Chapters 7, 8, and 9):

- Teaching questioning
- Data of some nature
- Student research
- Applied or laboratory exercises
- Lists of student generalizations

If you plan to use a deductive mode of presentation for some topic, then you'll be using other elements:

- Demonstrations
- Videos or films
- Student activities
- Guest speakers
- Assigned readings
- Student reports

Obviously, the range of instructional strategies that you can use in the classroom is limitless (Tate 2003). We urge you to start by planning your objectives or *what to teach*, and then plan *how to teach it*. By varying your weekly calendar of activities, you will accommodate the spectrum of individual learning differences in your classroom (see Lazear 2003). By using multimethodology, you do not get stuck in the usual rut. If you have to lecture, then break it up with activities, questions, or student-elicited summaries every ten minutes. Keep the focus on the content, but vary the pace and the instructional method of the lesson. If you adopt the concept of multimethodology, you'll have an instructionally rich classroom environment. (See Marzano, Pickering, and Pollock 2001 for a detailed discussion of effect sizes computed for various instructional methods.)

Break up lecturing with other
methods.

Teachers often feel compelled to "cover all the materials," but this is not a function of any style. One young middle school student made a profound observation: "Kids never really get to do anything with new school learning, except just get more of it." Textbooks set the pace for most teachers and learners, the Internet notwithstanding. But you will probably supplement the text with short presentations or demonstrations that provide students with missing skills or background information. One last note: Beverly Hill (2005) observes that with high-stakes the current norm, children who have a learning style or preference that is different from the test formats may be at great risk of failure. She suggests examining the structure of any test so you can help your students succeed.

You have been introduced to instructional sequencing, organizing, and multimethodology, but to use them appropriately, you will need additional training and classroom experiences in the specifics. Difficult and challenging instructional concepts can be taught and understood if you structure your lessons to be intentionally inviting to learners. It is your decision. Once you are able to sequence major blocks of information while keeping in mind all the differences in your students' learning and abilities, you will be able to implement any planning or learning model. Visit our website at **http://education. college.hmco.com/students** for data relating to the instructional effectiveness (effect size) of advance organizers, cues, graphic organizers, and task analysis.

---

reflect

A Closing Reflection

- Using one of the modes of reasoning (inductive or deductive), outline how you would teach one major concept in your teaching area.

- Select one major concept that is not usually taught but that you feel is important. Create a set of advance organizers and a hierarchy chart for it.

- How can task analysis be used to plan a daily lesson? Draft a list of steps for a lesson, beginning with a test to measure entry skills.

- Design a lesson that incorporates a concept with graphic organizers.

- To what extent have you seen or been exposed to the concepts of learning styles, multiple intelligences, and multimethodology? How has it affected your teaching philosophy so far?

- Which of the multiple intelligences on Gardner's list are your strongest? Imagine that you are the teacher of a student very much like you. What activities and approaches would you use for this student?

---

summary

1. Sequencing instructional activities provides a ladder for student success.

2. Facts, concepts, and generalizations form the basis of most content.

3. Inductive modes of presentation lead the student to generalizations by providing specifics first.

4. Deductive modes of presentation begin with a generalization and follow with specific points.

5. Task analysis allows you to determine what components of more complex instruction are needed for student success.

6. Sequencing isolated tasks provides a meaningful or logical pathway for student success.

7. Hierarchy charts and graphic organizers help teachers plan and students learn.

8. Advance organizers provide students with an instructional map of what is to be learned.

9. Teachers need to plan instruction to incorporate both right- and left-brain activities.

10. Planning, organizing, and sequencing instruction are fluid and flexible processes, not static ones.

11. Graphic organizers are intentionally inviting.

12. Multimethodology is a planning tool that accommodates individual intelligences and learning styles.

PrInT ResOurces

Hyerle, D. *A Field Guide to Using Visual Tools.* Alexandra, VA: Association for Supervision and Curriculum Development, 2000, 147 pp.

This small book presents information on and examples of many graphic organizers. It's one for your professional library.

Irvine, J. J., and D. E. York. "Learning Styles and Culturally Diverse Students: A Literature Review." In *Handbook of Research on Multicultural Education.* J. A. Banks and C. A. McGee Banks, editors. San Francisco: Jossey-Bass, 2001, pp. 484–497.

This singular chapter on the learning styles of culturally diverse students is mandatory reading and discussion by both students and instructors in any instructional methods course. The authors illustrate the complexity of the entire concept of styles and enumerate the "preferences" of African American, Hispanic, and Native American students. There is a note of caution about over-generalizing.

Sylwester, R. *A Celebration of Neurons: An Educator's Guide to the Human Brain.* Alexandria, VA: Association for Supervision and Curriculum Development, 1995, 167 pp.

After you read this book, you'll have an excellent understanding of the chemistry and environment under which the brain functions. This technical piece might make a good discussion stimulus for you and a few peers.

InTerneT ResOurces

Go to the website for this book to find live links to resources related to this chapter.

> A comprehensive website about learning styles is offered by the Island Adult Development Association of Victoria, British Columbia, Canada. Included are six broad categories, including multiple intelligences.
> **http://www.ldpride.net**

References

Ausubel, D. P. *Educational Psychology: A Cognitive View*. New York: Holt, Rinehart & Winston, 1968.

Bailey, V. "The Writing Trek," *TechTrends* 45(2) (2001): 14–15.

Baker, J. C., and F. G. Martin. *A Neural Network Guide to Teaching* (Fastback 431). Bloomington, IN: Phi Delta Kappa Education Foundation, 1998.

Banks, J. A. *Teaching Strategies for Ethnic Studies* (7th edition). Boston: Allyn and Bacon, 2003.

Banks, J. A., and C. A. McGee Banks, editors. *Handbook of Research on Multicultural Education*. San Francisco: Jossey-Bass, 2001.

Banks, J. A., and C. A. McGee Banks, editors, *Handbook of Research on Multicultural Education* (2nd edition). San Francisco: Jossey-Bass, 2004.

Baxendell, B. W. "Consistent, Coherent, Creative, The 3 C's of Graphic Organizers." *Teaching Exceptional Children* 35(3) (2003): 46–53.

Baylor, A., A. Kitsantas, and H. Chung. "The Instructional Planning Self-Reflective Tool: A Method for Promoting Effective Lesson Planning." *Educational Technology* 41(2) (2001): 56–59.

Black, S. "Stretching Students' Minds." *American School Board Journal* 188(6) (2001): 31–33.

Bowman, L. A., J. Carpenter, and R. A. Paone. *Using Graphic Organizers, Cooperative Learning Groups, and Higher Order Thinking Skills to Improve Reading Comprehension*. Unpublished Action Research Project. Chicago: Saint Xavier University, 1998. ED 420 842.

Bruer, J. T. "In Search of . . . Brain-Based Education." *Phi Delta Kappan* 80(9) (1999): 648–654.

Caine, R. M., and G. Caine. *Education on the Edge of Possibility*. Alexandria, VA: Association for Supervision and Curriculum Development, 1997.

Calhoun, S., and J. Haley. *Improving Student Writing Through Different Writing Styles*. Chicago: Saint Xavier University and Skylight Professional Development Field-Based Master's Program, 2003. ED 473 052.

Capretz, K., B. Ricker, and A. Sasak. *Improving Organizational Skills Through the Use of Graphic Organizers*. Chicago: Saint Xavier University and Skylight Professional Development, M.A. Research Project, 2003. ED 473 056.

Chang, K. E., Y. T. Sung, and S. F. Chen. "Learning Through Computer-Based Concept Mapping with Scaffolding Aid." *Journal of Computer Assisted Learning* 17(1) (2001): 21–33.

Chase, P. A., K. L. Franson, and A. An. "Discovery Maps: A Student-Centered Approach to Reinforcing the Curriculum." *American Journal of Pharmaceutical Education* 65(1) (2001): 74–77.

Culbert, E., M. Flood, R. Windler, and D. Work. *A Qualitative Investigation of the Use of Graphic Organizers*. Paper presented at the SUNY-Geneseo Annual Reading and Literacy Symposium. Geneseo, NY: State University of New York at Geneseo, May 1998. ED 418 381.

Cushner, K., A. McClelland, and P. Safford. *Human Diversity in Education: An Integrative Approach* (4th edition). New York: McGraw-Hill, 2003.

Dennis, S. *Multipurpose Poetry: Introducing Science Concepts and Increasing Fluency*. Newark, DE: International Reading Association, 2003. ED 480 244.

Dochy, F. J. R., and P. A. Alexander. "Mapping Prior Knowledge: A Framework for Discussion Among Researchers." *European Journal of Psychology of Education* 10(3) (1995): 225–242.

Eden, G. F., F. B. Wood, and J. F. Stein. "Clock Drawing in Development Dyslexia." *Journal of Learning Disabilities* 36(3) (2003): 216–218.

Eggen, P. D., D. P. Kauchak, and R. J. Harder. *Strategies for Teachers: Information Processing Models in the Classroom*. Englewood Cliffs, NJ: Prentice Hall, 1979.

Ekhaml, L. "Graphic Organizers: Outlets for Your Thoughts." *School Library Media Activities Monthly* 14(5) (1998): 29–33.

Erlauer, L. *The Brain-Compatible Classroom: Using What We Know About Learning to Improve Teaching*. Alexandria, VA: Association for Supervision and Curriculum Development, 2003.

Fitzhugh, W. P. "Magazine Geography: Using Magazine Pictures to Enhance Social Studies Instruction," 1995. ERIC Document Reproduction Service No. ED 390 784.

Forsten, C., J. Grant, and B. Hollas. "Reading to Learn: Are Textbooks Too Tough?" *Principal* 83 (2) (2003): 28–33.

Gagné, R. M., W. W. Wager, K. Golas, and J. M Keller. *Principles of Instructional Design* (5th edition). Belmont, CA: Wadsworth, 2005.

Gardner, H. *Frames of Mind: The Theory of Multiple Intelligences*. New York: Basic, 1985.

Gardner, H. *The Unschooled Mind: How Children Think and How Schools Should Teach*. New York: Basic, 1991.

Gardner, H. *Multiple Intelligences: The Theory in Practice*. New York: Basic, 1993.

Gardner, H. *Intelligence Reframed: Multiple Intelligences for the 21st Century*. New York: Basic, 1999a.

Gardner, H. "Who Owns Intelligence?" *The Atlantic Monthly* 283(2) (1999b): 67–76.

Gil-Garcia, A., and J. Villegas. *Engaging Minds, Enhancing Comprehension and Constructing Knowledge through Visual Representatons.* Paper presented at a Conference on Word Association for Case Method Research and Application, Bordeaux, France, June 29–July 2, 2003. ED 480 131.

Given, B. K. *Teaching to the Brain's Natural Learning Systems.* Alexandria, VA: Association for Supervision and Curriculum Development, 2002.

Guilford, J. P. *The Nature of Human Intelligence.* New York: McGraw-Hill, 1967.

Hellige, J. P. "Split-Brain Controversy." In *Encyclopedia of School Administration and Supervision.* R. A. Gorton, G. T. Schneider, and J. J. Fisher, editors. Phoenix: Oryx, 1988.

Hill, B. "Learning Styles and Standardized Test Scores: Is There a Connection?" *The Delta Kappan Bulletin* 20 (Spring 2005): 27–30.

Hines, T. "The Myth of Right Hemisphere Creativity." *Journal of Creative Behavior* 25 (1991): 223–227.

Hyerle, D. "Thinking Maps: Seeing Is Understanding." *Educational Leadership* 53(4) (1995–1996): 85–89.

Hyerle, D. *A Field Guide to Visual Tools.* Alexandria, VA: Association for Supervision and Curriculum Development, 2000.

Jensen, E. *Teaching with the Brain in Mind, 2nd edition.* Alexandria, VA: Association for Supervision and Curriculum Development, 2005.

Jensen, E. "Brain-Based Learning: A Reality Check." *Educational Leadership* 57(7) (2000): 76–80. Knapp, M. S., and S. Woolverton. "Social Class and Schooling." In J. A. Banks and C. A. M. Banks, editors, *Handbook of Research on Multicultural Education, 2nd edition. San Francisco: Jossey-Bass,* pp. 656–681.

Lazear, D. "Eight Ways of Teaching: The Artistry of Teaching with Multiple Intelligences" (4th edition). Glenview, IL: Skylight, 2003.

Lenz, K., and J. Schumaker. *Adapting Language Arts, Social Studies, and Science Materials for the Inclusive Classroom. ERIC/OSEP Digest.* Arlington, VA: ERIC Clearinghouse on Disabilities and Gifted Education, 2003. ED 480 433.

Marzano, R. J. *Building Background Knowledge for Academic Achievement: Research on What Works in Schools.* Alexandria, VA: Association for Supervision and Curriculum Development, 2004.

Marzano, R. J., J. S. Norford, D. E. Paynter, D. J. Pickering, and B. B. Gaddy. *A Handbook for Classroom Instruction That Works.* Alexandria, VA: Association for Supervision and Curriculum Development, 2001.

Marzano, R. J., D. J. Pickering, and J. E. Pollock. *Classroom Instruction That Works: Research-Based Strategies for Increasing Student Achievement.* Alexandria, VA: Association for Supervision and Curriculum Development, 2001.

Myrah, G. E., and L. Erlauer. "The Benefits of Brain Research: One District's Story." *High School Magazine* 7(1) (1999): 34–40.

Reigeluth, C. M., and B. J. Beatty. "Why Children Are Left Behind and What We Can Do About It." *Educational Technology* 43(5) (2003): 24–32.

Slavin, R. E. *Educational Psychology: Theory and Practice* (7th edition). Boston: Allyn and Bacon, 2003.

Stanford, P. "Multiple Intelligence for Every Classroom." *Interaction in School and Clinic* 39(2) (2003): 80–85. Sternberg, R. J. *Thinking Styles.* New York: Cambridge University Press, 1997.

Sungur, S., C. Tekkaya, and O. Geban. "The Contribution of Conceptual Change Texts Accompanied by Concept Mapping to Students' Understanding of the Human Circulatory System." *School Science and Mathematics* 101(2) (2001): 91–101.

Sylwester, R. *A Celebration of Neurons: An Educator's Guide to the Human Brain.* Alexandria, VA: Association for Supervision and Curriculum Development, 1995.

Tate, M. L. *Worksheets Don't Grow Dendrites.* Thousand Oaks, CA: Corwin, 2003.

Tippett, C. "Demonstrating Understanding in Science: Connection to Learning Styles." *Canadian Children* 28(1) (2003): 21–28.

Vasilyev, Y. "The Network of Concepts and Facts: Forming a System of Conclusions Through Reflection." *Thinking Classroom* 4(2) (2003): 29–33.

Weiss, R. P. "Brain-Based Learning." *Training and Development* 54(7) (2000): 20–24.

Wilson, W. J. *When Work Disappears: The World of the New Urban Poor.* New York: Knopf, 1996.

Winters, C. A. "Brain-Based Teaching: Fad or Promising Teaching Method." University Park, IL: Governor State University, April 13, 2001.

Instruction as a Dynamic Process in Classrooms

In Parts 1 and 2, we discuss the vitally important, yet somewhat passive, areas of preparation and instructional planning. We say these subjects are *passive* because the work is often done in isolation, after school, or with colleagues; it may or may not involve interacting with students. Now we present the *dynamic* parts of teaching, where students and teachers interact. In Part 3, we show you how to create an environment for learning. Chapter 6, "Managing the Classroom Environment," shows you how to keep the classroom ethos positive. Questioning and conducting highly involved recitations are the topics of Chapter 7. Conducting authentic small-group discussions is the principal subject of Chapter 8. In addition, we introduce you to a cooperative learning model that fosters learning for all in a small-group configuration.

Chapter 9 adds the complete inquiry model to your teaching repertoire. Here are methods that will help you teach students how to think. We close Part 3 with Chapter 10 on Classroom Assessment. All of these strategies will help you create a classroom that intentionally invites everyone to engage in learning at the highest possible level.

Managing the Classroom Environment

1

THE GOAL OF MANAGING A CLASSROOM

Changing Definitions of Discipline

Core Management Concepts

2

CLASSROOM ROUTINES

Planning and Preparation

Establishing Usable Rules

Getting Off to a Good Start

Providing Clear Directions

Monitoring the Classroom Environment

Keeping Records Efficiently

Managing Interruptions

4

SOCIETY AND CLASSROOM MANAGEMENT

Engendering Cooperation and Equity

Realizing the Importance of Parental Involvement

Dealing with Abusive Attitudes and Behaviors

3

A CONTINUUM OF MANAGEMENT SYSTEMS

Systems Based on Self-Discipline

Imposed-Discipline Systems

Today's math lesson in Mr. Davis's fourth-grade class involves adding three-digit numbers. All the students are busy writing puzzle problems for each other to solve. As each student comes up with a problem and a solution, Mr. Davis checks it for accuracy, and the student then challenges another student to solve the problem. As the students become increasingly involved in this activity and move around the room to challenge and be challenged, the murmur of activity gradually rises. The steady, loud drone is continually punctuated by cries of "Let me try!" "Did you get it?" "Who wants to try this one?" "Wow! That's not the solution I came up with, but you're right, too!" A stranger walking into the classroom might think that pandemonium reigned here.

What makes a good environment for all learners?

What's going on in this classroom?

Along with some laypeople, some educators might consider this classroom to be out of control. "Does Mr. Davis have a classroom management problem in this noisy, active place?" they might wonder. Is he using a conscious classroom management approach? Is this a good environment for all learners? Does his approach suit both boys and girls? How would Mr. Davis handle an emergency or an unanticipated interruption such as a fire alarm or a classroom visitor? This chapter helps you assess and learn to apply positive classroom management techniques to achieve desirable learning outcomes. As you move through this chapter, think about how you would answer the following questions.

- How will you establish a classroom environment that rewards appropriate behavior and deters inappropriate behavior?
- How can you tell when to intervene to prevent discipline problems?
- Which student-to-student behaviors are considered harassing? Abusive?
- How can you analyze a classroom management technique to determine its impact on student learning?
- How important are parents to achieving your goals as a teacher?
- How can you manage your classroom so that the learning environment is fair to all your students?

SECTION 1: THE GOAL OF MANAGING A CLASSROOM

Prospective teachers tend to focus their attention on preparing subject matter. Yet, according to a 1998 survey of more than 4,000 teachers, many feel inadequately prepared to maintain order and discipline in the classroom, and even fewer feel competent to address the needs of students from diverse cultural backgrounds (Loehrke 1999). This finding comes as little surprise. **Classroom management**, the way the teacher organizes, disciplines, and runs the class in order to ensure positive student behaviors conducive to learning, is a top concern of many experienced teachers. In this chapter, we present a variety of classroom management strategies for your analysis. Your task is to formulate a classroom management program that fits your teaching style and philosophy and that promotes successful classroom instruction. As you gain experience, you will observe more experienced teachers using the same tested techniques that are presented here.

Changing Definitions of Discipline

Why are classroom management issues of such concern? The *Davis* v. *Monroe County School Board* decision and the Columbine High School shootings may or may not be familiar events to you. However, these two events shook the pillars of education throughout the country. In the case of *Davis* v. *Monroe County School Board*, a Georgia elementary school failed to act to protect a fifth-grade girl whose classmate made unwanted physical contact and sexual remarks. The U.S. Supreme Court ruled in this case that educators who are deliberately indifferent to student-to-student sexual harassment might be liable under a federal antibias law (Greenberger 1999). If you, as a teacher, overlook some "children just being children" behavior that others deem harassment, you may be liable.

The 1999 Columbine High School incident, in which two Jefferson County, Colorado, students killed twelve fellow students and a teacher, displayed the gross inadequacies of educational institutions to address planned violence. The U.S. Department of Education's National Center for Educational Statistics showed that, in the 1996–1997 school year, 1 percent of schools had installed permanent metal detectors, 4 percent used hand-held metal detectors, 19 percent had drug sweeps, 24 percent controlled access to the grounds, 53 percent controlled access to the building, 80 percent had closed lunch (prohibiting students from leaving campus for lunch), and 96 percent required visitors to sign in. Education Department and Department of Justice statistics showed that the overall nonfatal victimization rate had declined (Kaufman et al. 2000). What can a teacher do to be proactive, knowing that some students are threatened and abused?

Discipline is usually defined as the preservation of order and the maintenance of control—the two traditional outcomes of classroom management techniques. However, this view of discipline is far too narrow. Teachers must make on-the-spot, split-second decisions and must react spontaneously to solve problems that arise in the classroom. As shown in Figure 6.1, classroom management techniques are determined by *teacher–student–situation* factors. The attitudes students develop in formal classroom settings are influenced by the teacher's classroom management skills. Your ideas about what a classroom should look like and how it should function will determine your classroom's atmosphere. Recall the level of activity and energy in Mr. Davis's classroom.

In the early twentieth century, the major emphasis of teacher preparation programs was classroom *control*. Accepted ideas about "mental discipline," physical punishment, order, and obedience provided educators with a consistent frame of reference that was enforced throughout the school. Later, in the 1950s, school administrators began to shift more of the burden for establishing classroom climate and managing student conduct to the individual teacher. While this shift in responsibility was occurring, the results of relevant studies of discipline by social and behavioral scientists began to be applied in the schools. The shift to individual responsibility, combined with social and behavioral research, set the stage for **democratic discipline**.

Recent events put classroom management in the news.

Classroom climate and student conduct are a teacher's responsibility.

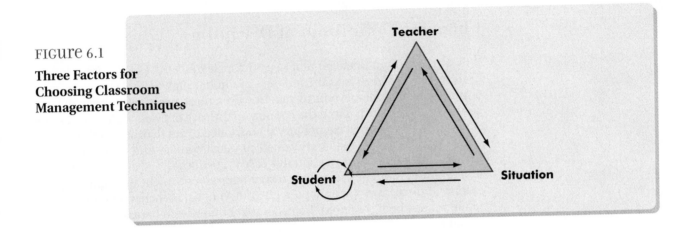

FIGURE 6.1

Three Factors for Choosing Classroom Management Techniques

Two principles are essential for the use of democratic discipline in the classroom:

- As the adult member of the class, the teacher must add the rational dimension to the rule-making capacities of the group.
- Rules administered by the teacher should reflect the wisdom and fairness and patience of a judge.

The change in classrooms was even more dramatic during the 1970s and 1980s. Four changes had a distinct effect on classroom management during that time. First, families became very mobile. It was not uncommon for even rather stable schools to show 25 percent annual student turnover. Such a high degree of turnover had an impact on both the learning environment and the expected patterns of student behavior and classroom systems. Thus today's classrooms tend to be relatively unstable social systems.

The second phenomenon was the so-called breakup of the nuclear family. More students now live with single parents than at any other time in history, and this number is increasing. Examining the population of U.S. households with children, the U.S. Census Bureau recorded that in 2003 married-couple families comprised 68 percent of the group. Single-mother families accounted for 26 percent, and single-father families made up 6 percent. Thus about one of three children in 2003 was living in a single-parent family (Fields 2004).

Third, an ethos developed among many students that viewed school as a place to "get through." Social promotion (promoting failing students with their age group) had firmly taken hold; as a result, students felt entitled to advancement. How can teachers motivate students if there was little threat of failure and little reward for achievement?

Fourth, urban schools experienced a distinct set of problems (gangs, violence, high dropout rates, poverty) that were quite different from the problems facing suburban and rural schools. One can no longer compile a single list of rules and expect it to apply to all schools.

Social trends may affect student behavior.

Core Management Concepts

Our approach to classroom management is based on a **humanistic orientation** toward the classroom environment, which views students as diverse individuals seeking acceptance and fulfillment. Teachers must be mindful of the fact that young minds and attitudes are shaped by both *overt* and *covert* teacher behaviors. Thus, in this section, we discuss three concepts that are both central to the principles of classroom management and an important influence on student development: *norms, power,* and *awareness.*

A **norm** is a behavioral rule or pattern accepted by most members of a group. For example, raising one's hand before speaking is a norm in many classrooms. Norms are usually not recorded the way the laws of a country are. However, there exists in the minds of group members an ideal standard directing how each member ought to behave under specific conditions. This shared standard introduces a high degree of regularity and predictability into their social interaction (see the box below). An observed deviation from the norm usually results in a negative response, and norms can change over time. For example, changes in the racial and ethnic makeup of a school or classroom can influence previously established norms.

Norm = accepted standard of behavior

key ideas

The Importance of Norms

- Norms are valuable to social relationships.
- Norms reduce the necessity for direct information and personal influence.
- Norms provide for the control of individual and group behavior without anyone overtly exerting power.

By virtue of your role and position in the classroom, you as teacher have influence, or **power**. Unrestrained use of that power creates insecurities and resistance among students, adversely affecting their learning. Students can retaliate against the teacher (and other students) by forming cliques, creating irritating disturbances, and making threats (see Table 6.1). To be an effective classroom manager, you must learn to exercise the least amount of power necessary to accomplish the desired academic results (see Leriche 1992) and maintain essential classroom norms.

The term **awareness** refers to a teacher's attention to and insight about the classroom environment. A class constantly gives its teacher verbal and nonverbal clues. Children's behaviors offer insights regarding student-to-student interactions (Power 1992). Furthermore, communication occurs both between the teacher and individual students and between the teacher and the class as a whole. The master teacher understands how to read this mixture of communications. Knowing which communications to ignore and which to attend to quickly separates the pro teachers from the rookies.

Awareness = use eyes and ears to read class's cues

Establishing classroom norms is practical for democratic management. © Suzie Fitzhugh

TABLE 6.1

Reported Crimes Against Students, 1993 and 2003.
While reports of crimes against students have dropped nationally, publicity of school crime has increased.

	Percentages	
Offense Reported	1993	2003
Threatened or injured with a weapon	7.3	9.2
Carried a weapon	11.8	6.0
In a physical fight	16.2	12.8

SOURCE: U.S. Department of Education, *Indicators of School Crime and Safety: 2004* (NCES 2005-002), Tables 4.1 and 5.1.

Initially, a teacher must determine how his or her class presents cues. The teacher who simply complains, "My class was particularly lousy today" has not adequately analyzed the information provided by the class. This teacher must define precisely what he or she means by "lousy." Did students recite inappropriately, not pay attention, or not accomplish the work requested? Were they just generally off task? Were they unprepared? Disorderly? The teacher must be able to specify what behaviors were demonstrated. Next, the teacher must be prepared to state what behaviors would be considered appropriate (see Evertson 1995).

For example, the cell phone has become an accessory item to our lives. Students and faculty carry them about like a quickdraw pistol—reflexively drawing at the first ring or vibration. Schools and teachers must understand how prevalent cell phones are and the impact they have on attention and learning. They should discuss appropriate and inappropriate uses (both when and where) of cell phones on school grounds. Ideally, all phones, including the teacher's, should be turned off and placed in a secure location during the instructional period.

We use the terms *discipline* and *classroom management* throughout this chapter. The box on this page describes how the two concepts differ operationally. The list for discipline shows reactive teacher behaviors. The list for classroom management shows teacher actions that are proactive. A proactive teacher is in charge of the classroom environment and establishes the climate for instructional activities.

INSTRUCTIONAL STRATEGIES

Discipline Versus Classroom Management: The Most Common Teacher Strategies

Discipline

Giving in-school suspensions

Sending misbehaving students to the office

Contacting parents

Using a check or demerit system

Taking away privileges

Classroom Management

Emphasizing rules at the start of the school year

Planning for smooth transitions; leaving minimal time between activities

Paying attention to the entire class; continuously scanning the group

Pacing activities effectively

Giving clear and concise instructions

Carefully designing the classroom environment

Organizing activities in advance

SOURCE: Based on information from Rita Seedorf. Used with permission.

reflect

- Research the Supreme Court's *Monroe County* ruling at **http://www. washingtonpost.com/wp-srv/national/longterm/supcourt/ 1998-99/davis.htm**. Do you agree or disagree with the Court's ruling on this case. Why? What discipline or classroom management techniques could prevent this type of situation in the future?

- Research the Columbine High shootings. Do you agree or disagree that the four national trends discussed on pages 173–174 may contribute to incidents of school violence? What discipline or classroom management techniques, or other solutions, could prevent these situations?

- To what extent do teachers have the responsibility to ensure classroom management under all circumstances, even if the results are contrary to the desires of some students?

section 2: classroom routines

Classroom management systems provide routine ways of managing instructional and behavioral interactions in the classroom (see Table 6.2). We focus here on the seven key elements the pros use to effectively manage their classrooms (see the box below).

video case

Find out which strategies work best for seasoned teachers in the Video Case "Classroom Management: Best Practices." Which of their techniques echo what you're learning in this chapter? Which are different? The bonus video gives tips for managing a technology-based lesson.

Seven Key Elements of Effective Classroom Management

1. Planning
2. Establishing usable rules
3. Getting off to a good start
4. Providing clear directions
5. Monitoring the classroom environment
6. Keeping records efficiently
7. Creating strategies for managing interruptions

Planning and Preparation

Planning is a top priority for effective time management. Detailed planning is initially time consuming, but teachers who make explicit plans are better organized and progress faster in achieving educational goals (Walsh 1992). Teachers who plan and communicate their expectations to their students

TABLE 6.2

What comes first, poor
procedures or the disruption?

Sources of problems in classroom management

If you observe several of these problems in a classroom, you likely will find lower
student achievement and poor student morale.

Motivation Problems

Insufficient activity for students
Student apathy
Difficulty getting students involved
Negative student attitudes
Daydreaming
Lack of student success
Negative teacher attitudes

Instructional Problems

Lack of variety in instructional techniques
Inadequately communicated goals and objectives
Bad pacing (too fast or too slow)
Lack of prerequisite skills, causing student failure
Student distress or anger over evaluations
Students not following directions
Failure to complete all assignments

Procedural Problems

Unclear assignments
Moving the class to a different room
Lack of a systematic routine for procedural activities
Failing to reserve a special room or space for an activity
Forgetting to check out projector or AV equipment
Failing to preview media, resulting in presentation of inappropriate material
Not having the necessary materials in the classroom
Failure to plan discussion groups in advance

Disruptive Problems

Excessive talking at beginning of class
Note passing
Cheating
Stealing
Vandalism
Attention seeking
Arriving late for class
Racial tensions
Teacher making value judgments about students' dress, home life, or parents
Teacher making unenforceable threats
Obscene language or gestures

Characteristics of well-prepared teachers

promote a positive academic environment. Thus teachers with an effective plan know what, whom, and how they will teach; they have materials ready for their students; they plan for smooth transitions between classes and activities; and they have additional activities ready for students who finish early.

Well-prepared teachers keep lessons moving at a brisk pace but do not ignore students who are having difficulties. They do not allow interruptions during a lesson, and they stress the importance of every lesson. They make a practice of critiquing their day's work. They jot a few notes into their lesson planning books to act as tips for future lessons. Their lesson plans are very brief and conceptual in nature, but they do carry out formal planning (see Martella and Nelson 2003).

Establishing Usable Rules

The purpose of establishing rules is to enhance students' academic and social achievement (see Marzano, Marzano, and Pickering 2003). Teachers who are effective managers explain the importance and need for each rule, teach students how to follow rules and procedures, and begin with the rules that are of the most immediate importance. (How do I get permission to leave the room? How do I ask a question?) They state rules clearly and enforce them consistently. On-again, off-again enforcement contributes to student behavior problems.

Rules must be applied consistently.

Effective teachers also make rules that are not related to discipline. These cover classroom routines for distributing materials, transitioning to new activities, starting and ending class, obtaining permission to leave the classroom, and accomplishing tasks such as sharpening pencils. Simplicity is the hallmark of effective rules. If your rules are complicated, you will not be able to enforce them, and students will become confused. Thus simplicity will allow you to easily explain and enforce your rules.

Getting Off to a Good Start

Effective classroom managers discuss classroom procedures with their students at the beginning of the school year and provide opportunities for students to practice them to ensure understanding (Lombardi 1992; Tauber 1999). During the first few days of school, your students will require frequent feedback. State your expectations often and give students positive or corrective responses. By the end of the third or fourth week of school, you can anticipate that transitions will be smoother and shorter and that reminders to your students on class routines can be greatly reduced (Evertson, Emmer, and Worsham 2000). It is much easier to be firm and precise in the beginning and then relax as you observe that students have adopted your rules. It is almost impossible to gain control once chaos takes over.

The first day of school is a testing period. Students will test your rules, your determination to apply them fairly, and your commitment to maintain-

**Simplicity is
the hallmark of
effective rules.**
© Jean-Claude Lejeune

ing them. Proper management is essential for learning and for student safety. Apply your rules immediately, fairly and with determination. Introduce, explain, reinforce, and repeat. The first day is also the best time to initiate routines. This is the day to establish a positive, caring, and businesslike environment.

Providing Clear Directions

Giving directions is a core skill (Anderson 2002). Whether the directions concern instruction or classroom procedures, give them clearly and succinctly. Even more important, their orientation must be positive. Directions such as

"Stop that" or "Cut that out" given to disruptive students omit the most important part: What is the student to do after he or she stops the disruptive behavior? Provide the student with a constructive alternative. For example, you might suggest that the student return to work, or you might provide some instructionally related activity to replace the disruptive behavior. For example, you might say, "Sam, please reduce your volume; turn to page 72 in your book and complete the questions following the unit's reading. I will review your answers in ten minutes."

Positive correcting: What should they do instead?

INSTRUCTIONAL STRATEGIES

Steps for Effective Directions

1. Give the directions
   - Get the class's attention
   - Deliver the directions in brief steps (both orally and in writing)
   - Explain expectations—what students will produce and when
   - Ask a student to restate the directions and expectations
   - Repeat the directions
2. Follow up the directions
   - Closely monitor selected individuals until satisfied that the directions are understood and being applied.
   - If the class or an individual student is having a problem, point out a positive example as an alternative to the problem.

Monitoring the Classroom Environment

Effective teachers monitor student behavior in the classroom. They make each student responsible for some work during the learning activity and then watch to see that it is actually accomplished. These teachers are strong student motivators (Wood 2001).

Room Arrangement   The arrangement of the room is an important part of a monitoring strategy. An orderly arrangement of desks and tables in a classroom contributes to a smooth, businesslike atmosphere that promotes effective use of instructional time. Two criteria for effective room arrangement are (1) your ability to see all students at all times and (2) the circulation patterns that you establish. It is important to be able to monitor all students from your desk and from all other areas where you are likely to be. Simply being visually close to a student can prevent many problems. This is your greatest deterrent against harassing and bullying behavior.

Sightline to all students prevents problems.

If the physical aspects of your classroom permit the rearranging of student seats, you might consider various small-group arrangements: circles, U shapes, or 50-50 splits. Often, a change in perspective results from the rearrangement of the classroom and may energize the students with a different perspective on the material and learning.

Questioning   Questioning is also an effective monitoring strategy (see Chapter 7). During learning activities, effective teachers ask questions and then look around the room before calling on a student. They call on volunteers as well as others and seem to get around to everyone, but not in a predictable manner. Effective teachers intersperse calls for group answers with solicitations of individual responses and occasionally throw out challenging statements such as "I don't think anyone can get this!" Finally, effective teachers monitor their classes by asking students to react to the answers of others. Such monitoring strategies promote a smooth-flowing, highly interactive learning environment with a high percentage of on-task student behavior.

Keeping Records Efficiently

Every teacher faces the tasks of recording grades, taking attendance, keeping track of students' class participation, recording disciplinary actions, and documenting other aspects of classroom life. For legality, fairness, and consistency, you need a comprehensive and systematic approach to record keeping.

Managing records essential to fair grading

Records management is an extremely important part of maintaining a fair and equitable grading system. After you have established reasonable guidelines for standards, quality, late work, missed assignments, bonus work, makeup tests, and class participation, you must be prepared to track each student's performance in each area reliably and consistently.

In addition, you should maintain objective anecdotal records (short objective notes about student actions) to document classroom incidents such as fights, inappropriate behavior, and cheating. Of course, you should also record acts of courage, ingenuity, and creativity. If you notice a rapid change in a student's dress, friends, language, or attitude, you should note the change and closely monitor it. Such behavioral change frequently indicates abuse of some nature (physical, gang, or drug). Record these acts when they happen. This record will provide you with a chronicle that may provide evidence to support or confront a student at some later date.

Managing Interruptions

Teachers spend a tremendous amount of time planning instruction: preparing lesson plans, selecting support materials, creating student activities, designing tests, and so on. Yet all too often the anticipated instructional period is drastically reduced by interruptions. Lost time! Studies have demonstrated that frequently 30 percent or more of the instructional day is lost to anticipated and unanticipated interruptions. These interruptions range from student misbehavior to announcements over the intercom. (We heard of one example of thirty such announcements in one day!) Whatever

Technology can save time and improve effectiveness.

TECHNOLOGY INSIGHT

Gradebook Software

Many schools and school districts make use of gradebook software to facilitate determining and recording students' grades. Gradebook software is essentially a combination of *database* and *spreadsheet* software. Most of these products make it relatively easy for a teacher to set up an electronic version of a traditional paper gradebook. The teacher creates a database of students with information that may include the student's name and parent/guardian contact information. Once the database is created, the software generates a spreadsheet—a series of columns and rows that form a grid in which text and numeric data can be stored and manipulated. The teacher can then designate specific assignments with days of the week that can be cross-referenced with each individual student. As with a paper gradebook, the teacher can then fill in each student's accomplishments for a specific assignment or day.

Gradebook software has at least two significant advantages over its paper counterpart:

1. Once a class database/spreadsheet is set up, the software can perform a variety of calculations to determine grade averages and final grades (for example, each assignment may be given a specific weight or percentage of the final grade). The software then performs all the necessary calculations.
2. If an entire school or school district is using the same software, a teacher can often submit a class's grades via computer. This saves time for both the teacher and the school administration.

Most gradebook software products also support the creation of printable student reports. These reports can be shared with students and their parents or guardians. A web search using the phrase "gradebook software" will provide access to a number these products. Any company that makes gradebook software will offer free trial versions of their products. These are usually limited versions of the software that either expire after a short time or do not allow a user to save work.

Interruptions steal time from teaching and learning.

its cause, lost time has a negative impact on student academic achievement and creates the conditions for student behavior problems (see Ysseldyke and Elliott 1999).

The ability to manage most interruptions is fully within teachers' control (see Leonard 1999). You simply need to anticipate and plan for them. You must plan for transitions in instruction (anticipated interruptions), and you must establish firm expectations regarding student behavior to reduce the instructional impact of unanticipated interruptions. Table 6.3 lists some examples of anticipated and unanticipated interruptions.

Anticipated Interruptions Twenty-one percent of class time is spent on transitions (Gump 1982), on ending one lesson or activity and beginning another. Effective teachers prepare their students for transitions (Cotton 2001). Besides making transitions from one activity to the next quickly, they are especially careful not to end one activity and begin a second and then return to the first. Abrupt endings to activities set the stage for numerous behavior problems. To become more efficient, give signals, set time limits, and provide very clear instructions—even modeling them as needed (Gump 1982).

Gaps in teacher directions before and after an instructional episode or interruption are a frequent cause of both classroom management problems and lost instructional opportunities. Frequently teachers get caught up in the physical requirements of lesson setup or breakdown, materials handling, and student assessment. While the teacher is focusing on these tasks, the class is left idle, which often leads to problems! Thus teachers must develop strategies for managing prelesson transitions, transitions that occur during a lesson, and postlesson transitions. Among other strategies, teachers should plan to use "fillers"—student activities or routines that fill the gaps created by transitions between instructional episodes and administrative activities.

1. **Prelesson transitions.** Delegate administrative tasks to students whenever possible. A routine should be made for managing attendance,

Be ahead of the game: Expect interruptions and plan for them.

TABLE 6.3

The Best Teachers Prepare for Anticipated and Unanticipated Interruptions
Anticipated Interruptions
Transitions between and during instructional episodes Equipment setup and breakdown Materials distribution/collection Changing from teacher- to student-centered activity Beginning/end of class or school day
Unanticipated Interruptions
Student illness Visitors Announcements/messages Student behavioral problems Equipment malfunctions Fire alarms/classroom evacuations Materials shortages

announcements, materials distribution and collection, and special activities as much as possible. Create a routine in which homework is checked by a peer or teacher's aide and deposited in student files. Rotate the students selected for such administrative support activities. Many teachers use the first few minutes of class and the last few minutes to encourage creative thinking activities, which are repeated each day. Puzzles, thought problems, computer games, or related art and media projects that can be quickly started and stopped are good fillers. Naturally, it is important to assign some value to these activities in terms of student grades (see Scofield 2000–2001 for ideas).

2. **Transitions that occur during a lesson.** Students rarely complete an activity in a uniform time span. A prepared teacher recognizes the likelihood of this and prepares supplementary activities or additional resources for the fast workers. Many teachers use peer tutor strategies or have fast finishers assist with administrative tasks (such as correcting tests) or prepare for the next instructional episode. The transition from a regular to a supplementary activity must be carefully thought out and the procedures explained to the class in advance. If you develop activities that can be used on a regular basis, be sure to state your expectations for their use clearly and then reinforce appropriate student behaviors.

3. **Postlesson transitions.** Teacher control of the classroom can easily break down at the end of an instructional episode, due to the many details a teacher must attend to before the class moves on. Frequently you will be involved with materials collection, equipment management, individual student assignments, or administrative chores. Prepare for such demands by developing routine student activities. Create a routine for the last five minutes of each class period or instructional episode. The routine will give you time to shift from one class or activity to the next. The ending activity should be self-paced and self-instructional for the students. The teacher should merely announce the beginning of the "curtain" (ending) activity, and everyone should know what to do. For such curtain activities, avoid student movement, materials distribution, and teaming. The activities should focus on the individual and provide an opportunity for relaxed exploration. Reading, writing, drawing, student planning, or journal writing are appropriate for the closing minutes. Avoid the rigorous, the active, the involved. *Slow things down. Your students need a breather before moving on to the next instructional episode,* just as you do.

Unanticipated Interruptions   During the course of a typical day, many unanticipated events occur. These events may be initiated by students, school personnel, visitors, or others. They include fire alarms, intercom announcements, broken equipment, problems with the school building, messages from the office, and untold other attention breaks. You can anticipate that such events will occur each day; however, you cannot anticipate when they will occur or how long they will last. For example, loss of electrical power is always an interesting instructional interruption with which to cope. All you can do is prepare yourself and your classes for such eventual-

Quick learners can be effective peer tutors during transitions.

ities. During the initial weeks of the school year, you should explain your expectations for how the class is to deal with unanticipated interruptions. Provide specific instructions concerning what students should do in an emergency (fire, injury, chemical spill, accident, electrical failure, earthquake), how they should behave for a visitor (parent, student, other), and how the class is to manage itself if your attention is required to resolve another issue or if you must leave the room. You may want to simulate these events. The expected behaviors should become part of your classroom's norms.

When explaining your expectations for interruptions and transitions, be sure to provide a detailed explanation of the importance of good behavior and ongoing academic effort. All too frequently, a teacher will establish a set of classroom rules but fail to explain their importance to classroom citizenship and learning.

Explain not just the rules but why they are important.

The specific way you approach planning for interruptions obviously will vary according to your students' maturity levels. Individual planning can help reduce the time loss caused by anticipated interruptions; however, many unanticipated interruptions are schoolwide or otherwise beyond the teacher's control (intercom messages, inappropriate classroom visitors). The teachers in a school must band together to address such interruptions and suggest ways to stop or greatly reduce them.

reFLeCT

- What impact do unanticipated interruptions have on students and their learning?

- To what extent do you believe that the gender of the teacher or the student has a role in classroom management considerations? What about the age of the teacher? How can you address these issues in your classroom?

section 3: A continuum of management systems

As you strive to maximize learning time for your students, you must choose from among a large number of classroom management strategies. We have arranged these strategies along a continuum ranging from those that rely on self-discipline to those that involve imposing discipline on your students (see Figure 6.2). *Self-discipline* implies voluntary adherence to norms that promote students' self-interest and protect the welfare of others. *Imposed discipline* suggests a student code of conduct prescribed by the teacher in the best interests of individual students and the class as a whole. Between self-discipline and imposed discipline there are numerous choices.

Discipline can be internal or external.

FIGURE 6.2

A Continuum of Classroom Management Systems

| Reality Therapy (William Glasser) | Assertive Discipline (Lee and Merlene Canter) | Desist Strategies (Jacob S. Kounin and Carl J. Wallen) |

Self-Discipline ⟷ Imposed Discipline

| Hierarchy of Needs (Abraham H. Maslow) | Moral Reasoning (Lawrence Kohlberg) | Behavior Modification (B. F. Skinner) |

To provide you with an overview of selected classroom management systems, we will discuss three theories that lean toward self-discipline: Maslow's hierarchy of needs, moral reasoning and character development, and reality therapy. On the imposed-discipline side, we will discuss desist strategies, assertive discipline, and behavior modification. Reality therapy, desist strategies, and behavior modification are highlighted because they are generic (that is, other systems have been developed from them).

Systems Based on Self-Discipline

VIDEO CASE

Adolescent anger can present difficulties for educators, parents, and teens themselves. The video "Social and Emotional Development: Understanding Adolescents" offers a discussion between a counselor and several teen boys. What coping strategies do they devise? Can these strategies be generalized to address other management issues?

Self-discipline strategies are based on the premise that the students' self-discipline depends heavily on effective teacher-student and student-student relationships. Advocates of self-discipline as a classroom management tool argue that to facilitate learning, teachers need to increase their involvement. Involvement requires that teachers demonstrate genuineness, empathy toward the student, and acceptance and trust of the student.

While success is attained with involvement, teacher involvement also means working with individual students on a one-to-one level to address behavioral or academic problems. While remaining in the "teacher role," the teacher helps the student make plans, carry them out, revise them, and strive continually for success. Involvement means that the teacher helps the student become more responsible for his or her behavior by having the student constantly state what he or she is doing. Involvement also means meeting with parents or guardians, if possible, and seeking their cooperation. Furthermore, it means meeting with other teachers to discuss the needs of certain students.

Additionally, self-discipline requires a positive perspective and *positive expectations* on the part of the teacher. Through positive feedback, self-discipline is expected and achieved by students (Cotton 2001). With these prerequisites in mind, let us examine classroom management strategies that focus on self-discipline.

Maslow's Hierarchy of Needs   Abraham H. Maslow's humanistic approach (1968) has had a major impact on educational theory and classroom management for decades. Maslow's *hierarchy of needs* theory (see Figure 6.3) assumes that an individual's behavior at any time is determined by his or her needs. For example, a hungry student will have a hard time focusing on learning skills. Maslow's theory suggests a teacher determine what need might be causing a behavior problem and then address that need. Naturally, teachers would like for self-esteem and self-actualization to direct student behavior, for then students could be truly self-regulated and time spent managing the classroom would not be required.

To use Maslow's ideas, you must truly believe in your students. Students need to be shown that they are valued and respected and are really important in the class. Structure, routines, and consistency are all hallmarks of this strategy. You help all students to develop a positive, constructive self-image. The classroom environment must be structured to be supportive. Even when someone is "in trouble," it is always the act that is corrected, not the person. Teachers stress the intrinsic value of each student and attempt to motivate all students to do the best they possibly can. Implementing Maslow's system requires a long-term commitment to classroom management and routines consistent with students' self-actualization.

Correct the act, not the person.

Moral Reasoning and Character Development   Many recent calls for educational reform have come from parents and community leaders who believe that the schools have ignored a responsibility to build the character and moral values of students. Researchers have also argued that the schools should focus more on students' moral reasoning and character development (Noddings 2002; Ryan and Bohlin 1999; Simon 2002). Others argue that the public schools have no role in character development and moral education, and that they should concentrate exclusively on developing

FIGURE 6.3

Maslow's Hierarchy of Needs

A well-managed classroom allows the students to focus on personal growth, not on safety and belonging.

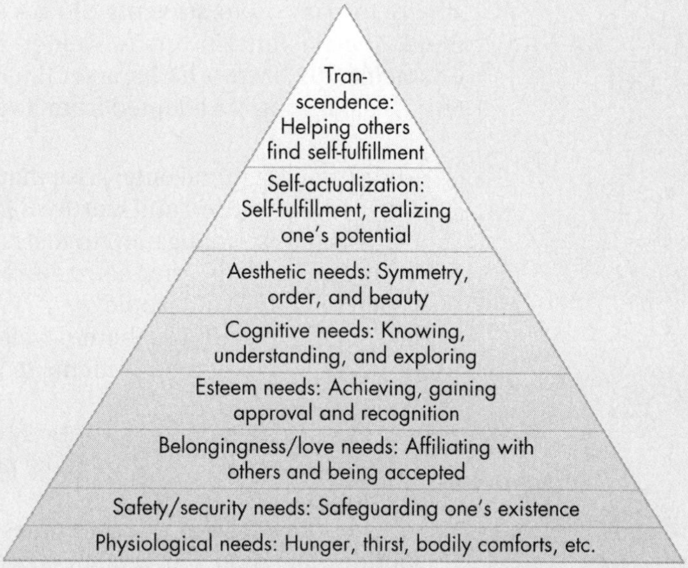

Tran-
scendence:
Helping others
find self-fulfillment

Self-actualization:
Self-fulfillment, realizing
one's potential

Aesthetic needs: Symmetry,
order, and beauty

Cognitive needs: Knowing,
understanding, and exploring

Esteem needs: Achieving, gaining
approval and recognition

Belongingness/love needs: Affiliating with
others and being accepted

Safety/security needs: Safeguarding one's existence

Physiological needs: Hunger, thirst, bodily comforts, etc.

students' cognitive skills. We believe that the process of schooling necessarily affects the way children think about issues of right and wrong, so it is important to purposefully address those issues.

A model for providing a moral education was developed by Lawrence Kohlberg (1975; Power, Higgins, and Kohlberg 1989). His model presents "moral dilemmas" in which students are faced with a personal choice. One such dilemma might be a group of students who are aware that a friend has a weapon in his locker and recently threatened another student. What action should the group take? How would the students feel if someone were injured or killed by the weapon? Such an exercise forces students to work through their values and develop and apply their moral compasses.

For such an exercise, the class is divided into groups for discussion. Kohlberg believes that these discussions will help students raise their consciousness and come to understand the motivation of others better. He stresses that the classroom should be a "just community" in which a democratic society is the model. Obviously, the dilemmas posed must be appropriate for the maturity of the class members. (See also Etzioni 1997; Myers 2001.)

There is a great deal of consensus surrounding moral development and positive classroom environments. The Josephson Institute of Ethics (2002), a nonprofit foundation, is a strong advocate of ethics and character development in schools, government agencies, and the business sector. The institute stresses "six pillars" of character:

1. Trustworthiness
2. Respect
3. Responsibility
4. Fairness
5. Caring
6. Citizenship

If the schools are to be reformed, they must reclaim their traditional responsibility to pass on to students the best of our culture's values. With this in mind, the Boston University Center for the Advancement of Ethics and Character (1997) wrote a Character Education Manifesto for U.S. schoolchildren. The following are adapted from its seven guiding principles.

1. Education is a moral enterprise that should guide students to know and pursue what is good and worthwhile.
2. Schools have an obligation to foster in their students personal and civic virtues such as integrity, courage, responsibility, diligence, and respect for the dignity of all people.
3. Character education is about developing virtues—habits and dispositions—that lead students to become responsible and mature adults.
4. All adults in a school must embody and reflect the moral authority that has been invested in them by parents and the community.
5. Schools must become communities of virtue in which responsibility and kindness are modeled, taught, expected, celebrated, and continually practiced.

6. Teachers and students must draw from the human community's reservoir of moral wisdom, much of which exists in our great stories, works of art, literature, history, and biographies.
7. Young people need to realize that forging their own character is an essential and demanding life task.

Character education is a fundamental dimension of good teaching, notes the Boston University Center Web home page (2005). For an elaborating discussion on this entire subject, see Sizer and Sizer 1999; Soder, Goodlad, and McMannon 2002.

Reality Therapy   Reality therapy is an approach that helps individuals take responsibility for solving their own problems. Reality therapy requires positive, genuine, human involvement that allows people to recognize their own reality and to begin to reshape their own behaviors to meet selected needs without any threats or implied punishments.

Accountability for own failures, responsibility for own success

The main premise is that an individual must acknowledge his or her own failures and be personally responsible for becoming successful. Toward this end, teachers must avoid labeling inappropriate behaviors with tags such as *disadvantaged, dysfunctional,* or *disabled.* Another premise is that examination of family or personal histories is not essential for change to occur.

Seven key principles form the basis for reality therapy.

Principle 1: Demonstrate Human Involvement   In the classroom setting, this means devising a structure that facilitates teacher–student and student–student involvement. Classroom management problems can then be solved in ways that express care and concern on the part of the teacher with direct student involvement. Thus small-group instruction on self-regulated learning is very much in concert with reality therapy.

Principle 2: Focus on Current Behavior   Although reality therapy does not deny emotions and their importance, its success depends on focusing on current behaviors—on what the student is doing *now.* Thus the teacher should ask a misbehaving student what he or she is doing. Rather than recall previous behavior ("Well, that's the seventh time today that you've interrupted without raising your hand"), the teacher should ask, "What are you doing?" Note that the emphasis is on the pronoun (*you*). There should be no misunderstanding concerning who is responsible for the misbehavior.

Principle 3: Examine Current Inappropriate Behavior   This means that the student who constantly misbehaves must be made to discuss his or her behavior and come to the conclusion that another type of behavior would be more appropriate. The teacher does not evaluate or label behaviors as good or bad, but simply indicates whether behaviors are appropriate or inappropriate in the classroom.

Principle 4: Create a Plan to Change   The student, with the help of the teacher, develops a plan to help meet his or her personal or educational goals. This plan becomes a contract between the student and the teacher. For example, a student who never studies should not be expected to begin studying two hours a night. Fifteen-minute sessions a few times a week would be more appropriate. Be certain that remedial plans are realistic for the particular student.

Principle 5: Demonstrated Student Commitment   After a reasonable plan has been devised, it must be carried out. Typically, the student prepares a plan in writing and signs it as a means of increasing personal motivation to maintain and fulfill the plan. This kind of commitment intensifies and accelerates the student's behavioral change.

Principle 6: Reevaluating the Plan   It is essential that both the teacher and the student be willing to reexamine the plan and renew or change it if it is in some way inappropriate. This does not mean that the teacher excuses the student's failure. When failure occurs, it must be mutually recognized that the responsibility lies with the student, either for not having fulfilled the plan or for not having planned appropriately in the first place.

Be prepared to examine and modify goals and plans.

Principle 7: Remove Punishment   William Glasser (1972; 1998) believes that punishment hinders the personal involvement that is essential between the teacher and the student. The purpose of punishment is to change an individual's behavior through fear or pain. Rather than punishment, Glasser suggests using a program of positive feedback to achieve success. In the reality therapy model, the teacher's praise of student success increases the involvement between the teacher and student and leads to more responsible student behaviors.

If you are philosophically against punishment, reality therapy may be a classroom management approach that you wish to explore further. Please glance through the reference section at the end of this chapter for additional reading.

KEY IDeas

Principles of Reality Therapy

- Teacher–student and student–student involvement is essential.
- The focus is on current student behavior.
- The student examines and evaluates his or her behavior.
- The student designs a plan to change.
- The student makes a commitment to change.
- The student owns the success or failure of the plan.
- A program of positive reinforcement is essential.

Reality Therapy and the Entire Class   Reality therapy may also be applied to an entire class through classroom meetings. A social problem-solving meeting involves a group discussion of classroom problems with the goal of reaching a mutually agreed-upon solution (see the Instructional Strategies box below). Such a meeting may be an extremely useful first step in resolving a seemingly intractable classroom-wide problem. Teachers can use many individual and group techniques in implementing a program of reality therapy. However, one requirement is essential to all of these techniques: being involved yourself. This takes training, patience, and, above all, perseverance.

INSTRUCTIONAL STRATEGIES

Elements of Social Problem-Solving Meetings

1. All group and individual problems in the class are eligible for discussion.
2. The session focuses on solving the problem, not finding fault or specifying punishment.
3. Meetings are conducted with all individuals positioned in a tight circle to foster interaction.

Imposed-Discipline Systems

Imposed-discipline systems are based on the teacher's recognized authority to set standards within the classroom and to dictate appropriate classroom behaviors and consequences of misbehavior. A teacher's authority derives from both state and local laws and societal expectations. When a teacher's responsibility is challenged, the teacher has the authority to use rewards or punishments to maintain classroom order and achieve educational goals.

In the following discussion, we describe three imposed-discipline strategies: *desist strategies*, *assertive discipline*, and *behavior modification*. Each of these strategies uses a variety of methods to exercise the teacher's authority within the classroom.

Desist Strategies   Of the imposed-discipline strategies we discuss here, the desist strategy is the most traditional. The term is derived from "desist techniques" suggested by Jacob S. Kounin and Paul V. Gump (1959). The **desist strategy** is a means of systematically communicating the teacher's desire for a student's behavior to stop or change. The communication may be accomplished by a command such as "Stop that!" or by a glance or movement. Numerous other terms have been used to describe such use of teacher authority in the classroom. However, because desist strategy is the "grand-daddy" of imposed-discipline approaches, we begin with it.

Basics   Desist strategies offer a systematic framework for applying the teacher's authority to maintain group norms. The technique of desist strategies involves two basic concepts. First, there are three levels of force—low, moderate, and high. Second, there are two types of communication of teacher desires—public and private.

In dealing with classroom discipline, it is usually best to use a low rather than a high level of force, and it is always better to use a private rather than a public form of communication. Occasionally, however, a situation calls for a high-level, public display of force. A classroom fight is one example. In the vast majority of cases, though, you will find it best to use private displays and low levels of force to handle "normal" discipline problems. Desist strategies are further explained in Tables 6.4 and 6.5.

The concept of the desist strategy is summarized by two principles first presented by Carl J. Wallen in 1968.

1. If a classroom activity is about to occur and you have not previously established standards of student behavior and your expectations, specify these expectations and behavioral standards before you begin the activity.
2. If, in a continuing activity, a student or group of students behaves in a manner contrary to specific expectations, use a desist strategy aimed at reaching the level of expectations while causing the least possible disruption to the classroom setting.

It is important that you specify the appropriate behavior for a particular activity. During a test, for example, you may decide that students should not speak out unless they raise their hands and are called on. During small-group

Start with the most private, least force.

TABLE 6.4

Desist Strategies

In general, the teacher should focus on low levels of force and private communications.

Level of Force	Definition	Desist Strategy
Low	Nonverbal, a signal or movement	Glancing at child, shaking head, moving over to child unobtrusively in the instructional activity
Moderate	Verbal, conversational, no coercion	Appealing to a child to act reasonably, removing disturbing objects, commanding the child to stop
High	Verbal and nonverbal, changed voice pitch, may use coercion	Raising voice and commanding child to stop, removing the child from group, threatening, punishing, physically restraining the child

Type of Communication	Definition	Desist Strategy
Public	Intended to be noticed by most of the children in a class	Acting and/or speaking in a way that commands attention
Private	Intended to be noticed only by small groups of children	Using unobtrusive actions or moving close to a child when speaking

SOURCE: From Wallen 1968, Appendix A, p. 15.

TABLE 6.5

Desist Strategies: Combining Force and Communication		
Force Level	Private Communication	Public Communication
1. Glance (low level)	Teacher shakes head so only one or two other children notice the action.	Teacher shakes head dramatically so most of class notices the action.
2. Appeal (moderate level)	Teacher moves close to child, asks child to act reasonably, and uses voice and manner so only one or two other children notice the action.	Teacher asks children to act reasonably, in a manner that most of the class notices.
3. Threat (high level)	Teacher moves close to child, tells what will happen if misbehavior continues, and uses voice and manner so only one or two other children notice.	Teacher tells what will happen if misbehavior continues, uses a loud and commanding voice that most of the class notices.

SOURCE: From Wallen 1968, Appendix A, pp. 15–16.

activities, students may be permitted to speak quietly. Your verbal statement of the appropriate behavior is the expected norm.

Punishments In contrast to reality therapy, desist strategies allow some form of punishment to be administered to nonresponsive students. Punishment entails consequences that reduce the future rate of undesirable behavior (Skinner 1953, 1974). *Loss of privilege* is the most common form (for example, loss of recess, sports pass, or an assembly).

George Sugai emphasizes, however, that "we also know that increasing the intensity of sanctions and excluding students for rule violations are insufficient solutions. Problem behavior often increases when only punitive discipline practices are used" (1996, p. 10).

Punishment: a consequence that reduces undesirable behavior.

Observations About Desist Strategies We should not leave the topic of desist strategies without including a short summary of one of the more important works on the topic. Kounin (1970) reported that more than half (55.2 percent) of perceived student misbehavior can be categorized as talking or other noisy behaviors. Off-task behaviors—for example, gum chewing—accounted for 17.2 percent of the total, and all other deviations from accepted norms—being late, not having homework, moving about the room without permission—accounted for the remainder (27.6 percent). According to Kounin's categories, the bulk of student misbehaviors would be regarded as low-level discipline problems.

Yet, when teachers were given the options of punishing, providing a suitable desist, or prescribing another form of productive activity in reaction to these misbehaviors, over half opted for high-level, public desists. The most interesting, or perhaps sad, finding in Kounin's study is that, in 92 percent of the cases, the teachers could give no reason for perceiving student behavior as being bad. Furthermore, in 95.6 percent of the cases, the teacher never provided the class with any knowledge of expected standards. This, of course, is an indictment of the teacher, not the students.

Assertive discipline is a form of behavior management.

In another study, Kounin (1970) noted the effects on the class of the way in which teachers either punished students or provided desists when a student or group misbehaved. After observing students in kindergarten through college, he collected data based on experimental conditions to show that the way the teacher provided a desist had, in fact, an accompanying effect on all of the class members. Kounin called this the *ripple effect*. As the students in a class observe the teacher confronting a student for apparent misbehavior, all other class members tend to be adversely affected as well. Kounin reported that the angry desist did not motivate the other students to behave better or to attend to the task; rather, it made them anxious, restless, and uninvolved.

reFLecT   The use of punishment as a classroom management tool has proponents and opponents. Are there any circumstances in which proponents of desist strategies and assertive discipline might agree on the use of punishment as a classroom management tool? Do you believe there are any circumstances in which punishment is permissible in our schools?

Assertive Discipline   **Assertive discipline** is a structured approach designed to assist teachers in running an organized, teacher-in-charge classroom environment. Lee and Marlene Canter (1992) created the original assertive discipline program after working with numerous school systems. Using their research and observation, together with behavior management theory, they developed an approach to help teachers become the stewards of their classrooms, while positively influencing their students' behavior.

A form of behavior management

A Discipline Plan   At the core of assertive discipline is a *classroom discipline plan*, a lesson plan that allows the teacher to detail classroom rules and the corresponding behaviors that are expected from students. Additionally, the lesson details what can be expected from the teacher in return. The aim of the plan is to have a fair and consistent way to establish a safe, orderly, positive classroom in which teachers teach and students learn. A discipline plan has the following three parts.

1. **Classroom rules.** The assertive teacher has clearly stated classroom rules and provides firm, clear, concise directions to students who are in

need of behavior management. Effective rules are limited in number (five at most), are observable (not vague), apply at all times of day, apply to behavior only and not to academics, and are written or chosen with student participation.

2. **Positive recognition.** During this phase of the lesson, the teacher focuses on building positive teacher–student relationships and the importance of cooperative behaviors for everyone. As discussed in the upcoming section on behavior modification, positive recognition can take many forms and should be appropriate for the age and the subject being taught. It may include giving frequent praise, sending positive notes home to parents, or motivating students with special privileges.

3. **Consequences.** When disruptive behavior occurs, the teacher must be prepared to deal with it calmly and quickly. Consequences should be organized in a hierarchy from the first time a student breaks a rule until the fifth time. A warning is the most common first consequence. Contacting parents and making administrative referrals should appear near the end of the hierarchy. The hierarchy should include a "severe clause" for severe misbehavior such as a fight or bullying.

Assertive discipline underscores the belief that teachers can mold a student's ability to control his or her behavior through a program of positive recognition and consequences.

reflect
• Using the guidelines presented in this section, create four classroom rules, along with positive recognition strategies and a hierarchy of consequences, appropriate to an eighth-grade classroom.

Behavior Modification   **Behavior modification** refers to the process of changing behavior by rewarding desired actions and ignoring or punishing undesired actions. It is a set of strategies you can use in establishing effective classroom management. The classroom teacher can select components of the behavioral approach while retaining a humanistic approach to learning and students. The basic steps in the technique are discussed below (adapted from Salvia and Ysseldyke 2004).

Phase 1: Charting Baseline Behaviors   During the baseline period, the teacher observes and records instances of the target behavior (the behavior to be changed). This phase provides evidence of whether the problem actually exists. Systematic observation may reveal that a student who has been labeled "disruptive" does not exhibit disruptive behavior more often than his peers. All data are recorded and tallied so that an established rate of occurrence may be determined. (See Figure 6.4, which illustrates one example of charting.)

Chart behaviors to create a baseline for comparison.

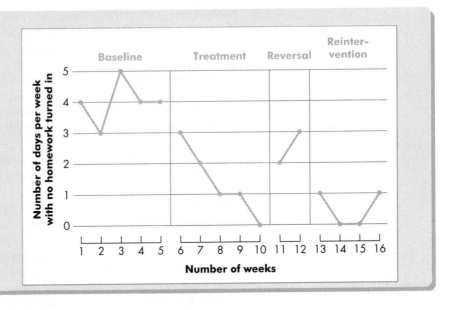

FIGURE 6.4

Charting an Effective Behavior Modification Strategy for "Turning in Homework"

INSTRUCTIONAL
STRATEGIES

Recording Classroom Behaviors: Make It Simple

Systematic Observation—Please incorporate the simple steps suggested below when charting in your classroom.

- Create a seating chart with students identified.
- Create a short-hand code for behaviors you wish to record:
  "O" Off-Task
  "P" Classroom Participation
  "I" Inappropriate Behavior
- Record the behaviors across at least three instructional periods.
- Analyze resulting data for trends. (For example: Is there a relationship between "off-task" and "classroom participation"? Could you change this outcome by redirecting questions to nonparticipating students?)

Phase 2: Intervention or Experimentation   The chart serves as a baseline in choosing an appropriate strategy and determining its effectiveness. For example, if the behavior occurs only two or three times during silent reading, you may select ways to increase the student's ability to read silently. Structure the day so that, during these periods, you are positioned near the student to administer verbal praise when the appropriate behavior (silent reading) occurs. If, after a few days of your increased attention, there is a decrease in the number of times the student talks to neighbors during a silent reading period, you can assume that the strategy is having a positive effect. In most cases, you will try to reinforce an appropriate behavior while ignoring or not responding to inappropriate ones.

Sometimes verbal reinforcers are adequate to modify the student's behavior. You may need to experiment to determine the set of reinforcers that changes the student's behavior with the least effort. In some cases, you need visible or material reinforcers such as stars on the student's papers, the student's name on the class "honor list," tokens, pencils, or special privileges. Whatever the reward, it is absolutely imperative that it follow the appropriate behavior immediately.

Reinforcement is defined as consequences that increase the future rate of a behavior. The use of **reinforcers**, or rewards that encourage students to repeat positive behaviors, is a critical component of behavior modification (see the box below). If you use the same set of reinforcers over an extended time, you may find that they lose their impact. After studying this problem, Roger Addison and Donald T. Tosti (1979) compiled a system and a list of reinforcers that can be applied with various motivational strategies in an education environment.

Sample Reinforcers for Classroom Situations

- Recognition
- Tangible rewards
- Classroom learning activities
- Classroom and school responsibilities
- Status indicators
- Incentive feedback
- Personal activities
- Social activities
- Relief from restrictive policies or procedures (for example, freedom to move around the classroom)
- Relief from restrictive classroom environments (for example, work independently or in small groups)

Reinforcers are very personal; a teacher may have to try various reinforcers with a specific student before finding the most powerful one (Addison and Tosti 1979). Obviously, there is no one universal reinforcer. Several of the above activities have been classified as being aspects of *student recognition programs* (see McElroy 2000). Such programs emphasize student success. Recognition helps create a positive climate and makes schooling intentionally inviting.

Select reinforcers to fit the student.

Phase 3: Reversal to Baseline Conditions   For most teachers, no further class manipulation is necessary once the appropriate reward or reinforcer is determined. However, to follow the behavior modification paradigm completely, you should return from the phase 2 conditions to those classroom conditions that were present during the original baseline period. Teachers often resist this requirement because it means returning to the original conditions that seemingly prompted the undesired behavior.

As in phases 1 and 2, in phase 3 data are consistently tabulated so that the behavioral patterns are quickly discernible. Phase 3 usually is conducted only long enough to effect a reversal of behavior to the baseline type. When you have again observed such behavior, go on to phase 4.

Phase 4: Reinstating the Intervention Conditions   The final stage reinstates the conditions used during phase 2. If the intervention caused a change in behaviors during the second phase, it should do so again at this time. But, if there is no change toward the desired behaviors, then you were just lucky in phase 2, and you will have to start all over again. Now you can understand why teachers dislike phase 3.

General Principles for Use of Classroom Management Strategies

1. **Accentuate the positive.** Schools have been criticized for being too "unpleasant" and teachers for being far too negative toward students. To change this image, the teacher must praise students, even if it is for the most inconsequential matter. Admittedly, it may be difficult to praise a student who continually disrupts the class, but it has been frequently demonstrated that simply admonishing a student will not reduce the inappropriate behavior. Praising some positive aspect of the student's behavior is more likely to bring about change (see Ellett 1993).

   How does the teacher use different forms of praise or social reinforcement? There are verbal, nonverbal, and tactile reinforcers. Several examples of positive verbal and nonverbal praise are listed in the box on page 201. We comment on tactile reinforcers in the next section.

2. **Identify productive behavior for the class.** Praise provides reinforcement not only for the student to whom it is directed but also for the entire class. Praise provides students with an explicit model of what you expect of them. To be sure, public praise can be embarrassing as well as reinforcing; therefore, you must learn what technique works best for each student—and hence for the whole class.

3. **Start small.** In most cases, students view major changes in behavior as unachievable. If a student hands in about 25 percent of the required homework assignments, there is little chance that reinforcement will result in 100 percent completion right away. However, you can still establish a definite contingency schedule by making a behavioral contract with the student. The student may complete two of five assignments in the first week. If so, move up the requirement to three of five assignments for the next week. Remember that the student probably did not reach the present level of academic deficiency in one step. Therefore, do not expect to remedy the problem in one great leap. Take small initial steps by increasing the quantity or the quality until the student reaches the agreed-upon criterion. This requires you to be patient and to give constant positive feedback to the student.

4. **Be consistent.** As you begin to use behavior modification in the classroom, whether on an individual or a group basis, keep your own behavior consistent and predictable. If you remain consistent in your responses to student stimuli, then you can better predict the reactions of class members. For example, ask that every student always raise his or her hand and wait to be called on to answer a question, and always wait until students do so before calling on them.

Finding something to praise is not always easy.

instructional strategies

Examples of Verbal and Nonverbal Praise

Verbal Praise

• All right	• Great	• Really great	• Very interesting
• Fantastic	• Nice work	• Dynamite	• Wonderful
• Mighty fine	• Terrific	• Keep it up	• Fabulous
• Splendid	• Clever	• Quite nice	• Marvelous
• Awesome	• Ideal	• A winner	• Yes
• Neat	• Unreal	• Excellent	• Wow
• Super	• Good job	• Lovely	• Beautiful

Nonverbal Praise

- Laughing
- Pointing with a smile
- Smiling
- Looking with interest
- Raising the eyebrows
- High-five
- Thumbs-up signal
- Moving toward student
- Signaling by lifting the palms
- Winking
- Nodding approval

key ideas

Basic Steps in Behavior Modification

1. Chart baseline behavior.
2. Use an intervention in which contingencies are changed or manipulated.
3. To test the intervention, revert to the baseline conditions by reinstating original contingencies.
4. Return to the intervention condition.

reflect

- Select the classroom management strategy with which you are most comfortable and provide a brief explanation for its selection and how you would implement it in your classroom.

section 4: society and classroom management

The classroom is a social and emotional environment as well as a learning environment. As teachers, we need to be certain that all students play a role in learning and other activities. If boys are always asked to lead or to set up schoolroom apparatus, or if girls are always asked to take notes and arrange things, then both boys and girls are being unfairly typecast. The manner in which a teacher engages every student has potential learning and achievement overtones. This means you must consciously address many of your personal mores and habits and avoid reinforcing social barriers and stereotypes. Helping every student feel the thrill of success and the value of "belonging" is what effective teaching is all about. And that goes for all students.

In this section, we approach the influences of society on the social and emotional environment of the classroom through three main topics: engendering cooperation and equity, realizing the importance of parental involvement, and dealing with abusive attitudes and behaviors.

If you look across the characteristics listed in Table 6.6, you will notice several that support the three topics we now approach in depth. They are useful in discussing academic and behavioral expectations with parents and as a yardstick for measuring your classroom management success.

Engendering Cooperation and Equity

When you establish classroom management strategies, remember that students are, for the most part, reasonable human beings who are anxious to make their classrooms cooperative and pleasant places in which to be (Johnson and Johnson 1989). By enlisting student aid in the formulation of classroom activities and regulations, you help prevent classroom management problems in three ways: (1) you are setting the stage for classroom equity

Teachers send a powerful message about which students belong.

TaBLe 6.6

Traits That Engender Cooperation, Equity, and Involvement While Reducing Abusive Attitudes and Behaviors

Academic Characteristics

- Clear instructional focus
- High academic time on task
- Frequent monitoring of student progress
- High expectations from the school
- Appropriate award structures
- Active teaching
- Few student absences

School Climate Indicators

- Orderly and safe environment
- Minimal instructional interruptions
- Few discipline problems
- Little time spent on classroom management
- Friendly ambience
- No graffiti
- Frequent contact with parents

SOURCE: Bickel 1999, pp. 959–983; Teddlie and Stringfield 1993.

Get student investment in setting up rules.

through a process of respect and understanding; (2) students tend to have a greater interest in the maintenance of these regulations when they have had a part in generating them; and (3) they have a greater understanding of the need for and the meaning of regulations when they help to develop them.

Gender and Race Issues   Teachers are often unaware that they project a bias toward or against some students because of sex, race, ethnic background, or perceived intelligence. Such bias has resulted in dramatically diminished numbers of girls and minorities in science and mathematics classes (see Graham 2001; Wood 2000). Additionally, low expectations and a lack of role models are considered main contributors to high dropout rates among boys and minorities.

Several studies have shown that teachers interact with boys more than girls in secondary science classes. Findings discovered that girl-initiated science interactions *declined* during the middle school years, teacher expectations favored boys, and racial minorities tended to be rejected more by teachers (Good and Brophy 2003). These situations are all *disinviting* to female and minority learners. Interestingly enough, both male and female teachers were found to be equally disinviting.

How can we recognize our own "disinviting behaviors" and avoid them in our classrooms? First, you or someone else can chart your interactions with students. Tabulate positive and negative feedback, nonverbal cues, use of male pronouns, and male bias. If bias is apparent, use a list of student names to conduct recitations on a regular schedule. Change your verbal and written communication patterns to use inclusionary language. (In case you need a model, this textbook is written with inclusionary, gender-neutral language.) Provide an equitable number of leadership positions to males, females, minority students, and students with disabilities. In short, become proactive by making the classroom environment equitable to all.

Ask a visitor to chart your interactions for fairness.

To enhance equity and promote achievement, Sam Kerman (1979) perfected a series of fifteen strategies that are collectively labeled TESA, "Teacher Expectations and Student Achievement" (see the box below and Phi Delta Kappa 1993). As you examine these fifteen elements, you will see that, in this chapter, we have stressed all but touch. Very young pupils do touch their teachers and vice versa; but we suggest that, beginning at middle school, you should be very cautious with teacher–student contact, especially with members of the opposite sex. The best intentions may be misinterpreted and might lead to charges of sexual harassment or physical abuse. Chapter 2 provides additional insights into issues affecting gender and racial equity. The most critical point is to be fair, impartial, and intentionally inviting to every student.

The TESA Program

Teachers that value equity incorporate these strategies in their classrooms.

Response Opportunities
1. Equitable distribution of participation
2. Individual help
3. Latency or wait time

Continued

The TESA Program—Cont'd

4. Delving
5. Higher-level questions

Feedback
1. Affirmation of correct responses
2. Praise
3. Reasons for praise
4. Listening
5. Accepting feelings

Personal Regard
1. Proximity of teacher to student
2. Courtesy
3. Personal interest and compliments
4. Touching (as a positive gesture)
5. Desist strategies

Educational Equity and Student Tracking   Most teachers enjoy working with academically gifted students. And why not? In most cases, academically gifted students virtually teach themselves. However, if schools were to use some measure of academic ability to group students of similar ability together, would this be a potential disadvantage to any students? Using any measure or set of measures (tests, grades, and teacher recommendations) to homogeneously group students is labeled "student tracking."

A great deal has been written in support of and against student tracking, but the greatest concern deals with teacher expectations of students placed in "lower" tracks. Once a student has been labeled as a low performer in any given subject or grade, that label has a tendency to follow that student throughout his or her academic career.

The most compelling evidence against tracking comes from a 1988 study by Adam Gamoran and Mark Berends. They concluded that tracking favors students in the high track, accounts for disparities in student achievement, produces a cycle of low expectations for low-track students, and creates poor morale among teachers and students.

Evidence supporting academic tracking at both the elementary and secondary levels, especially over long periods of time, has been inconclusive. Teachers have reported, however, that they *dislike* teaching low-ability classes, spend less time preparing for them, and schedule less-interesting or less-challenging activities for them (Good and Brophy 2003). Students in low-track classes are merely kept busy with mundane, irrelevant work. Not surprisingly, students in high-track classes have better attitudes toward school and better work habits, and they assume positions of greater leadership.

We recognize that specific classes will automatically draw motivated students (advanced placement calculus, foreign languages, music theory, and art history are several). Of course, some teachers in these classes may unwittingly discourage girls, students with disabilities, students from lower-income fam-

Low tracking may set student on a low-achievement course.

ilies, or minority students. Such incidents as these are commonly reported by university undergraduate students. In such cases, gender bias is closely related to tracking and, in our opinion, is extremely unprofessional educational behavior.

Robert E. Slavin (1991) provides the best interpretation of the evidence *against* tracking. His findings are summarized in the box below. This analysis will not receive rave reviews in most public schools—it runs counter to the myths that educators and school board members perpetrate about tracking. A 1992 report from the National Assessment of Educational Progress noted that, although approximately 25 percent of tested eighth-grade students were grouped by ability, their average proficiency score was not higher in any educationally significant manner than scores of students not grouped by ability. Significant differences did appear when the top 16 percent of eighth-graders were compared to the lowest 11 percent.

In middle and elementary schools, tracking has no professional defense (see Becker 1988). Review Chapter 8 for several tested strategies that will have a far more effective impact on student achievement, attitude, and quality of work in these grades. These include cross-age peer tutoring, cooperative learning, feedback, reinforcement, and mastery learning. To be sure, there are gifted-and-talented programs in most schools. Several use the "pull-out" model; that is, they pull these students out of regular classes for enrichment experiences. That such a model disrupts the regular class is often ignored. The real challenge is how to provide all children with that elusive "best of educations."

> No basis for tracking before high school

Realizing the Importance of Parental Involvement

Do you want to provide a pleasing, enriching, successful classroom experience? The path to such a learning experience is well known: Get parents involved. Active parents follow the development of their children, reinforce the expectations of the schools, and monitor student behavior and participation. Getting the parents into the schools is so important that it is the eighth goal in the Goals 2000 Educate America Act of 1994: "Every school will promote parental involvement and participation to promote social, emotional, and academic growth of children."

Slavin's Findings Against Tracking

- The top 3 to 5 percent of students benefit from acceleration but not enrichment.
- Enrichment programs may benefit very slightly from homogeneous placement, but such enrichments are beneficial to all students, not just the top 5 percent or top one-third of them.
- Low-track students tend to drop out of school more frequently than lower-achieving students in heterogeneous classes.
- Ethnic minority students tend to make up a disproportionate number of low-track classes.

Parents or other significant adults provide positive influences on student behavior. © Elizabeth Crews

It is rare for the parents of problem students to closely follow their children's educational achievement. There are few models parents can follow in deciding just what role they should play in their children's educational career. This lack of direction, coupled with the demands of two-career and single-parent homes, fosters poor parent participation.

Working Parents   Two working parents now represent the norm. This leaves little time and even less energy for oversight of children's schooling. Today's parents tend not to ask for school reports, monitor class assignments, or attend school activities. If you are a primary teacher, you have a good chance of encouraging parents to build an active school attendance record along with their children. However, you must call, call, call! Don't wait for participation; go out and get it. Such extra work will pay off in fewer classroom disruptions and better achievement.

Be proactive in contacting working parents.

Secondary teachers face too many years of parental inactivity to hope for much parental participation. Yet the teacher still has an obligation to keep parents informed. There are those committed parents who actively pursue a good education along with their children. These folks will demand your attention, and you will be glad to give it. Rejoice in this rarity.

What do parents wish to know? In a national survey (Horace Mann 2001) conducted among teachers in K–12 grades, there were five questions most frequently asked. See the box on page 207.

Questions Most Frequently Asked by Parents

- How do my children behave in school?
- How do my children interact with their peers?
- How important is reading in my child's life?
- Can you give me more information about homework assignments?
- How hard do my children work at school?

The Single Parent   In urban areas, the single parent is the norm. The *2005 Kids Count* report by the Annie E. Casey Foundation noted that in 2003 the percent of children in single-parent households ranged nationally from 22 to 62 percent by race, with the national average being 30 percent (*Kids Count,* Table 1, Race and Child Well Being, *p. 1; and* NCES, No. 2005-312). These parents work double-time to keep up with all the demands of their job, parenting, and personal life. Don't jump to the conclusion that the single parent is always female or young. Many parents share the custody of their children, so you may find a different parent present at consecutive school activities. Confusion for you and the student may be a frequent result. To make sure everyone in the family is well informed, be prepared when you meet with each parent to give him or her sufficient background on what you've already discussed with the other parent in earlier meetings.

Extended Families   Many children are being raised today by members of their extended family. This might be a grandmother, uncle, sister, or cousin. Don't ask questions; just build a relationship with any "parental" figure who demonstrates an interest in your student. *Concern* is the operative word here. If they are involved and concerned, then they are the parent and should be treated the same way you treat other parents.

Meeting Effectively with Parents   Most schools have some type of parent orientation night. This is a good time to meet as many parents as show up. In Chapter 10, we discuss a technique of having the student provide the parents with his or her work. If some problem seems to be chronic, initiate a parent conference. Of course, a working single parent will not be meeting during school hours, so some accommodations need to made—telephone, letter, e-mail.

INSTRUCTIONAL
STRATEGIES

Conducting a Teacher-Parent Conference

Here are some tips for preparing for your conference and making sure it runs smoothly.

- First, review school and district policies on parent conferences. Seek input from master teachers and school counselors on approaches to behavioral and academic issues that are relevant.

Continued

Conducting a Teacher-Parent Conference—Cont'd

- Provide adequate notification to the parent (or parents) of the time, location, and purpose of the conference. If possible, provide written examples of the academic problems you wish to discuss.
- Follow this conference process: (a) issues, (b) goals, (c) possible approaches, (d) parental input, and (e) agreement. Explain the five-step process before you begin.
- Encourage questions. Emphasize that you are both working toward a common purpose, the student's welfare.
- Before moving ahead with any plan or procedure, ensure that the parent understands the issues. Achieve agreement through consensus. Do not take any additional step until mutual commitment to a desired outcome is clear.
- Document the conference's outcomes and next steps and allow the parent to review the document and sign off on it. Discuss this last step with school administrators if you are concerned about possible repercussions such as a lawsuit or complaint.

VIDEO CASE

Peer pressure is often cited as a cause of drug and alcohol use in students. Watch the video "Social and Emotional Development: The Influence of Peer Groups" and the bonus segment "A Real Story About Bullying." How does teacher Voncille Ross help her students process these everyday pressures?

Most schools have specific, directive policies for reporting child abuse.

Dealing with Abusive Attitudes and Behaviors

Child Abuse All schools have policies relating to the role of the police in the schools and court referral systems. Teachers are not usually involved with these agencies, but you need to know about them, especially when child abuse is suspected. You are never wrong to request approval from the principal before permitting a police action or directive from occurring in your classroom. Your principal is trained in such law enforcement agency interaction and has prescribed procedures to follow. Obviously, concerns about a life-threatening situation overrule any prior-notice issues.

Every school has a strict written policy outlining the steps to be taken if child abuse is suspected by a teacher or reported to school personnel. These policies have been developed in conjunction with the courts to protect our most vulnerable citizens. A teacher has little recourse but to follow such policies exactly. Most school districts will provide an orientation to all new teachers regarding the policy and procedure for handling such cases and will expect all personnel to follow the guidelines rigorously. States such as Washington have laws requiring all school personnel to report suspected child abuse. Discuss this point with your principal on the first day of school!

Alcohol and Drug Abuse In today's schools, you almost certainly will come in contact with drug and alcohol abuse among your students (see Table 6.7). According to the Federal Substance Abuse and Mental Health Services Administration, any school of 1,500 can expect to have 195 students (13 percent of the student population) with serious emotional and/or drug problems, which block success and increase feelings of hopelessness. Without help, as many as 56 percent drop out and become adults with problems such as underemployment or unemployment.

As a teacher, you are responsible for encouraging students to understand and value our system of government and laws. Your role demands that you exhibit high ethical standards because the community has given you charge of its youth. Furthermore, professional ethics preclude your support of student use of alcohol or illegal drugs. On a personal level, we must do a better job of listening to and making time for our students. Plan regularly for after-school conference time to talk with your students. Encourage those you feel are at risk to drop by for a chat. Encourage at-risk students to become involved in after-school activities. Too frequently, children are raising themselves and are alone after school when the riskiest behaviors, including drug and alcohol use, sexual activity, and criminal activities, surface. The box below lists several early warning signs of alcohol and drug abuse.

Your leadership models the value of laws.

Early Warning Signs of Alcohol or Drug Abuse

- *Sudden behavioral changes.* Homework is lost, is not turned in, is copied, or declines in quality.
- *Attitude changes.* Comments are made to hurt others' feelings, or an "I-don't-care" demeanor emerges.
- *School problems.* Grades decline, difficulties with other teachers and school personnel appear, fights and arguments occur.
- *Changes in social relationships.* Student abandons old friends, becomes involved in a different social scene.
- *Self-destructive behavior.* Student develops injuries from "falls" or "fights" that he or she has difficulty recounting.
- *Avoidance.* Student withdraws or refuses to communicate, spends an inappropriate amount of time in isolation.

TABLE 6.7

Drug Use Among High School Seniors
Substance abuse in our schools is a major deterrent to learning.

Type of Drug	1980	1992	2002
Alcohol	87.9	76.8	71.5
Marijuana/hashish	48.8	21.9	36.2
Any illicit drug other than marijuana	30.4	14.9	20.9
Heroin	0.5	0.6	1.0
LSD	6.5	5.6	3.5
Cocaine	12.3	3.1	5.0
PCP	4.4	1.4	1.1

Figures are percentage of high school seniors who reported using drugs or alcohol any time during the previous year.

SOURCE: U.S. Department of Education, *Digest of Education Statistics 2003* (NCES 2005-025), Table 150.

All teachers must be cautious in handling students suspected of drug or alcohol abuse. An accusation may lead to a lawsuit by the student or his or her parents. Our advice is to check with school administrators on the accepted protocol for dealing with such problems (Zabel and Zabel 1996). The alcohol and drug problem is not simply critical—it is pandemic!

Bullying and Harassment   Bullying contributes to a climate of fear and intimidation in schools. In 2003, students ages twelve through eighteen were asked if they had been bullied (that is, picked on or made to do things they did not want to do) at school. About 7 percent of the students reported they had been bullied, with females as likely as males to report being bullied. Students in grade 6 tended to express bullying more than students in other grades. About 13 percent of students in grades 6 and 7 reported being bullied, compared with about 3 percent in grades 10 through 12 (*Indicators of School Crime and Safety* 2004). "Bullying is one of the most serious and yet underrated problems in school today," said Ronald Stephens, executive director of the National School Safety Center, a California nonprofit group that researches school crime and violence (Wicker 1999).

Educators are redefining violence to include all the time-honored tools of the schoolyard bully—ridicule and jokes, mean tricks, and exclusion. Bullying is a power issue. Although much of the bad behavior is limited to bathrooms, hallways, and the playground, it is also prevalent in the classroom. Many kids try bullying strategies at some time, but some use them regularly. Whereas boys typically use physical tactics, girls often bully with insults and by ostracizing and gossiping about others. In her book *Odd Girl Out,* Rachel Simmons (2002) discusses this covert aggression shown by girls against other girls. In addition, Emily White (2002) writes how labels and rumors about other girls' alleged sex lives create social ostracism and isolation. Elementary school bullies generally pick targets of their own gender, but as early as the fifth grade, bullies begin to target the opposite sex. Young bullies, left unchecked, are likely to move on to sexual harassment or physical violence when they get older. Children who seem friendless are such magnets for bullying that even one friend can make a difference. As a teacher, you need to be aware of even the subtlest social manifestations of bullying (see Garbarino and deLara 2003).

Teacher intervention must be consistent, thoughtful, and skilled (see below). Teachers should establish classroom rules regarding bullying and harassing behavior and enforce them. Inappropriate behavior should draw consequences designed to be as calm as possible. Remember, the bully wants attention! In some cases bullying behavior stems from being "bullied." No matter the cause of the behavior, seek assistance from your school's administrators, coun-

Difference in bullying styles of girls and boys

INSTRUCTIONAL STRATEGIES

Strategies for Overcoming Bullying

- Tell students that standing up to meanness takes more courage than fighting.
- Put up banners with antibullying slogans.

INSTRUCTIONAL STRATEGIES

Strategies for Overcoming Bullying—Cont'd

- Urge bystanders to speak up in defense of the victim, tell a teacher, and be sure not to encourage bullying behavior.
- Intervene when bullying or teasing behavior is observed.
- Clean up all graffiti as soon as it is discovered.
- Have zero tolerance for unwanted touching, verbal comments, name-calling, sexual rumors, and rude gestures, jokes, or cartoons.
- Assign older students to be "book-buddies" with new kids and with those students who demonstrate tendencies to be isolated during student activities.
- Organize breakfast clubs for new students to help them build friendships and support networks.

selors, psychologist and other teachers. Don't argue with the bully; instead, state the consequences for the action and walk away. Avoid eye contact. When bullying becomes boring, the bully will change. Would you call this behavior modification?

The effectiveness of any classroom management strategy depends on how much time, energy, and confidence you invest in it. A possible pitfall is moving quickly from one technique to another without expending the necessary time and energy to make any strategy succeed. Such efforts are likely to be counterproductive, thus confusing the student and making management problems more severe. The final selection and implementation of any one strategy or combination of strategies rest solely with you. But the ultimate criterion is student success. And, again, to aid you in determining how effective various management techniques may be, please go to our website at **http://education.college.hmco.com/students**.

Only you can transform the classroom into an interesting and positive learning environment. Structure that environment so that everyone is highly motivated to learn. It is the very least that you can do; perhaps the very most!

REFLECT

- What do you think will be the easiest and most enjoyable aspect of meeting with parents? What will be the most difficult?

- If you observed a case of bullying *off* the school campus, how responsible would you be for taking action? How might your action affect the students' attitudes toward school?

- If you suspected the use of an illegal substance by a student during school hours and harm is resulting, what teacher actions would be appropriate?

TECHNOLOGY INSIGHT

Managing Limited Computer Resources

Although virtually every public school in the United States has computing technology and Internet access available to its teachers and students, this most often means either a shared computer lab area or one or a few computers in each classroom. Many teachers find it difficult to manage these limited resources. One method of making sure that everyone has an equal opportunity to use the computing tools is to create a schedule or calendar (this can be a schedule that either informs students when they will have computing time or allows them to sign up for time).

Another strategy to reduce demands on limited computing tools is to require students to plan their use of the computer in advance, using paper and pencil to create "mockups" of their designs (if they are using the computer to create a presentation) or outlines of their research (if they are using the Internet to find information). Having students plan for their computer use in advance will greatly reduce the amount of time they will need to work with the computer itself.

SOURCE: T. D. Green and A. Brown, *Multimedia in the Classroom: A Guide to Development and Evaluation* (Thousand Oaks, CA: Corwin, 2002).

---

reflect

A Closing Reflection

- How can you judge the effectiveness of a classroom management strategy if you have yet to teach a class?

- What criteria can you use to help judge the effectiveness of your first days in front of a class?

summary

1. A positive classroom environment is based on adherence to norms and your awareness of and insight into the classroom environment.

2. A positive environment stresses equity as a major principle.

3. The seven core concepts of classroom routines are planning, establishing rules, getting a good start, providing clear direction, monitoring the environment, keeping essential records, and creating strategies for managing interruptions.

4. Self-discipline systems, which include the hierarchy of needs, moral reasoning, and teacher effectiveness training, stress personal responsibilities.

5. Imposed-discipline systems, such as desist strategies, assertive discipline, and behavior modification, stress teacher authority.

6. Behavioral systems require pinpointing specific behaviors and using reinforcers.

7. To apply behavior modification strategies in the classroom, it is necessary to identify positive behavior and use rewards consistently.

8. Homogeneous grouping may not be instructionally effective.

9. Parental involvement aids in achieving school expectations, so teachers should build positive relationships with parents.

10. Teachers must learn to recognize the signs of child abuse, drug and alcohol abuse, and bullying so that they can work with the proper authorities.

Print Resources

Algozzine, B., and P. Kay, editors. *Preventing Problem Behaviors: A Handbook of Successful Prevention Strategies.* Thousand Oaks, CA: Corwin, 2002, 247 pp.

This compilation of papers is under the auspices of the Council for Exceptional Children and covers a wide array of problems and solutions.

Brainard, E. "Classroom Management: Seventy-Three Suggestions for Secondary School Teachers." *Clearing House* 74(4) (2001): 207–210.

If you are looking for just one quick reference, this is it. The author provides extensive checklists on (1) relating to students positively, (2) preventing misbehavior, (3) handling discipline, and (4) providing classroom leadership.

Charles, C. M. *Building Classroom Discipline* (7th edition). Boston: Allyn and Bacon, 2002, 302 pp.

The author analyzes seventeen different models of school discipline. Case studies and historical precedents are included.

Daniels, V. I. "How to Manage Disruptive Behavior in Inclusive Classrooms." *Teaching Exceptional Children* 30(4) (1998): 26–31.

This short article provides very helpful tools for teachers with mainstreamed or inclusive students.

Rigby, K. *Stop the Bullying: A Handbook for Teachers.* Portland, ME: Stenhouse, 2001, 64 pp.

In just sixty-four pages, the author provides a practical and research-based guide for action.

The Journal of Moral Education

For detailed discussions about moral and character education, refer to current issues of this journal.

INTERNET RESOURCES

Go to the website for this book to find live links to resources related to this chapter.

> The Boston University Center for the Advancement of Ethics and Character website is rich with information relating to moral and character education.
> **http://www.bu.edu/education/caec**

> The Josephson Institute of Ethics organized "Character Counts," a coalition of schools, communities, and organizations to advance character education.
> **http://www.charactercounts.org**

> The following sites provide a rich dialogue about assertive discipline strategies, resources, and programs.
> **http://www.honorlevel.com/**
> **http://www.humboldt.edu/~tha1/canter.html**
> **http://www.adprima.com/assertive.htm**
> **http://maxweber.hunter.cuny.edu /pub/eres/EDSPC715_ MCINTYRE/AssertiveDiscipline.html**

> Alfie Kohn examines the negative aspects of assertive discipline and similar approaches in *Education Week*. A copy of the article is on-line at:
> **http://www.alfiekohn. org/teaching/edweek/discipline.htm**

REFERENCES

Addison, R., and D. T. Tosti. "Taxonomy of Educational Reinforcement." *Educational Technology* 19 (1979): 24–25.

Anderson, S. C. *Learning for All: Giving Effective Directions and the Peg System of Memorization. ERIC Digest.* Eugene, OR: ERIC Clearinghouse on Educational Management, 2002. ED 478 384.

Becker, H. J. *Addressing the Needs of Different Groups of Early Adolescents.* Baltimore: Johns Hopkins University Center for Research on Elementary and Middle Schools, 1988.

Bickel, W. E. "The Implications of the Effective Schools Literature for School Restructuring." In *The Handbook of School Psychology* (3rd edition). C. R. Reynolds and T. B. Gutkin, editors. New York: Wiley, 1999, pp. 959–983.

Boston University Center for the Advancement of Ethics and Character: Character Education Manifesto. Boston, April 13, 1997.

Boston University Center for the Advancement of Ethics and Character. Release, March 20, 2005. Retrieved at: *http://www.bu.edu/education/cace/*, page 1.

Canter, L., and M. Canter. *Lee Canter's Assertive Discipline: Positive Behavior Management for Today's Classroom.* Santa Monica: Lee Canter & Associates, 1992.

Cotton, K. "Schoolwide and Classroom Discipline." School Improvement Research Series (SIRS). Northwest Regional Educational Laboratory, 2001. Retrieved at http://www. nwrel.org/sepd/sirs/5/cu9.html

Ellett, L. "Instructional Practices in Mainstreamed Secondary Classrooms." *Journal of Learning Disabilities* 26(1) (1993): 57–64.

Etzioni, A. *The New Golden Rule: Morality and Community in a Democratic Society.* New York: Basic, 1997.

Evertson, C. M. "Classroom Rules and Routines." In *International Encyclopedia of Teaching and Teacher Education* (2nd edition). L. W. Anderson, editor. Tarrytown, NY: Elsevier Science, 1995, pp. 215–219.

Evertson, C. M., E. T. Emmer, and M. E. Worsham. *Classroom Management for Elementary Teachers* (5th edition). Boston: Allyn and Bacon, 2000.

Fields, J. U.S. Census Bureau. *America's Families and Living Arrangements: 2003 Current Population Reports, Population Characteristics*. Washington, DC: U.S. Government Printing Office, November 2004. P. 20-553.

Gamoran, A., and M. Berends. *The Effects of Stratification in Secondary Schools: Synthesis of Survey and Ethnographic Research*. Madison, WI: University of Wisconsin at Madison National Center for Effective Secondary Schools, 1988.

Garbarino, J., and E. deLara. "Words Can Hurt Forever." *Educational Leadership* 60(6) (2003): 18–21.

Glasser, W. "Reality Therapy: An Anti-Failure Approach." *Impact* 2 (1972): 6–9.

Glasser, W. *Choice Theory in the Classroom* (revised edition). New York: HarperPerennial, 1998.

Good, T. L., and J. E. Brophy. *Looking in Classrooms, MyLabSchool Edition* (9th edition). Boston: Allyn and Bacon, 2003.

Graham, M. "Increasing Participation of Female Students in Physical Science Class." Chicago: St. Xavier University, MA Action Research Project, 2001. ED 455 121.

Greenberger, R. S. "Justice Rules on School Bias and Land Use." *The Wall Street Journal*, May 25, 1999, p. A3.

Gump, P. V. "School Settings and Their Keeping." In *Helping Teachers Manage Classrooms*. D. Duke, editor. Alexandria, VA: Association for Supervision and Curriculum Development, 1982.

Horace Mann Educator Corporation. *Educator Survey, 2000–01*. Springfield, IL: Horace Mann Educator Corporation, 2001.

Indicators of School Crime and Safety, 2004 (NCES 2005-002). Washington, DC: U.S. Department of Education, 2005.

Johnson, D. W., and R. T. Johnson. *Cooperation and Competition: Theory and Research*. Edina, MN: Interaction, 1989.

Josephson Institute of Ethics. *Character Counts!* Marina del Rey, CA: Josephson Institute of Ethics, 2002. http://www.charactercounts.org/

Kaufman, P., X. Chen, S. P. Choy, S. A. Ruddy, A. K. Miller, J. K. Fleury, K. A. Chandler, M. R. Rand, P. Klaus, and M. G. Planty. *Indicators of School Crime and Safety, 2000* (NCES 2001-017/NCJ-184176). Washington, DC: U.S. Departments of Education and Justice, 2000.

Kerman, S. *"Teacher Expectations and Student Achievement."* Phi Delta Kappan 60 (1979).

Kohlberg, L. "The Cognitive-Developmental Approach to Moral Education." *Phi Delta Kappan* 56 (1975): 670–677.

Kounin, J. S. *Discipline and Group Management in Classrooms*. New York: Holt, Rinehart and Winston, 1970.

Kounin, J. S., and P. V. Gump. "The Ripple Effect in Discipline." *Educational Digest* 24 (1959): 43–45.

Leonard, L. J. "Towards Maximizing Instructional Time: The Nature and Extent of Externally-Imposed Classroom Interruptions." *Journal of School Leadership* 9(5) (1999): 454–474.

Leriche, L. "The Sociology of Classroom Discipline." *The High School Journal* 75(2) (1992): 77–89.

Loehrke, J. "Teacher Quality Trumps Quantity When It Comes to Helping Kids." *USA Today*, January 29, 1999, p. 13A.

Lombardi, T. P. *Learning Strategies for Problem Learners* (Fastback No. 345). Bloomington, IN: Phi Delta Kappa Educational Foundation, 1992.

Martella, R. C., and R. J. Nelson. "Managing Classroom Behavior." *Journal of Direct Instruction* 3(2) (2003): 139–165.

Marzano, R. J., J. S. Marzano, and D. Pickering. *Classroom Management That Works: Research-Based Strategies for Every Teacher*. Alexandria: VA: Association for Supervision and Curriculum Development, 2003.

Maslow, A. H. *Motivation and Personality*. New York: Van Nostrand, 1968.

McElroy, C. "Middle School Programs That Work." *Phi Delta Kappan* 82(4) (2000): 277–292.

Myers, R. E. "Taking a Common-Sense Approach to Moral Education." *Clearing House* 74(4) (2001): 219–220.

NCES: National Center for Education Statistics, 2005-312. *Characteristics of the 100 Largest Public Elementary and Secondary School Districts in the United States: 2002-2003*. Washington, DC: U. S. Department of Education, 2005.

Noddings, N. *Educating Moral People: A Caring Alternative to Character Education*. New York: Teachers College Press, 2002.

Phi Delta Kappa. *TE&SA: Teaching Expectations and Student Achievement*. Bloomington, IN: Phi Delta Kappa, 1993.

Power, B. M. "Rules Made to Be Broken: Literacy and Play in a Fourth-Grade Setting." *Journal of Education* 174(1) (1992): 70–86.

Power, F. C., A. Higgins, and L. Kohlberg. *Lawrence Kohlberg's Approach to Moral Education*. New York: Columbia University Press, 1989.

Ryan, K., and K. E. Bohlin. *Building Character in Schools: Practical Ways to Bring Moral Instruction to Life*. San Francisco: Jossey-Bass, 1999.

Salvia, J., and J. E. Ysseldyke. *Assessment: In Special and Inclusive Education* (9th edition). Boston: Houghton Mifflin, 2004.

Scofield, R. T., editor. *School-Age Notes, 2000–2001*. ED 455 000.

Simmons, R. *Odd Girl Out: The Hidden Culture of Aggression in Girls*. New York: Harcourt Brace, 2002.

Simon, K. G. *Moral Questions in the Classroom: How to Get Kids to Think Deeply About Real Life and Their Schoolwork.* New Haven, CT: Yale University Press, 2002.

Sizer, T. R., and N. F. Sizer. "Grappling." *Phi Delta Kappan* 81(3) (1999): 184–190.

Skinner, B. F. *Science and Human Behavior.* New York: Macmillan, 1953.

Skinner, B. F. *About Behaviorism.* New York: Knopf, 1974.

Slavin, R. E. "Are Cooperative Learning and 'Untracking' Harmful to the Gifted?" *Educational Leadership* 48(6) (1991): 68–71.

Soder, R., J. I. Goodlad, and T. J. McMannon, editors. *Developing Democratic* Character *in the Young.* San Francisco: Jossey-Bass, 2002.

Sugai, G. "UO and Public Schools Design Just-In-Time Learning Approaches to Find Solutions to Rising Student Discipline Problems." *Education Matters* 3(1) (1996): 10–11.

Tauber, R. T. *Classroom Management: Sound Theory and Effective Practice* (3rd edition). Westport, CT: Bergin and Garvey, 1999.

Teddlie, C., and S. Stringfield. *Schools Make a Difference.* New York: Teachers College Press, 1993.

2005 Kids Count Data Book Online. Baltimore: Annie Casey Foundation, Table 1, "Race and Child Well-Being," p. 1. Retrieved at http://www.aecf.org/kidscount/sld/auxiliary/race_child.jsp

U.S. Department of Education. *Digest of Education Statistics 2003* (NCES 2005-025). Washington, DC: U.S. Government Printing Office, 2005.

Wallen, C. J. "Establishing Teaching Principles in the Area of Classroom Management." In *Low Cost Instruction Simulation Materials for Teacher Education.* Monmouth, OR: Teaching Research, 1968. (U.S. Department of Health, Education and Welfare, Office of Education, Bureau of Research.)

Walsh, F. M. *Planning Behaviors of Distinguished and Award-Winning High School Teachers.* Unpublished doctoral dissertation, Washington State University, Pullman, 1992.

White, E. *Fast Girls: Teenage Tribes and the Myth of the Slut.* New York: Scribner's, 2002.

Wicker, C. "Educators Work to Rid Schools of Bullying Behavior." *The Salt Lake Tribune,* April 4, 1999, p. A14.

Wood, J. "The Girls Have It!" *Instructor* 109(6) (2000): 31–35.

Wood, M. M. "Preventing School Failure: A Teacher's Current Conundrum." *Preventing School Failure* 45(2) (2001): 52–57.

Ysseldyke, J., and J. Elliott. "Effective Instructional Practices: Implications for Assessing Educational Environments." In *The Handbook of School Psychology* (3rd edition). C. R. Reynolds and T. B. Gutkin, editors. New York: Wiley, 1999, pp. 497–518.

Zabel, R. H., and M. K. Zabel. *Classroom Management in Context: Orchestrating Positive Learning Environments.* Boston: Houghton Mifflin, 1996.

The Process of Classroom Questioning

Your mentor has suggested that you observe another teacher, Dee Ennis, because she is a master of the questioning technique. Dee begins her class with a series of questions and, in a businesslike manner, calls on a number of students for responses. She calls on as many as four students to respond to the same question. The students respond eagerly. Their responses are lengthy and thoughtful, and they seem to be carrying on the recitation among themselves with few verbal cues from the teacher.

"Wow," you say to yourself, "I'd like to know how to use this technique. My mentor was right to suggest this classroom for observation."

In this chapter, we set out the skills you will need to become a master questioner. As you read, think about how you would answer the following questions.

- How can I ask a variety of questions during a recitation period?
- How can I use a positive and humane approach to questioning?
- What techniques should I use to conduct effective recitations?

SECTION 1: THE Importance of Questioning

Next to lecturing and small-group work, the single most common teaching method employed in U.S. schools (and, for that matter, around the world) may well be the asking of questions. Questioning plays a critical role in teaching. Teachers must be knowledgeable in the process of *framing questions* so that they can guide student thought processes in the most skillful and meaningful manner. This implies that teachers must design questions that will help students attain the specific goals (that is, objectives or outcomes) of a particular lesson. Although written questions in textbooks and examinations contribute to the learning process, most classroom questions are verbal and teacher formulated. Questions can be critical elements for teachers to use to stimulate student thinking (see Brualdi 1998; Marzano, Pickering, and Pollock 2001).

Research on Questioning

Classroom questions and the process of teacher questioning have been studied for nearly a hundred years. Rather than listing these studies, we summarize the key findings and conclusions in the box on page 219.

Teachers ask a plethora of questions, but on average they do not systematically organize or classify the ways in which they ask classroom questions. In this chapter, we provide empirically tested and validated techniques that are easy to use and, more important, that invigorate classroom recitation. **Recitation** is a learning technique in which the teacher calls on different students to answer factual or knowledge-based questions that limit students to one "correct" response. In keeping with our concept of multimethodology, you will have options as to the models to use when you conduct questioning or recitation sessions.

Research Findings on Questioning

- Questioning tends to be a universal teaching strategy.
- A broad range of questioning options is open to you.
- Being systematic in the use and development of questioning tends to improve student learning.
- By classifying questions according to a particular system, you may determine the cognitive or affective level at which your class is working and make adjustments as needed.
- Through systematic questioning, you may determine students' entry skill and knowledge levels for specific content areas.
- Questions should be developed logically and sequentially.
- Students should be encouraged to ask questions.
- A written plan with key questions provides lesson structure and direction.
- Questions should be adapted to the students' level of ability.
- Questioning techniques that encourage the widest spectrum of student participation should be used.
- Statements rather than questions should also be used to promote student reactions.
- No one questioning strategy is applicable to all teaching situations.

An Overview of Questioning Techniques

Teachers use recitation and question-answer periods for a variety of reasons. One key reason is to determine what students have remembered or achieved as a consequence of some assignment. In this regard, you are conducting a brief *formative evaluation*—to which we devote an entire section in Chapter 10. This evaluation tells you what points everyone knows and, equally important, which students do not know or have misunderstood some element or concept. With this feedback, you can take corrective action immediately. Although formative checks tend to focus on low-level questions with factual answers, they can lead to higher-level questions that use skills in the top four categories in the cognitive taxonomy. George W. Gagnon (2001) illustrates how a teacher can bridge concepts and enhance student understanding with well-chosen questions. *Bridging* means that you or the students connect previously learned material to the new topic or concept being taught. Prompts such as "Think back to yesterday's assignment" and "How might we approach this problem from what we know?" help students to bridge.

Why use questioning?

Merely asking questions does not cause students to think. If you ask a low-level question, then you can expect a low-level response (see Dillon 1982a, 1982b). But your higher-level questions *invite* and encourage higher levels of critical thinking in students. Furthermore, it appears that if teachers systematically raise the level of their questioning, students raise the level of their responses correspondingly (Filippone 1998). This requires a carefully planned questioning strategy that may span several weeks of instruction (van Zee and

Teacher's expectation helps students reach for higher levels.

Minstrell 1997). Asking higher-level questions also requires an adjustment in your attitude toward your students. As a teacher, you hold high expectations for your students. Your attitude should be one of, *Yes, you can!*

Marilyn P. Arnone (2003) suggests that through appropriate questioning, student curiosity is fostered. Curiosity is an *affective* dimension of learning, which means that it deals with the emotions and with motivation. The emotions cannot be discounted in student performance. As we develop this chapter, you will observe how the art of questioning subtly encourages student curiosity, creativity, and reflectivity.

You should also consider an alternative to stimulate student responses, curiosity, and thinking: using *declarative statements* instead of questions. This technique elicits longer and more complex student responses. There is some evidence that students' verbal responses are of higher quality when they respond to statements rather than to questions alone (Dillon 1990). For example, a teacher might say, "It really doesn't matter what tense you use when writing." That statement predictably will evoke a wide range of student responses. Another example might be the statement, "Laboratory-based science instruction helps students to learn." Keep such statements short (about one sentence) and, when appropriate, seek comments from students. Using declarative statements requires some practice. One useful application of this technique is examining the complaints listed in the Declaration of Independence. The statements can become sources for student questioning and subsequent discussion (see "Declare the Causes," 2001). Microteaching—teaching a single concept to a small group of peers—and peer coaching are ideal ways to practice the declarative statement technique (see Glickman 2002; L'Anson, Rodrigues, and Wilson 2003).

"Questions" can be phrased as declarative statements.

Using Students' Questions and Summarizations

Even when using higher-level questions, it is important not to let yourself dominate the scene. Orient your class toward student communication, that is, toward giving students a chance to express their opinions and ideas and to originate questions of their own. Some evidence shows that teachers do most of the talking and questioning. Disturbingly few students ask questions during recitations, "nor are they encouraged to do so" (Swift, Gooding, and Swift 1995, p. 1). What an example of being intentionally disinviting! This is particularly unfortunate because encouraging student questions leads to higher-level questions, stimulates more students to interact, provides positive cognitive effects, and promotes analytic reasoning (see Gall and Artero-Boname 1995; Koegel et al. 1998).

Teachers need to try hard not to dominate classroom verbal interactions and thereby cause class members to become passive and dependent on the teacher. Student passivity hardly fosters ingenuity, creativity, or critical thinking—traits we all consider desirable. Nor is passive student behavior appropriate for a constructivist method of teaching; rather, the classroom should be highly interactive (Gagnon 2001).

Don't dominate verbal interactions.

One way to ensure that you are not too dominant in the discussion or recitation is to end appropriate sections of all lessons with student summaries. According to research, this is one of the nine most effective teaching strategies (Wormeli 2004). This simple technique shifts the burden of

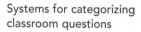

Encourage students to ask questions and to summarize.

reflecting and interpreting directly to the students and provides another form of formative evaluation.

Aiming for Critical and Higher-Level Thinking

If you want to stimulate critical thinking among your students, take a look at the way you use textbooks. Be aware of the advantages and disadvantages of your textbook materials. To involve students more, you may have to supplement the materials provided by the publisher. For example, you might teach lessons with focused questions that require students to compare or contrast items, persuade others, determine cause and effect, or even question the textual presentation. These processes are crucial to developing thinking skills (see Carpenter 2003). You can use questions to diagnose student progress, determine entry-level competence, prescribe additional study, and enrich an area (Gibson 1998).

Systems for categorizing classroom questions

Lelia Christenbury and Patricia P. Kelly (1983) have discussed seven different taxonomies or hierarchies of learning that can be used in formulating questions. One of these seven is Bloom's cognitive taxonomy, and three others are also "sequential hierarchies" with stages similar to his. Thus, for our purposes and for the sake of uniformity, we will simply rely on using Bloom's (1956) cognitive taxonomy as a means for classifying questions and their responses. Refer to Chapter 3 to review the six categories.

Higher-level questions do not *guarantee* higher-level responses; they only open a very important door to critical thinking for your students. Keep in mind the "if-then" strategy: *If you want to encourage a response at a particular level of thinking, then you must frame the question at the appropriate intellectual level.* This strategy also requires concomitant and continuous decision making and evaluation. It can be applied to *all* levels of instruction and with *all* types of students.

Use a questioning hierarchy as a plan for your recitations and discussion. This will allow you to structure facts, concepts, and generalizations within a framework for thinking—the hierarchy becomes a visible blueprint for action (see Buehl 2001). Note that a questioning hierarchy can also be used to plan declarative statements and to structure them in a hierarchical manner to elicit higher-level student responses. You'll find yourself asking fewer questions (see Barnette et al. 1995). Refer to Chapter 4 in which the Kaplan matrix illustrates a series of hierarchical statements. Your questions can be tailored after that model.

KEY IDEAS

Ways to Develop Higher Thinking

- Ask higher-level questions.
- Don't rely too heavily on a textbook.
- Frame questions appropriately.
- Use a questioning hierarchy.
- Encourage student verbal interactions in class.

Questioning is a highly interpersonal and interactive teaching strategy.
© Tom McCarthy/Photo Edit

professional voices from the field

)))

Jack Guske, Washtucna High School, Washtucna, Washington

Tapping Higher-Level Thinking for Community Improvement

As a project in the high school civics class, the students were asked to do a "walkabout" around our community, looking for neglected lots or areas that would benefit from improvement. Each student identified a spot, took digital pictures of it, sketched it, and designed a way of making it look better.

Soil Conservation Service helped us secure the assistance of an agency that specializes in helping small groups or towns in writing grants. They coached us through the entire process, making sure we did it all properly and in the right time line. We secured a small grant of $5,000 from the State Department of Natural Resources, which funded three student projects.

PROFESSIONAL
VOICES
FROM THE
FIELD

))))

*Jack Guske, Washtucna
High School, Washtucna,
Washington*

Tapping Higher-Level Thinking for Community Improvement—Cont'd

To celebrate Arbor Day, the students planted trees under the supervision of an arborist in three sites. One site became a half-acre park that previously had been an empty lot covered with weeds and broken glass. Several trees didn't make it, but were replaced later by the city. This attractive site has become a sense of community pride and will be for decades to come because the students did it all.

We submitted this project to the Arbor Day Foundation and got a commendation. The community was awarded the designation "Tree City USA" by the foundation. All of this was placed in the student portfolios for community service.

SECTION 2: QUESTIONING STRATEGIES

In this part of the chapter, we describe four basic questioning strategies: *convergent, divergent, evaluative* (Verduin 1967), and *reflective* questioning. If you assign a particular importance to the different types of questions you ask, then you will need a method for verifying that you are indeed using the desired questioning patterns. The classification scheme we present here will help you conduct goal-specific recitation periods.

Four distinct questioning strategies

Convergent Strategy

The convergent questioning strategy focuses on a narrow objective. When using a convergent strategy, you encourage student responses to converge, or focus, on a central theme. **Convergent questions** typically elicit short responses from students and focus on the lower levels of thinking—that is, the knowledge or comprehension levels. This does not mean that using a convergent technique is bad per se. In many situations, you will decide that your students need to demonstrate a knowledge of facts and specifics; in such cases, lower-level questioning strategies are appropriate. Remember that the appropriateness of any questioning strategy must be judged solely on the basis of its ability to fulfill your predetermined objectives (see Crespo 2002).

Convergent questions lead to a common set of responses.

So when might convergent questioning be the appropriate choice? If you use an inductive teaching style (proceeding from a set of specific data to a student-derived conclusion), then you will use a large proportion of convergent-type questions. Or you may wish to use short-response questions as rapid-fire warmup exercises (for example, when you are building vocabulary skills). Teachers in foreign language classes may use a convergent, rapid-fire pattern to help develop students' oral, vocabulary, and spelling skills. This technique also allows all students to participate. The same method may be used by a science teacher to build technical vocabulary. Thus a biology teacher may wish to use a convergent technique for the first few minutes of class to maximize participation and to generate constructive verbal motivation among the students.

The convergent technique is an ideal application of "teacher-directed instruction," or *direct instruction,* in which all students in class respond in unison to teacher-asked questions. Everyone gets to participate. A convergent questioning pattern is not an appropriate means of stimulating thought-provoking responses or classroom discussions; rather, it stresses the knowledge level (see Rowe 1996).

The box below includes examples of convergent questions. Note that these questions all meet two criteria: (1) they limit student responses to a narrow spectrum of possible options, and (2) they are more recall-oriented than analytical.

Examples of Convergent Questions

- In what works did Robert Browning use the dramatic monologue as a form for his poems?
- Under what conditions will water boil at less than 100°C?
- What helps bread dough rise?
- What rights are ensured by the First Amendment?
- Why do relatively few people live in the deserts of any country?
- Where and when was Fort Ticonderoga built?
- What's 5 to the third power?

Divergent Strategy

Divergent questions are the opposite of convergent questions. Rather than seeking a single focus, the goal in using a divergent questioning strategy is to evoke a wide range of student responses. Divergent questions also elicit longer student responses. The divergent technique is ideal for building the confidence of children with learning difficulties because divergent questions do not always have right or wrong answers (see Beamon 1997).

Divergent questions lead to an array of responses.

Eliciting Multiple Responses   If you want to elicit multiple responses, then you will want to use a multiple-response questioning technique. After asking a question, call on three or four students and then assume a passive role in the ensuing discussion. Such a technique teaches students to conduct a classroom recitation themselves. It is a rather sophisticated teaching strategy when used properly. The multiple-response technique also sharpens students' listening skills.

Accepting Diverse Responses   If encouraging creative responses to questions and novel solutions to problems is your goal, then the divergent method is also appropriate. Remember, though, that if you elicit diverse responses from students, you have a professional obligation to listen respectfully to them. To reinforce appropriate response behavior, you must demonstrate a high degree of acceptance for the responses of each student (van Zee and Minstrell 1997). This means that you may not use subtle put-down tactics, regardless of how outlandish a student's point of view may seem (or how different from what you expected). Again, this is a great technique for students with some learning difficulties because they get to become stars in the classroom.

Preparing Yourself and the Students   When you begin to use divergent questions, you will find it helpful to write out the questions ahead of time. Then examine them to ensure that they are clearly stated and convey the precise meanings you intend. You probably will find your initial class experience with divergent questions difficult or even disappointing, usually because students are not yet oriented toward giving longer or higher-level responses (see Savage 1998).

It takes a good deal of reshaping of student behavior patterns to elicit high-level student thinking and responses. From grade school through high school, over thousands of classroom hours, students have been conditioned to give short, low-level responses. When you begin to ask divergent questions, you must let your students know that the level of questions is changing and that you want the level of their responses also to change, quite drastically. You will soon find that students' responses will demonstrate higher-level thinking—application, analysis, and synthesis. They may even be prepared to conduct discussions themselves and to give longer and more diverse written responses (see Epstein 2003).

When you inform the students about your change in questioning strategy, you should also inform them that you expect multiple responses, with each student taking cues from other students' responses. For example, you might begin by stating, "Today, we are going to change how we recite. I am going to call on three of you, and after each of you has responded, I'll ask three more of you to react to your classmates' responses. Ready?" This means that, as a general rule, you do not repeat student responses to other class members, except when a student speaks too quickly or softly to be heard or when a statement needs some clarification. The rationale for not repeating responses is that, if students know that the teacher will repeat the previous response, they become conditioned to listening only for the teacher's repetition, and not to their fellow student's original words.

When using the divergent strategy, allow all students to present their responses without your interference. This has a positive effect on the class. Teachers tend to interrupt their students before students have fully explained their positions. When the teacher avoids interrupting, students realize that their responses are important and that they must be responsive to one another. As a result, the class's attending behavior improves. It does little good for a teacher continually to remind students that they are not paying attention; such negative comments make a class only less attentive. By encouraging students to listen to one another, you encourage them to participate in a dynamic fashion. You also encourage peer reinforcement of positive, constructive classroom behavior.

To get the best results, your emphasis must be on systematic development of questions over an extended time, with well-conceived, appropriate learning objectives (see Streifer 2001). Do not expect overnight miracles. It takes weeks,

Many responses to a single question

even months, to incorporate these techniques into the usual repertoire of teaching strategies.

Use of divergent questions requires you to help students locate different sources of information so that they can share a variety of viewpoints in class. The box below lists examples of divergent questions. Note that we have adapted a few of these from the previous list of convergent questions.

Examples of Divergent Questions

- What type of social and cultural development might have taken place if Christopher Columbus had landed on Manhattan Island on October 12, 1492?
- What would happen in a school if it had no personal computers?
- Explain the attitude that the Romantic poets had toward nature.
- What do you think are other effective methods of organic gardening that are not listed in the textbook?
- How does the environment affect human shelter-building?
- Why would you select arc welding over gas welding in creating art objects?
- What kinds of evidence would you seek if you were an opponent of the "Big Bang" theory?
- How would a government organized according to a parliamentary system have reacted to the Iran-Contra incident in the 1980s?
- Why was Fort Ticonderoga built where it was on Lake Champlain?
- Under what conditions are First Amendment rights abridged?

Evaluative Strategy

The third questioning strategy is based on the divergent strategy, but with one added component—evaluation. The basic difference between a divergent question and an **evaluative question** is that the evaluative question has a built-in set of **evaluative criteria**. For example, an evaluative question might ask why something is good or bad, why something is important, or why one theory explains the facts better than another. When you frame an evaluative question, emphasize the specific criteria on which students should base their judgments. As with divergent questions, you should accept all student responses to evaluative questions.

Helps students generate criteria for making judgments.

A major component of the teacher's role in the evaluative strategy is to help students develop a logical basis for establishing evaluative criteria. To illustrate this, we'll give you a classic example. You ask a question, and a student presents a response. You next ask, "Why?" and the student replies, "Because." You should recognize immediately from this response that the student does not understand how to frame a logical, consistent set of evaluative criteria. Again, you must never use sarcasm or any other disparaging approach; instead, reinforce the student in an environment conducive to the development of logical evaluative criteria. For example, you might suggest a number of criteria: "What happens when someone is convicted of a crime? What about situations of national emergency?" Provide a specific set of criteria from which students may develop their own criteria. Some students might be intimidated if you ask "Why?" It has been suggested that instead of asking why, ask *what*. For example, in an art class discussing backgrounds, the teacher might ask, "What type of background did Charles M. Russell usually use?" This would be more appropriate than, "Why did Charlie Russell use this background?" This is a subtle form of shifting the burden of proof from the student to the topic (see Dana et al. 1992). As an introduction to the evaluative technique, you might try a joint writing session in which the teacher and small groups of students collaboratively list criteria. Then, as you pose evaluative questions and students make responses, you and the students can classify the evaluative responses along a continuum ranging from "inappropriate" or "illogical" to "appropriate" or "logically developed." An alternative method would be to have the class develop a set of evaluative rubrics such as those shown in Table 10.1 (see page 355) (Eppink 2002; Jackson and Larkin 2002). Note that we have been using the term *responses*, not *answers*. *Answers* carry the connotation of being final or complete. To be sure, convergent questioning patterns may elicit such answers, but when you ask divergent and evaluative questions, students will not be giving you definitive or absolute answers. They will be providing responses that tend to be relative, tentative, or less than certain (see Martinello 1998).

Most student responses to evaluative questions will demonstrate a broad range of thought when rated on a set of evaluative criteria. You can classify them according to their logical development, internal consistency, and validity. Again, we suggest that you accept all student responses. When apparent logical inconsistencies develop, don't rush to bring them up. Discuss them *after* the student has had an opportunity to participate in classroom discourse.

The box below provides examples of evaluative questions. Some of the questions we previously designated as divergent have been converted now into evaluative questions. Remember that most evaluative questions are also divergent. The one characteristic that separates divergent questions from evaluative ones is that the latter rely on established judgmental criteria.

Usually no definitive, final answer

Evaluative Questions

- Why is the parliamentary system of government more responsive to citizens than our legislative system?
- Why is the world a better (or worse) place because of computers?
- Why will the federal position on welfare reform affect social and moral attitudes and behaviors?
- What reasons could be given to switch to either gasohol or hydrogen as fuel for our automobiles?
- What evidence is there that the federal system of interstate highways harmed our city environments?
- Defend (or criticize) the strip mining of coal in eastern Montana.
- Why is the "Big Bang" theory a more viable one than the "Cold Start" theory?
- What made the location of Fort Ticonderoga critical to early colonial development?

Reflective Strategy

The newest addition to the list is the *reflective* questioning strategy. This strategy draws its historical perspective from the classical Socratic method of questioning (Elder and Richard 1998). Reflective questions stimulate the wide range of student responses, as do divergent questions. Reflective questions also have an evaluative element. The major difference between this and the other three techniques is that the goal of the **reflective question** is to require your students to develop higher-order thinking: to elicit motives, inferences, speculations, impact, and contemplation. Rather than asking a student a "why" or "what," as with the evaluative strategy, you want the student to ponder, to think of implications, to search for unintended consequences (see Moutray, Pollard, and McGinley 2001; York-Barr et al. 2001). The box below includes the types of thought processes that can be stimulated through reflective questions.

Probes for implications

The process initiated by reflective questions can also be called *critical* or *analytical thinking*. A teacher doesn't bring students to this stage of intellectual development without carefully shaping the classroom environment and instructing the students as to what the process entails. Jim Minstrell (van Zee and Minstrell 1997) uses a technique that he calls the "reflective bounce." He bounces questions from the student back to the same student and others so that the student needs to provide an expanded version of a previous response, adding another dimension. In civics, a student might ask, "I wonder why 'Deep Throat' waited so long to be identified?" As teacher, you would "bounce" that question back to the originating student and then to another. The box on page 229 includes a few examples of other reflective questions. Jamie A. McKenzie (2005) has developed a very useful Questioning Toolkit in which he discusses seventeen types of questions. The following five exemplify reflective questions: *hypothetical, irreverent, probing, provocative,* and *unanswerable.*

Using reflective questions requires even more planning than using convergent or divergent ones. We recommend that you write out a cluster of several reflective questions that would be relevant to the content being taught and learned. In some cases, the reflective strategy approaches a constructivist perspective; that is, the students must construct their own meanings to the questions. You might also organize student teams to write a few reflective questions. This approach gives you double value: Students work cooperatively, and they have to think.

Stimulating Thinking Process with Reflective Questions

- Seeking motives
- Expanding a vision
- Listing implications
- Searching for unintended consequences
- Identifying issues
- Analyzing persuasive techniques
- Making unique interpretations
- Inferring values
- Challenging assumptions
- Seeking meanings

Reflective Questions

- What are some twenty-first-century implications of Manifest Destiny?
- What issues are unresolved by having security persons in our high school?
- What rationale is given to support interscholastic activities?
- What problems might you anticipate if algebra were to be made a required course for all eighth-graders?
- What values can we imply are important in our school by examining its entry showcase?
- What assumptions did we make when we constructed the interstate highway system?
- What impact have personal computers made on our school courses?
- What metaphors do your teachers use when describing school and what do they imply?

TECHNOLOGY INSIGHT

What the Computer Can Ask and Answer: Algorithms Versus Heuristics

It is often difficult to remember that computers do not think. Although they may seem intelligent, computers are just a collection of specific instructions. (A simplistic example is the instruction "If 'Dan' is typed on the keyboard, then place the response 'Hello Dan' on the monitor.") Computers are capable of completing algorithmic processes. An **algorithmic** procedure always provides the same result ("if 2 and 2, then 4"). The great strength of computers is the speed with which they are able to perform algorithmic procedures, and, unlike humans, they never tire of doing so.

Computers cannot handle **heuristic** procedures. That is to say, they cannot provide an answer to a question with a number of possible correct answers. A computer would be at a loss to answer the question "What makes a joke funny?"

Even professional programmers who know the exact capability of computers have trouble avoiding *anthropomorphizing* them (considering them as human). It is not easy, but it is important to keep in mind that computers can work only with questions and answers that operate using algorithms.

SOURCE: B. Reeves and C. Nass, *The Media Equation: How People Treat Computers, Television, and New Media Like Real People and Places* (New York: Cambridge University Press, 1996).

reFLecT

- How can you provide students with content knowledge so that they can respond to evaluative and reflective questions?

- What question have you been asked by a friend or classmate lately that elicited the longest, most thoughtful response? Which of the four question categories did it fall into?

- Reflect on the techniques discussed here and for what content areas they are most appropriate. Do you have any ideas for using questions in your content area? Please contact us with your thoughts. Write to: Don Orlich, c/o College Education, Houghton Mifflin Company, 222 Berkeley Street, Boston, MA 02116.

secTIon 3: APPROPRIATe QuesTIONING BeHaVIORs

To develop a repertoire of questioning skills, you must be aware of a wide spectrum of techniques for eliciting appropriate responses from students. The questioning skills that follow address specific kinds of problems that may arise in any class using questioning strategies.

Using Questioning Positively

The questioning in a recitation period, a tutorial period, or an inductive session (as we describe in Chapter 4) is always based on the assumption that some meaningful or purposeful learning activity will take place, allowing the student to gain another learning experience. For this to happen, questions must be asked in a positive, reinforcing manner—that is, so that the student will enjoy learning and responding. All students should receive positive reinforcement from the questions being asked as well as for the responses elicited. Thus questions should *never* be used for punitive purposes. The teacher who asks a question to punish a student is turning a positive learning situation into a negatively reinforcing one. The result is that the teacher not only "turns off" the learner but also shuts down the learning process. It is extremely important to avoid doing this, especially when working with students with learning disabilities or young students.

Questioning should enhance student enjoyment.

Framing Questions and Using Wait Times

A, P, C: Ask, pause, then call on

The basic rule for asking questions is to proceed in three steps: *ask the question, pause,* and *then call on a student.*

This rule is grounded in the psychological rationale that when you ask a question and follow it with a short pause, all students will attend to the communication. The nonverbal message—the pause—communicates that any student in the class may be selected for a response, so the attention level of the class remains high. If you do the opposite and call on a particular student before you ask a question, all the other students may ignore the question.

To be an effective questioner, you must be able to pose clear, concise, succinct questions. Avoid using "uhs," false starts, uncertain pauses, and ineffective transitions between topics. All such verbal behaviors by teachers ultimately cause student uncertainty (see Gettinger and Stoiber 1999). Thus the complete technique of **framing** a question entails asking a clear, succinct question, pausing, and then calling on a student. You can use this technique even when you intend to select several students to respond. Furthermore, once you and the students have mastered this technique, you can modify the third element to a nonverbal action of simply pointing or nodding to a student for a response. This technique becomes easy with a little practice.

Wait Time 1   The time between when you first ask a question and when you call on a student is called **wait time 1**. Why wait at all? There are several reasons to use the pause. First, it gives students a chance to think about their responses to the question. This is especially important when you ask higher-level questions.

Second, this pause gives you time to read students' nonverbal cues. With some practice, you can readily observe nonverbal signals indicating pleasure, apprehension, fright, excitement, joy, or shame. As you become more sensitive to humanitarian considerations in the classroom, this dimension of teaching becomes very important to gauging your students' well-being. It also allows you to pick up on how prepared the students are or how well they understand the material.

Waiting gives a window into nonverbal cues.

Wait Time 2   After the student has given a first answer to your question, wait again. **Wait time 2**, the pause after the student you have called has responded, is equally important because it gives the student additional time to think or allows other students to respond as well (Rowe 1969, 1980). If the teacher waits a while to respond after the initial student response, students will continue to respond—without prompting. Figure 7.1 illustrates the use of wait time.

The effectiveness of wait time has been well documented (see Stahl 1994). The box on page 232 lists the benefits to both teachers and students. However, many teachers are impatient with students when asking questions (Rowe 1969, 1974, 1978). Studies show that the wait time between asking a question and either answering it for the student or calling on another student is often only a few fractions of a second! Is it any wonder, then, that some students dread being called on? They fear that being called on will bring impatience from the teacher and that they will be "in hot water" again. It's important to note that while wait time has no effect on student responses to lower-level questions (Riley 1986), it has a significant effect on responses to higher-level questions. Lack of wait time with higher-level questions can cause students to give low-level responses.

Remember that classroom silence is not all bad—even when you are asking questions. So make the decision to wait—not only once, but twice, even three times, if students are interacting. With practice, you'll develop *the art of staying silent.*

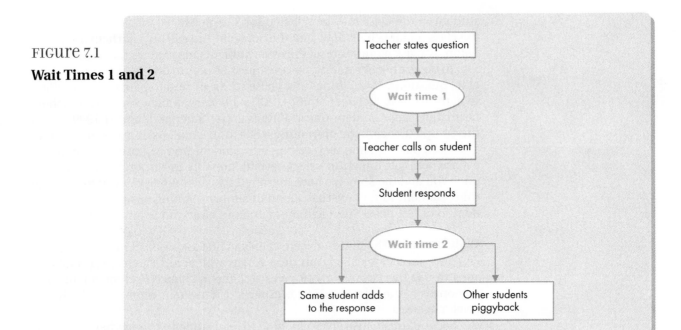

FIGURE 7.1
Wait Times 1 and 2

Benefits of Wait Time (Tobin 1987)

For the Teacher
- Less teacher talking
- Less repetition of questions
- Fewer questions per period
- More questions with multiple responses
- Fewer lower-level questions
- More probing
- Less repetition of students' responses
- More application-level questions
- Less disciplinary action

For the Students
- Longer responses
- More student discourse and questions
- Fewer nonresponding students
- More student involvement in lessons
- Increased complexity of answers and improved reasoning
- More responses from slower students
- More peer interaction and fewer peer interruptions
- Less confusion
- More confidence
- Higher achievement

Using Positive Prompting Techniques

Once you have asked a question and called on a student to respond, the student may not answer the question the way you want him or her to, or he or she may not answer at all. When this happens, you should prompt the student. You may do this by clarifying the question, by eliciting a fuller response, or by eliciting additional responses from the student to allow you to verify whether he or she comprehends the material (Dann 1995). As you develop prompting skills, you can follow many rules. However, to simplify matters, keep one rule foremost in mind: *Prompt in a positive manner.*

You may have to prompt a student many times during a questioning session to evoke a more complete or logical response. Always provide positive reinforcement so that the student will be encouraged to complete an incomplete response or revise an incorrect one. In many cases, a student will answer with a *partially* correct response. When you hear such a response, immediately begin to prompt the student so that the response can be completed, made more logical, reexamined, or stated more appropriately.

The Instructional Strategies box below and on page 234 illustrates two possible prompting techniques. Observe that, in the first example, the teacher tries to focus the student's ideas. In the second example, the student's response is recast to answer the question that was asked. In both cases, the teacher is trying to use some aspect of the student's responses to keep the episode positive.

Value partially correct responses.

INSTRUCTIONAL STRATEGIES

Prompting Techniques

Example 1

Teacher:	What did the English citizens and American colonists think a constitution should be like? (pause) Hector?
Hector:	Well . . . um . . . they figured it was a bunch of laws all written down in one place.
Teacher:	That's a good description of the American point of view. Now . . . what did the English think?
Hector:	They thought the laws should be written down in different places . . . sort of.
Teacher:	Okay . . . that's part of the answer. Now, did *all* the laws for the English constitution have to be written down?
Hector:	Some stuff was just rules that had been set up, and everybody knew what they were and followed them. But others were written down in many different . . . ah . . . documents.
Teacher:	Fine! Now, how about going back and listing the main points on what you've worked out so far?

Continued

instructional
strategies

Prompting Techniques—Cont'd

Example 2

Teacher:	Class, now let's examine the data that we collected on our experiment on absorption and radiation. What differences did you observe between the covered and uncovered shiny pans? (three- to five-second pause) Angela?
Angela:	The water in the covered pan had a temperature of 96 degrees.
Teacher:	At what point in the experiment was that temperature measured?
Angela:	After the pan had been covered for ten minutes.
Teacher:	What was the temperature of the water when you took the first reading?

The teacher prompts the student in a nonthreatening or neutral verbal tone (including all the nonverbal cues). The episode continues until the student provides all the necessary information for an appropriate closure.

Handling Incorrect Responses

No matter how skillful a teacher is at motivating students, providing adequate and relevant instructional materials, and asking high-quality questions, one continual problem will detract from both the intellectual and the interpersonal aspects of classroom questioning sessions—incorrect student responses.

As we discussed previously, you may use prompting techniques when students' responses are partially correct or stated incompletely. Prompting is an easy technique because you can reinforce the positive aspect of a student's response while ignoring the negative or incomplete component. However, when a student gives a totally incorrect response, a more complex interpersonal situation arises. First, it's hard to reinforce positively in such a case. But comments such as "No," "You are *way* off," or "That is incorrect" should be avoided because they all act as negative reinforcers and may reduce that student's desire to participate in a verbal classroom interaction. This is critical, especially with students whose first language is not English.

Second, if you respond negatively to an incorrect student response, there is a high probability that a **ripple effect** will occur (Kounin 1970). This effect describes the way in which students who are not themselves the target of a teacher's negative behavior are still negatively affected by what the teacher says or does to another class member. Therefore, when a student gives an

Avoid negative responses.

incorrect response, try to move to a neutral prompting technique rather than responding with "No, that is not at all correct."

How should you do this? Because the entire approach to this method is to stress the positive, you might first analyze the student's verbal response to determine whether any portion of it can be classified as valid, appropriate, or correct. After you make this split-second decision, you then provide positive reinforcement or praise for the correct portion of the response. For example, if you ask a general mathematics question and the student gives a totally incorrect answer, then you might state, "Your response is close to the answer, so do some recalculating." "Could you tell us how you arrived at your answer?" or "Could you rethink your solution and take another try at it?" These responses are *neutral*, not negative.

Another strategy is to rephrase the question, to remove from the student the onus for incorrectly answering the original question. You can carefully lead the student to a correct response with a set of convergent questions.

Always avoid being sarcastic or punishing. A putdown strategy provides negative reinforcers and ultimately has unpleasant residual effects because it causes students to ignore opportunities to respond verbally. A primary goal of schooling is to provide a positive and stimulating environment in which learning can take place. But learning can be blocked by insults and negative teacher responses. The student learns nothing by humiliation—except to despise the teacher and to hate school. Verbal abuse is never an appropriate or professional response.

When carrying out this strategy, you must be careful that nonverbal cues—such as frowning—do not show that you are upset or angered by the incorrect response. You must maintain congruency between your verbal and nonverbal behaviors when handling incorrect responses. (See Chapter 6 for a list of positive verbal and nonverbal responses.)

Another strategy for helping a student correct a response is to immediately assess the type and level of question you asked and then ask the student a similar, but less difficult, question, without making any other comments. Always react flexibly; give students the opportunity to show that they know *some* answer.

Interpersonal relationships between teachers and students are delicate and take time to build. After you have assessed each student's personality type, you may find that it is appropriate to use some negative as well as positive reinforcers with certain students. It is not uncommon for better students to clown or joke with the teacher or to kid the teacher. When you see such situations developing, you can predict fairly accurately how a specific student will react, and you can then humor that student. For example, if a top-performing student gives a response that you consider "off the wall," then you might comment, "Are you putting me on?" and then smile or laugh. This diffuses those tense moments.

The Instructional Strategies box on page 236 illustrates a number of ways to handle incorrect responses. Note that in these examples, the teacher's response does not criticize the student. We hope you will create an atmosphere in your classes that is supportive—one in which students can react freely without the fear of being wrong.

Reward partial correct answers; if you can't be positive, be neutral.

Teacher putdowns cause students to hate school.

INSTRUCTIONAL
STRATEGIES

Handling Incorrect Responses

Example 1

Teacher: What relationships did we find between the hypotenuse and sides of a right triangle? (pause) Peggy?

Peggy: Well, we did some squaring of a side. I forgot.

Teacher: Okay. Now think of the model that the class constructed. Can you visualize it in your mind? What did those constructions look like?

Example 2

Teacher: What was one of the military reforms instituted by Senator Harry Truman? (pause) Joe?

Joe: Didn't he want to stop building forts?

Teacher: What was it about building the forts that he challenged?

Joe: Was it something about costs and waste?

Teacher: You're on the right track now. What were some of the wasteful practices that he uncovered?

REFLECT

- Recall your own experiences as a student. To what extent did your teachers employ the positive behaviors discussed here?

- With a group of peers, act out a role-playing exercise in which you take turns responding to incorrect or completely illogical student responses. Do you find it difficult to prompt positively? Why?

SECTION 4: HOW QUESTIONING CAN CREATE A DYNAMIC LEARNING ENVIRONMENT

In Section 3 of this chapter, we discussed some prompting techniques you can use to help your students become more successful. Now let's focus on how you can increase student verbal interaction and reduce yours. You see, we want your students to go home tired from thinking and working—and you to go home refreshed.

Promoting Multiple Responses

As noted earlier, teachers typically conduct recitation periods by sequential questioning: They ask one student to respond, than another student to respond, and so on. For the most part, the teacher does the talking. Few students, if any, listen carefully to their peers' responses because at any one time there is a closed communication circuit between two individuals: the teacher and one student. We recommend that you avoid this closed technique and instead use **multiple-response questions**, which are questions to which at least three or four students respond. The key to increasing the number of students who respond to each question is to emphasize divergent and evaluative questions. These types of questions allow for many different responses. In the multiple-response technique, you ask a question, pause, and then call on three or four students to respond.

Of course, before you use the multiple-response technique, you must carefully explain it to the class. Also caution students that you will not repeat any student responses. Thus students must listen carefully to their peers' responses so that they will not repeat them.

The multiple-response strategy also allows the teacher to speak less. It is difficult for you to be an empirical observer of student behavior, direct a question-and-answer period, manage the classroom, and plan for appropriate questions—all at the same time. You cannot listen and talk simultaneously. But if you use divergent or evaluative questions coupled with the multiple-response strategy, you will have time to analyze the responses that are being given. In short, you will be able to make a qualitative evaluation of each student's response.

Shifts more activity to the students

You can modify this technique by subdividing the class into teams of three, four, or five students to add the motivating factors of small-group solidarity and identification. Once the groups are formed, you ask a divergent or evaluative question of the class. Each group discusses it, and then a spokesperson responds. This situation increases student-to-student verbal interaction. (You can further facilitate students' interaction by rearranging their desks.) Any competition that develops within the class will be peer oriented rather than between teacher and student. Friendly intraclassroom competition can be established by incorporating some type of game into the lesson (see MacKenzie 2001).

Teachers tend to be parsimonious with rewards. But by using this variation of the multiple-response strategy, you can reward one group for providing the most novel responses, another for the best responses obtained from an encyclopedia, another for the best nonverbal responses (pictures, cartoons, posters), and another for the best multimedia presentation. All these are motivational strategies that help make the classroom an enjoyable, creative, and interesting place. The Instructional Strategies box on page 238 illustrates the multiple-response technique. Notice how the teacher frames a question and then calls on three or four students to answer it.

When you use the multiple-response technique, you also build other communication skills in students. For example, when you start using this technique, you can ask students to write one-sentence summaries of each response given by their peers. Think of the implications of this simple teaching technique for improving listening skills; structuring logical discussions; identifying the main points in an oral discourse; enabling students to classify arguments, positions, or statements systematically; and learning to outline. Because questioning is such a widely used communication technique in the classroom, it follows that teachers should maximize the usefulness of questioning so that it improves other cognitive skills and processes as well. As with using reflective questions, we strongly recommend that you write out in advance questions that have multiple responses. By composing them ahead of time, you can phrase them in a manner that is clear and understandable for all students. Writing divergent, evaluative, reflective, and multiple-response questions helps you, as teacher, master the techniques.

The multiple-response strategy allows for longer student responses, greater depth in student statements, and greater challenges for all students. It is a logical precursor to student-conducted **discussions**. Student discussions are extremely difficult to conduct effectively because many students do not demonstrate the behaviors or skills needed. By using multiple-response questions, you subtly condition students to accept more responsibility for listening to one another and to modify their responses based on previous ones and begin to ease the class into student-led discussion. We recommend, however, that such discussions be postponed until the multiple-response technique is mastered by teachers and students alike.

Builds numerous communication skills

The multiple-response technique shifts more activity to the students.

Write out multiple-response questions before class.

INSTRUCTIONAL STRATEGIES

The Multiple-Response Technique

Teacher: Today I'm going to use a new technique that we'll continue using from here on. I'll ask you a question, pause for a few seconds, and then call on three or four of you for responses. Listen carefully, because I won't repeat the question. Furthermore, listen to your classmates as they respond, because I will not repeat any of their responses either. Any questions? Okay? Where might Christopher Columbus have landed if he had set sail from London and headed due west? (pause) Trudy, Raphael, Billy, Tommie.

Trudy: He'd have landed in Canada.

Teacher: (Smiles and points, without comment, to Raphael.)

Raphael: I think he would miss Canada and land near Boston, because the Pilgrims landed in that area.

Teacher: (Nods head and points to Billy, without verbal comment.)

Billy: You're both off. He'd have been blown to Greenland.

Tommie: That would not happen, either. Christopher Columbus would have been blown by the Gulf Stream winds right back to England.

Teacher: Those are all interesting ideas. Class, let's check the direction of the Gulf Stream and the air currents. Helen, will you please get the big map of ocean and air currents from the closet and give us a reading?

Helen: Okay.

Conducting Review Sessions

How can you review previously taught concepts using questioning strategies? One successful method is to reintroduce previously discussed concepts in the context of newly presented material. For example, if you are teaching a unit on transportation and you wish to review the topic of railroads, which has already been covered, you could compare the placement of airports and bus stations with that of railroad stations as part of a discussion on transportation infrastructures. Through questioning, you could elicit from students the fact that most railroad terminals, like airports, were initially built at the edges of cities. Students would then have the opportunity to demonstrate their comprehension of city growth, noting that transportation terminals became engulfed as cities expanded and that this, in turn, causes a set of problems unique to cities and the transportation industry.

What we are suggesting, as a viable alternative to separate, discrete review sessions, is continual review. Such review may be conducted at any level of Bloom's taxonomy. As students begin to relate previously learned skills or concepts to new ones, they may begin to perceive the relationships between old and new material. If you wish to use the true basic liberal arts approach, then you should relate the ideas of one discipline to those of other disciplines. But instead of *telling* students about subtle interdisciplinary relationships, you can direct them to the library or the Internet so that they may discover them on their own and report them to the class. This is particularly useful for those students who are always finished with their work and have "nothing to do"—except disrupt the class. (See Gagliardi 1996 for other examples.)

Build in continual review.

To use the **concept review questioning technique**, you must always be on the alert for instances that will allow you to establish meaningful relationships, reinforce previously learned concepts, or synthesize students' knowledge, and thereby create added motivation for the class. More importantly, you will be using the technique of "ideational scaffolding," or "bridging," that is, diagramming a concept map on the chalkboard and showing how other ideas or concepts relate to it.

The Instructional Strategies box on pages 241 and 242 illustrates the concept review questioning technique. The class is a group of new teachers studying the affective domain.

Encouraging Nonvolunteers

In most situations, you will not have much problem encouraging students to respond to questions. To be sure, if you kept careful records of which students respond to questions, you would find that a few students dominate recitation sessions. Furthermore, observation of any class tends to show that there are several students who do not volunteer responses, often because the teacher calls on students who are quick to respond. If your goal is to encourage verbal responses, then you must encourage nonvolunteers to respond. Such encouragement is most difficult at the beginning of a new term, when you are relatively new to the students. As you become more knowledgeable about your students' interests, it becomes easier to prompt nonvolunteers because you can ask questions that relate to their individual areas of interest. What, then, are some helpful strategies to motivate nonvolunteers to respond during questioning sessions?

1. Maintain a highly positive attitude toward nonvolunteering students. Allow them to respond appropriately or correctly each time they are called on. In other words, ask nonvolunteers questions that they will be likely to answer successfully. Once the student has responded appropriately, give generous positive feedback to encourage him or her to continue responding. Ask questions that require short responses *but lead to other questions that require longer responses*. Thus you will progress from a convergent frame of reference to a more divergent one. You may even begin by using easy evaluative questions because most students respond readily to questions that concern judgment, standards, or opinions.

Determine why and proceed accordingly.

2. Attempt to determine why each nonvolunteer remains quiet. Is the student merely shy, or is there a language disability? We do not mean that you should play the role of an amateur psychologist, but you should determine whether a specific student manifests a speech deficit and, if necessary, make an appropriate referral.

3. Occasionally, make a game out of questioning. For example, place each student's name on a card and draw cards at random to select respondents. Or, if certain students always raise their hands when you ask a question, you can politely ask these students to "hold all hands for the next three minutes" so that other students have an opportunity to respond. In this way you can shape the behavior of those students who are already adequately reinforced through verbal participation to allow other students to respond.

Provide prompts to encourage shy students.

4. There is nothing wrong with giving each nonvolunteering student a card with a question on it the day before the intended oral recitation period. Quietly hand these students their cards and tell them they may review the assignment so that they can summarize their responses for the next class period. This method begins to build a trusting relationship between teacher and student.

Implicit in this technique is the task of systematically recording who is volunteering responses in class recitations, and in what class situations. If time permits, it would even be desirable to keep a daily record of each student's verbal activity. You could appoint one member of the class to keep such a tally each day. At the end of a week, you will begin to see patterns for each student.

Calling on nonvolunteers should never be a punishment. Schooling ought to be a positive, enjoyable experience that makes students *want* to learn. As a general rule, the most effective way to encourage nonvolunteers to participate is to treat each student sincerely and as a human being. Many nonvolunteers have learned—sometimes painfully—that it does not pay to say anything in class because the teacher will put them down or make a joke at their expense. Be considerate and encouraging at all times.

INSTRUCTIONAL
STRATEGIES

Concept Review Questioning Technique

Teacher: How does the taxonomy of the cognitive domain, which we studied last month, differ from the taxonomy of the affective domain? (pause) Bill?

Bill: The cognitive domain is concerned with the intellectual aspects of learning, while the affective domain is more concerned with emotional outcomes.

Teacher: Good. Can you list some examples of these "emotional outcomes"? (pause) Mary?

Mary: Attitudes and values?

Teacher: Fine. Now, going back to my original question, how are the two taxonomies similar? (pause) Sally?

Sally: Well, because they both are called taxonomies, they both are classification systems, and both are hierarchical in nature.

Teacher: Excellent. What do we mean by "hierarchical" in nature? (pause) Bill?

Bill: I think it means that each category builds on the ones below it.

Teacher: Okay, could you give us an example of another kind of taxonomy that would illustrate your point?

Bill: Sure, the taxonomy of the animal kingdom. Each phylum supposedly is related in some evolutionary fashion to the one below it.

Teacher: Good. Does everyone see how that example applies to Bloom's taxonomy? Okay, let's take a second now and try to relate the module on the taxonomy to previous modules. In other words, how could we use the taxonomy with some of the other ideas we've talked about? (pregnant silence, which does not last for long) Let me try to be more specific. How could the taxonomy be used in constructing better lesson plans? (pause) Jim? Mary?

Jim: You can use the taxonomy to look at your performance objective and see if your procedure correlates with the terminal behavior.

Mary: (with emotion) You could also use the taxonomy to kind of judge whether the lesson is worth doing at all.

Teacher: How do you mean, Mary?

Mary: Well, if the lesson consists of nothing more than transmitting a lot of facts, maybe the teacher should ask if these facts are ever going to be used again in one of the higher categories. And if the facts are important, there are more effective ways of having the students master them than by recitation.

Continued

INSTRUCTIONAL
STRATEGIES

Concept Review Questioning Technique—Cont'd

Teacher:	Good. Anything else? (pause) How about the discussion module? Can you make any connections with the taxonomy? (pause) Al?
Al:	Kind of going along with what we said about lesson plans, the taxonomy might give teachers some new ideas about discussion topics.
Teacher:	Could you elaborate?
Al:	Well, sometimes it's easy to get in a rut. Though teachers aren't likely to use discussions with performance objectives at the knowledge level, they may not be aware of the full range of possibilities open for discussion topics.
Teacher:	Excellent. Anyone else?
Tina:	Also, the taxonomy might be useful in analyzing why discussions bog down.
Teacher:	In what respect?
Tina:	If the students are attempting thought processes at the higher levels and don't have the background at the lower levels, there's likely to be a lot of confusion because the students don't "know" or "comprehend" what they're talking about.

Developing Students' Questioning Skills

The techniques discussed so far all are oriented toward improving your questioning skills. But there is great value in attempting to teach students how to frame *their own* questions.

For the most part, unfortunately, teachers neither encourage nor teach their students to ask questions. Some teachers are even upset when students do ask questions (see Commeyras 1995). However, if you, as an educator, desire to encourage critical or reflective thinking, or thinking of any sort, then you must develop your students' skill at framing questions (Ciardiello 1993). One technique is to play a game of Twenty Questions. In Twenty Questions, participants ask questions in order to identify something. The teacher thinks of some problem, concept, place, or historical figure, and students attempt to discover it through questioning. For example (if it is a place), "Does it still exist under its original name?" "Does it have a democratic form of government?" The teacher can respond with only yes or no answers. Initially you will conduct the session, but as students master the technique and develop their questioning skills, you can let them conduct the entire session. This will leave you free to analyze their interactions.

Another technique is to demonstrate some phenomenon and have the students raise questions about what is happening. Here the teacher plays a

Twenty Questions

passive role while the students actively generate questions that the teacher must answer. For example when teaching about the transfer of energy, a teacher might have a tray of marbles in a row. The teacher rolls one marble into the rest and only one marble rolls from the other end. Students begin asking the teacher what they think happened. The teacher only gives a yes or no response. This technique causes other students to continue asking questions until the concept of momentum and transfer of energy has been correctly described by the students (see Suchmann 1966).

When this technique is first used, students tend not to ask the teacher logical questions because much of schooling requires little logic, causing initial results to be discouraging. However, the teacher should review each lesson and then give students precise and detailed directions on how their questioning logic can be improved. As one alternative, if it will not be too slow, the teacher may write each student's question on a chalkboard or transparency. This will allow students to accumulate information and skills gradually and in a systematic manner. (See Chahrour 1994 for an extension of this technique.)

Of course, to develop effective questioning skills, it is imperative that students have the ability to formulate questions that address a specific point, not some vague one. The teacher can demonstrate how to develop this ability by moving from a general point of reference to a specific one. (In other words, use a deductive logic questioning process, and encourage students to do the same.)

Model effective questioning for students.

A third method of developing students' questioning skills is to have them prepare study or recitation questions ahead of time about the subject being studied. Select a few students each day to prepare a series of questions for their peers. You might even share with students a few of the questioning techniques discussed here, such as following Bloom's taxonomy. To be sure, most students will be oriented only toward the knowledge level because that is what is reinforced the most in their schooling. But a skillful teacher will continually reinforce those questions that are aimed at higher-level thinking skills and will ultimately help students prepare appropriate higher-level questions.

As you begin to encourage class members to ask questions of one another, you will see a subtle shift of responsibility away from the teacher and toward the students (Rallis et al. 1995). This shift implies that responsibility is a learned behavior. As a teacher, you owe it to your students to help them become articulate and thinking individuals. You have a splendid opportunity to do so when you transfer more responsibility for classroom questioning to them (see Richetti and Sheerin 1999). Additionally, you will be creating the conditions necessary for student-initiated learning (Callison 1997; Commeyras and Sumner 1996).

After conducting extensive research, Cynthia T. Richetti and Benjamin B. Tregoe (2001) summarized five reasons why students should develop their own questions. The box on page 244 lists them.

Like all new methods, this one must be explained carefully to students and then practiced for a few class periods. Then, once a week or more often, students can conduct questioning sessions on their own. This method is a prerequisite experience to student-led discussions. If you teach children with learning disabilities or exceptional children, they can display their responses (and questions) on cards (Heward 1996).

A very novel technique for creating a more interactive questioning session is to have the students question the author of the texts they have read for class. Isabel L. Beck and Margaret McKeown (2002) illustrate how you can encourage students to do this, just as if the author of the text were standing in the classroom. Students are shown how to initiate queries in three forms:

1. What is the author trying to say?
2. What did the author say to make you think that?
3. What do you think the author means?

These queries are then followed with other student questions as they construct the author's meaning (see Kucan and Beck 1997). This technique is very handy when you study complex topics or when the textbook is difficult to comprehend. Now you have one more way to create an active learning environment in what is traditionally a dull one!

You and the class may generate a set of criteria on which to base student-framed questions. The criteria may also be applied to a broader context. Students can be requested to evaluate the kinds of questions that are asked on various television quiz shows as a means of improving their own skills in data collection and interpretation.

All the teachers we have worked with have been pleased with the results of the techniques described here. More important, they were all amazed at how much they had underestimated their students' potential. We are not suggesting that these techniques are simple to implement; they take much work and planning. But the attendant rewards make both teaching and learning more worthwhile.

Reasons to Develop Student Questioning

- Increases motivation to learn.
- Improves comprehension and retention.
- Encourages creativity and innovation.
- Teaches how to think and learn.
- Provides a basis for problem solving and decision making.

Make every effort to encourage students to ask questions.

---

reflect

- With a small group of your peers, discuss which of these questioning techniques you are likely to try during your first year on the job. Do you have other ideas as well? Try them out on your peers.

- What fears, concerns, or reservations do you have about allowing students to take more responsibility for the questioning and discussing that takes place in the classroom? How can you overcome these concerns?

Include student-led questioning periods as part of your unit plans.

SECTION 5: COMMON CHALLENGES OF QUESTIONING

Avoiding Teacher Idiosyncrasies

Up to this point, we have been discussing only those teacher behaviors associated with questioning that are positive and encouraging. We hope we haven't made you think that you need only a few tricks and a smile to achieve instant success. Unfortunately, inappropriate teacher behaviors specific to each teacher can interfere with smooth verbal interaction in the classroom. These behaviors, or **idiosyncrasies**, include repeating the question, repeating all student responses, answering the question yourself, not allowing a student to complete a long response, not attending to the responding student, and always selecting the same student respondents. Why these pitfalls are dangerous and how to avoid them are discussed next.

Be vigilant about possibly harmful habits.

Repeating the question. This habit conditions students to catch the "replay" of the question instead of attending to it the first time, either cognitively or intuitively. It also causes a loss of valuable time and does not help the teacher efficiently manage the classroom. Repeating a question is sometimes appropriate: when the class is in a very large room with poor acoustics, when the question is multifaceted, when the question was not adequately framed the first time (often a difficulty for beginning teachers), or when the question is being dictated for the class to write down. In most cases, though, avoid repeating a question.

Repeating students' responses. An equally distracting and time-wasting habit is that of repeating all or nearly all of your students' verbal responses. Not only is this a waste of time, it causes class members to ignore their peers as sources of information and to wait until the word comes from the "fount of all wisdom," you. If you are sensitive to the need to build positive student self-images, you will not want to be the center of verbal interaction: You will keep the focus on the responding student. After all, if it is important to call on a student and require a response, then it ought to be equally important to listen to that response.

Make an exception for large-group sessions held in rooms with poor seating arrangements and for students with very soft voices. But if students are to develop prediscussion behaviors, then they must learn to take cues from one another.

Answering the question yourself. Have you ever observed or participated in a class in which the teacher carefully frames a question, pauses, calls on a student, and then answers the question him- or herself? This idiosyncrasy is a morale defeater. How can students be encouraged to think or to volunteer when they know that the teacher will not allow them to voice their opinions? If a question is so complex that no one but you can answer it, rephrase it, begin prompting, or assign it as a research project.

Not allowing a student to complete a long response. One very distracting, inappropriate, and rude teacher idiosyncrasy is to ask a question and then interrupt the student by completing the response or by adding personal comments.

Teacher:	What impact has the Iraq War had on our young people? (pause) Arnie?
Arnie:	Well, I sure don't trust . . .
Teacher:	Right, you kids really don't have the confidence in our government that my generation did. Why, I can remember when I was in high school . . .

Such interruptions discourage participation and do not allow students to develop logical response systems.

Not attending to the responding student. When you call on a student, show that you are attending to (that is, listening to) him or her. You must model good listening habits for your students. How would you feel if you were responding in class and the teacher was gazing out the window or counting some loose change?

Exhibiting favoritism. One frequently heard student complaint is that "my teacher never calls on me" or that "the teacher has a few pets who are always being called on." These statements typify the frustrations of students who recognize partiality when they see it. The teacher who calls on only a few (usually highly verbal and successful) students provides a negative reinforcer to the majority of the class members, makes them lose interest in the subject, and causes serious erosion of group morale.

Consider the classic study conducted in a Chicago elementary school. A teacher in a primary grade exhibited great bias in selecting students for class recitations (Rist 1970). Fewer and fewer individuals were called on by the teacher, until only a select few were. To make matters worse, the teacher began to move the responding pupils up to the front seats and the nonrespondents to the rear of the room. Needless to say, there were tremendous disparities between the educational achievement of the students in the front rows and that of the other students. This may be an extreme case, but similar situations do arise. For example, in mathematics classes, there is a tendency to call on boys more than girls. You can avoid bias by giving equal opportunity to every student in the conduct of recitations, regardless of what questioning technique you use.

Many teachers exhibit strong biases against academically poorer students. The box on page 247 lists a few of the *intentionally disinviting* teacher behaviors exhibited toward these students.

It is tempting to call on students who often volunteer and who will give you the "right" answer, so that you will appear to be an effective teacher. But if you wish to encourage all your students to be winners, then you must accord them an equal opportunity to respond. A quick way to determine whether you show bias is to ask a different student each day to list the number of times that you call on each student. A quick tally at the end of the week will provide the data. If students are hesitant about responding, then you must gear your questions to their needs and abilities so that they too can enjoy the feeling of success and positive reinforcement.

Equity is the goal.

How Teachers Treat Low Achievers

- Giving them less time to answer a question
- Giving them answers, or calling on others rather than trying to improve the low achievers' responses by giving clues or repeating or rephrasing questions
- Reinforcing inappropriately: rewarding their inappropriate behavior or incorrect answers
- Criticizing them more often for failure
- Praising them less frequently than high achievers for success
- Failing to give feedback to their public responses
- Paying less attention to them or interacting with them less frequently
- Calling on them less often to respond to questions or asking them easier, nonanalytical questions
- Seating them at a distance from the teacher
- Using less eye contact and other nonverbal means of communicating attention and responsiveness (such as leaning forward and nodding the head) in interactions with them

SOURCE: T. L. Good and J. E. Brophy, *Looking in Classrooms* (9th edition). Published by Allyn and Bacon, Boston, MA. Copyright © 2003 by Pearson Education. Adapted by permission of the publisher.

Leading the Way with Questioning

All these questioning strategies provide you with important tools of the trade. But they are just that—tools. Each technique must be used appropriately and must be congruent with your objective for a specified student, group of students, or class.

Questioning sessions in classrooms ought to be constructive and cheerful experiences in which students' opinions are respected, their interests stimulated, and their minds challenged. Questioning is a valuable tool for ensuring instructional equity.

Despite the fact that the techniques described in this chapter have powerful effects on student achievement, thousands of teachers and principals refuse to adopt them. Unquestionably, school culture can be very anti-intellectual and way behind the times in helping kids to learn. Maybe you can help by demonstrating to your future peers the efficacy of this empirically validated interactive method. As you begin your teaching journey, keep in mind that it will take you much practice, microteaching, even rehearsals to become proficient in using all the aspects that are presented. We encourage you to work with your principal or a colleague as you incorporate these skills into your everyday lesson and recitation periods. You will then receive feedback and quickly master the art of asking questions.

Proven techniques are underutilized.

reflect ## A Closing Reflection

- Describe the questioning techniques you have observed in your teacher education courses. How do they compare to the techniques described here?

- Arrange to microteach lessons to practice the art of questioning. What do you discover about the art of questioning?

- What kinds of lessons lend themselves to convergent, divergent, evaluative, and reflective questions?

- Why is it useful to apply a taxonomy to your questions?

- Examine the effects on students of wait time 1 and wait time 2 in your classes by collecting data on student responses. What is the effect on higher-level responses when teachers use wait time?

- Review a few studies relating to teacher responses to incorrect student answers. Do you find any conclusions that differ from what you read in this chapter?

- Give some of your own ideas as to how you can attain instructional equity in questioning.

summary

1. The convergent strategy elicits short or even one-word responses.
2. The divergent strategy elicits varied student responses.
3. The evaluative strategy elicits a divergent response plus a rationale.
4. The reflective strategy helps students actively develop a concept.
5. Hierarchies or taxonomies may be used to categorize questions.
6. Students need to be encouraged to ask questions in class and summarize lessons.
7. Using wait time is a powerful technique to aid student learning.
8. Teachers need to develop skills in prompting, handling incorrect responses, prompting multiple responses, framing review questions, and encouraging nonvolunteers.
9. Positive responses to incorrect answers encourage continued student participation.
10. Stress the positive and avoid sarcasm and cynicism.
11. Teachers can avoid the idiosyncrasies that interfere with student learning.
12. It's important to provide opportunities for equity in responding.

PRINT RESOURCES

Below are three carefully selected resources that will provide you with an expanded knowledge base about the art of questioning.

Buehl, D. *Classroom Strategies for Interactive Learning* (2nd edition). Newark, DE: International Reading Association, 2001, 170 pp.

This book provides forty-five skill-building strategies for learning middle through high school content.

McKenzie, J. A. *Learning to Question to Wonder to Learn.* Bellingham, WA: FNO Press, 2005, 180 pp.

This may be one of the most comprehensive books written about the processes of questioning. The "Questioning Toolbox" cleverly addresses the scope of the technique.

Wormeli, R. *Summarizing in Any Subject: 50 Techniques to Improve Student Learning.* Alexandria, VA: Association for Supervision and Curriculum Development, 2004, 226 pp.

Here is a practical handbook that illustrates how summarization strategies can be easily implemented to improve student comprehension.

INTERNET RESOURCES

Go to the website for this book to find live links to resources related to this chapter.

> Jamie McKenzie provides a treasury of question-related material.
> **http://www.fno.org**

> The following URL provides leads into several different topics associated with questioning. You will find "Topical Syntheses," or research findings, "Close-Ups" on specific techniques, and "Snapshots" describing effective schooling practices.
> **http://www.nwrel.org/scpd/sirs/**

REFERENCES

Arnone, M. P. *Using Instructional Design Strategies to Foster Curiosity. ERIC Digest.* Syracuse, NY: ERIC Clearinghouse on Information and Technology, 2003. ED 479842.

Barnette, J. J., S. Orletsky, B. Sattes, and J. Walsh. *Wait-Time: Effective and Trainable.* Paper presented at the annual meeting of the American Educational Research Association, San Francisco, April 18–22, 1995. ED 383 706.

Beamon, G. W. *Sparking the Thinking of Students, Ages 10–14: Strategies for Teachers.* Thousand Oaks, CA: Corwin, 1997.

Beck, I. L., and M. G. McKeown. "Questioning the Author: Making Sense of Social Studies." *Educational Leadership* 60(3) (2002): 44–47.

Bloom, B. S., editor. *Taxonomy of Educational Objectives. Handbook I: Cognitive Domain.* New York: McKay, 1956.

Brualdi, A. C. *Classroom Questions. ERIC/AE Digest.* Washington, DC: ERIC Clearinghouse on Assessment and Evaluation, 1998. ED 422 407.

Buehl, D. *Classroom Strategies for Interactive Learning.* Newark, DE: International Reading Association, 2001.

Callison, D. "Key Term: Questioning." *School Library Media Activities Monthly* 13(6) (1997): 30–32.

Carpenter, L. P. "A Teaching Note: Getting Started in a Course on Historical Method." *Teaching History: A Journal of Methods* 28(1) (2003): 37–42.

Chahrour, J. "Perfecting the Question." *Science Scope* 18(2) (1994): 8–11.

Christenbury, L., and P. P. Kelly. *Questioning: A Critical Path to Critical Thinking.* Urbana, IL: ERIC Clearinghouse on Reading and Communications Skills and the National Council of Teachers of English, 1983.

Ciardiello, A. V. "Training Students to Ask Reflective Questions." *The Clearing House* 66(5) (1993): 312–314.

Commeyras, M. "What Can We Learn from Students' Questions?" *Theory into Practice* 34(2) (1995): 101–106.

Commeyras, M., and G. Sumner. *Questions Children Want to Discuss About Literature: What Teachers and Students Learned in a Second-Grade Classroom.* Athens, GA: National Reading Research Center, 1996. ED 390 031.

Crespo, S. "Praising and Correcting: Prospective Teachers Investigate Their Teacherly Talk." *Teaching and Teacher Education* 18(6) (2002): 739–758.

Dana, N. F., K. L. Kelsay, D. Thomas, and D. J. Tippins. *Qualitative Interviewing and the Art of Questioning: Promises, Possibilities, Problems and Pitfalls.* Paper presented at the Qualitative Research in Education Conference, Athens, GA, January 1992. ED 343 308.

Dann, E., et al. "Unconsciously Learning Something: A Focus on Teacher Questioning," 1995. Paper presented at the Annual Meeting of the North American Chapter of the International Group for the Psychology of Mathematics Education. Columbus, OH: October 21-24, 1995. ED 389 618.

"Declare the Causes: The Declaration of Independence—Understanding Its Structure and Origin." Washington, DC: National Endowment for the Humanities, EDSITE, 2001. ED 455 517.

Dillon, J. T. "Cognitive Correspondence Between Question/Statement and Response." *American Educational Research Journal* 19 (1982a): 540–551.

Dillon, J. T. "Do Your Questions Promote or Prevent Thinking?" *Learning* 11 (1982b): 56–57, 59.

Dillon, J. T. *The Practice of Questioning.* London: Routledge, 1990.

Elder, L., and P. Richard. "The Role of Socratic Questioning in Thinking, Teaching and Learning." *Clearing House* 71(5) (1998): 297–301.

Eppink, J. A. "Student-Created Rubrics: An Idea that Works." *Teaching Music* 9(4) (2002): 28–32.

Epstein, A. S. "How Planning and Reflection Develop Young Children's Thinking Skills." *Young Children* 58(5) (2003): 28–36.

Filippone, M. *Questioning at the Elementary Level.* M.A. Research Project. Union, NJ: Kean University, 1998.

Gagliardi, C. "Changing the Rules (Teaching Idea)." *English Journal* 85(3) (1996): 86–90.

Gagnon, G. W. *Designing for Learning: Six Elements in Constructivist Classrooms.* Thousand Oaks, CA: Corwin, 2001.

Gall, M. D., and M. T. Artero-Boname. "Questioning." In *International Encyclopedia of Teaching and Teacher Education* (2nd edition). L. W. Anderson, editor. Tarrytown, NY: Elsevier Science, 1995, pp. 242–248.

Gettinger, M., and K. C. Stoiber. "Excellence in Teaching: Review of Instructional and Environmental Variables." In *The Handbook of School Psychology* (3rd edition). C. R. Reynolds and T. B. Gutkin, editors. New York: Wiley, 1999, pp. 933–958.

Gibson, J. "Any Questions, Any Answers?" *Primary Science Review* 51 (January–February 1998): 20–21.

Glickman, C. D. *Leadership for Learning: How to Help Teachers Succeed.* Alexandria, VA: Association for Supervision and Curriculum Development, 2002.

Good, T. L., and J. Brophy. *Looking in Classrooms* (9th edition). Boston: Allyn and Bacon, 2003.

Heward, W. L. "Everyone Participates in This Class: Using Response Cards to Increase Active Student Response." *Teaching Exceptional Children* 28(2) (1996): 4–10.

Jackson, C. W., and M. J. Larkin. "Rubric: Teaching Students to Use Grading Rubrics." *TEACHING Exceptional Children* 35(1) (2002): 40–45.

Koegel, L. K., S. M. Carmarata, M. Valdez-Menchaca, and R. L. Koegel. "Setting Generalization of Question-Asking by Children with Autism." *American Journal on Mental Retardation* 102(4) (1998): 346–357.

Kounin, J. S. *Discipline and Group Management in Classrooms.* New York: Holt, Rinehart & Winston, 1970.

Kucan, L., and I. L. Beck. "Thinking Aloud and Reading Comprehension Research: Inquiry, Instruction and Social Interaction." *Review of Educational Research* 67(3) (1997): 271–299.

L'Anson, J., S. Rodrigues, and G. Wilson. "Mirrors, Reflections and Refractions: The Contribution of Microteaching to Reflective Practice." *European Journal of Teacher Education* 26(2) (2003): 189–199.

MacKenzie, A. H. "Brain Busters, Mind Games, and Science Chats." *Science Scope* 24(6) (2001): 54–58.

Martinello, M. L. "Learning to Question for Inquiry." *Educational Forum* 62(2) (1998): 164–171.

Marzano, R. J., D. J. Pickering, and J. E. Pollock. *Classroom Instruction That Works: Research-Based Strategies for Increasing Student Achievement.* Alexandria, VA: Association for Supervision and Curriculum Development, 2001.

McKenzie, J. A. *Learning to Question to Wonder to Learn.* Bellingham, WA: FNO Press, 2005.

Moutray, C. L., J. A. Pollard, and J. McGinley. "Students Explore Text, Themselves, and Life through Reader Response." *Middle School Journal* 35(5) (2001): 30–34.

Rallis, S. F., G. B. Rossman, J. M. Phlegar, and A. Abeille. *Dynamic Teachers: Leaders of Change.* Thousand Oaks, CA: Corwin, 1995.

Richetti, C., and J. Sheerin. "Helping Students Ask the Right Questions." *Educational Leadership* 57(3) (1999): 58–62.

Richetti, C. T., and B. B. Tregoe. *Analytical Processes for School Leaders.* Alexandria, VA: Association for Supervision and Curriculum Development, 2001.

Riley, J. P., II. "The Effects of Teachers' Wait-Time and Knowledge Comprehension Questioning on Science Achievement." *Journal of Research in Science Teaching* 23 (1986): 335–342.

Rist, R. C. "Student Social Class and Teacher Expectations: The Self-Fulfilling Prophecy in Ghetto Education." *Harvard Educational Review* 40 (1970): 411–451.

Rowe, M. B. "Science, Silence and Sanctions." *Science and Children* 6(6) (1969): 11–13.

Rowe, M. B. "Wait-Time and Rewards as Instructional Variables, Their Influence on Language, Logic and Fate Control. Part I: Fate Control." *Journal of Research in Science Teaching* 11 (1974): 81–94.

Rowe, M. B. "Wait, Wait, Wait." *Science and Mathematics* 78 (1978): 207–216.

Rowe, M. B. "Pausing Principles and Their Effects on Reasoning in Science." *New Directions for Community Colleges* 31 (1980): 27–34.

Rowe, M. B. "Science, Silence, and Sanctions." *Science and Children* 34(1) (1996): 35–37.

Savage, L. B. "Eliciting Critical Thinking Skills Through Questioning." *Clearing House* 71(5) (1998): 291–293.

Stahl, R. J. *Using "Think-Time" and "Wait-Time" Skillfully in the Classroom. ERIC Digest.* Bloomington, IN: ERIC Clearinghouse for Social Studies/Social Science Education, May 1994. ED 370 885.

Streifer, P. A. "The 'Drill Down' Process." *School Administrator* 58(4) (2001): 16–19.

Suchmann, J. R. *Inquiry Development Program in Physical Science.* Chicago: Science Research Associates, 1966.

Swift, J. N., C. T. Gooding, and P. R. Swift. "Using Research to Improve the Quality of Classroom Discussions." *Research Matters . . . to the Science Teacher,* No. 9601. Cincinnati: The National Association for Research in Science Teaching, 1995.

Tobin, K. "The Role of Wait-Time in Higher Cognitive Level Learning." *Review of Educational Research* 57 (1987): 69–95.

van Zee, E., and J. Minstrell. "Using Questions to Guide Student Thinking." *Journal of the Learning Sciences* 6(2) (1997): 227–269.

Verduin, J. R., Jr. "Structure of the Intellect." In *Conceptual Models in Teacher Education.* J. R. Verduin, Jr., editor. Washington, DC: American Association of Colleges of Teacher Education, 1967, pp. 85–94.

Wormeli, R. *Summarization in Any Subject: 50 Techniques to Improve Student Learning.* Alexandria, VA: Association for Supervision and Curriculum Development, 2004.

York-Barr, J., W. A. Sommers, G. S. Ghere, and J. Montie. *Reflective Practice to Improve Schools: An Action Guide for Educators.* Thousand Oaks, CA: Corwin, 2001.

Small-Group Discussions and Cooperative Learning

Your principal has just informed you that a demonstration lesson is being planned at the Harry S Truman Professional Education Development Center. Your substitute takes over your class, and off you go.

On arrival and check-in you observe a classroom with thirty-two students. Their desks are arranged in circular groups, with eight students to a group. A buzz of meaningful noise emanates from the room. The teacher walks about the room, sitting in with each group but not participating verbally. After a bit, students begin to give reports to the class. Students then prepare summary statements on sheets of newsprint, and there is more interaction among them.

As the lesson ends, you are impressed with the level of responsibility and control the students have exhibited, as well as with the amount of real learning they have achieved. You wonder how to organize similar work groups in your classroom.

Using small groups is one of the best ways to promote student autonomy, cooperation, and learning in your classroom. This chapter shows you how to organize discussion, small-group, and cooperative learning experiences for your students. As you read, think about the following questions.

- How can I organize my class for small-group discussions?
- What kinds of small groups are there, and how can I use them in my classroom?
- How can I use cooperative learning in my classroom?

SECTION 1: ORGANIZING AND INITIATING DISCUSSION GROUPS

VIDEO CASE ⏪ ▶ ⏩

Joshua Lawrence uses both traditional and online discussion formats to teach the Greek myth "The Judgment of Paris," as shown in the video "Middle-School Reading Instruction: Integrating Technology." What traditional discussion techniques translate well to an on-line environment?

A major tenet of the constructivist philosophy of education is the importance of an active learning environment. If every student were always active in the classroom, however, chaos would soon reign. Therefore, you can implement active learning by organizing the class into small groups of students who can work harmoniously, foster their own learning strategies, and create an atmosphere in which information sharing can take place.

The Discussion Method Defined

Discussion is a purposeful learning exchange, *not* recitation.

What exactly do we mean by a "discussion" in the context of schooling? As we said in an earlier chapter, discussion is a teaching technique that involves an exchange of ideas, with active learning and participation by all concerned.

The discussion method requires the teacher to develop a viewpoint and to tolerate and facilitate the exchange of a wide range of ideas. Discussion is an active process of student-teacher involvement in the classroom environment (see Gauthier 2001). Discussion allows a student to discover and state a personal opinion or perspective, not merely repeat what the teacher or text has already presented. Janet I. Angelis (2003) observed that achievement gains in middle school literacy could be attributed to well-planned classroom discussions. In discussion groups, students are active learners (Bond 2001).

For example, a previously tracked Advanced Placement high school English class was opened to all interested students. The teacher changed her technique to use small groups, tutoring, and role playing (all discussed later). These processes gave students more responsibility for learning and created an opportunity for some to experience learning that had previously been denied to them (Cone 1992). This is an example of being intentionally inviting.

Besides promoting meaningful personal interaction, discussion promotes a variety of learning, including content, skills, attitudes, and processes. It is an appropriate way to improve both the thinking and the speaking skills of students. Discussions can also be a means of enhancing students' analytical skills (Furinghetti, Federica, and Domingo 2001; George and Becker 2003; Rex 2001). If you desire to have different students doing different tasks or activities at the same time, all leading to meaningful goals, then discussions are suitable. If you want to practice indirect control of learning, then discussion is the technique to use.

Before we discuss the specific links between classroom discussion and the use of small groups, we focus on a fundamental skill that you and your students must develop to participate in successful discussions.

Teaching Good Listening Skills

All discussions involve verbal interaction. This means that without good listeners, a meaningful discussion cannot take place. Being a good listener is partly a matter of positive attitude and partly a matter of listening skill, so you and your students have two things to practice. From our work with students and others (see Carico 2001), we have gathered tips that can help you become systematic and thorough in fostering listening in the classroom.

Listening can be taught by modeling.

1. Begin by modeling excellent listening habits for your students. Observe yourself: Do you lean forward, make eye contact, and show interest in students? Or do you fidget, look away, show boredom, or walk around the classroom? The former behaviors are indicators of listening; the latter indicate that you couldn't care less. You must give your students nonverbal feedback when they talk to you. Your nonverbal posture is the only way that they have of determining if you really heard and understood what was said. Also observe whether you reinforce students for listening to one another (Smith 2003).

2. Support your modeling with sound instructional practices. First, use short and simple directions. Children in the early grades can usually remember only one or two directions. Even older students forget if you give long directions or a series of directions at a time. (Write detailed sets of directions on paper and hand them out to students.) Second, do not keep repeating and explaining the directions. Expect students to listen the first time. Third, to help students develop into listeners, check to see that unnecessary noises, such as talking and equipment noises, are reduced (see Owca, Pawlak and Pronobis 2003).

When students know that there are concrete reasons for listening, they will improve. If you give them practical listening experience, some of what they learn will show up in their discussion activities. Honing students' listening skills will improve their academic achievement in all subject areas. Carl Glickman (1998) suggests that teachers also develop these skills.

Listening is a learned behavior, and the teacher's attitude is what illustrates to the student that listening is important (Gehring et al. 2003; Mosher 2001). The Instructional Strategies box below contains a number of additional techniques that teachers have told us work well.

INSTRUCTIONAL
STRATEGIES

Tips for Teaching Listening

Deliver a short, well-organized lecture and have the class outline it. Review the content to identify main topics and main points.

Ask a question. Have students paraphrase the question and recite these paraphrases in class.

Conduct oral tests frequently.

Limit or avoid repetition of directions, questions, and comments.

Allow students to conduct recitations.

Have students summarize television programs they have seen.

List good listening habits on the blackboard (at the end of each class, each student could list one good listening habit).

Post a bulletin board display relating to listening skills.

Appoint a class recorder to provide a summary of recitation or discussion activities.

Appoint one or two students to listen for any grammatical errors spoken in a class.

Ask a student to paraphrase instructions, directions, or a student's previous response to a question.

Key Elements of Small-Group Discussions

Because they encourage interaction among students, small-group settings are particularly appropriate for the exchange of ideas and to provide a focus on processes—in short, they are ideal for classroom discussion. This section explains what is involved in conducting successful **small-group discussions**, verbal exchanges of ideas and information in groups of four to eight students. But first, we will put this in a context for you and describe how long a time period you may typically expect this process to take. As you'll see, it doesn't happen overnight! (See Karen S. Evans 2001 for her insights and experiences.)

It takes time to develop the skills that *both teachers and students* must master before implementing student-led discussion techniques effectively. Our work with teachers shows that it takes approximately eight weeks to practice all of the discussion elements (although it can be done in as little as four weeks). However, the first steps using discussions are based on the divergent and reflective questioning strategies we consider in Chapter 7; thus the needed skills must be identified, and they must be practiced repeatedly so that students will understand the routines and support one another's

Discussion techniques may take eight weeks to develop.

Successful groups do not just happen.

learning. By having students perform the process, the teacher can better discover problems and effectively resolve them.

The teacher who claims that small-group discussions just don't work ("I tried one once during the first week of school, and my students wouldn't even participate") does not understand them. *Effective* small-group discussions do not take place accidentally; they are learning activities that develop from carefully structured student behaviors.

Let's look at four key elements of organizing small groups in your classroom: goals and objectives, ideal group size, room arrangement, and choice of topics and applications.

Goals and Objectives Learning processes of discussions include groups making time lines, observing courts in session, taking field trips to museums. The value is in the experience. Small-group learning is especially suited to focus on processes such as these for which the most important learning outcome is the process itself, not its end result. For such outcomes, teachers write **process objectives**, which require the learner to participate in some technique, interaction, or strategy. Whereas performance objectives, which we discuss in Chapter 3, indicate a specific desired achievement, process objectives usually call for the gradual and more openly defined development of skills and attitudes.

The first task in planning a successful process-oriented learning activity is to develop a set of long-range priorities or goals. From these you will derive process objectives, which will help you to focus individual lessons. Each process objective in turn will require carefully planned learning experiences and ample time for student practice. A teacher who wishes to develop students' writing skills, for example, must give them guidance, feedback, *and* repeated opportunities to practice their writing. The same applies to building students' discussion skills. Students need practice and cumulative experience

Students can learn the skills to work in harmony toward achieving meaningful goals. © Suzie Fitzhugh

Integrate process skills into
your unit plans.

within a carefully planned framework to gain the skills necessary to be successful in these areas (see Tate 2003).

Ideal Group Size   In this chapter, we make a distinction between small-group discussions and whole-class recitations. Group size is an important variable that influences learner participation. There is no absolute minimum or maximum number of persons that must be included in a small group to ensure a successful discussion. Small groups can number anywhere from three to fifteen (Miller 1986). Some suggest that two to five is the ideal size (Cohen, Lotan, and Holthuis 1997; Schmuck and Schmuck 2001); others assert that six is the maximum (Johnson, Johnson, and Holubec 1994, 1998). Our own observations suggest that the optimal group size is from six to eight students. When four or fewer individuals are involved in a discussion group, the participants might pair off rather than interact with all members.

Group size affects
participation.

On the other hand, we have found that, when a group consists of ten or more participants, student interaction begins to diminish. With larger groups—that is, fifteen or more—a few students participate actively, a few participate in a more limited way, and most remain silent or passive. Therefore, we suggest that you divide the class into groups of not more than eight before you initiate a small-group discussion (the above suggested sizes preclude paired-learning or tutorial instruction).

Room Arrangement   Probably the optimal physical arrangement for small-group discussion consists of several discussion centers located within a large room. You can partially isolate the centers from the rest of the room with bookshelves or folding room dividers. Another simpler way is to turn student desks so that participants face one another and are not distracted by activities in the rest of the room. Students will normally block out noise from the other groups if each circle is enclosed so that students make eye contact only with members of the same group. By converting the room into "centers," you can conduct several types of activities simultaneously without disruptions. Circular or semicircular seating arrangements offer an optimal configuration.

Rooms can easily be
rearranged to promote
discussion.

Choice of Topics and Applications   Discussion topics may arise from ongoing class work, or they may follow students' interest in a selected area. The usefulness of the discussion depends in large part on group members' ability and willingness to define the problem.

Discussions can be held in any classroom, on appropriate subject matter, and among students of any age or developmental level. The topic chosen should both be pertinent to classroom studies and be able to hold students' interest. The issue being discussed should be sufficiently difficult to sustain interest and require serious, creative thinking. In short, the topic must have relevance to those discussing it. Sufficient information should be available to class members, either in print or via the Internet, to keep the discussion going. Controversial issues and moral dilemmas are excellent topics for small-group discussions (see Soja and Huerta 2001 for a clever model).

Students need to learn how to express their ideas effectively and to incorporate this skill into their personality. For example, the National Council of Teachers of Mathematics published a series of case studies and questions that are appropriate for children in grades K–5 (Bush, Dworkin, and Spencer 2001).

Group discussions can occur as early as kindergarten.

By referring to this resource, you will have mind-stretching experiences for young pupils.

Introducing a new topic is appropriate for small groups as would be seeking alternative solutions to problems or respecting the viewpoints of others on controversial issues (see also Scotty-Ryan 1998).

What kinds of sharing experiences do you want your students to have? Some of you will probably focus immediately on multicultural experiences—on sharing customs related to dress, games and recreation, family activities, and religion. Or you might think about the need for students to display and share their unique talents or the benefits of sharing the experiences of students who are socioeconomically impoverished or who have disabilities (see Sapon-Shevin 2001).

Discussions promote instructional equity: Everyone participates.

Making this decision is important because most of you will be teaching in classes where mainstreaming or school policy mandates the placement of students with disabilities within regular class settings (see Chapter 1). Others of you will be involved with gifted and talented classes, and all of you will be faced with the challenge of providing a nongender-biased, multiculturally oriented education for your students. Being adept at handling small-group discussions will help you meet these challenges.

> **reflect**
> - How might process skills and content work together when you create a small-group discussion project for your class?
> - What are some ethical or moral dilemmas that you might present for small-group discussion in the grade you plan to teach?
> - What are the most effective room arrangements for facilitating student interactions when conducting discussions? Can you think of other possible arrangements than the ones we've discussed so far? Draw a sketch of a possible classroom arrangement.

Basic Small-Group Concepts

As you initiate small-group discussions, you need to understand four basic concepts: process, roles, leadership, and cohesion.

Process and Interaction   As we have already discussed in earlier sections of this chapter, the essence of process in small-group discussion is verbal interaction. Communication processes are most vital for successful discussion. Students must be taught and encouraged to listen to what each person is saying and to respond appropriately. Involvement by everyone is part of the process.

Roles and Responsibilities   Every member of a discussion group has a **role**. Group members may be assigned roles by the teacher or by the group as it matures. Each role has specific attendant privileges, obligations, responsibilities, and powers. As the teacher, your own role is best described by the term *facilitator*. A **facilitator** gives students the skills, materials, and opportunities they need to direct their own learning experiences. As facilitator, you need to walk around the class, listening, observing, and encouraging every student to participate (see Ngeow and Kong 2003). In most discussion groups, other roles typically include a leader and a recorder, for example, and additional roles are assigned as needed. All class members must be rotated through the roles so that everyone gets experience as the leader and in the other roles. It is your responsibility to provide all students with the opportunity to participate in a variety of roles (see Schmuck and Schmuck 2001). Roles are discussed in more depth in Section 3 of this chapter.

Rotate students through leader and other roles.

Leadership   The single most important role in a small group is that of the leader. The leader is the person in authority—the spokesperson for the group. Leadership is a learned quality. So, as teacher, you have to model how a leader opens the discussion, calls on participants, clarifies statements, and seeks everyone's comments. Leaders have to be taught how to plan the discussion, organize the group for maximum efficiency, direct the discussion, and coordinate different individual assignments.

When you begin to use small-group discussions, you may choose the initial student leaders on the basis of leadership abilities already observed in class situations. Attributes that enhance leadership ability may include personal popularity, academic standing, temperament or sociability, thinking ability, and speaking ability.

Ideally, leadership develops through experience, but it is wise to discuss with the class early in the semester what qualities a leader must have to help the group work together. At first, appoint leaders. As new leaders emerge, they should then be rotated in. It is your responsibility to help students develop the desired leadership behaviors and competencies. For example, leaders will need time to learn how to ask questions, how to report a summary, how to involve nonvolunteers, and how to restrain dominating volunteers without using aversive techniques. Ultimately, every class member should have an opportunity to develop those skills and be a leader. You must emphasize the main functions of the small-group leader and provide the leaders with special training (see Miles 1998). Leader functions are summarized in the box below.

KEY IDeas

Functions of the Discussion Leader

- *Initiating.* Getting the group going and keeping it moving when it becomes bogged down or goes off on a dead-end tangent (for example, by clarifying certain statements or asking questions that call for more than a yes or no answer).
- *Regulating.* Influencing the pace of the discussion (by summarizing or pointing out time limits).
- *Informing.* Bringing new information to the group (but not by lecturing).
- *Supporting.* Making it easier for members to contribute (by harmonizing opposing viewpoints, voicing group feelings, varying members' places in the group, helping group members get acquainted).
- *Evaluating.* Helping the group evaluate process goals (by testing for consensus or noting the group's progress in some area).

The Four Basic Concepts Related to Small-Group Methods

- *Process:* The interactions that take place within the group
- *Roles:* Each group member's specific responsibilities within the group
- *Leadership:* The capacity to guide and direct others in a group setting
- *Cohesion:* Group members' support for one another

Cohesion: The "We" Attitude   The final concept is group **cohesion**—the tendency of a group to stick together and support its members. A cohesive group displays a "we" attitude: The members support one another and show pride in belonging. The tone the teacher sets is all-important here. In fact, possibly the most important criterion for predicting your ability to facilitate small-group discussions is your own set of attitudes and feelings. Mastering small-group discussion methods requires an appreciation of the atmosphere or emotional setting of the classroom. As the teacher, you must believe that students can accept responsibility and that your actions are closely related to the manner in which the students respond.

Attitude begins with teacher's belief.

Evaluation in Small-Group Settings: Providing Positive Feedback

Why use positive feedback in a small-group setting? First, as we have already seen in Chapter 7, positive feedback increases responses. Many students do not respond because they are afraid of giving an incorrect reply and receiving a negative teacher reaction. If they give a partially correct response, some positive feedback from you usually will motivate students to try again (see Chapters 7 and 10). This feedback can also come from the group leader. To many students, especially at the middle and secondary levels, peer approval or feedback is even more important than teacher approval.

Second, students need to learn to cooperate with and support others. Students *can* and *will* learn to give positive feedback to one another, but only if you are not the only one giving feedback. Gradually shift the responsibility for providing feedback to the group. This helps to promote activity and harmony within the group, as well as to give the students practice with the valuable leadership skill of providing feedback to others (see Weissglass 1996).

Evaluative processes should provide feedback concerning group members' progress in discussion skills and processes, and they should inform the teacher about how the group is progressing in relation to process objectives and group goals. You (or the group leader) and each student need to assess individual group members' progress. Evaluation should be nonthreatening

Base evaluation on learning objectives.

and varied, and it should be based on specific learning objectives. Students need to know, before the discussion or group project, on what they are being evaluated.

Figures 8.1 and 8.2 show forms we've used when collecting feedback in discussions. The process is cyclical. You collect, tabulate, and summarize the data and then share the results with the entire class for its collective reaction. Remember that it takes planning, time, and experience to develop smoothly functioning small groups in any setting.

Benefits of Small-Group Discussions

Small-group discussions have been proven to be beneficial to students, particularly if the groups are involved in tasks requiring higher-level thinking, decision making, problem solving, or positive social behaviors and attitudes. One summary of several research studies noted significant gains by students who worked collaboratively in groups (Fillmore and Meyer 1992).

FIGURE 8.1

Personal Data Check Instrument

PERSONAL DATA CHECK

Name _____

Directions: Keep track of the number of times that you participate orally in the small-group activity. Then insert the total number in the place provided in Item 1. After the discussion is over, place an X next to the statement that best describes your reaction to each of the questions.

1. Tally the number of times that you participated verbally in the small-group discussion.

   _____ Your Tally

2. To what extent did you participate in the discussion?

   _____ a) I really dominated it.
   _____ b) I participated as much as the others did.
   _____ c) I didn't participate as much as I would have liked.

3. To what extent would you like to contribute more to the group discussion?

   _____ a) I'd like to contribute more.
   _____ b) I'm contributing just about the amount I'd like.
   _____ c) I'd like to contribute less.

4. How would you rate the extent to which your group encourages all of its members to participate fully?

   _____ a) The group encourages everyone to participate fully.
   _____ b) The group could encourage its members to participate more.
   _____ c) The group discourages individuals from participating.

Modify the form to match your process objectives.

FIGURE 8.2

Discussion Evaluation Form: Individual Participant Rating

DISCUSSION EVALUATION FORM

Group _____

Participant's Name _____

Directions: Rate your own participation in your group by circling one of the numbers in the scales (from 1 to 5) for each criterion stated at the left.

Criteria	Very Ineffective	Somewhat Ineffective	Not Sure	Somewhat Effective	Very Effective
1. What overall rating of effectiveness would you give this discussion session?	1	2	3	4	5
2. How effective was the background event in getting you interested in the discussion topic?	1	2	3	4	5
3. How effectively did your group seem to be working together by the conclusion of the discussion?	1	2	3	4	5
4. How effective were the decisions your group reached?	1	2	3	4	5
5. How effective was the group in considering every idea that you contributed?	1	2	3	4	5
6. How effective was the leader in making it easier for you to say something?	1	2	3	4	5
7. How effective were you in encouraging others to speak or to become involved?	1	2	3	4	5

A simple form such as this gives each participant some idea of his or her strengths or weaknesses in the group activity. The recorded information can provide a focus for the improvement of small-group discussion processes. Modifications of the form can be made for specific needs.

More chances for students to prove themselves

Moreover, small-group discussions may be a way to turn on your turned-off students. Because small-group learning requires varied activities and interactions, it gives students more chances for success. For example, a student who is a flop at initiating discussion but is highly perceptive may be called on for analysis or to craft a compromise. The class member who is a poor reader has a chance to excel in reporting or visualizing.

The now classic HumRRO study noted five benefits to the learners associated with discussion (Olmstead 1970). These are listed in the box on page 263.

The Key Ideas box on page 263 summarizes some of the important points we have covered about small groups so far.

Learner Benefits from Discussion

- Increased depth of understanding and grasp of course content
- Enhanced motivation and greater involvement with the course
- Positive attitudes toward later use of material presented in the course
- Problem-solving skills specific to content of the course
- Practice in the application of concepts and information to practical problems

KEY IDeas

Attributes of Discussion Formats

- Active learning can be implemented in small groups of students (preferably six to eight).
- Achieving process objectives requires active student involvement and interaction.
- Discussions are highly interactive, not teacher-led recitations.
- Discussions cannot be used for any topic—they are selectively incorporated into teaching units.
- A positive classroom environment is essential for collaborative work.
- Everybody in a discussion group is assigned some responsibility.

TECHNOLOGY INSIGHT

The Computer as Communicator

A computer connected to the Internet allows students and teachers to communicate with a variety of people in a variety of geographic locations, creating communities of learners that extend beyond the classroom. One of the most famous examples of this is the coordinated observation of the monarch butterfly migration, with students, teachers, and scientists communicating via the Internet to observe and record the butterflies' travels (to learn more, start with the University of Kansas's Monarch Watch site: http://www.monarchwatch.org/).

Another excellent resource for teachers interested in participating in extended learning communities is TERC, a well-established organization that offers teachers and students opportunities to work with scientists and mathematicians on a variety of projects that use the Internet to maintain communication: http://www.terc.edu/.

Continued

TECHNOLOGY INSIGHT

The Computer as Communicator—Cont'd

You can also set up communications between individual students, student groups, or entire classes by participating in the KeyPals Club sponsored by teaching.com (**http://www.teaching.com/keypals/**). The KeyPals Club lets teachers set up e-mail versions of pen pals between individuals or groups around the world.

REFLECT

- How does your role as small-group facilitator differ from your traditional role as teacher?

- Parents are often concerned that small group learning destroys individual initiative. How would you address this issue?

- Plan a unit that could be taught using discussions. How does the plan differ from one you might write if you were using other techniques?

- How might you plan to include all students in a discussion?

SECTION 2: SIX BASIC SMALL-GROUP DISCUSSION TYPES

In this part of the chapter, we present six basic types of small-group discussion: brainstorming, tutorials, task-directed, role playing, simulations, and inquiry-centered. From this list, you should be able to find at least one type of discussion that will fit your instructional and process objectives at any given time.

One method for classifying (and remembering) discussion types is to use the variable of control or domination. When implementing small-group discussions, you must decide on the proper amount of teacher control for the activity: You can dominate the activities of the groups almost totally, you can act in an egalitarian manner, or you can choose not to participate at all. Likewise, you must decide how much control you want the group leaders to exert within their groups. Table 8.1 illustrates the basic types of discussion groups we have identified, viewed along a continuum from greater control (at the top) to lesser control (at the bottom).

In addition to deciding on the proper amount of control, there are two other important decisions you must make when choosing a discussion type for a particular situation: the desired or anticipated process or skill to be learned and the desired or anticipated product of the discussion. Group work

How much control do you want?

TABLE 8.1

A Taxonomy of Discussion Group			
Type of Discussion	General Instructional Purposes	Orientation	Knowledge, Skills, and Control Continuum
Brainstorming	Creativity Stimulation Idea generation Role building Listening	Processes	Lowest need of discussion skills and moderate probability for teacher control
Tutorial	Individual skills Questioning Basic competencies	Processes and products	
Task group	Delegation of responsibility Initiative Achievement Planning skills Group learning Affective consequences Reflection Evaluation	Product and processes	
Role playing	Evaluation Reflective thinking Values analysis Situation presentation	Processes	
Simulation	Inquiry Decision making Application of skills	Processes and product	
Inquiry group	Analysis Synthesis Evaluation Student initiative	Processes	Highest need of discussion skills and lowest probability for teacher control

always has a goal, such as the completion of a given task. This goal is the *product*. How the members interact with one another during the discussion is the *process*. These two objectives must be taught to the students so that they will learn the ropes. Let's proceed to those basic techniques.

Brainstorming

Brainstorming is a simple and effective skill-building technique to use when a high level of creativity is desired. The entire class can participate in a brainstorming activity, but the shorter the time available for discussion, the smaller should be the number of participants (which should, in any case, be within five to fifteen persons).

The leader begins the brainstorming session by briefly stating the problem under consideration. The problem may be as simple as "What topics would the group like to consider this semester?" or as complex as "How can the school lunchroom be arranged to maximize efficiency?" Every school subject has some elements that require students to do some freewheeling thinking. This is when you want to use a brainstorming group.

After the topic has been stated and before interaction starts, it is crucial to select a method for recording the discussion. It can be taped, or one or two students who write quickly can serve as recorders. The leader should stress to the group that *all* ideas need to be expressed. All group participants need to realize that *quantity* of suggestions is paramount. Refer to Chapter 5 to review the topic of graphic organizing because it is an effective way to display and organize participants' suggestions.

There are some very important rules to follow for brainstorming sessions. The box below summarizes them. All the students should be oriented to the rules ahead of time, and the student leader should enforce them.

Brainstorming is an initiating process; it must be followed by some other activity. For example, the group might use the ideas generated in the brainstorming session as the basis for another type of discussion. After the brainstorming session, the ideas should be categorized and evaluated, and as many as possible should be used by students in follow-up activities. The group may arrange the elements in priority order; for example, members may evaluate the suggested topics according to their importance for future study.

A structure for freewheeling thinking

Rules for Brainstorming

- All ideas, except for obvious jokes, should be acknowledged and recorded.
- No criticism is to be made of any suggestion.
- Members should build on one another's ideas. In the final analysis, no idea belongs to any individual, so encourage "piggybacking."
- The leader should solicit ideas or opinions from silent members and then give them positive reinforcement.
- Quality is less important than quantity, but this does not relieve group members of the need to think creatively and intelligently.

Tutorial

The **tutorial discussion group** is most frequently used to help students who have difficulties learning or processing information at a satisfactory rate. The group is very small (usually four or fewer) and focuses on a narrow range of materials. Teachers of such subjects as reading, mathematics, home economics, art, and business often use the tutorial group for remedial instruction. In the social studies, language arts, math, and sciences, the tutorial group is often used to help students grasp a concept, again with the purpose of remedying a learning difficulty (see Berry 2002). Physical education and primary grade teachers employ a tutorial mode frequently in the area of motor development. It is an excellent way to facilitate student handling of manipulatives, allowing the teacher to evaluate students' motor skills and helping students understand the relationships between movement and body functions (see Davies 1999). Peer tutoring is an excellent technique for *inclusive* class use (see Bond and Castagnera 2003; Kennedy 2003).

The tutorial leader performs three major functions: questioning the students to pinpoint the exact problem that has blocked learning, providing feedback or skills to facilitate learning, and encouraging students to ask questions and to seek answers among themselves. It has been demonstrated that students often learn as well as from one another as they do from the teacher (Cracolice and Deming 2001). We caution, however, that, before you use student tutors, you must be satisfied that each potential student tutor has mastered the necessary competencies—such as the skills of questioning, giving positive reinforcement, and analyzing work tasks.

Many school districts currently use student tutors and are finding them to be invaluable resources for the classroom teacher. Although it is most often used for remedial work, the tutorial discussion group is also an excellent method by which to encourage independent projects or advanced learning (see Mastropieri et al. 2001). Many gifted students find it a challenge to explain their projects to other students.

The person who leads the tutorial discussion needs skills in giving feedback and encouragement. The leader must also keep the group moving toward its goal, accept feedback from students who learn slowly, and prod group members who do not contribute. It may be helpful to give your student leaders a brief review of the questioning techniques we cover in Chapter 7. (See also Berry 2002 for details on developing a tutoring program.)

Tutoring that combines feedback and formative evaluation is such a powerful instructional technique that tutored students can gain 98 percent more than students in conventional classes, as measured by achievement tests (Bloom 1984; Walberg 1999). This critical finding validates the instructional efficacy of the tutorial. No other instructional variable—homework, advance organizers, conventional classes—surpasses tutoring in increasing achievement.

We have been discussing the use of adults, peers, or older students as tutors. It is also possible to prepare a tutorial in advance, on which a student may work privately and individually as a form of programmed instruction. Printed workbooks are available that use the elements of programmed instruction to help teach a wide variety of subject matter. Another form of programmed instruction comes in the form of computer software that can be used for drill, practice, or remediation. (See Grabe and Grabe 2007 for details.) Computer software has the advantage of being completely reusable (printed workbooks often required students to fill in blanks), and if well designed, software may be perceived by the student as something that behaves very much like a live tutor.

Peers, older students, adults, and computers can all be tutors.

Task-Directed Discussion

One of the least complex types of small groups used for discussion is the **task group**. Each student in a task group can make significant contributions to the discussion. A prerequisite to using task groups is to specify clearly defined tasks for all group members. A task group has clearly defined goals and clearly identified individual assignments and roles—for example, recorder, library researcher, artist, leader, and evaluator. It may be beneficial for you to establish a work schedule for the groups and a way to internally monitor participants' achievements and, initially, even to provide all the learning resources that are necessary to accomplish the identified tasks (see Choe and Drennan 2001 for an example using the "jigsaw" technique).

Task groups tend to begin as teacher-dominated groups, insofar as the teacher usually selects the tasks and assigns each group member to accomplish a specific role. You will find that this is an especially efficient group type for helping students learn to interact positively in small work groups. You may also observe how selected students work with one another and how responsibly they tend to accomplish the assigned task. Recall from Chapter 7 the *reflective questioning strategy* that we introduced. This is an ideal technique to use with task groups. Each team would be given the challenge to generate one reflective question on which the class could ponder—individually or in small groups.

We must end with a cautionary note. Even though you give a specific assignment to each task group member, do not assume that he or she will completely finish it. Students must ultimately learn to accept responsibility, but it is your job to help them set appropriate goals, to motivate them, and to monitor each student's activities to help all students achieve their assigned goals (see Anderson 2001).

Role Playing

Role playing is a process-oriented group technique in which students act out or simulate a real-life situation. It may involve almost any number of participants, although seven to ten is ideal. To use this type of group, you should be well acquainted with role-playing techniques. Students also need some coaching to use the technique effectively. The box on page 269 lists the basic elements of role playing.

Thorough preparation will help students enjoy the process and experience of role playing. A key point to emphasize with your class is that they should *not be overly concerned* about interactions that might, in other situations, be perceived as personal attacks. It is especially important for participants to understand the difference between regular acting and psychodrama. Role players and all students who participate in the follow-up discussion should abstain from psychoanalyzing anyone or pretending that they are psychologists. In role playing, as we are using the term, the emphasis is not on the psyche of any participant, but on reenacting or dramatizing a situation and demonstrating how different characters would react in that situation.

Each role-playing group discussion is a unique experience, but there are some common criteria on which you can base your evaluation of a group's effort: Did students who are usually quiet take an active part? Did the role playing lead to a better understanding of the topic being investigated? Was the situation resolved (if the topic of study involved a problem)? Did the participants take their roles seriously? Did they avoid making self-serving comments during the discussion phase?

Establish goals, individual tasks, schedules.

VIDEO CASE

Find out more about using task groups by watching the Video Case "Cooperative Learning in the Elementary Grades: Jigsaw Model." How much teacher control is evident at each stage of learning about the Greek Olympics? How much student control?

Not an opportunity to psychoanalyze

Role playing can be used with students at all grade levels and all levels of academic achievement, and it can be used to investigate almost any situation or topic (see McCormick 1998). In a unit on environmental problems, for example, students can be assigned specific roles to play as they explore the complexities of scientific or mathematical issues (see Mesmer 2003; Resnick and Wilensky 1998). The U.S. Constitution is a great topic for role-playing groups, especially the First Amendment and how it affects schooling (Vessels 1996). A complete lesson plan that uses the stated grievances in the Declaration of Independence can be easily adapted for role playing and other discussion techniques (see "Declare the Causes" 2001). Role playing can also be effective in developing students' social skills (van Ments 1999). Teachers can also easily use role-playing groups to help assess students' competency levels. Your own creativity and that of your students are the only limits to using role playing as a powerful learning and evaluation tool.

Role playing allows for some drama in the classroom.

Steps of Role Playing

- *Briefing students:* Explaining the topic and establishing the situation in understandable terms for each student
- *Conducting the drama:* That is, behaving as an actor in the described situation
- *Debriefing:* Analyzing how the roles were played and identifying what concepts were learned

---

Simulation

A **simulation** is a representation or recreation of a real object, problem, event, or situation. Although it mirrors reality, a simulation removes the possibility of injury or risk to the participants. The learner is nevertheless an active participant, engaged in demonstrating a behavior or previously acquired skills or knowledge. Interactive simulations may be special cases of role playing. Simulations can be used to motivate students, provide information, enhance conceptual development, change attitudes, assess performance, and provide interdisciplinary activities (see Alsup and Altmyer 2002; Lauer 2003; McGee, Corriss, and Shia 2001; Verkler 2003).

Although simulation groups have long been used in the military, in business, in medicine, and in administrative planning, their introduction into the schools is a more recent event. But we should remember that teachers have for years used play stores and school councils as instructional devices to reflect selected dimensions of reality. Some goals of instructional simulation are listed in the box on page 270.

Simulation exercises should be selected for specific learning objectives for which they are appropriate. Usually you cannot achieve all of the goals listed in the box with a single simulation. All simulation exercises should stimulate learners to learn more through independent study or research. Furthermore, as students engage in relevant simulation exercises, they may begin to perceive that knowledge learned in one context can become valuable in different

Select simulations to suit learning objectives.

situations. One paper-and-pencil example compares the United States and Europe. Five data sets are provided by which to make comparisons—climatic, economic, political, demographic, and quality of life. Thinking, analyzing, and communication skills are stressed (Richburg and Nelson 1991).

In our use of simulations, we have observed that students become immersed in the activities almost immediately. Simulations are great icebreakers for diverse groups of students. There is also an element of risk taking for all participants. Even though there is no penalty for "wrong" answers, participants tend to view simulations in a serious, personal way, especially those that require decisions. For example, whereas middle and high school students *simulate* investment decisions as illustrated in the box, the D. A. Davidson Company of Great Falls, Montana, provides cash grants to several universities in the Northwest to learn about stock investing. In these instances, there is a reality of actually making (or losing) real money. The step from simulated classroom learning to real capitalism is just one grade level away (Davidson 2005). Jane Lopus and Dennis Placone (2002) identify a website for stock market simulations. Simulations seem to be applied more easily to the study of issues than processes. The simulation encourages students to express, in their own words, the basic arguments for the various sides of an issue (see Boston 1998).

Applications include investments practice.

Three easy to use computer-aided simulations include "The Oregon Trail," "Sim City," and "The Stock Market Game"™. Perhaps one of the better applications of computer technology is the use of simulations. A computer simulation can be "played" by just one student or by a small group of students if the classroom has networking capabilities. One student could even play a simulation with students in several different classrooms.

While on the topic, it is important to note that networked computer communication offers one more dimension for human interaction. The Internet allows students to participate in discussions locally, regionally, or internationally. Students may interact with others synchronously (in real time) by participating in chat rooms (examples include ICQ, Netmeeting, and AOL Instant Messenger). They may also interact **asynchronously** by reading and replying to short messages that are part of a larger, continuous discussion (examples include threaded discussions on sites, blackboard.com, e-mail listservs, and usenet groups) but not in a scheduled class period.

Whether simulations will work for you depends on your goals and objectives. If you want to teach processes associated with decision making, then simulations provide alternatives to the usual classroom routines. Simulations are also appropriate if you wish to promote human interaction. If you want to provide experiences that students may not get from the routine application of learning skills or principles, then simulations can achieve this end. With some ingenuity, knowledge of your subject, initiative, and imagination, you, too, can design an effective small-group simulation (Brown 1999).

Goals of Simulation

- Develop changes in students' attitudes.
- Change specific behaviors.
- Prepare participants for assuming new roles in the future.

Goals of Simulation—Cont'd

- Help individuals understand their current roles.
- Increase students' ability to apply principles.
- Reduce complex problems or situations to manageable elements.
- Illustrate roles that may affect students' lives but that they may never assume.
- Motivate learners.
- Develop analytical processes.
- Sensitize individuals to other persons' life roles.

PROFESSIONAL VOICES FROM THE FIELD

))))

Dennis Griner, Garfield-Palouse High School, Palouse, Washington

A Simulation for Teaching Economics

I use a stock-exchange simulation learned at a summer economics institute to introduce the Stock Market Crash and the Great Depression to my U.S. History classes. First, I create a trading floor by spreading the chairs apart and making space in the center of the room. I divide the class and designate half as buyers and half as sellers. Each student picks up an order form. The buyer order form lists the maximum price buyers are to pay per share of stock, and the seller form lists the minimum amount sellers are to accept.

The simulation begins when a bell rings to open trading. Students buy or sell their stock by shouting out the price they are willing to pay or accept. Once they agree, both buyer and the seller come to the recorder (me or a designated student) to record the sale on the "big board," which can be a chalkboard, overhead, or interactive white board. After ten minutes, I ring the bell to signify the end of a trading day. Students use a buy/sell sheet created in Excel to record their goals and transactions.

While they complete their sheets to determine how much money they made or lost for the day, the recorder averages the overall price using the information on the big board. If the activity is used over a three-day period, students will see the average price of the stock rise and fall.

Students tell me how much they enjoy this simulation. As an introductory exercise, it involves students at all levels of academic ability in a positive learning activity. The simulation introduces the ideas of stock, stock trading, profit and loss, market fluctuations, daily averages, and other basic concepts. It also establishes a common knowledge base for later discussion of margin buying, margin calls, stock pools, speculative buying, and the Dow Jones Industrial Average.

(For detailed instructions on making the materials for Dennis Griner's simulation activity, see our textbook website.)

Inquiry-Centered Discussion

If you wish to emphasize problem solving, then you will find the *inquiry discussion group* extremely valuable. Any number of students may be in the discussion group, but six students per team is ideal. The purposes of an **inquiry discussion group** are to stimulate scientific thinking, develop problem-solving skills, and foster the acquisition of new facts through a process of discovery and analysis (Sparapani 1998). The teacher may be the leader of this type of group. If, however, you have a student who has demonstrated good questioning skills and understands the concept under consideration, then allow that student to be the leader.

Inquiry groups are used to stimulate students to become skillful askers of questions. They also allow students to test the validity of hypotheses, to determine by direct experience whether they are valid. Inquiry groups are most appropriate for those disciplines that lend themselves to problem solving— science and social science (George and Becker 2003; Yell 1998).

Emphasis on questions

Before you introduce the inquiry-group technique, your students should have mastered the skills of observing and inferring. You can encourage these behaviors by having students ask questions based on selected observations of phenomena, by having them collect data, and by having them summarize and draw conclusions. After you and the students have identified the problems to be explored, subdivide the class into small inquiry groups to complete the investigation of each problem. In the box below are several suggestions for inquiry-group topics.

To make the inquiry-group exercise most meaningful, plan an activity that has some degree of authenticity. For example, the inquiry-group technique can be used effectively when students are studying about the general subject of human and civil rights. A group can role-play an episode in which a civil right has been violated and then, through inquiry discussion, isolate specific aspects of the violation or solve the problem in other ways. Student hypotheses should be testable; for this reason, situations that affect students directly are excellent sources of material. For example, an inquiry group could study a specific area in which students' rights are seen as jeopardized.

How to evaluate an inquiry group is fairly obvious. What you need to know, and what students need to know, is how well they ask questions. Were they able to ask higher-order questions that could lead to hypothesis making and testing? Of course, you also will want to know whether they learned the concept being discussed. How the students ask questions may be tabulated by listing higher-order questions, lower-order questions (refer to Chapter 7), formal statements of hypotheses, and miscellaneous statements. We suggest that the evaluation be accomplished simply. See the Instructional Strategies box on page 273 for suggestions.

Plan to evaluate every discussion.

Selected Topics for Inquiry Groups

- How are the commercials on television presented to the viewers, that is, what graphical representations deliver the message?
- What major issues or topics occupy newspaper headlines right now?
- How much food is consumed or wasted in the school lunchroom?

> ## Selected Topics for Inquiry Groups—Cont'd
>
> - Which school intersections carry the heaviest traffic when students arrive at or leave school?
> - What themes are most repeated by persons seeking political offices?

INSTRUCTIONAL STRATEGIES

> ## Three Ways to Evaluate an Inquiry Group
>
> 1. Maintain a continuous checklist as each participant comments during the discussion (similar to taking minutes at a meeting).
> 2. Videotape the discussion and evaluate student performance during playback. Examine questioning skills and accuracy of information exchange.
> 3. Invite a colleague or train a student to tabulate selected behaviors during the discussion sessions.

REFLECT

> - What means would you use to evaluate students' performance during a simulation experience?
>
> - What situations might you suggest as role plays in the grade you plan to teach? What kinds of role plays would you avoid? Why?
>
> - Under what circumstances might you employ any of these discussion groups when teaching?

SECTION 3: COOPERATIVE LEARNING

So far we have described a variety of tested discussion methods. The purpose of all these methods is to involve students actively in thoughtful verbal exchanges. Cooperative learning has much in common with the methods already discussed. **Cooperative learning** is learning based on a small-group approach to teaching that holds students accountable for both individual and group achievement. Five characteristics of cooperative learning are shown in the box on page 274 (Johnson and Johnson 2004).

Students accountable for their own and group's achievement

Rationales for Cooperative Learning

Cooperative learning takes many forms within classrooms. Its essential characteristic is that it fosters positive interdependence by teaching students to work and learn together in a small-group setting. Traditional cooperative learning groups consist of three to four students who work on an assignment or project together in such a way that each group member contributes to the

> ## key ideas
>
> ## Characteristics of Cooperative Learning
>
> - Uses small groups of three or four students (microgroups).
> - Focuses on tasks to be accomplished.
> - Requires group cooperation and interaction.
> - Mandates individual responsibility to learn.
> - Supports division of labor.

learning process and then learns all the basic concepts being taught. Cooperative learning provides unique learning experiences for students and offers an alternative to competitive models of education. It is especially beneficial to students who learn best through social or group learning processes (including a large number of students of color who come from cultures where learning often takes place in social contexts). It offers opportunities for students to learn through speaking and listening processes (oral language) as well as through reading and writing processes (written language).

Cooperative learning offers many benefits: For students, it improves both academic learning and social skills; for teachers, it is an aid to classroom management and instruction (see Cohen, Brody, and Sapon-Shevin 2004). Cooperative learning enhances students' enthusiasm for learning and their determination to achieve academic success (Lan and Repman 1995; Mueller and Fleming 2001). It has been shown to increase the academic achievement of students of all ability levels (Stevens and Slavin 1995a, 1995b) in reading, writing, mathematics computation and application, comprehension, critical thinking, and physical education (Bramlett 1994; Dyson and Grineski 2001; Hart 1993; Megnin 1995; Nattiv 1994; Stevens and Slavin 1995a; Webb, Trooper, and Fall 1995). Time on task and engagement increase in cooperative learning settings because each student is a necessary part of the whole group's success (Mulryan 1995).

Cooperative learning is great for social studies classes (Morton 1998). For learning groups to be effective, students must learn to honor and respect one another's differences, to support one another through learning processes, to communicate effectively with one another, and to come to a consensus or understanding when needed. Thus cooperative learning provides valuable training in skills needed to become effective citizens, to engage in group problem solving, and to attain and keep employment. It has also been shown to improve interpersonal relations and strengthen conflict resolution skills (Megnin 1995; Zhang 1994; Zuckerman 1994). It improves students' emotional well-being, self-esteem, coping skills, and attitudes toward schoolwork (Patrick 1994; Patterson 1994). Students engaged in cooperative learning experiences have been able to identify an increase in their own knowledge and self-esteem, trust of peers, problem-solving and communication skills (see Elliott, Busse, and Shapiro 1999), and technology proficiency (McGrath 1998).

Promotes citizenship, social skills

African American, Hispanic, and Native American children often learn by socializing with their extended family and community members. Many cultures also have strong oral traditions that foster creativity, storytelling, and kinesthetic expression of language in students, skills that go unrecognized in those school settings in which students are expected to work primarily as individuals through written work. Although most cultures value cooperation, group loyalty, and caring for extended family and community members, these values may clash with the values of individual accomplishment, competition, productivity, and efficiency dominant in U.S. schools and workplaces. Cooperative learning has been specifically shown to increase school success for Hispanic students (Losey 1995). Cooperative and social learning is also the preferred learning style for many students of European descent. Obviously, students still learn by studying on their own. But some learn better in settings in which they can share ideas, ask questions, and receive feedback.

Cooperative learning experiences have also been shown to improve the relationships among diverse students, when teachers are careful to construct groups of students from various cultures (see Gallego and Cole 2001) and levels of physical need and ability (Stevens and Slavin 1995b).

Cooperative learning benefits you as a teacher in terms of classroom management and instruction. When you teach the whole class and students are not allowed to interact or assist one another, it is up to you to provide individualized assistance to students who have not understood a given concept, have difficulty following directions, lack skills needed to begin a task, or have trouble following classroom routines. Much valuable student learning time is lost when students must wait for the teacher to circulate through the classroom.

Cooperative learning provides exciting learning opportunities across content areas. Students can work in cooperative groups to research topics, write reports, and plan and implement class discussions, debates, and panels. Students can also use cooperative groups to read materials, write summaries, find specific information, and answer questions. They can work together to study for tests, memorize information, and articulate concepts. Students can receive feedback and editing assistance from peers. They can engage in hands-on projects, experiments, and practical applications. They can design and implement school and community service projects. (For more examples, see Coelho 1998; Johnson and Johnson 1996; Lord 2001; Slavin 1995; and Webb, Trooper, and Fall 1995).

You can increase student learning time and reduce your own stress level and workload by teaching students to help one another with learning and organizational tasks and to monitor one another's progress. This allows you to become a facilitator of learning and allows students to become responsible for their own learning and that of their peers. Some other benefits of cooperative learning are listed in the box below.

Taps into diverse cultural values

Frees the teacher, increases learning time

Cooperative learning works well in multicultural classrooms.

Cooperative learning enhances students' academic, management, and social skills.

Benefits of Cooperative Learning

- Improvement of comprehension of basic academic content
- Reinforcement of social skills
- Student decision making allowed
- Creation of active learning environment
- Boosted student self-esteem
- Celebration of diverse learning styles
- Promotion of student responsibility
- Focus on success for everyone

Features of Cooperative Learning

Traditional models of cooperative learning include, at least, the following five distinct features (Johnson and Johnson 2004; see also Jacobs, Power, and Loh 2002).

Positive Interdependence   In traditional classrooms, where competition is emphasized, students experience **negative interdependence**—a management system that encourages competing with one another for educational resources and academic recognition. Competition encourages better students to hoard knowledge and to celebrate their successes at the expense of other students. In cooperative learning classrooms, students work together to ensure the success of each student. **Positive interdependence** is a management system that encourages students to work together and teaches students that school life for each one of them is enhanced when everyone succeeds.

Face-to-Face Interaction   In cooperative learning situations, students interact, assist one another with learning tasks, and promote one another's success. The small-group setting allows students to work directly with one another, to share opinions and ideas, to come to common understandings, and to work as a team to ensure each member's success and acceptance.

Individual Accountability   In cooperative learning settings, each student is held accountable for his or her own academic progress and task completion, apart from the accomplishments of the group as a whole. In traditional models of cooperative learning, individuals are asked to sign statements describing their contribution to a particular project. Individuals may also be held accountable by means of grades based on their academic achievement and social skills and by evaluations conducted by the teacher, their peers, or themselves.

Development of Social Skills   Cooperative learning offers students a chance to develop the interpersonal skills needed to succeed at school, at work, and within the community. Primary among these skills are effective communication, understanding and appreciation of others, decision making, problem solving, conflict resolution, and compromise. As the teacher, you must actively teach and monitor the use of social skills. You need to actively teach social skills on a daily basis, ask students to practice those skills within their cooperative groups, and have students provide feedback on group interactions and social processes (Abruscato 1994; Kagan 1999; Wolford, Heward, and Alber 2001).

Group Evaluation   Groups of students need to evaluate and discuss how well they are meeting their goals, what actions help their group, and what actions seem to hurt group interactions. They may articulate these evaluations during class discussion or provide the teacher with written progress reports. Students should also have a way of alerting the teacher to group problems. As a teacher, you should develop plans for engaging students in problem solving and conflict resolution.

Initiating Cooperative Learning in the Classroom

Providing cooperative learning opportunities is not simply a matter of placing students in groups and assigning tasks. Teachers must carefully select student groups, plan cooperative learning activities, set both academic and social goals for group work, and monitor individual student progress and group learning and social processes. It will take you about one year or longer to master the model (see Ishler, Johnson, and Johnson 1998).

Patience is required.

Selecting Student Groups   Several details should be considered when you form cooperative learning groups. Groups may be formed on the basis of academic skill level, interests, personality characteristics, social skills, or a combination of these factors. Groups usually contain students of varying ability levels who support one another in multiple ways. Traditionally, cooperative learning groups have been set up to contain one above-average, two average, and one below-average student. One difficulty with this is that it blatantly categorizes students when all students have areas of greater and lesser ability. In addition, it ignores the importance of considering the whole student. It ignores the fact that coping and social skills affect students' academic performance and that performance can vary from day to day based on emotional factors.

Avoid blatant ability placements.

You might also form groups and have them pursue different activities based on students' interests. One group might paint pictures while others plan a play, develop a presentation, conduct experiments, or work as a group of reporters. In science, each group might decide to spearhead a different project to increase environmental awareness. In home management, each group might create a different portion of a family budget. In art, each group might design a different project to beautify the city or town. Note how the above activities are applications of multiple intelligences, which are highlighted in Chapters 4 and 5.

Multiple intelligences come into play.

It is essential to group students carefully whenever cooperative learning groups are first formed, so that student experiences can be positive and reinforcing. As the year progresses and students become accustomed to working together, group membership should become less of a factor in success. Students should try as many roles as possible. In this way, they are allowed to share their strengths, learn new skills from peers, and then try them out in a small-group setting.

Cooperative learning groups often remain together for two to six weeks; at that time, group membership changes to allow students to experience cooperation and caring with other peers. How long students should stay in a group depends on the characteristics of the students in the class and the nature of the tasks or projects on which they are working.

You may assign specific roles to each group member. Typical roles might include group leader (facilitates group discussion and makes sure group sets goals and works to meet them), monitor (monitors time on task and ensures that everyone gets equal opportunity to participate), resource manager (gathers and organizes materials), recorder (keeps a written or taped record of group activities), and reporter (shares group findings and plans in whole-class discussions). Setting student roles allows teachers to influence the workings of the group, to capitalize on student strengths, and to encourage students to take risks by assuming new roles. On the other hand, group roles often evolve, with students falling into natural roles. Although this may create spontaneous and natural interactions, it may also lock students into negative roles based on behaviors and social status. Keep in mind that it will take from three to nine weeks of experience before a class begins to maximize the benefits of cooperative learning.

Planning Activities   Many types of learning can take place in cooperative settings. Many learning activities allow for both individual and collaborative work, for small-group interaction followed by whole-class discussion and analysis (see Zuckerman, Chudinova, and Khavkin 1998). For example, students might read a history text and articles as individuals, then convene in small groups to review the materials and discuss the causes of the Great Depression, and then share their findings with the whole class to generate a comprehensive list of causes. Later, students might be asked to write individual essays to show their understanding of the causes of the Great Depression.

Setting Academic and Social Goals   You must carefully set academic and social goals for cooperative groups, and articulate these goals to students on a daily to weekly basis. Especially when first using cooperative learning, students will need specific training and monitoring. Seasoned teachers suggest that it is essential to teach social skills within the classroom and to model these before cooperative groups begin their work. As with other kinds of group work, it is important to help develop communication skills. It has been reported that students with poor communication skills benefit less from cooperative learning (Kramarski and Mevarech 2003). In addition, it is helpful to emphasize one or two social skills each day or week and to remind students to practice them within their group. Examples of such skills are listed in the box below.

Track subordinate objectives for academic and social skills.

Academic as well as social learning must be subdivided into meaningful tasks and goals. A teacher who wants students to choose a project, do research, write a report, and present the results to the class must teach students how to set group goals, brainstorm options, choose a viable topic, assign group member tasks, find and access resources, write meaningful and well-organized exposition, and execute effective oral presentations.

Key IDeas

Key Social Skills

- Knowing how to brainstorm with others
- Making sure each person has an equal opportunity to participate
- Solving problems cooperatively
- Choosing roles
- Knowing what to do when one group member fails to contribute
- Knowing how to handle conflict with other group members

VIDEO CASE

Gretchen Brion-Meisels teaches a unit on Costa Rica that culminates in a student PowerPoint presentation in the Video Case "Multimedia Literacy: Integrating Technology into the Middle School Classroom." How does she apply the jigsaw approach to this group project?

TECHNOLOGY INSIGHT

Multimedia Production and Cooperative Learning

Multimedia projects tend to generate excitement among students. Learners of all ages have found multimedia production projects to be satisfying and fun (Green and Brown, 2002). Presentations created using software such as PowerPoint or HyperStudio, or the creation of class webpages can be wonderful learning experiences that encourage students to work cooperatively in small and large groups.

Green and Brown (2002) have developed guidelines for planning a cooperative learning activity that focuses on a multimedia project:

1. Set clear objectives for the group(s). Be specific about what the group must complete. Be sure to focus on the content of the presentation. For example, instead of saying "You are going to make a PowerPoint presentation about George Washington Carver," state "Your group is going to make a presentation on the contributions George Washington Carver made to science and society." This will help students avoid the pitfall of creating a presentation that is all "flash" with no substance.
2. Have individuals in the group take a specific role. Have the group act as a production team, with individuals taking responsibility for various aspects of the production. Roles include writer, fact-checker, graphics designer, tester (the person who makes sure the product works the way it is supposed to), and production manager.
3. Plan opportunities for group members to talk about their experiences with students outside their own group. Meetings could be role-based: Have all the writers meet to discuss their experiences, and have the production managers meet to talk. It is important that students get to see and hear about how other groups go about solving problems similar to their own group's.
4. Monitor the group(s) carefully. Students are learning how to work together in a novel situation. Make sure that no single student or subgroup is taking over the entire project. Make sure students are resolving their differences in a productive manner.
5. Find ways to offer positive feedback to groups that are performing well. Look for opportunities to recognize and celebrate students developing abilities and the successful resolution of problems.

Cooperative activities and multimedia projects both take a little extra time; be sure to plan for this in advance. Also, be sure to plan time to show off a little! Invite parents, friends, and administrators to see what your class has created, and give students an opportunity to be recognized for their work.

Students doing online research for an oral history project. © Susie Fitzhugh

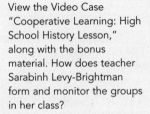

VIDEO CASE ⏪ ▶ ⏩

View the Video Case "Cooperative Learning: High School History Lesson," along with the bonus material. How does teacher Sarabinh Levy-Brightman form and monitor the groups in her class?

Methods for gauging individual and group progress

Monitoring and Evaluating Individual and Group Progress

It is essential to monitor and evaluate the progress of both individual students and working groups as a whole. You need to assess both (1) the academic progress, social functioning, and emotional well-being of individual students, and (2) the productivity and social functioning of the working groups. Individual academic progress may be measured by assessing the portion of the group project completed by a given student or by giving students individual assessments apart from their group work. Individual social functioning and emotional well-being may be assessed through teacher observation and group or self-evaluations that give feedback on how members are functioning within the group. Evaluations of group productivity may be made by assessing time logs, progress reports, and final group projects. Assessment of group social functioning may be made by teacher observations, conferencing with groups, group self-evaluations, or requests for teacher assistance (see Johnson and Johnson 2004).

With the teacher as facilitator, a cooperative learning group encourages individual and group efforts. © Elizabeth Crews

Cooperative learning supports the process of *authentic assessment,* in which students produce summative essays, creative works, and projects that allow them to use critical thinking, application, synthesis, analysis, and evaluation skills (Crotty 1994). Students might write essays, photo journals, or editorials; design public information pamphlets, posters, videos, or home pages; create works of visual or performing art; or design and implement community service projects (see Tate 2003).

Cooperative groups should be presented with real challenges.

Criticisms of Cooperative Learning

Several criticisms have been leveled at the concept of grouping together students of varying abilities. Advocates for gifted children believe that heterogeneous grouping may hold back those with the greatest academic talent. Advocates for students with learning difficulties state that children with disabilities may not get a chance to improve their reading, writing, and math skills when they receive so much assistance from peers. Research tends to refute this, showing significant academic gains for students who are gifted and students with learning disabilities in cooperative settings (Johnson and Johnson 1992; Slavin 1990; Stevens and Slavin 1995a, 1995b).

Do only typical students benefit?

In addition, there are several counterpoints to these concerns. First, *all* students have areas of lesser and greater abilities. Academically gifted students, for instance, may lack essential social skills, feel separate from peers because of unique abilities, or fear class presentations, while students with reading disabilities may have outstanding oral language and listening comprehension skills. Cooperative learning allows students to share their diverse talents and learn new skills.

Second, cooperative learning provides benefits to students beyond academics, including the teaching of social skills essential to working in families, schools, communities, and workplaces. All students benefit from learning cooperative processes and social skills (see Baloche 1998; Gabriele and Montecinos 2001).

Third, the *type* of task assigned influences whether all students will benefit from a cooperative learning situation. Tasks that focus on finding information generally do not provide much benefit to gifted students. But, if the assignment also involves understanding essential concepts, exploring new meanings, thinking critically, and synthesizing information, each group member can provide ideas that will contribute to emergent, constructivist learning (see Kagan 1994; Vermette 1998).

Fourth, whether students benefit from group work seems to be a function of the classroom climate, which must be one of support, trust, and caring. Of greatest concern is whether students are building a sense of efficacy and self-esteem, both prerequisites to continued, successful academic learning.

Last, cooperative learning groups should not remain static, nor should they always be based on heterogeneous grouping. Certainly, gifted students need opportunities to work, think, and learn together, and students with special needs need time to work together on essential reading, writing, and mathematics skills.

Another frequently heard criticism of traditional models of cooperative learning concerns the practice of rating, grading, or rewarding students on the basis of group accomplishment. Parents have cited instances where one student did his or her part of the group work but received a low grade because some other student in the group failed to follow through. Such a system seems to foster an atmosphere of blame. In addition, awarding privileges on the basis of group performance once again sets up a competitive process, subtly undermining the ethic of cooperation and success for all (Kagan 1996). However, a teacher may assign both a group and an individual grade by using specific assessment criteria for each. And although some students do need extrinsic rewards for work they accomplish, most can learn to appreciate the intrinsic benefits derived from group work. You can learn of the instructional benefits that students may derive from different discussion techniques at our website: **http://education.college.hmco.com/students**.

Research shows gains for all.

reflect | **A Closing Reflection**

- Parents are often concerned that cooperative learning destroys individual initiative. How would you address this issue?

- Plan a unit that could be taught using cooperative learning. How does the plan differ from one you might write if you were using other techniques?

- List the factors that will support your attempts to use small-group discussions and those that will hinder you.

summary

1. Using small-group discussions can promote student autonomy, cooperation, and learning.

2. Small-group discussions and cooperative learning are ideal for accomplishing process objectives.

3. The ideal size for a small group is six to eight students.

4. Students learn and gain experience by functioning in various roles within the group.

5. The six basic small-group discussion techniques are brainstorming, tutorials, task-directed, role playing, simulations, and inquiry-centered.

6. Cooperative learning requires much time, organization, and structure, but it is an ideal way to focus group work on specific tasks and to mandate individual responsibility.

7. Cooperative learning requires positive interdependence, face-to-face interaction, individual accountability, student involvement, and good listening skills.

8. Collect feedback to analyze small-group efforts.

Print Resources

We have listed some references below that will expand your knowledge base on cooperative learning, simulations, and discussions.

Hyslop, N. B., and B. Tone. *Listening: Are We Teaching It and If So, How? ERIC Digest Number 3*. Bloomington, IN: ERIC Clearinghouse on Reading and Communication Skills, 1988. ED 295 132.

In three short pages, you will have a foundational knowledge on developing listening skills.

Jacobs, G. M., M. A. Power, and W. I. Loh. *The Teacher's Sourcebook for Cooperative Learning: Practical Techniques, Basic Principles, and Frequently Asked Questions*. Thousand Oaks, CA: Corwin, 2002, 168 pp.

Here is a very helpful compendium for anyone using cooperative learning.

Johnson, D. W., and R. T. Johnson. *Assessing Students in Groups: Promoting Group Responsibility and Individual Accountability*. Thousand Oaks, CA: Corwin, 2004, 206 pp.

This is a must handbook for any teacher who wants a practical lesson on initiating and maintaining cooperative learning, plus addressing fairness when assessing students

Jones, K. *Simulations: A Handbook for Teachers and Trainers, 3rd Edition*. East Brunswick, NJ: Nichols, 1995, 145 pp.

This revised and improved handbook is a minilibrary for anyone who wants to use or design simulations in the classroom.

Kagan, S. *Cooperative Learning*. San Clemente, CA: Kagan, 1994.

One could consider this work as a definitive statement on the topic.

Lord, T. R. "101 Reasons for Using Cooperative Learning in Biology Teaching." *American Biology Teacher* 63(1) (2001): 30–38.

Drop the word *biology* from the title of this must-read article and you have a memo that can be sent home to parents concerned about this technique. Includes a one-page list of 101 referenced findings that summarizes the research on cooperative learning.

Race, P., and S. Brown. *500 Tips for Tutors* (2nd edition). London: RoutledgeFalmer, 2005, 136 pp.

If you want a quick orientation to the processes of tutoring, this book does it.

van Ments, M. *The Effective Use of Role-Play: Practical Techniques for Improving Learning* (2nd edition). London: Kogan Page, 1999, 196 pp.

The entire spectrum of role playing is presented in an easy-to-adopt format.

Internet Resources

Go to the website for this book to find live links to resources related to this chapter.

> Roger T. Johnson and David W. Johnson direct the Cooperative Learning Center at the University of Minnesota. Their website is a rich resource for this model.
> **http://www.clcrc.com/**

> The Schreyer Institute for Teaching Excellence at the Pennsylvania State University provides an extensive array of materials focusing on teaching methods for active learning, which includes discussion techniques and other related topics.
> **http://www.schreyerinstitute.psu.edu/Resources/**

References

Abruscato, J. "Boost Your Students' Social Skills with This 9-Step Plan." *Learning* 22(5) (1994): 60–61, 66.

Alsup J. K., and D. J. Altmyer. "Bullish on Mathematics: Using Stock Market Simulations to Enhance Learning." *Mathematics Teaching in the Middle School* 8(2) (2002): 112–117.

Anderson, R. P. "Team Disease Presentations: A Cooperative Learning Activity for Large Classrooms." *American Biology Teacher* 63(1) (2001): 40–43.

Angelis, J. I. "Conversation in the Middle School Classroom: Developing Reading, Writing, and Other Language Abilities." *Middle School Journal* 34(3) (2003): 57–61.

Baloche, L. A. *The Cooperative Classroom: Empowering Learning*. Upper Saddle River, NJ: Prentice Hall, 1998.

Berry, J. D. *Success . . . One Child at a Time*. Tampa, FL: Plan for Social Excellence, 2002. ED 466 308.

Bloom, B. S. "The 2 Sigma Problem: The Search for Methods of Group Instruction as Effective as One-to-One Tutoring." *Educational Researcher* 13(6) (1984): 4–16.

Bond, R. J., and E. Castagnera. "Supporting One Another: Peer Tutoring in an Inclusive San Diego High School." In *Inclusive Urban Schools*. D. Fisher and N. Frey, editors. Baltimore: Brookes, 2003, pp. 119-142.

Bond, T. F. "Giving Them Free Rein: Connections in Student-Led Book Groups." *Reading Teacher* 54(6) (2001): 574–584.

Boston, J. "Using Simulations." *Social Studies Review* 37(2) (1998): 31–32.

Bramlett, R. K. "Implementing Cooperative Learning: A Field Study Evaluating Issues for School-Based Consultants." *Journal of School Psychology* 32(1) (1994): 67–84.

Brown, A. "Simulated Classrooms and Artificial Students: The Potential Effects of New Technologies on Teacher Education." *Journal of Research on Computing in Education* 3(2) (1999): 307–318.

Bush, W. S., L. Dworkin, and D. B. Spencer, editors. *Mathematics Assessment Cases and Discussion Questions for Grades K–5 Set*. Reston, VA: National Council of Teachers of Mathematics, 2001.

Carico, K. M. "Negotiating Meaning in Classroom Literature Discussions." *Journal of Adolescent and Adult Literacy* 44(6) (2001): 510–518.

Choe, S. W. T., and P. M. Drennan. "Analyzing Scientific Literature Using a Jigsaw Group Activity: Piecing Together Student Discussions on Environmental Research." *Journal of College Sciences Teaching* 30(5) (2001): 328–330.

Coelho, E. *All Sides of the Issue: Activities for Cooperative Jigsaw Groups*. San Francisco: Alta Book Center, 1998.

Cohen, E. G., C. M Brody, and M. Sapon-Shevin, Eds. *Teaching Cooperative Learning: The Challenge for Teacher Education*. Albany: State University of New York Press, 2004.

Cohen, E. G., R. A. Lotan, and N. C. Holthuis. "Organizing the Classroom for Learning." In *Working for Equity in Heterogeneous Classrooms: Sociological Theory in Practice*. E. G. Cohen and R. A. Lotan, editors. New York: Teachers College Press, 1997, 31–43.

Cone, J. K. "Untracking Advanced Placement English: Creating Opportunity Is Not Enough." *Phi Delta Kappan* 73 (1992): 712–717.

Cracolice, M. S., and J. C. Deming. "Peer-Led Team Learning." *Science Teacher* 68(1) (2001): 20–24.

Crotty, E. "The Role of Cooperative Learning in an Authentic Performance Assessment Approach." *Social Science Record* 31(1) (1994): 38–41.

Davidson, I. B. Personal communication, April 27, 2005.

Davies, P. *70 Activities for Tutor Groups*. Brookfield, VT: Gower, 1999.

"Declare the Causes: The Declaration of Independence—Understanding Its Structure and Origin." Washington, DC: National Endowment for the Humanities, 2001. (*Note:* Collective author of annotated lesson plan.) ED 455 517.

Dyson, B., and S. Grineski. "Using Cooperative Learning Structures in Physical Education." *Journal of Physical Education, Recreation & Dance* 72(2) (2001): 28–31.

Elliott, S. M., R. T. Busse, and E. S. Shapiro. "Intervention Techniques for Academic Performance Problems." In *The Handbook of School Psychology* (2nd edition). C. R. Reynolds and T. B. Gutkin, editors. New York: Wiley, 1999, pp. 664–685.

Evans, K. S. *Literature Discussion Group in the Intermediate Grades: Dilemmas and Possibilities*. Newark, DE: International Reading Association, 2001.

Fillmore, L. W., and L. M. Meyer. "The Curriculum and Linguistic Minorities." In *Handbook of Research on Curriculum*. Philip W. Jackson, editor. New York: Macmillan, 1992.

Furinghetti, F., O. Federica, and P. Domingo. "Students Approaching Proof Through Conjectures: Snapshots in a Classroom." *International Journal of Mathematical Education in Science and Technology* 32(3) (2001): 319–335.

Gabriele, A. J., and C. Montecinos. "Collaborating with a Skilled Peer: The Influence of Achievement Goals and Perceptions of Partners. Competence on the Participation and Learning of Low-Achieving Students." *Journal of Experimental Education* 69(2) (2001): 152–178.

Gallego, M. A., and M. Cole. "Classroom Culture and Culture in the Classroom." In *Handbook on Research on Teaching* (4th edition). V. Richardson, editor. Washington, DC: American Education Research Association, 2001, pp. 951–997.

Gauthier, L. R. "Coop-Dis-Q: A Reading Comprehension Strategy." *Intervention in School and Clinic* 36(4) (2001): 217–220.

Gehring, T., K. McGuire, K. A. Parr, and D. Wiles. *Improving Language Arts Skills through Use of Modeling and Grade Appropriate Comprehension Activities*. Chicago: Saint Xavier University and

Skylight Professional Development Field-Based Master's Program, 2003. ED 479 375.

George, L. A., and W. G. Becker. "Investigating the Urban Heat Island Effect with a Collaborative Inquiry Project." *Journal of Geoscience Education* 51(2) (2003): 237–243.

Glickman, C. D. *Revolutionizing America's Schools.* San Francisco: Jossey-Bass, 1998.

Grabe, M., and C. Grabe. *Integrating Technology for Meaningful Learning* (5th edition). Boston: Houghton Mifflin, 2007.

Green, T. and A. Brown. *Multimedia Projects in the Classroom: A Guide to Development and Evaluation.* Thousand Oaks, CA: Corwin, 2002.

Hart, L. D. "Some Factors That Impede or Enhance Performance in Mathematical Problem Solving." *Journal for Research in Mathematics Education* 24(2) (1993): 167–171.

Ishler, A. L., R. T. Johnson, and D. W. Johnson. "Long-Term Effectiveness of a Statewide Staff Development Program or Cooperative Learning." *Teaching and Teacher Education* 14(3) (1998): 273–281.

Jacobs, G. M., M. A. Power, and W. I. Loh. *The Teacher's Sourcebook for Cooperative Learning: Practical Techniques, Basic Principles, and Frequently Asked Questions.* Thousand Oaks, CA: Corwin, 2002.

Johnson, D. W., and R. T. Johnson. *Assessing Students in Groups: Promoting Group Responsibility and Individual Accountability.* Thousand Oaks, CA: Corwin, 2004.

Johnson, D. W., and R. T. Johnson. "What to Say to Advocates for the Gifted." *Educational Leadership* 50(2) (1992): 44–47.

Johnson, D. W., and R. T. Johnson. "Cooperative Learning and Traditional American Values: An Appreciation." *NASSP Bulletin* 80(579) (1996): 63–65.

Johnson, D. W., R. T. Johnson, and E. J. Holubec. *The New Circles of Learning: Cooperation in the Classroom and School.* Alexandria, VA: Association for Supervision and Curriculum Development, 1994.

Johnson, D. W., R. T. Johnson, and E. J. Holubec. *Cooperation in the Classroom, 7th edition.* Edina, MN: Interaction, 1998.

Kagan, S. *Cooperative Learning.* San Clemente, CA: Kagan, 1994.

Kagan, S. "Avoiding the Group-Grades Trap." *Learning* 24(4) (1996): 56–58.

Kagan, S. *Building Character Through Cooperative Learning.* Port Chester, NY: National Professional Resources, 1999. Videocassette.

Kennedy, C. H. "Commentary. Peer-to-Peer Relationships as a Foundation for Inclusive Education." In *Inclusive Urban Schools.* D. Fisher and N. Frey, editors. Baltimore: Brookes, 2003, pp. 143–149.

Kramarski, B., and Z. R. Mevarech. "Enhancing Mathematical Reasoning in Classroom: The Effects of Cooperative Learning and the Metacognitive Training." *American Educational Research Journal* 40(1) (2003): 281–310.

Lan, W. Y., and J. Repman. "The Effects of Social Learning Context and Modeling on Persistence and Dynamism in Academic Activities." *Journal of Experimental Education* 64(1) (1995): 53–67.

Lauer, T. E. "Conceptualizing Ecology: A Learning Cycle Approach." *American Biology Teacher* 65(7) (2003): 518–522.

Lopus, J. and D. Placone. "Online Stock Market Games for High Schools." *Journal of Economic Education* 33(2) (2002): 192.

Lord, T. R. "101 Reasons for Using Cooperative Learning in Biology Teaching." *American Biology Teacher* 63(1) (2001): 30–38.

Losey, K. M. "Mexican-American Students and Classroom Interaction: An Overview and Critique." *Review of Educational Research* 65(3) (1995): 283–318.

Mastropieri, M. A., et al. "Can Middle School Students with Serious Reading Difficulties Help Each Other and Learn Anything? *Learning Disabilities: Research and Practice* 16(1) (2001): 18–27.

McCormick, K. *Plays to Ponder for Grades 6–8: Prompting Classroom Discussion Through Dramatic Play.* Torrance, CA: Good Apple, 1998.

McGee, S., D. Corriss, and R. Shia. "Using Simulations to Improve Cognitive Reasoning." Paper presented at the annual meeting of the American Educational Research Association, Seattle, April, 10–14, 2001. ED 470 975.

McGrath, B. "Partners in Learning: Twelve Ways Technology Changes the Teacher-Student Relationship." *T.H.E. Journal* 25(9) (1998): 58–61.

Megnin, J. K. "Combining Memory and Creativity in Teaching Math." *Teaching PreK–8* 25(6) (1995): 48–49.

Mesmer, K. "Hire a Scientist." *Science Scope* 25(6) (2003): 42–44.

Miles, M. B. *Learning to Work in Groups* (2nd edition). Troy, NY: Educator's International Press, 1998.

Miller, D. P. *Introduction to Small Group Discussion.* Urbana, IL: ERIC/RCS and SCA, 1986. DRS ED 278 037.

Morton, T. *Cooperative Learning and Social Studies: Towards Excellence to Equity.* San Clemente, CA: Kagan, 1998.

Mosher, R. S. "Silence, Listening, Teaching, and the Space of What Is Not." *Language Arts* 78(4) (2001): 366–370.

Mueller, A., and T. Fleming. "Cooperative Learning: Listening to How Children Work at School." *Journal of Educational Research* 94(5) (2001): 259–265.

Mulryan, C. M. "Fifth and Sixth Graders' Involvement and Participation in Cooperative Small Groups in Mathematics." *Elementary School Journal* 95(4) (1995): 297–310.

Nattiv, A. "Helping Behaviors and Math Achievement Gain of Students Using Cooperative Learning." *Elementary School Journal* 94(3) (1994): 285–297.

Ngeow, K., and Y. Kong. *Learning through Discussion: Designing Tasks for Critical Inquiry and Reflective Learning. ERIC Digest.* Bloomington, IN: ERIC Clearinghouse on Reading, English, and Communication, 2003. ED 477 611.

Olmstead, J. A. *Theory and State of the Art of Small Group Methods of Instruction.* Alexandria, VA: Human Resources Research Organization, 1970.

Owca, S., E. Pawlak, and M. Pronobis. *Improving Student Academic Success through the Promotion of Listening Skills.* Chicago: Saint Xavier University and Pearson Skylight Field-Based Masters Program, 2003. ED 478 233.

Patrick, J. "Direct Teaching of Collaborative Skills in a Cooperative Learning Environment." *Teaching and Change* 1(2) (1994): 170–181.

Patterson, V. E. "Introducing Co-Operative Learning at Princess Elizabeth Elementary School." *Education Canada* 34(2) (1994): 36–41.

Resnick, M., and U. Wilensky. "Diving into Complexity: Developing Probabilistic Decentralized Thinking Through Role-Playing Activities." *Journal of the Learning Sciences* 7(2) (1998): 153–172.

Rex, L. A. "The Remaking of a High School Reader." *Reading Research Quarterly* 36(3) (2001): 288–314.

Richburg, R. W., and B. J. Nelson. "Where in Western Europe Would You Like to Live?" *The Social Studies* 82(3) (1991): 97–106.

Sapon-Shevin, M. "Schools Fit for All." *Educational Leadership* 58(4) (2001): 34–39.

Schmuck, R. A., and P. A. Schmuck. *Group Processes in the Classroom* (8th edition). New York: McGraw-Hill, 2001.

Scotty-Ryan, D. L. *An Investigative Study of How Cooperative Learning Can Benefit High-Achieving Students.* M.S. thesis, State University of New York at Brockport, 1998.

Slavin, R. E. *Cooperative Learning: Theory, Research and Practice.* Englewood Cliffs, NJ: Prentice Hall, 1990.

Slavin, R. E. *Cooperative Learning: Theory, Research and Practice* (2nd edition). Boston: Allyn and Bacon, 1995.

Smith, C. B. *Skills Students Use When Speaking and Listening: ERIC Topical Bibliography and Commentary.* Bloomington, IN: ERIC Clearinghouse on Reading, English, and Communication, 2003. ED 480 895.

Soja, C. M., and D. Huerta. "Debating Whether Dinosaurs Should Be 'Cloned' from Ancient DNA to Promote Cooperative Learning in an Introductory Evolution Course." *Journal of Geoscience Education* 49(2) (2001): 150–157.

Sparapani, E. F. "Encouraging Thinking in High School and Middle School: Constraints and Possibilities." *Clearing House* 71(5) (1998): 274–276.

Stevens, R. J., and R. E. Slavin. "The Cooperative Elementary School: Effects on Students' Achievement, Attitudes and Social Relations." *American Educational Research Journal* 32(2) (1995a): 321–351.

Stevens, R. J., and R. E. Slavin. "Effects of a Cooperative Learning Approach in Reading and Writing on Academically Handicapped and Non-Handicapped Students." *Elementary School Journal* 95(3) (1995b): 241–262.

Tate, M. L. *Worksheets Don't Grow Dendrites: 20 Instructional Strategies That Engage the Brain.* Thousand Oaks, CA: Corwin, 2003.

van Ments, M. *The Effective Use of Role-Play: Practical Techniques for Improving Learning* (2nd edition). London: Kogan Page, 1999.

Verker, K. W. "Simulations: Interdisciplinary Instruction at its Best." *Hispania* 86(2) (2003): 322–325.

Vermette, P. J. *Making Cooperative Learning Work: Student Teams in K–12 Classrooms.* Upper Saddle River, NJ: Merrill, 1998.

Vessels, G. "The First Amendment and Character Education." *Update on Law-Related Education* 20(1) (1996): 26–28.

Walberg, H. J. "Productive Teaching." In *New Directions for Teaching Practice and Research.* H. C. Waxman and H. J. Walberg, editors. Berkeley, CA: McCutchan, 1999.

Webb, N. M., J. Trooper, and R. Fall. "Constructive Activity and Learning in Collaborative Small Groups." *Journal of Educational Psychology* 87(3) (1995): 406–423.

Weissglass, J. "Transforming Schools into Caring Learning Communities." *Journal for a Just and Caring Education* 2(2) (1996): 175–189.

Wolford, P. L., W. L. Heward, and S. R. Alber. "Teaching Middle School Students with Learning Disabilities to Recruit Peer Assistance During Cooperative Learning Group Activities." *Learning Disabilities: Research and Practice* 16(3) (2001): 161–173.

Yell, M. M. "The Time Before History: Thinking Like an Archaeologist." *Social Education* 62(1) (1998): 27–31.

Zhang, Q. "An Intervention Model of Constructive Conflict Resolution and Cooperative Learning." *Journal of Social Issues* 50(1) (1994): 99–116.

Zuckerman, G. A. "A Pilot Study of a Ten-Day Course in Cooperative Learning for Beginning Russian First Graders." *Elementary School Journal* 94(4) (1994): 405–420.

Zuckerman, G. A., E. V. Chudinova, and E. E. Khavkin. "Inquiry as a Pivotal Element of Knowledge Acquisition Within the Vogotskian Paradigm: Building a Science Curriculum for the Elementary School." *Cognition and Instruction* 16(2) (1998): 201–233.

Inquiry Teaching and Higher-Level Thinking

1

HELPING STUDENTS BECOME BETTER THINKERS

Defining Thinking (and Higher-Level Thinking)

How Successful Have We Been at Teaching Thinking?

Structuring Instruction for Success in Teaching Thinking

2

INQUIRY TEACHING

The Basic Elements of Inquiry Teaching

Inductive Instructional Models

3

METHODS FOR DEVELOPING HIGHER-LEVEL THINKING SKILLS

Problem Solving

Discovery Learning

Techniques for Developing Critical Thinking Skills

Assessing Higher-Level Thinking Activities

Kuni Ozone's social studies class is the designated site for your in-school observations. As you approach the room, you hear the buzz of meaningful noise. Students are working in small groups of three to five; a few students are at the computer center, which is neatly arranged in the far corner of the room; and the teacher is helping a small group of students with learning disabilities align their data on a large poster. The walls of the room are covered with the students' work. Their projects resemble the posters at a professional convention.

A student invites you to work with the group. You observe the division of labor among the students. After about thirty minutes, Kuni calls everyone together, and the recorders from three groups give short oral reports to the class. Students question the presenters, and a lively verbal interaction occurs. The teacher then writes a few specific assignments on the chalkboard, and students begin individual seat-work.

"Wow," you say to yourself, "I wonder if I can pull this style off?"

Traditionally, teachers present knowledge to students, who passively absorb it, and this pattern becomes both the means and the end of education. Is it any wonder, then, that students get bored? As an alternative to routine lectures and recitations, we offer an instructional strategy that is not new but is centuries old. The generic term for the strategy is **inquiry teaching**, an investigative learning process that asks students to pose questions, analyze data, and develop conclusions or generalizations. It can also be referred to as *discovery, problem solving, reflective thinking,* and *inductive teaching,* among other terms. It is associated with teaching techniques and methods that all have one thing in common: encouraging higher-level thinking. In this chapter, we discuss these techniques and describe their major characteristics. After you finish studying it, you'll be able to answer the following questions.

- Can we really teach kids how to think?
- What is inquiry teaching?
- How can I use it in my classroom?
- What techniques are associated with inquiry teaching?

SECTION 1: HELPING STUDENTS BECOME BETTER THINKERS

Although few people would disagree that educating students to become good learners and responsible citizens means that they must also be good thinkers, the road toward that goal is not automatic. Helping students reach that goal takes knowledge, awareness, and planning on the part of the teacher. We use this first section to examine three key aspects of the effective teaching of thinking skills. First, we explore the concept of thinking itself; then we examine just how successful our schools have been thus far in encouraging the development of thinking skills; and finally we present our own framework for how this essential goal might be better accomplished.

Defining Thinking (and Higher-Level Thinking)

What do we mean by *thinking*? The word is a construct, a label we apply to processes we can observe only indirectly through actions or products. In other words, when someone behaves in a careful, prudent manner, we infer that the behavior resulted from deliberate thought. When we observe an example of complex problem solving—space flight, for instance—we infer the incredible amounts of reasoning that were necessary.

Attempts to define thinking—beyond such synonyms as *reasoning* or *forming an idea*—become clouded by differences of psychological position. Despite the lack of consensus on the definition of thinking, we can still characterize it and suggest ways to make it more effective.

We propose that thinking is a combination of knowledge, skills or processes, and attitudes. Knowledge is involved, of course, because thinking requires an object. One must think about *something*. The more knowledge one has in any area, the more effectively one can think about it (Shayer and Adey 2002; Sternberg and Spear-Swerling 1996).

Effective thinking also requires particular attitudes, such as a disposition to perceive and relate to one's surroundings in particular ways. Some people, for instance, are curious about their environment; others are not. Attitude determines in part *what* we think about and in *what ways* we think about it (see the box below).

Combination of knowledge, skills, and attitudes

Attitudes That Promote Effective Thinking

- Willingness to suspend judgment until sufficient evidence is presented
- Tolerance for ambiguity
- A tendency to question rather than simply accept authority
- Willingness to believe credible evidence

Thus we arrive at the following definition: **thinking** is a complex act comprising attitudes, knowledge, and skills that allows the individual to shape his or her environment more effectively than intuition alone.

Now let us focus on higher-level thinking skills. Think back to our discussion of Bloom's cognitive taxonomy (Chapter 3). Recall that two of Bloom's higher levels are analysis and synthesis. **Higher-level thinking** skills, also known as critical thinking, consist of the application of these two levels. Critical thinking is a multistage construction of meaning. It is rational and logical and results in high levels of student achievement (see Marzano, Pickering, and Pollock 2001; Walberg 1999). To learn critical thinking skills, your students need to learn the skills listed in the box below.

Higher-level skills in Bloom's taxonomy

Thinking is a multifaceted process, not a singular one.

Elements of Critical Thinking

- Identifying issues
- Identifying relationships between elements
- Deducing implications
- Inferring motives
- Combining independent elements to create new patterns of thought (creativity)
- Making original interpretations (creativity)

How Successful Have We Been at Teaching Thinking?

National Data   It is one thing to identify and define thinking and higher-level thinking skills; it is quite another to successfully teach them to students. The single best source for standardized and nationally collected data on the general topic comes from the National Assessment of Educational Progress (NAEP). Since 1969, the NAEP has intermittently tested nine-, thirteen-, and seventeen-year-olds (grades 4, 8, and 11) in civics, science, mathematics, reading, and writing.

We recognize that fourth-graders may not be cognitively developed to process formal thinking questions (see Table 2.1, page 33), which are posed at the three upper levels of Bloom's taxonomy and the NAEP levels. Fourth-graders do very well at the two lower cognitive levels, again corresponding developmentally to the concrete operations levels. Eighth- and eleventh-graders truly shine at these levels.

International Comparisons   It may have escaped notice due to lack of publicity, but compared to other nations' students, U.S. students are doing a lot better than critics of our education system give them credit for. In fact, there is cause for qualified joy. In 1992, the National Science Foundation compared the achievement of thirteen-year-old mathematics students in the United States states with performance of other nations (Suter 1996). Taiwan was tops, followed by Iowa, South Korea, North Dakota, and Minnesota. Twelve of the top twenty were United States states, including Idaho, Utah, Wyoming, and Colorado.

In much the same way, a 1998 report issued by the National Center for Educational Statistics compared thirteen-year-old science students in individual states against each other and against students in other nations. It showed that United States states held fourteen of the top fifteen places in the world, if the data were disaggregated by state(Johnson and Siegendorf 1998).

Three other important studies should be touched on here. The *Programme for International Student Assessment* (PISA) is a report issued by the Organization for Economic Cooperation and Development that focuses on reading literacy in thirty-two countries. It found that

- Finland, which led all countries, and the United States had scores that were at the mean national level indicator, that is, among the higher group.
- Children in the United States were among the highest scorers in reading, yet were among the "least engaged" readers in the world.
- Worldwide students whose parents had higher-status jobs tended to have the best reading attitudes and habits (*Reading for Change* 2002).

A study called *Comparative Indicators of Education in the United States and Other G-8 Countries: 2002* provides an interesting snapshot of student achievement in the eight most powerful economies of the world: Canada, France, Germany, Italy, Japan, the Russian Federation, the United Kingdom, and the United States. Data sources were assembled from several different surveys, including the PISA, already discussed (Sherman et al. 2003).

The study of these so-called G-8 nations is a veritable library of information about schooling and student achievement at various levels. Here's what it reveals about the United States' standing compared to its economic peers.

- In fourth-grade mathematics and science achievement, only Japanese children were ahead of U.S. children. (Note, however, that in some G-8 nations, fifth-graders took the exam.)
- Eighth-grade math and science achievement found U.S. children at about the median. (Keep in mind at grade 8, most G-8 nations have already segregated students into academic and vocational tracks. This is not so in the United States.)
- The fourteen-year-olds in the United States led the G-8 nations in total civic knowledge and civic skills. These same children reported they would be "active citizens" and would be voters.
- In all G-8 countries, those students who completed higher education showed significantly higher relative earnings when compared to those without higher education.

The third study is the recently released *Progress in International Reading Literacy Study* (PIRLS), which surveyed thirty-five countries. It found that only Sweden outperformed the Netherlands and the United States in reading literacy (Mullis et al. 2003).

David C. Berliner (2004) summarizes the findings this way: "The fundamental premise underlying the legislation known as the No Child Left Behind Act (NCLB) is that the public schools of the United States are failing. But that is a half-truth at best" (p. 167).

Findings challenge NCLB.

Here's more good news. On July 11, 2001, the College Board announced, "A new study of the TIMSS International Study Center shows that Advanced Placement students [in the United States] who score three or higher [on a five-point scale] on physics and calculus AP Exams outperform physics and advanced math students from the United States and other countries in mathematics and science achievement" (*College Board News* 2001). Lee Jones, executive director of the College Board's Advanced Placement Program, stated, "These results demonstrate that students who do well on the AP Calculus and Physics Exams are indeed at the top of the world in academic achievement."

So teachers must be doing something right. We'll spend some time in the following discussion examining what you as a teacher can and should do "right" as you approach the teaching of thinking skills. (See Orlich 2000, 2002, 2003 for a critical analysis and interesting perspective about the issue of developmentally inappropriate tests.)

Structuring Instruction for Success in Teaching Thinking

First, what does it mean to teach thinking? Nearly all writers agree on the generic aspects of thinking highlighted in the box on page 294 (Lyons and LaBoskey 2002; Wallace and Bentley 2002; Weinbaum et al. 2004). These five skills are core skills. To build these skills requires careful teacher planning, appropriate sequencing, and a continuous building of cognitive and attitudinal factors.

> ## Core Skills of Thinking
>
> - Perception of a problem or issue
> - Ability to gather relevant information
> - Competence in organizing data
> - Analysis of data patterns, inferences, sources of errors
> - Communication of the results

Three aspects of thinking can be identified and taught to students—knowledge, skills, and attitudes. The assumption, of course, is that students will think more effectively as a result of learning these three aspects—that they will be able to relate to and alter their environment better than they otherwise would. Considerable empirical evidence supports this view (see Selwyn and Maher 2003; Wakefield 1996). In fact, we would go as far as saying that helping students identify and use these skills must be a basic part of instruction in *all* classes if students are to benefit from schooling.

Teach knowledge, skills, attitudes.

So, more specifically, what do we mean when we say you can help students become more effective thinkers? Do teachers need to add a new course in thinking to the curriculum? Do teachers need to teach a new content area or a new group of process skills?

The answer isn't simple. Instead, we believe that teachers need to take a threefold approach to the teaching of thinking, especially the teaching of higher-level or critical thinking. First, you need to develop an overall awareness—a kind of infusion of the need to focus on thinking in all classes at all times. In other words, you must systematically and continually instruct them in ways to think more effectively. Thinking must be taught across all subjects and all grade levels. Teachers must stress meaningfulness, but children must be taught how to understand and think (see Jones 2003 for a rich resource). For example, you might have the students ask one *reflective question* (Chapter 7) after they read some passage for study. Or, after you have introduced concepts, such as *infer, classify, hypothesize,* you might challenge the class to use those process skills in some pending assignment. By continuously reviewing thinking skills, you establish a base of knowledge and an attitude of inquiry (see Shayer and Adey 2002).

Second, we believe the adoption of an inquiry-based teaching strategy will greatly facilitate your teaching of thinking skills. At the core of this approach is an emphasis on student exploration and understanding. Third, you should know how to use some specific methods and teaching techniques that are themselves offshoots or "relatives" of the inquiry model; we present a number of these at the end of the chapter (Martin-Hansen 2002).

You should always bear in mind that the teacher is the most important factor in thinking instruction (Shayer and Adey 2002). Prepared texts, workbooks, preplanned programs, and drill exercises may be useful instructional aids, but by themselves they are insufficient to induce thinking abilities. The most effective instruction emanates from a teacher who is knowledgeable about both subject matter and thinking processes, who continually demonstrates the skills and attitudes involved in thinking, and who demands systematic, rigorous thought from students—both in speaking and in writing. In this regard, it is the teacher who can add the dimension of meaning. Make your students think about what meaning they might derive from school subjects. It is up to you to provide the bases for meaning when new topics and concepts are introduced. For example, Jacqueline N. Glasgow (2001) shows how easy it is to use political issues, such as social justice, to develop student critical thinking skills.

Also, realize that many—perhaps most—of the students you will teach will belong to minority ethnic or cultural groups. You can help them achieve at the highest academic levels if you demand it *and* if you try to relate the content, skills, or knowledge you are teaching to some artifact in their culture. Meaning is derived by moving from the known to the unknown. Be sensitive to the needs of all students, and be aware of teachable moments for students you may label as "minorities" (see Banks 2003).

Finally, reflect on how you can incorporate the concept of multimethodology into the entire realm of inquiry and critical thinking. There is really no limit to the number of ways that you may approach these powerful teaching strategies.

Teacher adds meaning to the materials.

Critical thinking is for every student.

reflect

- What topics or units in your teaching field would be appropriate for stressing thinking processes?

- Examine your state's and school district's NAEP data for selected subjects. What can you conclude about the level of thinking skills shown?

- How can you structure classroom questions to stimulate student thinking development?

SECTION 2: INQUIRY TEACHING

In this section, we first present several underlying bases for inquiry-based teaching and take a brief look at its relationship to the constructivist philosophy. We then explore in detail how two different instructional models based on the inquiry strategy can be used for instruction in your classroom.

The Basic Elements of Inquiry Teaching

Theoretical Bases of Inquiry Methods   All inquiry methods are predicated on specific assumptions about both learning and learners. The box on page 296 provides a synthesis of the views on the subject by several scholars (Bigge and Shermis 2004; Holcomb 2004; Joyce and Calhoun 1998; van Zee et al. 2001).

video case

To develop higher-level thinking, put students in charge of their own learning. Innovative teacher Jenerra Williams applies this approach to poetry writing in the Video Case "Elementary School Language Arts: Inquiry Learning." How do her techniques follow the points in the box "Basic Tenets of Inquiry Teaching"?

Basic Tenets of Inquiry Teaching

- Inquiry methods require the learner to develop various processes associated with inquiry.
- Teachers and principals must support the concept of inquiry teaching and learn how to adapt their own teaching and administrative styles to the concept.
- Students at all ages and levels have a genuine interest in discovering something new or in providing solutions or alternatives to unsolved questions or problems.
- The solutions, alternatives, or responses provided by learners are not found in textbooks. Students use reference materials and textbooks during inquiry lessons just as scientists and professionals use books, articles, and references to conduct their work.
- The objective of inquiry teaching is often a *process*. In many instances, the end product of an inquiry activity is relatively unimportant compared to the processes used to create it.
- All conclusions must be considered relative or tentative, not final. Students must learn to modify their conclusions as new data are discovered.
- Inquiry learning cannot be gauged by the clock. In the real world, when people think or create, it is not usually done in fifty-minute increments.
- Learners are responsible for planning, conducting, and evaluating their own efforts. It is essential that the teacher play only a *supportive* role, not an active one (that is, the teacher should not do the work for the students).
- Students have to be taught the processes associated with inquiry learning in a systematic manner. Every time a "teachable moment" arrives, the teacher should capitalize on it to further the building of inquiry processes.
- Inquiry learning complicates and expands the teacher's work, owing to the many interactions that may emanate from inquiry teaching and learning.

Inquiry teaching requires a high degree of interaction among the learner, the teacher, the materials, the content, and the environment. Perhaps the most crucial aspect of the inquiry method is that it allows both student and teacher to become persistent askers, seekers, interrogators, questioners, and ponderers. The end result occurs when your students pose the question every Nobel Prize winner has asked: "I wonder what would happen if . . . ?" It is through inquiry that new knowledge is discovered. It is by becoming involved in the process that students become historians, scientists, economists, artists, businesspersons, poets, writers, or researchers—even if only for an hour or two, in your class.

Teacher and students as seekers, askers

Recall that in Chapter 7 we urged you to develop the question-asking skills of all students. In this chapter, we take questioning a step further, for it plays a crucial role in both the teaching and learning acts associated with the inquiry mode of learning. The investigative processes of inquiry learning involve the student not only in formulating questions but also in limiting them, selecting the best means of answering them, and conducting the study.

Basic Inquiry Processes   The basic processes of inquiry learning are listed in the box below somewhat in order of complexity.

VIDEO case

Science teacher Richard Cho uses hands-on inquiry techniques for a lesson on the Grand Canyon in the video "Middle School Science Instruction: Inquiry Learning." Compare what you see to the list of inquiry processes on this page. Are they compatible?

Inquiry Processes

1. *Observing.* Identifying objects, object properties, and changes in various systems; making controlled observations; ordering series of observations
2. *Classifying.* Making simple and complex classifications; tabulating and coding observations
3. *Inferring.* Drawing conclusions based on observations; constructing situations to test these conclusions
4. *Using numbers.* Identifying sets and their members and then progressing to higher mathematical processes
5. *Measuring.* Identifying and ordering lengths and then areas, volumes, weights, temperatures, and speeds
6. *Using space-time relationships.* Identifying movement and direction; learning rules governing changes in position
7. *Communicating.* Constructing graphs and diagrams to describe simple and then more complex phenomena; presenting written and oral reports
8. *Predicting.* Interpolating and extrapolating from data; formulating methods for testing predictions
9. *Making operational definitions.* Distinguishing between operational and nonoperational definitions; constructing operational definitions for new problems
10. *Formulating hypotheses.* Distinguishing hypotheses from inferences, observations, and predictions; constructing and testing hypotheses
11. *Interpreting data.* Describing data and inferences based on them; constructing equations to represent data; relating data to hypotheses; making generalizations supported by experimental findings
12. *Controlling variables.* Identifying independent and dependent variables; conducting experiments; describing how variables are controlled
13. *Experimenting.* Interpreting accounts of scientific experiments; stating problems; constructing hypotheses; conducting experimental procedures

Note that each **inquiry process** requires progressive intellectual development and that as this development takes place for one process, it spurs development on other processes. Development of observing, classifying, and measuring skills, for example, speeds development of inferring skills.

These processes are found in every learning episode that involves inquiry. Inquiry is not simply asking questions; it is a process for conducting a thorough investigation, and as such, it applies to all domains of knowledge.

Each inquiry process—that is, the thirteen processes in the box on page 297—must be carefully developed and systematically practiced. This means that you must decide how much of *each lesson* will be devoted to building cognitive skills and how much to mastering processes—just as you did when you planned small-group discussions (see Chapter 8).

Constructivism and Inquiry Teaching   In Chapter 2, we introduce the topic of constructivism. In our opinion, there is a near perfect match between the notion of constructivism and the inquiry model of learning (see Ishii 2003).

Being "constructive" means that your students apply those thirteen process skills just presented. You, as the teacher, must make the invitation to students to learn through inquiry, and you must direct them to the proper tools. In Chapter 8, we refer to a cooperative lesson in world geography in which students compare the United States and Europe (see Richburg and Nelson 1991). Although the exercise was created for cooperative learning groups, it is precisely the kind of experience that can be adapted for inquiry and constructivist teaching. The exercise encourages active learning: Students must synthesize data, classify information, make inferences, communicate individual findings to everyone else, and evaluate their ideas or conclusions.

Inquiry as constructivism and active learning

An important tenet of the constructivist philosophy is that knowledge is constructed by different thought processes and patterns of thinking (Phillips and Soltis 2004). As you read this chapter, you will observe the development of the elements contained in all inquiry-based learning, including problem solving, discovery, and critical thinking skills that require information to be processed and new patterns or ideas to emerge.

Another tenet of constructivism is that learners construct knowledge through active engagement or experiences. This does not preclude memorization of key facts or events; however, the learner needs to *do* something— read, study, observe, write, discuss, chart, graph, map, or communicate. Jack Uldrich (2004) illustrates how the Lewis and Clark Corps of Discovery can become an active classroom experience. This kind of dynamic experimentation is also an essential part of the inquiry method.

Experiences are key.

Finally, in a constructivist approach to education, *the student assumes responsibility for acquiring knowledge*. As you become experienced at conducting inquiry-oriented classes, you will allow more student-initiated learning; this is definitely an example of using a constructivist notion.

It is important to recognize that constructivism is not an instructional model, such as direct instruction; it is a theoretical model about how learners come to know (Airasian and Walsh 1997). We also caution that, unlike inquiry methods that have been used in the sciences for centuries, constructivism does not entail a set of procedural steps.

Inquiry teaching takes time and much teacher energy. In our experience, we have never seen inquiry-oriented teachers sitting at their desks—they are on the go, and so are their students. Constructivist teachers behave the same way. We recognize that there are differences in social interpretations of the two approaches, but that is a topic for another book. Virginia Richardson (2003) provides a critical analysis of constructivist pedagogy showing its many interpretations and practices. See the box below for a synthesized set of commonalities between constructivist and inquiry-oriented teachers.

Points of Agreement Between the Constructivist and Inquiry-Oriented Approaches

- The focus is on the student.
- The pace of instruction is flexible, not fixed.
- Students are encouraged to search for implications.
- Students are encouraged to generate multiple conclusions.
- Students must justify their methods for problem solving.
- Neither constructivism nor inquiry sees itself as the sole learning model for all content.
- Nature provides the objects, and humans classify them.

---

reflect

- Locate any book about the constructivist teaching philosophy. Compare the list in the box on page 296, on basic tenets of inquiry teaching, to lists developed by constructivist writers. What do you find?

- Show the list of thirteen processes to peers who are studying art, history, or literature. Ask them to relate those processes to their respective disciplines.

Inductive Instructional Models

We have established the basics of inquiry as a teaching strategy. Now let's look at models of **empirical epistemology**: gaining knowledge through observation or experiment. In Chapter 5, we introduced inductive teaching. Remember that induction is a thought process wherein the individual observes selected events, processes, or objects and then constructs a particular pattern of concepts or relationships based on these limited experiences. **Inductive inquiry** is a teaching method in which teachers ask students to infer a conclusion, generalization, or pattern of relationships from a set of data or facts. Inductive inquiry may be approached in at least two different ways: guided and unguided. If you provide the specifics—that is, the data or facts—but want the students to make the generalizations, then you are conducting **guided inductive inquiry** (Tamir 1995). If you allow students to discover the specifics themselves before they make generalizations, the process is **unguided inductive inquiry**. In most cases, you will begin with guided experiences. This way you will know there is a fixed number of generalizations or conclusions that can reasonably be inferred, and you can then help

Guided (you provide the specifics) or unguided

students make them from the data provided. The guided method provides an easy transition from expository teaching to less expository teaching.

Inductive inquiry is appropriate at all levels of instruction, from preschool to university graduate schools. At any level, the processes of observing, making inferences, classifying, formulating hypotheses, and predicting are all sharpened (or reinforced) by the students' experiences (see Haury 2002).

Guided Inductive Inquiry   Pictures are usually the easiest way to introduce the concept of inductive inquiry. For young children, show different pictures of the same scene to the class. Ask the children to tell what they see in the pictures and to describe patterns they observe. Have them state these patterns as generalizations. Ask questions that require students to do some generalizing themselves, such as "What could cause this type of track in the snow?" or "Where have we seen this before?"

Distinguish clearly between statements based on observations and those based on inferences. Begin the lesson by explaining and demonstrating the difference between observations and inferences. As the children respond to your questions, ask, "Is that an inference or an observation?"

The process of inductive thinking is developed gradually. As the lesson progresses, prepare a simple chart or list on the blackboard of students' observations and inferences. Students' understanding of each process will gradually develop from studying these examples. This strategy was applied even to students who were challenged to describe combinations of pizza toppings and then construct a math theorem that could predict the number given the ingredients. (see Nord, Malm, and Nord 2002).

At all levels, ask students to make a list their observations and, beside them, their inferences or generalizations. The Instructional Strategies box below lists the steps to be used in arriving at generalizations through guided inductive inquiry.

INSTRUCTIONAL STRATEGIES

Steps for Guided Inductive Inquiry

1. Decide on the generalization(s) students should make during a particular unit of study.
2. Organize the learning activities and materials in a manner that exposes the strands or parts of the generalization(s) to students.
3. Ask students to write a summary of the content that will form the basis of the generalization(s).
4. Ask students to identify sequences or patterns of events, objects, or other data in the content.
5. Ask students to summarize these sequences or patterns in one sentence.
6. Ask students to offer proof that their statement is, in fact, a generalization by applying it to other events, objects, or data.

SOURCE: James G. Womack, *Discovering the Structure of Social Studies.* Copyright © 1966 Benziger Brothers. Reprinted with permission.

reflect	• Search the literature or the Internet for two types of inductive inquiry experiences that you can use in your teaching. • Examine a textbook published in the past three years. What inquiry exercises or experiences do the authors provide? • Explain this quote: "When you teach with the inquiry model, you teach less, but your students learn more."

Time Requirements   When you first use any type of inquiry activity in your classes, plan to spend at least twice as much class time on each lesson as you normally would. This time is spent on in-depth analyses of the content by the students. Inquiry methods demand greater interaction between the learner and the learning materials, as well as greater interaction between the teacher and the students (see Boss 2003).

At the same time, be prepared to reduce the amount of content you will cover because you will use more time developing process skills and less time covering facts. *You cannot maximize thinking skills and simultaneously maximize content coverage.* If you wish to build higher-order thinking skills, you must reduce some of the content and substitute processes instead (see Eylon and Linn 1988). By doing so, however, you will provide important instructional experiences that the student can apply across all disciplines.

Steps in Guided Inductive Inquiry   Figure 9.1 shows six major steps in the inquiry system it illustrates: (1) identifying the problem, (2) developing tentative research hypotheses or objectives, (3) collecting data and testing the tentative answers, (4) interpreting the data, (5) developing tentative conclusions or generalizations, and (6) testing, applying, and revising the conclusions. This model can be adapted to other inquiry models, such as problem solving (discussed later). These steps form the basis of what is called "the scientific method." (Strictly speaking, our models are adaptations of the Hypothetico-Deductive Model described by Sir Karl R. Popper, 1975.)

Inquiry learning cannot be rushed.

You will usually follow these steps for introductory guided inductive lessons. Recall that the process objectives are to observe, to infer, and to communicate. The problem, in this case, is to find a meaningful pattern in an array of events or objects. All inferences must be supported by some evidence—that is, observations or data. The latter may be obtained from some standard reference source such as the *Statistical Abstract of the United States,* almanacs, yearbooks, reports, or encyclopedias. The data become the focal point of the inquiry session and thus serve as a common experience for the entire class (see Holcomb 2004; Orlich 1989). Guided inductive inquiry includes the seven characteristics listed in the box on page 302.

Students must find the pattern.

Characteristics of Guided Inductive Inquiry Model

1. Learners progress from specific observations to inferences or generalizations.
2. The objective is to learn (or reinforce) the process of examining events or objects and then arriving at an appropriate generalization from the observations.
3. The teacher controls the specifics of the lesson—the events, data, materials, or objects—and thus acts as the class leader.
4. Each student reacts to the specifics and attempts to structure a meaningful pattern based on his or her observations and those of others in the class.
5. The classroom is to be considered a learning laboratory.
6. Usually, a fixed number of generalizations will be elicited from the learners.
7. The teacher encourages each student to communicate his or her generalizations to the class so that others may benefit from them.

FIGURE 9.1
A General Model of Inquiry

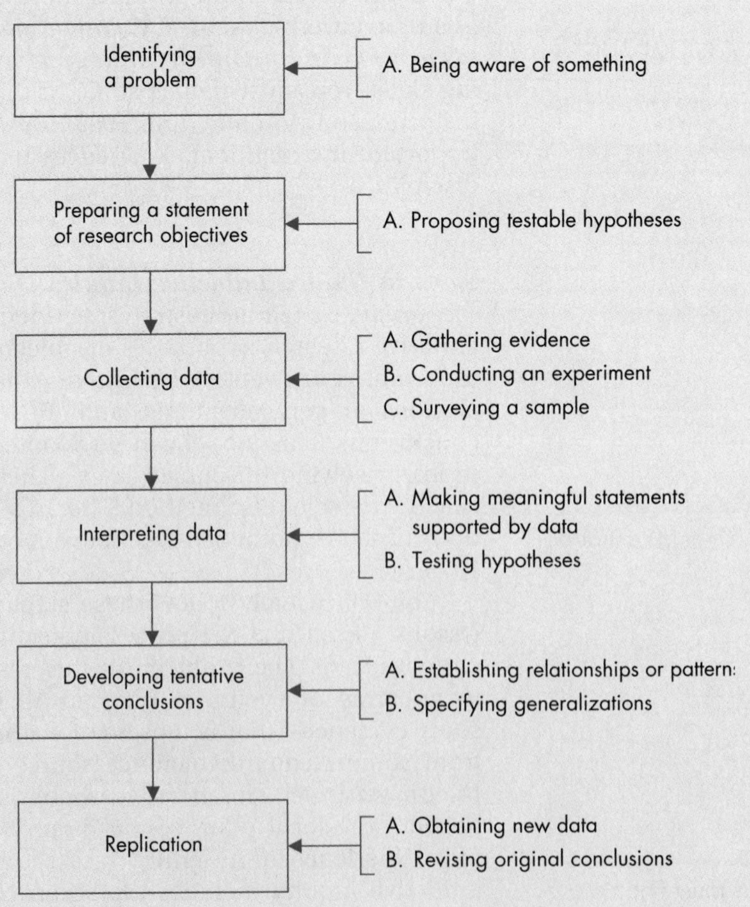

Identifying a problem
A. Being aware of something

Preparing a statement of research objectives
A. Proposing testable hypotheses

Collecting data
A. Gathering evidence
B. Conducting an experiment
C. Surveying a sample

Interpreting data
A. Making meaningful statements supported by data
B. Testing hypotheses

Developing tentative conclusions
A. Establishing relationships or pattern:
B. Specifying generalizations

Replication
A. Obtaining new data
B. Revising original conclusions

At this point, you may be thinking, "This certainly sounds like constructivism to me." For the most part, you would be correct. Constructivism is based on the idea that learners construct knowledge from their own thoughts, activities, and experience. What learners understand may be quite different from what the teacher understands. By scheduling time for children to ask questions and share their observations with one another, you will help them construct a more empirical sense of reality. By using inquiry, you challenge the student to ask questions and seek solutions (see Patrick 2003b).

Examples of Guided Inductive Inquiry An example of guided inductive inquiry is presented in the Instructional Strategies box below. This example is a clever guided inquiry exercise that allows students to learn about paper towel strength from their own observations. This activity demonstrates how easy it is to adapt elements of guided inductive inquiry to consumer issues. Sharon Brendzel (2002) provides sample questions, topics for discussion, and methods to determine absorbency in a classic guided inductive experience.

INSTRUCTIONAL STRATEGIES

Adapting Guided Inductive Inquiry to Consumer Issues: Best Deal in Paper Towels

- Provide sheets of different brands of paper towels.
- Ask students to design an absorbency test.
- Students work in small inquiry groups.
- Students share results.
- Students reach conclusions based on data.

The Role of Questioning Within Guided Inductive Inquiry We have noted that teacher questioning plays an important role in inquiry methods because the purpose of inquiry is to pursue an investigation. The teacher thus becomes a question asker, not a question answerer. Teachers who are masters of guided induction inquiry state that they spend their time interacting with students but provide very few answers (see Phillips and German 2002).

What kinds of questions should a teacher ask? The boxes on page 304 list relevant question stems or lead-in questions for teachers who want to have a more inquiry-oriented class environment (Orlich and Migaki 1981). These question stems are suitable for use in social studies, literature, science, and mathematics—any class in which the teacher wants to stress the process of inquiry. Note that the first box is oriented to dynamic situations. These stems are probably best classified as prompting questions, similar to those described in Chapter 7. If you are examining more static living or nonliving objects, the stems shown in the second box will prove very useful. Again, note that these prompting questions help the student to examine all kinds of interrelationships—one of the desired goals of inquiry teaching and constructivism.

Questions can be adapted to all subject areas.

Question Stems: Dynamic Subjects

- What is happening?
- What has happened?
- What do you think will happen now?
- How did this happen?
- Why did this happen?
- What caused this to happen?
- What took place before this happened?
- Where have you seen something like this happen?
- When have you seen something like this happen?
- How could you make this happen?
- How does this compare with what you saw or did?
- How can you do this more easily?
- How can you do this more quickly?

SOURCE for both boxes: Reprinted with permission from D. C. Orlich and J. M. Migaki, "What Is Your IQQ—Individual Questioning Quotient?," NSTA Publications. Copyright © 1981 National Science Teachers Association. Reproduced with permission of National Science Teachers Association via Copyright Clearance Center.

Question Stems: Static Subjects

- What kind of object is it?
- What is it called?
- Where is it found?
- What does it look like?
- Have you ever seen anything like it? Where? When?
- How is it like other things?
- How can you recognize or identify it?
- How did it get its name?
- What can you do with it?
- What is it made of?
- How was it made?
- What is its purpose?
- How does it work or operate?
- What other names does it have?
- How is it different from other things?

Table 9.1 provides examples of guided inductive inquiry in social studies at four different grade levels. The examples for grades 2, 7, and 10 are static, but think about how they could be connected to dynamic lessons. For grade 12 U.S. government classes, the examination of current events provides an easy application of dynamic inquiry teaching episodes. Be advised that several of the examples shown in Table 9.1 are very similar to actual test items used in the NAEP 1994 U.S. History Assessment (Beatty et al. 1996). The authors of

TABLE 9.1

Guided Inductive Inquiry: Social Studies Lessons

Grade Level	Materials	Questions	Processes
2	Magazine pictures of houses from around the world	What traits can you identify in these pictures?	Observing Inferring Communicating
7	Pamphlets and posters about World War II	What explicit and implicit messages are communicated by these materials?	Inferring Hypothesizing
10	Political cartoons	What are the key ideas and meanings conveyed by these cartoons? What is their context? What biases do they reveal?	Inferring Hypothesizing Making contextual references
12	A controversial court decision	What actions caused this case? What do you think will happen next? Have we studied any events similar to those in this case?	Analyzing Predicting Comparing

that report also stated, "The NAEP 1994 U.S. History Assessment was rigorous; many tasks demanded knowledge of complex events and concepts and *abilities to analyze and interpret*" (p. 74, emphasis added).

REFLECT

- Think of a lesson with which you are familiar and create a guided inductive inquiry experience for use in teaching it.

- How can you restructure curriculum materials to make them more inquiry oriented for your students?

- How is thinking enhanced by guided inductive inquiry experiences?

Unguided Inductive Inquiry   As we have seen, during guided inductive inquiry, you, the teacher, play the key role in asking questions, prompting responses, and structuring the materials and situations. Again, using guided inductive inquiry is an excellent way to begin the shift from expository or deductive teaching to teaching that is less structured and more open to alternative solutions. Once the class has mastered the techniques of guided inductive inquiry, you can introduce or allow for student-initiated situations that enable the students to take more responsibility for examining data, objects,

More student initiated than teacher initiated

and events. Because the teacher's role is minimized, the students' activity increases. The Key Ideas box below summarizes the major elements of unguided inductive inquiry.

KEY IDeas

Elements of Unguided Inductive Inquiry

1. Learners progress from making specific observations to making inferences or generalizations.
2. The objective is to learn (or reinforce) the processes of examining events, objects, and data and then to arrive at appropriate sets of generalizations.
3. The teacher may control only the materials provided or encourage student-initiated materials. He or she poses a question, such as "What can you generalize from . . . ?" or "Tell me everything that you can about X after examining these . . ."
4. The students, using the materials provided and without further teacher guidance, ask all the questions that come to mind.
5. The materials are essential to making the classroom a laboratory.
6. Meaningful patterns are generated by students through individual observations and inferences and through interactions with other students.
7. The teacher does not limit the generalizations students make.
8. The teacher encourages all students to communicate their generalizations so that all may benefit from each individual's unique inferences.

When you begin to use unguided inductive inquiry, a new set of teacher behaviors must come into play. You must now begin to act as the **classroom clarifier**, guiding students to develop logical thinking skills. As students start to make their generalizations, gross errors in student logic are bound to appear: Students will make generalizations that are too broad, infer single cause-and-effect relationships where there are several, and perceive cause-and-effect relationships where none exist. When such errors occur, you must patiently question the learner in a *nonthreatening* manner to verify the conclusion or generalizations. If errors exist in the student's logic or inferences, point them out. But you should *not* tell the student what the correct inference is, for this would defeat the purpose of any inquiry episode. These types of errors might appear in guided inquiry, but in that model the teacher is controlling the flow of information and can be more subtly directive through questioning (see Hoge 2003). There is much less direct teacher probing in unguided inquiry.

Teacher clarifies, but does not provide inference.

Inquiry techniques lead to student excitement when discovering concepts not found in a textbook. © Joel Gordon.

We suggest that you have students work alone during initial unguided inductive experiences. When students work alone, they tend to do most of the work themselves. When they work in pairs or triads without training as discussed in Chapter 8, one in the group usually takes the leadership role and dominates the group's thinking, so that there are really only one participant and two observers. When students demonstrate the necessary aptitude to use the inductive method successfully in an unguided fashion, you can assign small groups to work together.

Techniques for Unguided Inductive Inquiry   What are some tested ideas that can be used as prototypes for teachers wishing to incorporate appropriate inductive, unguided learning experiences into an ongoing lesson? Table 9.2 gives a few ideas that are expanded into a matrix of student tasks.

reflect

- Examine both the guided and the unguided inductive instructional models. What areas are common to both? What areas are different?

- Use the Internet to conduct a search of the ERIC database for ideas on using newspapers as sources of material in inductive inquiry lessons.

- How can lessons and activities in art, physical education, social studies, and literature be made more inductive for learners?

TABLE 9.2

Unguided Inductive Inquiry: A Matrix of Tasks

Content Area	Lesson Goal	Material	Student Questions	Student Summaries, Patterns, Inferences	Student Generalizations
Social studies	To understand regional difference in the U.S. culture	Recycled telephone books	"How many different churches are there in Boston, Tulsa, Nashville, Salt Lake City?"	1. Lists from Yellow Pages 2. Lists of different denominations 3. Percentages computed 4. Inferences listed	1. Students list and discuss generalizations
History, art	To interpret a classic artwork	Bayeux tapestry Encyclopedias	"What events are shown?" "What order is there to the tapestry layout?"	1. Events listed 2. Scenes counted and classified into categories 3. Types of persons identified 4. Chronology determined	1. Students interpret major themes. 2. Students draw conclusions. 3. Class discusses historical events. 4. Class compares means of communications.
Science	To learn about weather patterns	Recycled newspapers TV news	"How do weather systems usually hit the United States?" "What effect does the jet stream have on weather systems?"	1. Maps constructed showing major fronts 2. Patterns listed 3. Data collected north and south of jet stream paths	1. Students chart weather patterns. 2. Class analyzes patterns. 3. Students make conclusions and present them to class.

SECTION 3: METHODS FOR DEVELOPING HIGHER-LEVEL THINKING SKILLS

By now you should realize that, as a classroom teacher, you can never be too aware of thinking skills. The encouragement of your students' active observation and exploration should be infused throughout your teaching, so that you are not merely transmitting information, but also enhancing thinking abilities. You have been introduced to the basic elements of inquiry teaching and can now play a direct (guided inquiry) or indirect (unguided inquiry) role in classroom inquiry experiences. Within these overall contexts of teaching from an inquiry-based point of view, you also should know about several variations on the theme—that is, specific teaching approaches and techniques that are either directly related to or are themselves considered inquiry methods. The three approaches we focus on here have proven effective across many subject areas. They are problem solving, discovery learning, and techniques that emphasize higher-level critical thinking skills. We conclude by taking a brief look at classroom assessment, which we cover in depth in the next chapter.

Problem Solving

Problem-solving models of instruction are based on the ideas of John Dewey (1916, 1938). Among his major educational contributions was his advocacy of a curriculum *based on problems*. He defined a **problem** as anything that gives rise to doubt and uncertainty. Dewey held that a problem, to be an appropriate topic of study, had to meet two rigorous criteria: It had to be important to the culture, and it had to be important and relevant to the student.

Dewey's definition of *problem*

Many curriculum projects developed between 1958 and 1970 in science, mathematics, and social studies were based on Dewey's problem-solving approach. In addition, most contemporary curricula and a large majority of textbooks suggest "problems" to be solved by students. Some of the curricula that you may encounter will stress elements of inquiry, discovery, or problem solving. Contemporary curricula, especially interdisciplinary ones such as environmental studies, rely heavily on the two criteria Dewey first suggested. If you assign research reports to your students, you are using elements of problem-solving instruction.

This technique, like any inquiry method, requires careful planning and systematic skill building. Implicit within the problem-solving framework is the concept of **experience**, or the idea that the totality of events and activities that students carry out under the school's direction as part of the planned learning processes will produce certain desirable traits or behaviors that will better enable them to function in our culture. Furthermore, the experiences provided by the schools should articulate the content and the process of

Problem solving through experience

knowing. Both knowing *what is known* and knowing *how to know* are important objectives for the learner (see Martinez 1998).

This description shows that problem solving contains many elements of the constructivist model. As we use it here, **problem solving** refers to an inquiry learning process in which students seek answers to a question relevant to themselves and their culture. The constructivist philosophy requires the learner to be actively engaged in the learning process. Through the interaction of all those elements, the learner makes sense out of something. You, as the teacher, help by providing the environment that allows the student to participate and interact in regular classroom activities or on the Web (see Gordon et al. 2001; Kirk and Orr 2003; Munson et al. 2003).

The Teacher's Role   As the clarifier or definer, your role is to help the learners define precisely what is being studied or solved. Problem-solving methodologies focus on systematic investigation: Students set up the problem, clarify the issues, propose ways to obtain needed information, and then test or evaluate their conclusions. In most cases, learners will establish written hypotheses for testing. Students need your continual monitoring. In a problem-solving model, you must continually receive progress reports from students engaged in the investigative process.

Remember clarifying role

Students are not simply allowed to follow their whims. Problem solving requires building close relationships between students and teacher (see Delisle 1997; Verduin 1996). It also involves systematic investigation of the problem and the proposing of concrete solutions.

Steps in Solving Problems   Problem solving implies a degree of freedom (to explore a problem) and responsibility (to arrive at a possible solution). One tackles a problem to achieve objectives, not simply to use the process of inquiry per se. The steps listed in the Instructional Strategies box below comprise the problem-solving technique, although students may not follow them in strict linear fashion. Compare the steps to those of the inquiry model in Figure 9.1.

Student freedom and responsibility

INSTRUCTIONAL STRATEGIES

Steps for Problem Solving

1. Becoming aware of a situation or event that is labeled a "problem"
2. Identifying the problem in exact terms
3. Defining all terms
4. Establishing the limits of the problem
5. Conducting a task analysis so that the problem may be subdivided into discrete elements for investigation
6. Collecting data that are relevant to each task
7. Evaluating the data for apparent biases or errors
8. Synthesizing the data for meaningful relationships
9. Making generalizations and suggesting alternatives to rectify the problem
10. Publishing the results of the investigation

If you decide to use a problem-solving experience in your classes, you must realize that it will usually last for days or even weeks. During that time, other learning may be accomplished as well—for example, using reference books, requesting information, interpreting data, presenting progress reports to the class, and taking responsibility for the conduct of a task.

Examples of Problem Solving   Let's look at two case histories of real problem solving that took place in Washington, D.C., and Massachusetts elementary schools.

Our first example is taken from one federal education official's personal efforts to help break the poverty cycle and to instill an appreciation for basic school subjects that can ultimately improve students' economic well-being. Recall that in Chapter 8 we briefly discuss the national stock market simulation. Robert Radford (1991) of Washington, D.C., wanted to help children attending the Amidon Elementary School do the following:

- Gain insights into the U.S. economic system.
- Understand the concepts of compounding interest, increasing the value of money over time, and capital appreciation.
- Practice the concept of delayed gratification (to break the poverty cycle).

In the Amidon project, intermediate grade students were introduced to economics and business principles in practical ways. To demonstrate understanding, each student had to provide an example of the topics or concepts being discussed. Next, stock market activities were introduced. Students examined *Investor's Daily*, *Value Line Survey*, and *Barron's Financial Weekly*. The students read and reported on findings and even computed the Dow Jones Industrial Average.

Through hands-on experiences, they studied and discussed business cycles. They tracked selected stocks, graphed fluctuations in prices, and compared industrial stock profiles to that of the market as a whole. These real-life activities made a vivid impression on the children of their need to master arithmetic, reading, social studies, and language arts.

Teachers and students decided together to purchase Philadelphia Electric Company common stock (currently called PECOEnergy, a subsidiary of the Exelon Corporation). Money to purchase the shares came from gifts from seventy-five individuals who wanted to help in this project, plus the support of seventeen companies and corporations. Each graduating class purchased a number of shares of common stock of PECOEnergy, which were then placed into trust accounts for each student.

Authentic example: stock market

To take the exercise a step further, several students attended the annual stockholders' meeting. With their peers' proxies in hand, the delegates cast their votes and presented issues to the stockholders at large.

Accompanying the real-life component of this project was a stock market simulation game. Each child received a hypothetical $50,000 portfolio containing ten different stocks. Students tracked their portfolios each week and thus acquired additional drill and practice in arithmetic and decision making.

Is this an example of real problem solving? John Dewey would applaud it. The project illustrates how students can be exposed to an *experientially* rich curriculum that helps them understand how to better themselves in *their own immediate future*. Having a trust fund will undoubtedly encourage these children to pursue socially valued occupations and professions.

Finally, the Amidon project illustrates how *affective* objectives may be integrated into the curriculum. Every kid feels like a winner, both intellectually and financially. And those feelings have a carryover effect on student behavior, ultimately sparking positive student actions.

In another example, students in a Massachusetts elementary school collected data and presented it to their local school board to show that a major intersection was a grievous safety problem. The students then showed how a pedestrian overpass could be constructed; they even contacted architects to obtain cost estimates. The school board was impressed—and so was the city council, for the walk was constructed later just as the schoolchildren had proposed.

There are many other examples of how teachers and students can use problem solving in the real world. For instance, a class might observe problems in the immediate school environment—parking shortages, long lunch lines, crowded locker rooms, noise—and investigate them with the goal of creating alternative situations. Or you could give students in high school English classes the problem of generating at least three criteria for determining which works of U.S. literature should be added to or retained in the curriculum. Students will learn the difficulties associated with canon building, values, and curricular decision making.

Jennifer Nelson (1998) uses investigative techniques of problem solving by having her students study problems associated with the history of their own school. In a similar vein, Carol E. Murphy (1998) shows how the five themes of geography—location, movement, place, region, and human environment—are used to solve problems associated with the school site. John Harrell, Edwin Christmann and Jeffrey Lehman (2002) illustrate how the Internet can be incorporated in inquiry lessons. Regardless of whether you undertake an ambitious, large-scope problem-solving project with your students or a lesser one, we urge you to initiate problem-solving skills on day one. Doing so makes schooling an enjoyable, exciting, and worthwhile experience.

Let's add one more problem-solving model to your knowledge base. George Polya (1957), internationally famous mathematician at Stanford University, designed a process that students could use based on classroom experience. His model has four parts: (1) understand the problem, (2) devise a plan, (3) carry out the plan, and (4) look back or reflect (see Stephenson 2000). You will quickly observe that Polya synthesized most of the elements of inquiry teaching that have been conveyed in this chapter. Alice P. Wakefield (2001) illustrates a combination of constructivism and Polya's model in teaching young children mathematics.

---

reflect

- What elements of problem solving can be applied to any school-taught topics?

- Select a problem to be solved. To use problem solving most efficiently, sketch a task analysis chart showing the necessary student skills.

- Prepare a lesson that incorporates some real problem solving for students.

Discovery Learning

Who really discovered America? Native American people had been here for upwards of 13,000 years, and although Leif Ericson seems to have been the first European to visit our shores, Christopher Columbus got the credit for the discovery simply because he announced it first (Strike 1975). But the territory is named for the map maker Amerigo Vespucci because he knew Columbus had landed on a brand-new continent rather than in India. In this vein, Strike's comprehensive analysis of methods associated with **discovery learning**—an inquiry process in which learners pose questions and seek answers—may be of use. Strike (1975) establishes two categories of discovery: absolute discovery and relative discovery. *Absolute discovery* refers to those classic "firsts" in which something is discovered for all humankind—the discovery of the DNA molecule's reproduction mechanism; the discovery of new planets, theories, or synthetic materials. *Relative discovery* means that although a concept or fact is already known by others, an individual has learned it or found it out *for him- or herself* for the first time.

Strike (1975) also presents four modes of discovery:

1. Knowing that
2. Knowing how
3. Discovering that
4. Discovering how

Absolute vs. relative discovery

Finally, he provides a basic criterion that is essential for any act to be labeled a discovery. The discoverer must communicate both the *what* and the *how* to others. Thus, if you discover the Lost Dutchman Mine in Arizona but do not tell a single individual, you have not made a discovery.

Strike's four modes of discovery are consistent with the thirteen major inquiry processes and Polya's model described above. For example, communicating is a major inquiry process and is very much a part of discovery. Also, the model that Strike describes implies that learners must "know" something before they can "discover" something. Content, knowledge, fact, and processes are all very much a part of the discovery strategy.

Although there is much luck involved in discovery, Louis Pasteur's statement that "chance favors the prepared mind" is still valid. The most important discoveries made by scientists—including social and behavioral scientists—are the result of careful observation and systematic research. Discovery makes use of the same processes and skills we describe as being part of inductive inquiry and problem solving. This should come as no surprise because inquiry requires systematic conduct, not haphazard bungling.

Environmental education is a rich arena for discovery learning and problem solving. Students can collect water-quality data using standard, scientifically accepted practices and collect data to be analyzed and discussed. They *construct* meaning from data (Orlich et al. 1999).

On February 1, 2002, Oliver Huang, a student at Butte (Montana) High School, communicated directly with astronaut Dan Bursch, who was working at the international space station high above Earth. Oliver asked whether chemical reactions that normally precipitate on Earth do the same in microgravity, the gravitational conditions found in space. Bursch, in performing the experiments, explained in detail how some chemical reactions work differently aboard the space station because the densities of various compounds cause unexpected results. Other students asked equally interesting questions to discover their answers.

Is this an example of problem solving or discovery? We think that it fits in the category of *absolute* discovery because it was the first time that anyone had communicated the problem and completed the research. Oliver's science teacher, Sandra Shutey, encouraged her students to generate research questions for the astronauts and, in conjunction with the National Aeronautics and Space Administration (NASA) and her local Worldcom Internet provider, got her students involved in a real-time exchange with the space station scientists. This demonstrates the partnership that develops when learners and teachers share in the excitement of inquiry.

Authentic example: space experiments

Challenge your students to explore selected themes from history (Wilson 2002), genetics (Echevarria 2003), or another area (Kalayci and Cohen 2003). The key point is that critical thought comes before action.

Not all discovery learning needs to be as dramatic as NASA experiments. One common way to generate the fun and discipline of discovery is to use an overhead projector to present an event that requires student analysis. In the Mystery Island activity, the teacher makes a set of overlays that depict an unnamed island (Zevin 1969). The initial transparency shows the outline of the island. The map contains some standard clues to the island's general location, such as topographical symbols, rivers, and latitude and longitude symbols. This device is used primarily to focus the learner's attention on the event or to motivate inquiry. And with PowerPoint technology, the excitement can be continuous because students enjoy working on computers and a challenge makes school work, more fun.

The teacher usually begins the activity by telling the class that the island is uninhabited and that they are going to be the first persons to land on it. The students' first task is to choose where they will settle and to justify their choice. Ultimately they are given other tasks, such as to find the places that may be the best for farming, industries, railroads, harbors, airports, resorts, and the like. The students must make inferences concerning rainfall, winds, deserts, and other natural phenomena. Following Strike's four elements (1975), the activity requires students both to *know* and to *discover* "that" and "how." The opportunities for inquiry are limitless.

Creating discovery media: "desert island" simulation

The entire arena of inquiry and thinking, including problem solving and discovery approaches, naturally lend themselves to technology applications. We present one interesting example in the Instructional Strategies box below.

INSTRUCTIONAL STRATEGIES

Computer Applications to Enhance the Development of Thinking Skills

Nancy Ridenour, who taught at the Bridgeport, Washington, Middle School, used the inquiry model for student small-group research projects. Students visited the local Marina Park, located on the Columbia River. They decided on the topic for their research question and the method of

INSTRUCTIONAL
STRATEGIES

Computer Applications to Enhance the Development of Thinking Skills—Cont'd

data collection. The students prepared a written plan, which Nancy evaluated. Obviously, safety and appropriate science techniques are double-checked. The student teams collect data during the semester and make PowerPoint presentations. The students integrate photographs into the system using a digital camera. By placing the projects on-line, the students share their data and presentations with other students and community members. They are also available for examination anywhere in the world. This application of inquiry and computer technology is only one of many possibilities. We suggest reviewing Mark and Cindy Grabe's excellent resource, *Integrating Technology for Meaningful Learning* (5th edition) (2006) for a wealth of ideas associated with computers and inquiry.

REFLECT

- Compare and contrast discovery learning and problem solving.
- Prepare a lesson that incorporates discovery learning.

Techniques for Developing Critical Thinking Skills

Implicit in the techniques we present in this section is the assumption that information-processing psychology and schema theory are the most useful explanations of how students learn. **Information-processing psychology** asserts that learning is an interactive process between the learner and the environment, a process to which both contribute; that is, the learner is not just a passive receiver of stimuli (see Wakefield 1996 for discussion). Schema theory, as we have already seen, asserts that we organize what we learn according to patterns, or *schemas*, that help us make sense of the multiple stimuli we constantly receive. Learning becomes an *individual meaning-building process*, in which the student either relates new data to existing patterns or creates new schemas to understand (see Marzano 1998). These are also basic assumptions of the constructivist approach. Starting from this base of instructional assumptions, the teacher behaviors in the Instructional Strategies box below can help students improve their thinking processes. These techniques have proven useful across a broad range of subjects, from primary grades to graduate school.

INSTRUCTIONAL
STRATEGIES

Ten Teacher Behaviors That Encourage Thinking Skills

1. *Plan for thinking.* Develop units and lessons based on concepts and generalizations.
2. *Teach for meaning.* Connect each lesson to students' experience.

Continued

INSTRUCTIONAL
STRATEGIES

Ten Teacher Behaviors That Encourage Thinking Skills—Cont'd

3. *Ask thought-provoking questions.* "How do you know?" "What is the main idea?" "What alternatives can we think of?"
4. *Make students aware of their mental processes.* "From your observations about prices in this chart, what might we infer about supply and demand?"
5. *Explain your thought processes frequently.* "On this tape, I recorded my thoughts as I planned today's lesson. As you listen to it, identify examples of the following thinking skills."
6. *Keep data before students.* Summarize and record student answers on the board or a transparency.
7. *Call on students to explain.* Give students frequent opportunities to explain what they do or don't understand.
8. *Encourage credibility as a criterion.* "Does this make sense?" "Why not?"
9. *Be consistent.* Thinking instruction should be part of each lesson, each day.
10. *Be patient.* Significant change requires at least a semester.

The first behavior, which is of primary importance, is to plan your instruction to emphasize thought processes. The resulting plan may bear little relationship to a standard content outline. Most history texts, for instance, organize facts chronologically; however, such a structure does not resemble the way people think critically about history. A more *effective* organizer is to arrange historical facts around selected basic concepts and generalizations, such as elections, economic cycles, events, or technological inventions. Facts must be related to broader concepts or generalizations before they have significance. Thus effective instructional planning first determines the primary concepts and generalizations relevant to a unit or a course. These become the subjects of discrete lessons, which are planned around the facts needed to understand each concept. If you do use the instructional strategies carefully and consistently, with an emphasis on students' understanding rather than on rote memorization, you will develop their thinking skills effectively, and your content coverage will have a meaningful pattern for students.

Plan instruction around
thinking processes.

Strategic Learning Skills   Critical thinking skills are also called **strategic learning**, meaning that students develop a capacity to accelerate their own learning (see Gettinger and Callan Stoiber 1999, p. 952). In the box on page 317, these researchers provide four major assumptions under which we operate when developing student strategic learning skills.

> ## Assumptions About Learners and Learning
>
> 1. New skills, knowledge, competencies, and interests are built on previous ones.
> 2. Information is remembered when it is meaningful and gained through active and enjoyable learning.
> 3. Motivation is reinforced when learners feel competent.
> 4. Opportunities must be provided to practice critical thinking and problem solving in various formats.

Following are three specific techniques that you can use to help your students build their critical thinking and strategic learning skills.

1. Integrated Approach   Consider a high school unit in U.S. history that focuses on the colonial period. One way to combine content and thinking-skills coverage is to have students prepare a large wall chart listing specific characteristics of several colonies. These might be geographic features, economic characteristics, or social backgrounds and attitudes. From these data, students could infer and hypothesize about colonists' possible attitudes toward future events, such as declaring independence, providing free public education, or abolishing slavery. Similarly, science teachers could help students create a periodic table of the elements through observing, inferring, and generalizing rather than simply by studying a given example.

Note that these activities tend to reinforce many of the thinking skills listed earlier in the chapter. Depending on the instructional emphasis, students could be involved in virtually all thinking processes, from low-order skills (observing and classifying) to high-level skills (distinguishing relevant from irrelevant statements). Proponents of this integrated approach assert that such flexibility—the applicability of virtually any subject matter to teach a full range of thought processes—is its primary strength (see Gore 2004; Jones 2003).

2. Think-Aloud Modeling   Another method is to use your thought processes as examples. This will help make students aware of their own thought processes (see the fourth and fifth teacher behaviors in the Instructional Strategies box on page 316 and the related discussion of metacognition on page 319). Share with students the thinking steps you follow in planning a lesson, making a conclusion, or performing any relevant activity. Have your students identify the particular skills you use and suggest other strategies you might follow. Such demonstrations can take the forms of printed handouts, audiotapes, or even an unrehearsed problem-solving exploration of a student's question.

Lest you think this idea is simply a theory, we offer Professor Glenn Crosby, who taught graduate-level physical chemistry classes by narrating his thought processes as he worked out problems on the chalkboard. You can use this method to interpret O. Henry, President George W. Bush's speeches, or Langston Hughes, as well as chemistry.

Show students how you think.

Once students understand the think-aloud process, they can pair up and practice it, using selected topics related to classroom issues and the subject matter being studied. A useful exercise is for pairs of students to explain to each other their understanding of an assignment and the steps they will follow in completing it. This exercise uncovers ambiguities in assignments and helps students identify productive thinking and study strategies. Two considerations, though, are paramount in all thinking-aloud exercises: Each student must have as much practice as possible, *and the process of thinking is more important than the product of thinking*—the objective is to identify effective thinking steps, not necessarily to find a particular solution. This technique is ideal for open-ended activities.

3. Student Summaries   Another technique that has been found generally useful for encouraging thinking behaviors is to have students summarize. Ask students to outline the steps in a math solution, list the causes of a social condition, give reactions to an assembly speaker, and so on. Your imagination is the only limit to the choices. The summary can be made in writing or presented orally.

Considerable evidence (see Wormeli 2004) suggests that the act of writing is itself both an exercise of thinking skills and a generator of those skills. We must think to write—but in addition, when writing, we frequently come up with new statements and ideas we did not think up beforehand. Thus any writing is probably useful in learning. Writing summaries is particularly effective, however, because it forces the student to develop **criteria**—characteristics used to organize or evaluate ideas or products—for identifying some ideas as more important than others. This activity stimulates and reinforces the highest-level thinking skills (Nickelsen and Glasscock 2004).

Oral summaries are also effective in helping students develop speaking skills that will readily transfer beyond school. Moreover, oral summaries can be part of class discussions that are also essential activities for developing critical reasoning (see Patrick 2003a). As you incorporate student oral summaries in your teaching style, remember to subtly shift your efforts to an inactive instructional role while the class members assume an active one. Only you will know the difference.

When you assign a summarizing activity to a student, observe the four rules listed in the box below.

> Summaries challenge students to rate ideas.

Rules for Summarizing

1. To stimulate understanding of the material summarized, insist that students use their own words, not quotations.
2. Limit the length of the summary, whether written or oral, to ensure that students have judged the relative importance of ideas.
3. Have students discuss their summaries, especially the criteria they used for including and excluding information.
4. Have students discuss the summarizing process: What steps did they follow? What dead ends did they come to? What problems developed?

VIDEO Case

For a real-life example, view the Video Case "Metacognition: Helping Students Become Strategic Learners." Teacher Julie Craven supports students in reading a difficult newspaper article about China. To what extent are students aware of what they *don't* know? What prevents them from becoming discouraged?

Thinking about thinking

Metacognitive Skills Metacognition means being aware of your thought processes while you are thinking (see Leat and Lin 2003 for an extended treatment). Thinking aloud is one example. Research indicates that effective problem solvers subvocalize; that is, they talk to themselves (see Blakey and Spence 1990), constantly restating the situation, rechecking their progress, and evaluating whether their thinking is moving in an appropriate direction. Undoubtedly you will have students with special needs in your classes. Harvette M. Robertson, Billie Priest, and Harry L. Fullwood (2001) provide a series of metacognitive techniques to assist these students—and other learners as well.

The following are several techniques that are useful for helping students become accustomed to thinking about and stating their thoughts.

Describing Self-Thought   Perhaps the most effective technique is simply to have students describe what is going on in their minds while they are thinking (Block 2004). Have students practice this technique in pairs for three to five minutes several times a week to overcome awkwardness with the method (and even to practice cooperative learning). Once they are accustomed to the process, students can recall their thinking processes in larger groups or before the entire class to maintain the skill. You should also model this behavior as often as possible, of course. Connect this technique with the basic questioning model in Chapter 7. Rather than simply stating, "Your response is incorrect," you can ask the student, "How did you arrive at that answer?" That question engages metacognitive action (see King 2002).

Identifying What Is Known and Not Known   Another approach to metacognitive instruction is to have students identify what is known about a situation or problem, suggest what needs to be learned, and list steps required to obtain the information (Wray 2003). For example, Wray used this type of approach in class to determine whether science is a young person's game; that is, he had his students examine twenty-four revolutionary scientific figures to determine if young scientists are more likely to make important discoveries than are older ones. Such exercises, done frequently and with attention to identifying relevant processes, will help students use similar steps in their own thinking.

Students identify what is known and what they need to know.

Reciprocal Teaching   One more technique helpful to the metacognition package is **reciprocal teaching**, in which students and teachers switch roles in a lesson. This model was designed by Annmarie Sullivan Palincsar (in Gettinger and Callan Stoiber 1999). Her approach has been used successfully with middle-level students and improves reading comprehension. (Remember the concept of teaching for understanding, Chapter 3.) Note how this strategy synthesizes several aspects of discussions, inquiry, thinking, and metacognition.

When using reciprocal teaching, the teacher leads the discussion or recitation period on the material the students have read. At that point, the students are given four tasks: (1) predict what comes next in text, (2) generate self-testing questions, (3) summarize the information read, and (4) clarify any misunderstandings or unclear points. Following these steps, the teacher becomes a class participant and students assume the role of "teacher." This is also a great technique for generating personal interaction (see Hashey and Connors 2003; Oczkus 2003; Puchner 2003; Seymour and Osana 2003).

Analyzing Others' Thinking   You can also encourage metacognition by having students study how others think, particularly persons who are famous for their thinking. Students may be surprised to discover that high I.Q. is not necessarily associated with achievement; the application of intellect is what matters. They could explore and discuss how Curie or Mozart worked, what steps they took, and what things were important to them in achieving. Students can interview accomplished people from their own community, or such individuals can visit the class to discuss what thoughts go through their head while they paint a picture, run a race, or write a newspaper article.

Students get into the mind of a great achiever.

Monitoring Academic Behavior   Teaching metacognition can also include having students monitor their own academic behavior. Do they have test-taking strategies? Are the strategies effective? Might they be improved? What about learning strategies? Do they know whether they learn better from visual, auditory, or kinesthetic stimuli? Do they have strategies to help in each area? All of these questions are relevant to students' school experience. All are areas that you can explore with students as you help them share with one another and provide useful information (see Gallagher 1998; Tanner and Casados 1998). The result will be improved metacognition and application of selected thinking processes.

TECHNOLOGY INSIGHT

Thinking and Inquiring: Web-Based Resources and Activities

One of the nicest things about being a teacher is the fact that you can be a learner for your entire career, and you can help your students become lifelong learners as well. Using the World Wide Web reinforces this; because it is impossible to know everything that is available on the Web, one must constantly maintain a learner's point of view. Although we cover many different topics, all under the rubric of inquiry or thinking skills, there are a few Internet sources that provide ideas and resources for inquiry, thinking skills, and metacognition.

Probably the most famous web-based, inquiry-oriented classroom activities are found on San Diego State University's Web Quest site (http://webquest.sdsu.edu/webquest.html). Bernie Dodge is generally considered the master of the site, which is very popular with teachers and teacher-educators.

TECHNOLOGY INSIGHT

Thinking and Inquiring: Web-Based Resources and Activities—Cont'd

Kathleen Cotton of the Northwest Regional Educational Laboratory has developed a series of materials that can help teach those skills associated with thinking. You can find these at http://www.nwrel.org. Go to the search box on the NWREL home page and type in "thinking" to view several sites on the topic.

Assessing Higher-Level Thinking Activities

We saved the toughest part until last. The challenge of using any higher-level strategy—inquiry, problem solving, critical thinking—is that, in most learning episodes, there may be no one right answer. Thus you assess the *processes*.

In Chapter 10, we will introduce the technique of using rubrics to evaluate student work. In using rubrics, you establish a set of criteria by which to assess a product, paper, argument, conclusion, or methodology (see Busching 1998; Taggart et al. 1998). The overarching method of inquiry is interaction. Chapter 8 includes two forms (Figures 8.1 and 8.2) that you can adapt to fit higher-level thinking lessons. Perhaps the most critical aspect of assessment is simply to provide feedback to all students, so that they continually improve their use of logic and become more systematic in solving any problem.

In closing this chapter, we want to acknowledge how much time and effort it takes to teach thinking as an integral part of the curriculum, especially with all the conflicting demands of standards-based models. We hope that all educators will begin to integrate the best teaching and thinking strategies into the curriculum systematically and diligently. We have confidence that you will address the challenge as one that is intentionally inviting. And, once again, we invite you to our website to examine reported effect sizes on several inquiry and thinking techniques. Go to **http://education.college.hmco.com/students**.

reflect A Closing Reflection

- How can you integrate the different types of inquiry and the host of skills associated with thinking into your classroom instruction?

- In what ways can metacognitive techniques help student thinking?

- Review the list of ten teacher behaviors that encourage thinking skills. How can you incorporate those steps into an already crowded curriculum?

- If you want to stress the development of thinking skills in your teaching, who else in your school or community must you involve? How can you involve them?

summary

1. The goal of inquiry methods is to encourage students to ask questions, seek information, and become better thinkers.

2. The basic processes of inquiry learning include observing, classifying, inferring, measuring, communicating, predicting, formulating hypotheses, interpreting, and experimenting.

3. Inquiry teaching shares many characteristics with constructivism. These include a focus on the student, flexibly paced instruction, encouragement of multiple conclusions, and an emphasis on process.

4. Two models for inquiry teaching are guided inductive inquiry and unguided inductive inquiry. Both are based on inductive reasoning, a method of thinking that moves from the specific to the general.

5. Three other methods of inquiry learning instruction are the problem-solving method, discovery learning, and the use of specific critical thinking techniques. All these methods may be used to infuse critical thinking skills into the curriculum.

6. Classroom use of any inquiry model or method increases the amount of student-engaged time needed to complete a lesson and adds complexity to unit or lesson planning.

7. Using the integrated approach, think-aloud modeling, and summarizing helps students build their critical thinking and strategic learning skills.

8. Describing self-thought, identifying what is and is not known, reciprocal teaching, analyzing others' thinking, and monitoring academic behavior help students become accustomed to thinking about and stating their thoughts.

print Resources

This subject is so rich that we found it very difficult to designate only a few references as "must" reading. You may want to review these before you begin using inquiry or thinking strategies.

Campbell, J. R., K. E. Voelkl, and P. L. Donahue. *Report in Brief: NAEP 1996 Trends in Academic Progress* (NCES 98-530). Washington, DC: National Center for Educational Statistics, revised August 1998, 29 pp.

The National Assessment of Educational Progress (NAEP) is the sponsor of a series of tests in English, mathematics, science, art, writing, civics, and history that are administered to samples of fourth-, eighth-, eleventh- and twelfth-graders and students aged nine, thirteen, and seventeen. We consider these tests to be the best indicators of the levels of thinking at which students achieve and teachers teach. Examine the most current reports to understand our plea for higher-level teaching and for ideas on how to reach those levels.

Shayer, M., and P. Adey. *Learning Intelligence: Cognitive Acceleration Across the Curriculum from 5 to 15 Years.* Buckingham, England: Open University Press, 2002, 209 pp.

The authors have a long line of developmental research that will inform any teacher who desires to develop age-appropriate cognitive skills.

Starko, A. J. *Creativity in the Classroom: Schools of Curious Delight.* Mahwah, NJ: Erlbaum Associates, 2005, 499 pp.

Creativity is the top of the scale when it comes to thinking. This book provides you with more than enough information on how to encourage that trait in your classes.

Sternberg, R. J., and L. Spear-Swerling. *Teaching for Thinking.* Washington, DC: American Psychology Association, 1996, 163 pp.

This short book is a mind stretcher for the novice, but the authors critically examine thinking and creativity.

Wormeli, R. *Summarization in Any Subject: 50 Techniques to Improve Student Learning.* Alexandria, VA: Association for Supervision and Curriculum Development, 2004.

The author, a seasoned teacher, illustrates how you can use one of the more powerful learning techniques in any subject.

Internet Resources

Go to the website for this book to find live links to resources related to this chapter.

> The School of Chemical Engineering at Washington State University has a website featuring several teacher-designed modules that illustrate inductive, problem-solving, and discovery models for grades 7–12.
> **http://www.che.wsu.edu/home/modules/index.html**

> Mid-continent Research for Education and Learning (McREL) maintains a site covering topics from constructivist teaching to technology integration. Their index is a useful search tool.
> **http://www.mcrel.org/**

> Higher-Order Thinking Strategies for the Classroom are found at the Critical Thinking website, maintained by the faculty at Longview Community College.
> **http://www.kcmetro.cc.mo.us^^ /longview/ctac/corenotes.htm**

> The University of Toronto offers a short course relating to metacognitive techniques.
> **http://snow.utoronto.ca/Learn2/introll.html**

References

Airasian, P. W., and M. E. Walsh. "Constructivist Cautions." *Phi Delta Kappan* 78(6) (1997): 444–449.

Banks, J. A. *Teaching Strategies for Ethnic Studies* (7th edition). Boston: Allyn and Bacon, 2003.

Beatty, A. S., C. M. Reese, H. R. Persky, and P. Carr. *NAEP 1994 U.S. History Report Card: Findings from the National Assessment of Educational Progress* (NCES 96-085). National Center for Education Statistics. Washington, DC: U.S. Government Printing Office, 1996.

Berliner, D. C. "If the Underlying Premise for No Child Left Behind Is False, How Can That Act Solve Our Problems?" In *Saving Our Schools: The Case for Public Education in America*. K. Goodman, Y. Goodman, R. Rapoport, and P. Shannon, editors. Oakland, CA: RDR Books, 2004, pp. 167–184.

Bigge, M. L., and S. S. Shermis. *Learning Theories for Teachers* (6th edition). New York: Longman, 2004.

Blakey, E., and S. Spence. *Developing Metacognition. ERIC Digest.* Syracuse, NY: ERIC Clearinghouse on Information Resources, 1990. ED 327 218.

Block, C. C. *Teaching Comprehension: The Comprehension Process Approach.* Boston: Allyn and Bacon, 2004.

Boss, S. "Course of Discovery: Educators Living Along the Route Traveled by Lewis and Clark Infuse Their Teaching with Modern Tools for Exploration." *Northwest Education* 8(4) (2003): 8–13.

Brendzel, S. "Science on a Roll. Part One: Absorbing Inquiry." *Science Scope* 25(5) (2002): 18–20.

Busching, B. "Grading Inquiry Projects." *New Directions for Teaching and Learning* 74(1) (1998): 89–96.

Campbell, J. R., K. E. Voelkl, and P. L. Donahue. *Report in Brief: NAEP 1996 Trends in Academic Progress.* NCES 98-530. Washington, DC: National Center for Educational Statistics, revised August 1998.

College Board News 2000–2001. "AP Students with a '3 or Higher' Outperform Advanced Math and Physics Students both in U.S. and Abroad." New York City, July 11, 2001. *Full Report:* E. J. Gonzales, K. M. O'Connor, and J. A. Miles. *How Well Do Advanced Placement Students Perform on the TIMSS Advanced Mathematics and Physics Tests?* Boston: The International Study Center, Lynch School of Education, Boston College, June 2001.

Delisle, R. *How to Use Problem-Based Learning in the Classroom.* Alexandria, VA: Association for Supervision and Curriculum Development, 1997.

Dewey, J. *Democracy and Education.* New York: Macmillan, 1916.

Dewey, J. *Experience and Education.* New York: Macmillan, 1938.

Echevarria, M. "Anomalies as a Catalyst for Middle School Students' Knowledge Construction and Scientific Reasoning During Science Inquiry." *Journal of Educational Psychology* 95(2) (2003): 357–374.

Eylon, B., and M. C. Linn. "Learning and Instruction: An Examination of Four Research Perspectives in Science Education." *Review of Educational Research* 58 (1988): 251–301.

Gallagher, S. A. "The Road to Critical Thinking: The Perry Scheme and Meaningful Differentiation." *NASSP Bulletin* 82(595) (1998): 12–20.

Gettinger, M., and K. Callan Stoiber. "Excellence in Teaching: Review of Instructional and Environmental Variables." In *The Handbook of School Psychology* (3rd edition). C. R. Reynolds and T. B. Gutkin, editors. New York: Wiley, 1999, pp. 933–958.

Glasgow, J. N. "Teaching Social Justice Through Young Adult Literature." *English Journal* 90(6) (2001): 54–61.

Gordon, P. R., A. M. Rogers, M. Comfort, N. Gavula, and B. P. McGee. "A Taste of Problem-Based Learning Increases Achievement of Urban Minority Middle-School Students." *Educational Horizons* 79(4) (2001): 171–175.

Gore, M. C. *Successful Inclusion Strategies for Secondary and Middle School Teachers: Keys to Help Struggling Learners Access the Curriculum.* Thousand Oaks, CA: Corwin, 2004.

Harrell, J., E. Christmann, and J. Lehman. "Technology-Based Planetary Exploration." *Science Scope* 25(4) (2002): 8–11.

Hashey, J. M., and D. J. Connors. "Learn From Our Journey: Reciprocal Teaching Action Research." *Reading Teacher* 57(3) (2003): 224–232.

Haury, D. L. *Fundamental Skills in Science: Observation. ERIC Digest.* Columbus, OH: ERIC Clearinghouse for Science, Mathematics and Environmental Education, 2002. ED 478714.

Hoge, J. D. *Teaching History for Citizenship in the Elementary School. ERIC Digest.* Bloomington, IN: ERIC Clearinghouse for Social Studies/Social Science Education, 2003. ED 479 891.

Holcomb, E. L. *Getting Excited About Data: How to Combine People, Passion and Proof, 2nd edition.* Thousand Oaks, CA: Corwin, 2004.

Ishii, D. K. *Constructivist Views of Learning in Science and Mathematics. ERIC Digest.* Columbus, OH: ERIC Clearinghouse for Science, Mathematics and Environmental Education, 2003. ED 482 722.

Johnson, E. G., and A. Siegendorf. *Linking the National Assessment of Educational Progress and the Third*

International Mathematics and Science Study: Eighth Grade Results (NCES 98-500). U.S. Department of Education, National Center for Education Statistics. Project Officer, G. W. Phillips. Washington, DC: U.S. Government Printing Office, May 1998.

Jones, S. J. *Blueprint for Student Success: A Guide to Research-Based Teaching Practices K-12.* Thousand Oaks, CA: Corwin, 2003.

Joyce, B. R., and E. F. Calhoun. *Learning to Teach Inductively.* Boston: Allyn and Bacon, 1998.

Kalayci, N., and M. R. Cohen. *Integrating Problem Solving with Theme-Based Learning in the "Key Learning Community."* Paper presented at annual meeting of Education of Teachers, St. Louis, January 26 – February 2, 2003. ED 472 968

King, A. "Structuring Peer Interaction to Promote High-Level Cognitive Processing." *Theory into Practice,* 41(1) (2002): 33–39.

Kirk, J. J., and R. L. Orr. *A Primer on the Effective Use of Threaded Discussion Forums.* 2003. EDRS, ED 472 738.

Kong, Y. S.. *Learning to Learn: Preparing Teachers and Students for Problem-Based Learning. ERIC Digest.* ERIC Clearinghouse on Reading, English and Communication. Bloomington, IN: 2001. ED 457 524.

Leat, D., and M. Lin. "Developing a Pedagogy of Metacognition and Transfer: Some Signposts for the Generation and Use of Knowledge and the Creation of Research Partnerships." *British Educational Research Journal* 29(3) (2003): 383–415.

Lyons, N., and V. K. LaBoskey, editors. *Narrative Inquiry in Practice: Advancing the Knowledge of Teaching.* New York: Teachers College Press, 2002.

Martin-Hansen, L. "Defining Inquiry: Exploring the Many Types of Inquiry in the Science Classroom." *Science Teacher* 69(2) (2002): 34–37.

Martinez, M. E. "What Is Problem Solving?" *Phi Delta Kappan* 79(8) (1998): 606–609.

Marzano, R. J. "What Are the General Skills of Thinking and Reasoning and How Do You Teach Them?" *Clearing House* 71(5) (1998): 268–273.

Marzano, R. J., D. J. Pickering, and J. E. Pollock. *Classroom Instruction That Works: Research-Based Strategies for Increasing Student Achievement.* Alexandria, VA: Association for Supervision and Curriculum Development, 2001.

Mullis, I. V .S., M. O. Martin, E. J. Gonzalez, and A. M. Kennedy. *PIRLS 2001 International Report: IEA's Study of Reading Literacy Achievement in Primary Schools.* Chestnut Hill, MA: Boston College, 2003.

Munson, B. H., R. Huber, R. Axler, G. Host, C. Hagley, C. Moore, and G. Merrick. "Field Trips Online." *Science Teacher* 70(1) (2003): 44–49.

Murphy, C. E. "Using the Five Themes of Geography to Explore a School Site." *Social Studies Review* 37(2) (1998): 49–52.

Nelson, J. "Get to Know Your School: Involving Students in the Historical Process." *Southern Social Studies Journal* 23(2) (1998): 37–42.

Nickelsen, L., and S. Glasscock. *Main Idea and Summarizing.* New York: Scholastic Teaching Resources, 2004.

Nord, G., E. J. Malm, and J. Nord. "Counting Pizzas: A Discovery Lesson Using Combinatorics." *Mathematics Teacher* 95(1) (2002): 8–14.

Oczkus, L. D. *Reciprocal Teaching at Work: Strategies for Improving Reading Comprehension.* Newark, DE: International Reading Association, 2003.

Orlich, D. C. (2003). "An Examination of the Longitudinal Effect of the Washington Assessment of Student Learning (WASL) on Student Achievement" *Education Policy Analysis Archives,* 11(18) June 12, 2003. Retrieve at: http://epaa.asu.edu/epaa/v11n18/

Orlich, D. C. "Education Reform and Limits to Student Achievement." *Phi Delta Kappan* 81(6) (2000): 468–472.

Orlich, D. C. "Science Inquiry and the Commonplace." *Science and Children* 26 (1989): 22–24.

Orlich, D. C. "Something Funny Happened on the Way to Reform." *Northwest Professional Educator* 1(1) (2002): 1–3.

Orlich, D. C., J. C. Horne, C. Carpenter, and J. Brantner. "Water Plus Science Equals Active Student Learners (W + S = ASL)." Presentation at the National Science Teachers Association National Convention, Boston, March 27, 1999.

Orlich, D. C., and J. M. Migaki. "What Is Your IQQ—Individual Questioning Quotient?" *Science and Children* 18 (1981): 20–21.

Patrick, J. J. *Teaching About the Louisiana Purchase. ERIC Digest.* Bloomington, IN: ERIC Clearinghouse for Social Studies/Social Science Education, 2003a. ED 479 236.

Patrick, J. J. *Teaching the Declaration of Independence. ERIC Digest.* Bloomington, IN: ERIC Clearinghouse for Social Studies/Social Science Education, 2003b. ED 472 017.

Phillips, D. C., and J. F. Soltis. *Perspectives on Learning* (4th edition). New York: Teachers College Press, 2004 .

Phillips, K. A., and P. J. Germann. "The Inquiry 'I': A Tool for Learning Scientific Inquiry." *American Biology Teacher* 64(7) (2002): 512–520.

Polya, G. *How to Solve It.* Garden City, NY: Doubleday and Co., Inc., 1957.

Popper, K. R., Sir. *The Logic of Scientific Discovery.* London: Hutchinson (8th Impression.), 1975.

Puchner, L. D. *Children Teaching for Learning: What Happens When Children Teach Others in the*

Classroom? Paper presented at annual Educational Research Association, Chicago, April 21–25, 2003. ED 478 759

Radford, R. "Young Investors Forum: A Tutorial for Children and Parents." *Washington Parent*, September/October 1991, p. 11.

Reading for Change: Performance and Engagement Across Countries. Programme for International Student Assessment (PISA). Washington, DC: Organization for Economic Cooperation and Development, 2002.

Richburg, R. W., and B. J. Nelson. "Where in Western Europe Would You Like to Live?" *The Social Studies* 82(3) (1991): 97–106.

Ridenour, N. Private communication with authors. November 15, 1999.

Robertson, H. M., B. Priest, and H. L. Fullwood. "20 Ways to Assist Learners Who Are Strategy-Inefficient." *Intervention in School and Clinic* 36(3) (2001): 182–184.

Selwyn, D., and J. Maher. *History in the Present Tense: Engaging Students Through Inquiry and Action.* Portsmouth, NH: Heinemann, 2003.

Seymour, J. R., and H. P. Osana. "Reciprocal Teaching Procedures and Principles: Two Teachers' Developing Understanding." *Teaching and Teacher Education* 19(3) (2003): 325–344.

Shayer, M., and P. Adey, editors. *Learning Intelligence: Cognitive Acceleration Across the Curriculum from 5 to 15 Years.* Buckingham, England: Open University Press, 2002.

Sherman, J. D., D. Steven, S. Honegger, and J. L. McGivern. *2003 Comparative Indicators of Education in the United States and Other G-8 Countries: 2002* (NCES 2003-026). U.S. Department of Education, National Center for Education Statistics. Project Officer: Mariann Lemke. Washington, DC: U.S. Government Printing Office, 2003.

Starko, A. J. *Creativity in the Classroom: Schools of Curious Delight.* Mahwah, NJ: L. Erlbaum Associates, 2005.

Stephenson, C. "Teaching Problem Solving and Design." Toronto: University of Toronto, August 2000.

Sternberg, R. J., and L. Spear-Swerling. *Teaching for Thinking.* Washington, DC: American Psychological Association, 1996.

Strike, K. A. "The Logic of Learning by Discovery." *Review of Educational Research* 45 (1975): 461–483.

Suter, L. E., editor. *Indicators of Science and Mathematics Education 1995* (NSF 96-52). Arlington, VA: National Science Foundation, 1996.

Taggart, G. L., S. J. Phifer, J. A. Nixon, and M. Woods. *Rubrics: A Handbook for Construction and Use.* Lancaster, PA: Technomic, 1998.

Tamir, P. "Discovery Learning and Teaching." In *International Encyclopedia of Teaching and Teacher Education* (2nd edition). L. A. Anderson, editor. Tarrytown, NY: Elsevier Science, 1995, pp. 149–155.

Tanner, M. L., and L. Casados. "Promoting and Studying Discussions in Math Classes." *Journal of Adolescent and Adult Literacy* 41(5) (1998): 342–350.

Uldrich, J. *Into the Unknown: Leadership Lessons from Lewis & Clark's Daring Westward Adventure.* New York: AMACOM, 2004.

van Zee, E. H., M. Iwasyk, A. Kurose, D. Simpson, and J. Wild. "Student and Teacher Questioning during Conversations about Science." *Journal of Research in Science Teaching* 38(2) (2001): 159–190.

Verduin, J. R., Jr. *Helping Students Develop Investigative, Problem Solving and Thinking Skills in a Cooperative Setting.* Springfield, IL: Thomas, 1996.

Wakefield, A. P. "Teaching Young Children to Think About Math." *Principal* 80(5) (2001): 26–29.

Wakefield, J. F. *Educational Psychology: Learning to Be a Problem Solver.* Boston: Houghton Mifflin, 1996.

Walberg, H. J. "Productive Teaching." In *New Directions for Teaching Practice and Research.* H. C. Waxman and H. J. Walberg, editors. Berkeley, CA: McCutchan, 1999, pp. 75–104.

Wallace, B., and R. Bentley, editors. *Teaching Thinking Skills Across the Middle Years: A Practical Approach for Children Aged 9–14.* London: David Fulton, in association with the National Association for Able Children in Education, 2002.

Weinbaum, A., et al. *Teaching as Inquiry: Asking Hard Questions to Improve Practice and Student Achievement.* New York: Teachers College Press; Oxford, OH: National Staff Development Council, 2004.

Wilson, H. C. "Discovery Education: A Definition." *Horizons* 19 (2002): 25–29.

Womack, J. G. *Discovering the Structure of the Social Studies.* New York: Benziger Brothers, 1966.

Wormeli, R. *Summarization in Any Subject: 50 Techniques to Improve Student Learning.* Alexandria, VA: Association for Supervision and Curriculum Development, 2004.

Wray, K. B. "Is Science Really a Young Man's Game?" *Social Studies of Science* 33(1) (2003): 137–149.

Zevin, J. "Mystery Island: A Lesson in Inquiry." *Today's Education* 58 (1969): 42–43.

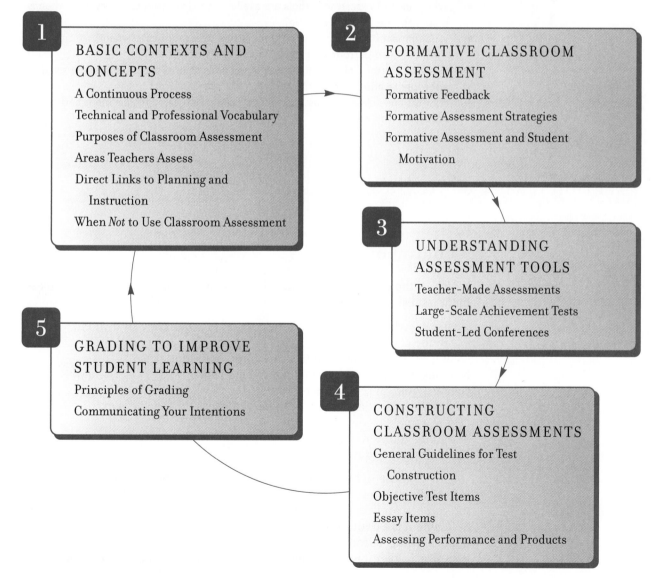

Classroom Assessment

CHAPTER

10

1 BASIC CONTEXTS AND CONCEPTS
A Continuous Process
Technical and Professional Vocabulary
Purposes of Classroom Assessment
Areas Teachers Assess
Direct Links to Planning and
    Instruction
When *Not* to Use Classroom Assessment

2 FORMATIVE CLASSROOM ASSESSMENT
Formative Feedback
Formative Assessment Strategies
Formative Assessment and Student
    Motivation

3 UNDERSTANDING ASSESSMENT TOOLS
Teacher-Made Assessments
Large-Scale Achievement Tests
Student-Led Conferences

5 GRADING TO IMPROVE STUDENT LEARNING
Principles of Grading
Communicating Your Intentions

4 CONSTRUCTING CLASSROOM ASSESSMENTS
General Guidelines for Test
    Construction
Objective Test Items
Essay Items
Assessing Performance and Products

Jane Jones, a new teacher at Emerson Middle School, has been reviewing the school board's policy on assessment and testing: "Teachers are expected to provide an objective evaluation of all students enrolled in their classes. Although some testing will be norm referenced and objective in format, we encourage the use of essay and criterion-referenced tests as well. Further, we encourage all teachers to use, as appropriate, portfolios, authentic measures, and performance assessments. This policy does not preclude the use of other indicators in the evaluation process." Jane silently muses on how she'll plan this process for her social studies and English classes.

You have already had considerable experience with assessment: You were assessed in most classes in elementary and secondary school; you probably took the SAT or other entrance exams before college; and you are likely being assessed in your present classes. But now it's time for you, like Jane, to start thinking of assessment from the teacher's point of view. This chapter will help you answer these questions.

- How do I coordinate planning, instruction, and assessment?
- What kinds of assessment tools are available to classroom teachers, and when is it appropriate to use each one?
- What impact has educational reform had on classroom assessment?
- How can I use performance assessments in my classroom?
- How can I communicate the results of my assessments to students, parents, and appropriate administrators?
- How do I use classroom assessment to enhance student achievement and academic well-being?

SECTION 1: BASIC CONTEXTS AND CONCEPTS

A Continuous Process

Which of the classroom activities listed below do you consider to be assessment issues?

Observing which students work best together when they sit near each other in the classroom
Asking students a question to check understanding
Noticing a student who seems not to hear well
Giving a quiz on recent instruction
Noticing that students seem bored and restless during a lesson
Giving a final test covering a unit
Assigning grades to students
Reviewing yesterday's lesson

All of these activities are examples of what teachers do—formally and informally—to monitor and guide student learning. They gather information, interpret it, and then make decisions of whether and how to respond. Thus assessment is a continuous process whose primary purpose is to improve student learning (Gronlund 2006). This chapter is offered to help you plan, organize, implement, and interpret classroom assessments to become a more

Main purpose: to enhance student learning

effective teacher. This chapter will help you think about classroom assessment as a powerful tool to enhance student learning. There are many reasons it is important for you to know about assessment to be an effective teacher. Several of them are noted in the box below.

Reasons for Classroom Assessment

1. To provide feedback to students
2. To make informed decisions about students
3. To monitor, make judgments about, and document students' academic performance
4. To aid student motivation by establishing short-term goals and feedback
5. To increase retention and transfer of learning by focusing learning
6. To evaluate instructional effectiveness
7. To establish and maintain a supportive classroom learning atmosphere

---

Technical and Professional Vocabulary

Before proceeding, let's clarify several terms. It is customary to distinguish among the terms *assessment, test,* and *measurement* in the following ways (Linn and Miller 2005, pp. 26–27): **Assessment**, the most general term, includes a broad range of processes by which teachers gather information about student learning. These processes include paper-and-pencil tests, performance and project ratings, and observations. Assessment is in part a qualitative description—making a value judgment in response to the question: How well does the student perform? Assessment can also include testing instruments, such as standardized or large-scale achievement tests.

A broad range of processes

A **test** is simply a particular type of assessment, usually a set of questions that all students must answer in a fixed period of time and under similar conditions to demonstrate learning. Teachers use tests to determine how well students perform on a specific set of tasks and to obtain comparative measurements of students' performance.

Measurement is a process that assigns numbers to assessment results, such as the number of correct answers or points on a project. It is a quantitative description and makes no statement about the quality of a student's performance. Measurement, as a concept, is typically associated with large-scale achievement tests.

A **norm-referenced standardized test**, such as the SAT or the Iowa Test of Basic Skills, is usually a paper-and-pencil test that has been developed by a major test publisher, standardized for a large population (called a "norming group"), and administered under the same conditions and time limits to all takers. The purpose of a standardized test is to rank each individual's score by comparing it to the scores (using measurement) of the entire norming group. Both the norming process and the fact that the same test is given to all takers under identical conditions make the test "standardized."

Two other terms—*validity* and *reliability*—need clarification (see Nitko 2004, pp. 36–76 for a full discussion).These characteristics are of the utmost importance in all assessments, both standardized and classroom assessments. The discussion that follows is focused on standardized, measurement-oriented tests and assessments. In a later section, reliability and validity for classroom assessments are addressed.

Validity refers to the degree to which a test measures what it is intended to measure. A ruler, for instance, is a valid tool to measure the dimensions of a table. The measurements it provides can be trusted in making decisions about where the table will or won't fit, for example. However, a ruler would be useless for measuring the weight of the table; for this task, it is an invalid tool.

Does the test measure what it's supposed to?

Now consider a math test that includes verbal problems. To what extent do the measurements that such problems provide reflect students' reading abilities as well as their math knowledge? To the extent the test measures more of a student's reading ability, it is less valid as a test purely of math skills. Is there an easy solution to this dilemma? None that we know of—no test is a completely valid measure of achievement constructs or domains. The fundamental question to ask is, "What evidence do I have that the test I'm giving, whether I made it or not, is measuring what I intend it to measure?" Notice also that validity is relative to purpose—a test may be valid for one purpose but not for another.

Reliability refers to the consistency of test results. If the same group of students could be retested several times and get about the same scores, then the test can be considered reliable. Obviously, you can't use this method to determine a test's reliability because students would learn from each retaking. However, several statistical methods are available for estimating test reliability that test publishers use when documenting the technical (e.g., reliability and validity) characteristics of the tests they produce (see the Print Resources section at the end of this chapter). One general rule for you to remember is that reliability increases with test length. That is, the more questions asked on a test, the more information is available on students. As a consequence, uncertainty about student achievement is reduced, which in turn increases consistency or reliability. The box below lists questions you should ask in determining an assessment instrument's validity and reliability.

Are the test's results consistent?

Key Ideas

Validity and Reliability

Validity
- Does this test measure what it is intended to measure?
- Can I make sound decisions about achievement on the basis of these test scores?
- Does this test sample a representative portion of the content being assessed?

Reliability
- Does this test give similar results with each use?
- Are the results of this test consistent with those of other measures?

reflect

• Consider a test you took recently to determine its validity and reliability. Did the test measure what it claimed to measure? Did it assess a reasonable portion of the content? If you repeated the test, with no learning gain, would the results be similar?

Purposes of Classroom Assessment

As a skilled teacher, you will use classroom assessment in four major ways to accomplish four different, important purposes. These four purposes are discussed below and summarized in the Key Ideas box on page 333.

Placement   Recall Benjamin Bloom's assertion in Chapter 4 that 50 percent of the variability in student achievement results from lack of sufficient knowledge or skill to begin new instruction. Therefore, before beginning instruction, many effective teachers use a **pretest** to assess their students' current knowledge. There are at least three reasons for doing so. First, such a test will identify students who do not know enough to begin the new material; the teacher can then provide these students with prerequisite work. Second, assessing the general level of students' prior knowledge helps determine where to begin instruction and what to present. Finally, scores on a valid and reliable pretest can serve as a baseline from which to measure progress. Depending on the material and the objectives, both multiple-choice and performance measures can be useful as pretests. Placement tests are generally produced by test manufacturers, although they can also be made by teachers.

Pretest is for placement.

Diagnosis   Another purpose of assessment is to determine specific areas of learning difficulty. The tool used, a **diagnostic test**, is most often a commercial product, although teachers may sometimes make it. Its purpose is to identify students' strengths and weaknesses, specifically what students need to learn in designated subjects. Typically, diagnostic tests are used in conjunction with specialists—teachers of reading, foreign language teachers, special educators, or counselors and psychologists—to identify problems or to screen for problems.

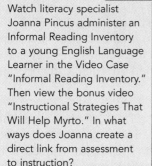

video case

Watch literacy specialist Joanna Pincus administer an Informal Reading Inventory to a young English Language Learner in the Video Case "Informal Reading Inventory." Then view the bonus video "Instructional Strategies That Will Help Myrto." In what ways does Joanna create a direct link from assessment to instruction?

Diagnosis identifies strengths and weaknesses.

Formative Assessment   At the heart of your job as a teacher is your students' growing competence and their successes in learning. Therefore, perhaps the most important kind of classroom assessment you will engage in is that of *formative* evaluation—ongoing assessments to monitor your students' progress. The purposes here are first, to verify that learning is occurring and that the curriculum is appropriate. In this instance, the primary user of the information is the teacher. Evaluation need not be a formal assessment. Systematic, recorded observations of each student by the teacher (called "anecdotal records" and discussed later in this chapter) can also used.

Formative assessment is also used to provide feedback to students, to answer their need to know "How am I doing?" and "Am I meeting expectations?" The form of the assessment will be whatever can most reasonably answer this question for the student and provide the quickest possible feedback. Usually formative assessments consist of daily quizzes, homework, and short tests. Current research shows that timely, relevant feedback, is one of the most important factors for improving student achievement (Marzano, Pickering, and Pollock 2001). After analyzing almost 8,000 studies, John Hattie (1992, p. 9) offers this perspective: "The most powerful single modification that enhances student achievement is feedback." Section 2 of this chapter is devoted entirely to formative assessment.

Formative assessment lets students know how they're doing.

Summative Assessment   Finally, *summative assessment* is used to make evaluative judgments and to certify completion of projects, classes, and programs. The users of summative evaluation (which often consist of a letter grade) include not only students but also their parents and perhaps future schools and employers. We devote the final section of this chapter to the process of grading because it is perceived by all those people to be a major part of schooling. Formative and summative tests are usually made by teachers, although they may be included in the supplementary materials that accompany textbooks.

Summative assessment includes letter grades.

Areas Teachers Assess

Now that you are familiar with a teacher's primary *purposes* for assessment, it will be helpful for you to know about the *kinds* of behaviors, activities, and knowledge you will be evaluating. (As you read this section, you might ask yourself which areas would be most suited to one or more of the purposes of assessment.)

Recall that, in Chapter 3, you studied three domains of learning—cognitive, affective, and psychomotor. Effective teachers make assessments in each domain. However, as you probably noticed in reading that chapter, many activities involve more than one domain. Making a wall poster, for instance, is in part a psychomotor activity, but the poster's quality depends in part on the students' knowledge of what to include and on their feelings about or motivation for making it. The discussion below, then, uses the term *areas* to identify what you assess, and each area involves one or more of the domains. (These areas are listed again in the box on page 333.) The areas and techniques are suggestive but not comprehensive. The techniques mentioned in each category are explained later in the chapter.

Effective teachers assess in the cognitive, affective, and psychomotor domains.

Knowledge and Conceptual Understanding   This, of course, is the usual area we associate with testing. It is a very broad area, however, and you will use different assessment methods for different types of knowledge. It is particularly important to identify objectives here before considering assessment methods (see Chapter 3). If, for instance, the objective was memory work—math facts, perhaps—then you should test students' recall of information, either orally or in writing. However, if conceptual understanding was the objective (of a concept such as photosynthesis, for instance), such understanding is best evaluated by having students explain the concept in their own words, either orally or written; by having them identify examples of the concept; or by having them create new examples of it. Ask yourself, "How can each student demonstrate understanding?"

Thinking We place this domain in a separate category, although some teachers refer to thinking as a skill. In the sense that one can improve one's performance at it, thinking *is* a skill. However, thinking seems to be much more than just a skill, and assessment can involve multiple-choice tests, problem-solving exercises, and oral or written explanations. Make sure that you have a definition of thinking that works for you. "What indicators will I look for to know that students are thinking?"

Skills There are many types of skills—physical, learning, social, thinking, math, problem solving—and a wide variety of tools can be used to assess them. Various kinds of paper-and-pencil tests may be appropriate for math or problem solving, whereas a demonstration is a reasonable way to display physical education skills. Portfolios may well be the assessment tool of choice for art, composition, or drafting classes, whereas performance may be the first choice for a music class. The point is to consider all the areas in your curriculum that involve any kind of skill, and then ask yourself, "What can each student do to indicate progress?"

Attitudes Especially in relation to building a group spirit and sense of interdependence in a class (see Chapter 8), it is useful to inquire about students' feelings toward one another and about school in general. Sociograms, attitude inventories, anecdotal records, and checklists can provide considerable data without compromising confidentiality or privacy rights. Ask yourself, "What evidence or student behaviors show positive attitudes in class?"

KEY IDEAS

Purposes of Classroom Assessment

- *For placement.* To determine whether the student has prerequisite skills to begin instruction
- *For diagnosis.* To determine causes (physical, intellectual) of persistent learning problems
- *For formative assessments.* To monitor learning progress, provide feedback to reinforce learning, correct learning errors
- *For summative assessments.* To determine final achievement for assigning grades or certifying mastery

SOURCE: Adapted from Linn and Miller 2005, p. 35.

Areas Teachers Assess

- Knowledge and conceptual understanding ("How can students demonstrate understanding?")
- Thinking ("What indicators show what and how students are thinking?")
- Skills ("What can each student do to indicate progress?")
- Attitudes ("What evidence or student behaviors show positive attitude in class?")

Direct Links to Planning and Instruction

Now that you understand several core concepts about classroom assessment and the primary contexts for your decisions about that assessment, we want to take another brief look at planning and how it relates to assessment.

Ideally, assessment planning should be an integral part of your instructional planning, not a process added on at the conclusion of instruction. Done carefully, such "whole-package" planning will ensure that instructional outcomes are clear to both you and your students; that instruction is sequenced rationally; that instruction and assessment are congruent; and that your assessment measures all the outcomes you intended. Recall from Chapter 3 that this process is called "curriculum alignment." When all three elements match—that is, when instruction and assessment focus on stated objectives—alignment exists.

Build it into instructional planning.

The other point that is critical for you to remember is that all three instructional processes inform one another. That is, your planning decisions will undoubtedly require adjustment once you actually teach from them and reflect on the day's instruction. Likewise, your ongoing observing and monitoring of your students' learning—daily classroom assessment—should directly affect instructional decisions. Have students learned the intended concepts well? If not, where does the problem lie—in the instructional methods, in students' background preparation, or perhaps elsewhere? Which of the methods you have selected seems to generate the most motivation and interest among students? What are an individual student's strengths and weaknesses in a specific area? The answers to all of these questions, gleaned through assessment on a continuous basis, will affect both the next lesson's planning and its instruction.

A few other comments about assessment and the planning process are in order. Some teachers find it useful, once they have written their objectives, to begin their planning with the assessment phase. They specify how students will demonstrate achievement of the objectives and then work back and forth between the instructional plan and the assessment plan to determine what must be included in the teaching (see Wiggins and McTighe 2005).

Sometimes teachers enter the instructional planning cycle at the learning activity phase. Having found an activity that stimulates student interest and enthusiasm, the teacher specifies which objectives the activity will attain and develops assessments to monitor and measure achievement.

Teach what you test, and test what you teach.

Keeping in mind that planning the assessment while you are planning a unit's instruction and activities is the best way to be sure that all the parts fit together and support one another. Study the following two general pointers about assessment and planning.

Begin with Report Cards   One practical way to plan assessments is to begin with the report cards that you will eventually be expected to prepare. What information is expected there? How often? Are letter grades used? Do you need to prepare comments? Are there check-off items? What sorts of data will you need to prepare report cards? How might you obtain all the required information? Does your school district key its standards to specific lists that form the report card?

These questions may sound simplistic and obvious, but we have seen many instances in which beginning teachers didn't ask about report cards until a few days before they had to prepare them—which is too late! Because you will be expected to document student progress at least four times a year, both practicality and professional responsibility require that you prepare adequately.

Teachers at different grade levels tend to use different types of assessments (Daniel and King 1998). Elementary teachers depend much on observations of students, periodic quizzes, and worksheets, supplementing sometimes with standardized tests of basic skills. A glance at the report card explains why. Elementary curriculum involves many skills and behaviors that are quite standard across districts (basic reading, writing, spelling, math). A checklist approach is an effective method of providing feedback.

Through the middle school and secondary years, the curriculum becomes much more content oriented and less basic skill oriented than in the elementary programs. Checklists seem less useful, and the traditional response has been a letter grade to indicate achievement. Grading is discussed at the end of the chapter, but the point here is that examining report cards is an efficient way to determine at least part of what you need to assess, in what form, and how often.

Consider the Timing   Timing of assessments is a next step in preliminary planning. Four strategies for using tests to maximize their contribution to learning are offered (Dempster and Perkins 1993). First, newly introduced material should be tested relatively soon. In this way, students are motivated to begin study immediately, and you, as the teacher, have information on student progress. Second, frequent testing encourages continuous study and reduces test anxiety. This strategy helps to maintain student motivation to study and obtain the learning expectations (rather than to procrastinate and worry about failure). Third, tests should be cumulative—including some material from earlier assignments. Fourth, testing helps in aiding retention.

The effective teacher, then, builds a preliminary calendar around required assessments for administrative purposes and necessary assessments for maximum learning gains.

Test often; test new material quickly.

When *Not* to Use Classroom Assessment

Overwhelming evidence shows that, when used appropriately, classroom assessment has a powerful influence on student achievement. Paul Black and Dylan Wiliam (1998), for example, did a review of studies spanning grade levels, subjects, and countries, and found that effective use of classroom assessment could boost student achievement as much as 15 percentile points as measured by standardized achievement tests. This is as strong a message about the link between classroom assessment and instruction that can be made.

When classroom assessment is not used with student well-being in mind, however, teachers can damage students' academic well-being and, ultimately, their achievement. This occurs when teachers use assessments for classroom control and student punishment—purposes for which assessments are not designed and should never be used. Unfortunately, many teachers, for many years, have used classroom assessments as a classroom management tool. Examples include "pop" quizzes to punish an unruly class and "settle them down" or taking away credit on a project to punish a student for goofing off. The net effect of using assessments to control and punish is that students learn to avoid tests and other assessments because they are never quite sure of their purpose. You as a teacher may want to use them for legitimate instructional purposes, while your students, given their previous experiences, think you may be using assessments for some other reason, such as punishment. Students stop striving for excellence because they are no longer willing to risk trying for a target that could become a weapon, and you lose a potential 15 percentile point gain on standardized tests. In addition, if you use classroom assessments for manipulative reasons, students may begin to lose trust, as well as respect, in you as their teacher. The negative consequences are simply too great to use assessments as tools of punishment.

Punitive testing damages motivation.

reflect

- The four questions below address important issues in classroom assessment. Pool your thoughts with a small group and then present your findings to the class.

    1. Why is continuous assessment valuable?

    2. What facts might make a classroom test or tests either invalid or unreliable?

    3. In your experience as a student, what purpose did classroom assessment serve? How does this compare to the purpose it should serve?

    4. List the ways that assessment methods might differ in the cognitive, affective, and psychomotor domains.

- Can you recall a time as a student when a teacher used classroom assessment deliberately to punish you or your classmates? How did this make you feel? How do you think it affected your or your classmates' willingness and ability to learn?

section 2: Formative classroom assessment

Classroom assessment can be productively used for far more that the collection of achievement information to assign grades. Of course, assigning grades is an important task teachers must perform. However, when teachers begin to think of assessment *for learning* rather than *of learning*, the power of assessment as an instructional tool is released into the classroom. Paul Black and colleagues (2004) argue that assessment for learning occurs when assessment is used to enhance student achievement.

Assessment not of learning, but for learning

Formative assessment is a type of classroom assessment devoted entirely to the enhancement of student learning and achievement. This chapter offers a variety of assessment strategies that can be used for this purpose. This section (1) provides a definition of feedback and discusses its importance, (2) describes three formative assessment strategies, and (3) connects formative assessment to student motivation.

Formative Feedback

Much has been written about the connection between assessment and feedback. For students, **feedback**, particularly formative feedback, is information that illustrates the gap or difference between what the student currently knows and understands and what the teacher's expectation is for this knowledge and understanding. Royce Sadler (1998) unravels the concept of feedback into simple terms teachers can apply in the classroom. In short, for teachers to assess the quality of student work and provide formative feedback, teachers must (a) have a clear idea of the standard or goal students are expected to achieve, and (b) be able to judge the quality of student work relative to the standard.

To achieve the full benefit of feedback, students must ultimately hold the same understanding of the standard as does the teacher. Students must also be able to assess their individual work and apply a variety of self-monitoring strategies to revise and enhance their work in order to meet the standard.

This is no small task. It requires several years of teaching to fully understand appropriate expectations for students, apply criteria to judge the quality of student work, and model strategies students can use to meet the standard. However, there are approaches teachers can employ that help to foster the benefits of formative assessment.

Students and teacher must have same expectations

Formative Assessment Strategies

Here is a short list of essential formative assessment strategies you can use in the classroom to enhance student learning (see Black et al. 2004 for more detail). When and how much to use each technique is a judgment you will need to make based on the class, content of the instructional unit, your teaching style, and your comfort with the procedure.

Questioning. A key aspect of formative feedback is questioning. Questioning is so important that we devote all of Chapter 7 to it. You have learned already that asking thoughtful questions about the learning task and providing sufficient wait time for students to think and generate responses lie at the heart of questioning for formative feedback. This type of questioning can bring all students, not just the high achievers, into the learning process.

Peer Assessment. Ultimately, for students to obtain high achievement, they need to be able to self-assess and, when necessary, to employ corrective measures to meet the standard. Self-assessment is typically fostered by feedback to students from the teacher. However, feedback from teachers may not always be received well by students, particularly students who have not achieved well in their schooling. Students can sometimes be more receptive to peers than to teachers, so developing tasks and feedback sessions between and among students could be used productively to enhance student learning. To do this well, teachers need to explain to students how to give useful feedback, perhaps by modeling. For example, suppose a teacher gave a writing assignment to students with a set of criteria for gauging the quality of the writing. Using a student essay from a previous class, the teacher could model the use of the criteria and how to give feedback on performance. With this knowledge and understanding, students could then give one another feedback, feedback that illustrates the gap between the current quality of the essay and the expected quality embodied in the criteria.

Feedback through Grading. Grading is clearly a task you must understand and do well. This includes not only the development of semester grades but also the grading of tests, reports, and projects (grading is discussed later in this chapter). The downside of grading is that it can reinforce achievement differences among students. Successful students see grades as connected to effort, while unsuccessful students view grades as evidence that they are losers in the educational system. This is most true when grades are provided without additional feedback.

Studies have shown that written feedback about performance on the tasks, in addition to a grade, can be a powerful means of enhancing student learning. It can help to encourage students to think about their own performance and achievement, rather than serve as evidence of who wins and who loses. It is not the amount but the type of feedback that has the greatest impact on student learning. Teachers need to have a clear idea of what they want from students, be able to judge students' work objectively against the expectation, and effectively communicate how the student performed (Sadler 1998).

> Students may be more open to peers' feedback.

Formative Assessment and Student Motivation

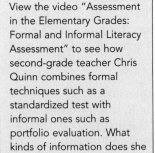

VIDEO CASE

View the video "Assessment in the Elementary Grades: Formal and Informal Literacy Assessment" to see how second-grade teacher Chris Quinn combines formal techniques such as a standardized test with informal ones such as portfolio evaluation. What kinds of information does she get from each approach?

Providing clear feedback to students about their achievement can increase student motivation to succeed. In particular, clarifying the goal or standard and helping students develop a representation of this standard for themselves helps students to take ownership for their success. When students understand what it means to succeed in your classroom, success is no longer a mystery or something held only by the teacher. With shared understanding of success, students are less likely to blame you or something else outside themselves for not meeting the standard. They are more likely to take responsibility when they do not meet a standard on a particular unit and take steps to obtain the goal.

These ideas have the greatest potential for low-achieving students. In an environment with little feedback except, for example, grades, low-achieving students see achievement as a futile guessing game and often stop trying. However, with formative feedback students are more likely to try and meet achievement challenges. Thus, the connection between formative assessment and student motivation should be at the forefront of any teacher's thinking and planning of classroom assessment.

> Low achievers can grasp the rules of the game.

Examples of Teacher Feedback

Insufficient feedback (vague; does not help students improve their performance)
- "Good effort"
- "Nice work"
- "Needs revision"

Useful feedback (gives specific information students can use to improve performance)
- "With this report, consider using shorter sentences. Your message is lost with such long sentences."
- "When solving these equations, use a different line for each step. Then you'll be able to monitor the progression you've used to solve the equation."

reFLecT

- Think about a teacher you had in high school whom you believe was a good instructor. Did this teacher use assessment to promote student achievement? How was this accomplished?

- At what point did you feel as though you understood what "success" meant in this classroom? Did you then notice a positive difference in your performance?

SECTION 3: UNDERSTANDING ASSESSMENT TOOLS

Classifying assessment tools is similar to classifying animals or plants—there are many ways to proceed. We saw earlier how assessment can be organized and categorized according to the purposes a classroom teacher needs to consider. Here we lay out a different kind of grouping of assessment tools, organized according to the nature and characteristics of the tools.

Teacher-Made Assessments

As your experience no doubt confirms, most classroom assessments involve teacher-made tests. There are good reasons for this. First, the teacher has monitored the learning experiences in the class and thus has a much better idea than anyone else what needs to be assessed. Second, we assess the learning based on what we taught. If we taught for memory of facts, that's what we assess. If we taught for application, we assess for that. A third reason is that the teacher is familiar with the students as well as the instruction, which may affect the what and how of assessment.

How exactly *do* teachers make assessments? A major section of this chapter (Section 4, "Constructing Classroom Assessments") details that process, but here we offer some overall guidelines to help you produce valid, reliable measures of your students' achievement.

First, as we've mentioned, plan the test as you plan instruction rather than waiting until the instruction is over. Knowing in advance how and what to assess can be an important aid in instruction, especially in keeping it focused and not dwelling too long in some areas and omitting others.

Second, remember that the overall context for classroom assessment involves a variety of methods. You will also be letting students demonstrate their skills and understandings in a variety of valid ways—reports (oral and written), posters, videos, music, plays, stories, models, performances. Sometimes, however, a paper-and-pencil test created by the teacher *is* the most appropriate assessment choice.

Third, weave assessment throughout the instruction; don't tack it on at the end. If students are assessed throughout the duration of a unit, you and they will have a much more realistic picture of their understanding than a single test at the end of the unit will provide.

As mentioned earlier, notions of reliability and validity are important for classroom assessments. Publishers of standardized or large-scale assessments use statistically oriented procedures to quantify reliability and validity. Teachers typically don't have the time and training to perform these statistical procedures. Assessments occur many times throughout the year and are often not standardized, and sometimes, classes have too few students to warrant statistical computation. However, this does not relieve the teacher of the responsibility of ensuring reliability and validity. Richard Stiggins (2005) offers five questions you can ask about your assessments to gauge their quality.

> Be flexible and creative in deciding on assessment formats.

> Is the assessment appropriate?

1. What is the purpose of the assessment?
2. Does this assessment assess clear learning targets?
3. Am I using a method that makes sense given the purpose and targets?
4. Do I have enough information for the given purpose?
5. Have I taken steps to control for mismeasurement of student achievement?

In sum, keep in mind that, as a teacher, you are using assessments to communicate to students about their achievement. These questions help to ensure that you are communicating effectively.

Large-Scale Achievement Tests

Large-scale achievement testing is a big topic, and you'll find many books devoted to it. Excellent coverage of the technical aspects of these tests and interpretation of the several kinds of scores they generate are found in John Salvia and James E. Ysseldyke's *Assessment* (2004), cited in Print Resources at the end of the chapter. The following section discusses the strengths of these tests and how you might use their results in your instructional decision making. Then we treat some of the questions, concerns, and reforms related to standardized tests.

Strengths and Potential Uses   Schools use large-scale achievement tests mainly to assess districtwide and statewide curricula, monitor student achievement, and assess student aptitudes prior to high school graduation. The primary consideration in using these tests is to be sure that there is congruence between what is taught (the curriculum) and what the test measures. A close study of the test itself and its supplementary manuals will reveal this.

As you teach, always remember that no single test gives (or even claims to give) a complete picture of a student's achievement. Test scores must be supplemented with samples of student work, observation of students, and the quizzes, tests, and assignments that you create for your students. Only then can a professional evaluation of achievement be made.

Here are the strengths of large-scale achievement tests (adapted from Herman, Aschbacher, and Winters 1992; Linn and Miller 2005, pp. 39–416; Madaus and Kellaghan 1993; Worthen 1993).

Strengths of large-scale tests

1. *Technical excellence in questions.* The questions on standardized tests are written by specialists, reviewed by experts on the subject matter being tested, reviewed for bias, and field-tested for flaws.
2. *Extensive technical data.* Standardized tests are accompanied by extensive helpful data on norming, validity, and reliability.
3. *Cost-efficiency.* The development costs of most standardized tests have long since been recovered, which means they can deliver the highest technical proficiency at the least cost per pupil. By contrast, most alternative assessments are not cost efficient.
4. *Easy-to-use data.* Standardized tests provide separate printouts for class records, individual student reports, reports to parents, and many other uses. They provide a variety of scores—percentiles, grade equivalencies, stanines—for use in comparing each student's score to the norming group's scores. In addition, scores are available to show mastery or non-mastery of specific skills and objectives.
5. *Ease of administration and scoring.* Unlike alternative and most teacher-made tests, standardized tests are extremely easy to administer and score.
6. *Customization.* Standardized tests can be custom-crafted to fit a district's specified objectives.

Questions, Concerns, and Reform   In the 1980s and 1990s, there was a great deal of dissatisfaction with standardized testing. In essence, this dissatisfaction stemmed from the inappropriate use of such testing—using test results to drive the curriculum, using test scores as the *only* indicator for high-stakes decisions, and overemphasizing basic skills in instruction as a result of standardized test results.

Another core problem was that many of the higher-level thinking processes are difficult to assess using a multiple-choice test. For instance, a math test might ask the student to select the correct response from four choices. Does doing so demonstrate the use of the same mental processes as calculating the answer? Many argued that it did not and that the only realistic way to assess such skill is by demonstration. The same arguments were made in many areas, including composition, speaking, foreign language, and music.

Weaknesses of large-scale tests

As a result of these and related concerns, reformers began demanding increased attention to many issues left out or ignored by the standardized testing movement—instructional emphasis on thinking and problem solving, local determination of learning outcomes, alignment of what is tested with what is taught, and fostering lifelong learning rather than stressing rote memorization of content. The result of teachers' continued dissatisfaction with testing, coupled with school reform efforts of the early 1990s, was a significant change in goals, processes, governance, curriculum, and assessment in the schools (see Linn 1998; Popham 1999).

The primary change, in both assessment and curricula (the two cannot logically be separated), was a shift in focus. For many decades, schools had concentrated on classifying and sorting students—ranking them and placing them in various groups. Standardized achievement tests, normed on a national sample, effectively accomplished this. The process was reinforced by a grading system in which the final result was a grade point average and a ranked class standing.

Reform efforts turned away from using numerical scores and averages as indicators of success and toward a focus on each student's competency in the skills that will be most useful in life—being a critical thinker, knowing how to analyze and solve problems, working productively in groups, monitoring one's own learning, and evaluating one's own efforts (see Stiggins 2005, pp. 20–37, for a detailed account). In addition, many of today's achievement tests are not norm-referenced but are *standards-referenced*. That is, the tests are built to reflect achievement targets, typically within a state. Scores derive meaning not by comparison to a norm group but by comparison to a fixed standard.

Today, the use of large-scale testing has become more complex and controversial as reform efforts continue into the twenty-first century. Nearly every state mandates statewide assessments with consequences for performance. Known as **high-stakes tests**, these testing policies seek to motivate and challenge students to excel, and hold teachers and administrators accountable for results. The federal government has weighed in with its own set of high-stakes testing requirements (U.S. Department of Education 2002).

The problem with this approach is that the teaching and learning process is often corrupted (see Madaus 1998; Nichols and Berliner, 2005). Teachers often overfocus on test preparation, skew instruction to the test, and pay particular attention to the form in which tests are constructed by teaching to this form. Because large-scale, standardized tests are predominantly multiple choice in form, teachers teach to this format. Ironically, much of the impetus for education reform in the first place is undermined. Teachers don't focus on problem solving and complex thinking. They focus on facts and those achievement targets tested through multiple-choice formats. Keep in mind that it is not the form that is the problem. Multiple-choice formats are quite useful and valid when used appropriately. It is the use of the tests to make high-stakes decisions about students and teachers that is problematic. This testing practice compels teachers to narrow their curriculum and instruction to focus on learning targets, which can be tested on current achievement tests, leaving many valuable learning targets out of the curriculum because they are not part of the test.

As a teacher, you will have plenty to keep you busy, necessitating careful choices about outside activities. However, the use of high-stakes tests has direct consequences for you and your students. Thus working through your local union to understand more about large-scale testing practices and what can be done to improve them will be time well spent. George Madaus (1998) has several recommendations that could be pursued in this context.

Student-Led Conferences

One of the great recent breakthroughs in classroom assessment is recognition of the power that student-led conferences have on student achievement. Although these conferences can take many forms, they are typically done at midterm as a progress report and include the student, teacher, and parent(s). These assessments are used to discuss a student's performance on various projects, essays, tests, or quizzes. This discussion includes the quality of the student's work, the ways in which the student performed well, and what might be done to improve on his or her work or performance.

In a student-led conference, the student takes major responsibility for discussing and evaluating his or her current level of achievement relative to the standard. While this is typically an oral evaluation for the teacher and parents, a student might also convey the assessment in written form.

The benefits of using student-led conferences are, first, that students learn to take ownership for their learning and are held accountable for it. Second, communication among the three stakeholders in student success—student, parents, and teacher—is enhanced. Student-led conferences foster coordination among these individuals, with student academic well-being at heart.

Many teachers have known about the power of this technique for some time and have used it successfully for years. On the surface, you might say that student-led conferences could require a lot of work by the teacher. However, there are documented strategies from experienced teachers that can be used to efficiently conduct student-led conferences. Anne Davies, Caren Cameron, Colleen Politano, and Kathleen Gregory (1992) provide an excellent guide to developing student-led conferences. Some of their ideas include ways to get parents involved; strategies to coordinate conference activities in crowded, busy school buildings; and instructional tips to help young children talk about their achievement. These authors have clearly thought through all of the logistical considerations with this tool.

Student-led conferences build accountability.

SECTION 4: CONSTRUCTING CLASSROOM ASSESSMENTS

Having considered why and what to assess, as well as the steps in test planning, we now have a foundation for writing specific test items. Such writing is in part an art, but with some basic techniques, persistence, and practice, the skill develops rapidly. This chapter can include only a small portion of available information. However, supplement your learning with suggestions from the Print Resources section.

We begin with some general guidelines to help you as you map out and structure your test. Then we take a finer, more detailed look at writing actual test items. We divide item types into the following categories and discuss them in that order:

1. Short-answer, matching, and true-false items, for measuring knowledge-level outcomes
2. Multiple-choice items, for measuring both knowledge-level and more complex learning outcomes
3. Interpretive items, for assessing complex, higher-level objectives
4. Essay items, for assessing higher-level outcomes

General Guidelines for Test Construction

Your work in writing a specific test will be greatly facilitated if you follow these six steps.

1. Determine how much importance and instructional time you will give to the major topics to be tested and then make the number of test items for each topic proportionate. For example, if you plan to teach four main ideas and devote equal time to teach, 25 percent of the questions on your test should relate to each topic. However, if time constraints caused you to give two of the topics less attention, decrease their coverage on the test. Yes, you should test on what you taught, even if it differs from what you planned.
2. Decide on the format and item type you will use. Remember: Test the format that you taught. If you teach for concept understanding, don't test for factual recall. Doing this is more difficult to do than it appears. Fact and recall questions are much easier to write and score than understanding questions—and far more common on tests. Up to 90 percent of secondary school test questions are at the lowest level (knowledge) of Bloom's cognitive taxonomy (Daniel and King 1998).
3. Determine a balance between the available testing time and the number of questions to include. How many questions a student can reasonably answer in a given time is a variable that you will understand with experience. The average high school student can complete two true-false items, one multiple-choice item, or one short-answer item per minute of testing time. Essay items require more time (Linn and Miller 2005, p. 237). However, remember that some students work more slowly than others, and time is needed to both begin and end the test. You will get a more valid picture of achievement if you allow plenty of time, even if it means dividing the assessment over several days—another reason for more frequent testing. You must also remember the special needs of your students with disabilities and your non–English-speaking students.
4. Use a matrix, such as the Kaplan's matrix shown in Tables 4.1 and 4.2 (pages 122–123), to help organize your planning. One method is to list main ideas on the left, with headings that indicate the anticipated cognitive level across the top. The Instructional Strategies box on page 345 illustrates the concept with a unit on the U.S. Civil War. The example refers only to objective questions such as multiple choice or matching. Essay items would be relevant, but we've omitted them for clarity. Notice the strengths of the format in the matrix. Identify main ideas so you can

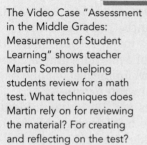

VIDEO CASE

The Video Case "Assessment in the Middle Grades: Measurement of Student Learning" shows teacher Martin Somers helping students review for a math test. What techniques does Martin rely on for reviewing the material? For creating and reflecting on the test?

Timing formula for test items

Use matrix to chart content
and level.

emphasize them in instruction and review them before the test. Note cognitive levels so you don't unintentionally use too many recall items. You can then estimate the time necessary to take the test.

5. Plan an activity for those students who finish early. Don't wait until test time for this; it always happens.

6. Develop the test items. (We discuss this next.)

Instructional Strategies

Example of Planning Matrix

Unit Test, Causes of Civil War

Major Ideas	Number of Knowledge-Level Questions	Number of Understanding-Level Questions	Total Number of Questions
Political factors	3	4	7
Economic factors	2	3	5
Geographic factors	2	3	5
Social factors	3	3	6
Total items	10	13	23

Objective Test Items

Objective items are so called because they have a single best or correct answer. There is no (or very little) dispute about the correct responses to objective items. No professional judgment is required to score them; the real skill involved here is at the other end—in constructing them carefully, fairly, and systematically. Objective items come in two types: the *selection* type, in which a response is chosen from among alternatives given, or the *supply* type, in which the student supplies a brief response. If no clear choice between supply or selection items is specified by the learning outcome, use the selection type. It provides greater control of the response and more objective scoring. But remember to test the format you taught.

Objective items have one
best answer.

True-False Items   True-false, matching, and short-answer items are three types of comparatively simple items useful mostly for measuring knowledge-level achievement. Of the three, the **true-false question**, or *alternate choice question,* is perhaps the least useful. Because these items have only two possible options, students who guess have a 50-percent chance of getting a correct response. The examples in Figure 10.1 illustrate possible formats and uses for these items. Note especially the specificity of the directions.

True-false susceptible to
guessing

Matching Exercises   **Matching exercises** are a variation on the true-false format. They, too, assess mostly recall. Their best use is in identifying relationships within homogeneous material. The same cautions and shortcomings apply to matching exercises as to true-false ones. The example in Figure 10.2 illustrates a matching test. Again, note the instructions.

FIGURE 10.1
Sample True-False Format Questions

Directions: Read each statement. If the statement is always true, circle the T. If it is always false, sometimes false, or partially false, circle the F.

T   F   **1.** Water always boils at 100 degrees centigrade.
T   F   **2.** 51% of 40 is more than 20.

Directions: Read each statement. If the statement is a fact, circle the F. If the statement is an opinion, circle the O.

F   O   **1.** Other countries should have a Bill of Rights like ours.
F   O   **2.** A red light requires a motorist to stop.

Directions: Circle the correct choice inside each pair of parentheses.

1. Give it to (whoever, whomever) you please.
2. Submit the papers to either the principal or (me, myself).

Be careful when writing matching questions. First, use only homogeneous material—don't mingle people, events, book titles, and geographic regions in the same lists. This is confusing to the student and tends to provide clues to the test-wise. Keep your lists to about eight items and use more options than there are items to be matched. Finally, be sure there is one best option for each item.

Short-Answer and Completion Items   **Short-answer** and **completion items** are supply-type rather than selection-type items. They generally require the student to provide a word, phrase, or symbol. Students are asked not simply to identify a correct choice but to retrieve it from memory—a different, perhaps intellectually more complex, process. Science and math teachers are particularly fond of this format because it seems to directly measure computational and problem-solving skills and can conveniently allow students a place to display their work. Figure 10.3 illustrates various formats.

Completion items can measure comprehension level.

Multiple-Choice Items   The **multiple-choice item** is generally considered the most useful objective test item. It can measure both knowledge and higher-level learning outcomes.

Multiple-choice items consist of two parts: a question or problem and a list of possible solutions. The problem, called the **stem**, may be phrased as either

FIGURE 10.2
Sample Matching Questions

Directions: On the line to the left of each name in Column A, write the letter of the statement in Column B that best identifies that person. Statements in Column B may be used once, more than once, or not at all.

Column A

_____ **1.** Cook
_____ **2.** Columbus
_____ **3.** Da Gama
_____ **4.** Hudson
_____ **5.** Magellan

Column B

A. The first European to navigate a southern route around South America.

B. He made four voyages to the New World.

C. The first European to sail the length of Africa's west coast.

D. His major discoveries were in eastern North America.

E. He located and conquered the Aztecs.

F. The first European to locate Australia.

G. The first European to navigate the Northwest Passage.

FIGURE 10.3

Sample Short-Answer and Completion Questions

Directions:
For each statement, write the correct word or numbers in the blank. If computations are needed, show your work on this paper, numbered appropriately. Spelling will not be counted in your score.

1. A ship is sailing on a compass heading of southwest. If it makes a ninety-degree turn to the left, in what direction will it now be sailing? _____

2. Walnut furniture wood sells for $4.12 per board foot. You need 31 board feet to complete a project. What will the wood cost? _____

3. Write the formula that describes the relationship among current, resistance, and energy in electrical problems. _____

4. What device is used to measure current? _____

5. In the statement $2x + 3 = 6 - 4x$, what number does x represent? _____

an incomplete statement or a question. The possible responses to the stem are called the **alternatives**. The correct alternative is the answer; the remaining ones are called **distractors**. Their function is to distract the unknowing student from the answer while not confusing the knowing student. Creating effective distractors is one of the most difficult parts of writing multiple-choice items.

There are many ways of effectively using multiple-choice questions to assess almost any level of achievement (Bloom et al. 1971). The examples in Figure 10.4 illustrate multiple-choice questions at several cognitive levels. The first question tests factual recall. The second question tests knowledge of a principle. The third question tests application of a principle.

Essay Items

Essays can measure complex outcomes.

The essay item is an excellent way to assess students' higher thinking processes—comprehending and analyzing—as well as skills in organizing and presenting one's ideas.

FIGURE 10.4

Sample Multiple-Choice Questions

Directions: Circle the best choice for each question.

1. **Who was the second president of the United States?**
   A. James Buchanan
   B. Thomas Jefferson
   C. James Madison
   D. John Adams

2. **Boyle's Law shows a relationship between**
   A. Density and pressure of gases
   B. Pressure and volume of a gas
   C. Density and molecular weight of a gas
   D. Pressure and temperature of liquids

3. **What should you do if the car you are driving starts to skid on a rain-slicked highway?**
   A. Steer into the direction of the skid
   B. Apply the hand brake to slow down gradually
   C. Turn the wheels in the opposite direction of the skid
   D. Quickly apply the foot brake

FIGURE 10.5
Sample Essay Items

Restricted-Response Essay Questions

1. Explain two reasons leading to the conflict in which Magellan was killed.
2. In one paragraph, explain how sailing vessels proceeded when the wind failed.
3. In no more than one page, explain in detail why Cook and other early explorers had great trouble finding again the islands they had "discovered" in the Pacific Ocean.

Extended-Response Essay Questions

1. A paved, four-lane highway of about thirty miles is to be built across Washington's temperate rain forest. Discuss the possible ecological consequences.
2. Compare England's experience during the American Revolution to the U.S. experience in Vietnam. Note specifically the concluding phases of both wars.

Types of Essay Items   In general, there are two types of essay items: restricted response and extended response.

1. *Restricted response.* This is the item of choice when your objective is to assess students' abilities to explain, interpret, and apply information. It focuses on specifics, and the question must be phrased to restrict the response in that way. Note the examples in Figure 10.5. (See Verma and Chhatwal 1997 for an extension of this concept.)
2. *Extended response.* When you wish to sample your students' abilities to select, organize, and evaluate ideas, this is an appropriate format. As the examples in Figure 10.5 show, the student has great latitude in all of these areas. However, this makes it an inefficient way to measure factual knowledge.

Scoring Responses to Essay Questions   After reading the examples in Figure 10.5 (both the restricted- and the extended-response questions), consider how you would assess them if you were the teacher. Your assessment might well differ from that of your colleagues. Reliability of grading (different graders giving the same grade, or the same grader giving the same grade over several readings) is a major concern with essay items. Extensive experience has shown that consistency of grading (reliability) is not easy to achieve with essay questions, but with careful planning and much experience, a reasonable level of reliability can be attained.

Before writing the questions, decide what learning outcomes are to be assessed (organizing ability, selection of relevant data, comprehension). Then be sure the question is phrased to elicit this objective.

Prepare a sample response, which should include the major points you expect to see, the appropriate format or organization, and the amount of credit to be given for each part or question. Many teachers also extend the sample into a rubric that shows what superior, adequate, and inadequate responses will contain. (See Table 10.1 for an example.)

Use **holistic scoring** for extended-response items. The outcomes being assessed here are global ones, such as organization and selection of relevant material. Since each paper will demonstrate these in different ways, it is neces-

Prepare sample responses or a rubric

sary to judge each response on its overall quality. Arranging the students' papers into perhaps five categories of acceptability for each question provides as much precision and reliability as you are apt to get. You then total the scores on the separate questions to determine an overall grade. When the categories are carefully defined, and raters understand the categories, considerable reliability is achieved (see Herman, Aschbacher, and Winters 1992, Chapters 5 and 6, for a thorough discussion and numerous examples of rubrics and ways to ensure reliable scoring).

Use **analytic scoring** for restricted-response items. Because of the restrictions, you can directly compare responses to the scoring rubric and assign points. As a general rule of grading, it is useful to use quantitative scores (5 points, 4 points) rather than descriptive words (excellent, needs improvement) or symbols (+, smiley face). You will eventually have to combine your judgments about individual tests and projects into an overall assessment of achievement—a grade. You can do this more fairly, we believe, through a consistent use of numbers.

Develop a coding system that conceals the students' names. This reduces the tendency to evaluate on personal qualities or other work the student has done. Some teachers assign students an arbitrary identification number to use for essay responses. Whatever system you use, you will likely soon recognize particular students' papers. Try not to let that influence your evaluation.

If there is more than one essay question, read all student answers to question 1 before going on to question 2, and so forth. This reduces the **halo effect**—the teacher's tendency to assess a student's performance based on the quality of earlier performance rather than an objective assessment. Also, reading all responses to one question first gives you an overall impression of misconceptions, well-learned areas, and areas needing further instruction.

Avoid the practice of giving students a choice of items (such as having them write on any three of four questions) or, similarly, handing out a list of topics a few days before the test, with instructions to be prepared to write on the questions. Particularly when you use restricted-response questions, giving students a choice means you will not be assessing all students on the same objectives and will thus lose comparability of scores as well as some validity (see Weber and Frary 1995).

Holistic scoring assesses work in its entirety.

Analytic scoring uses a rating system.

REFLECT

- To what extent is matching each assessment item to a specific objective essential?

- Obtain a sample unscored essay response from your school to share with a group of your peers. Evaluate and score the essay without discussing it. Now compare answers. How were your assessments similar? How did they differ?

- What techniques can you use to ensure greater fairness in the scoring of essay tests?

- To what extent are both objective and essay test questions subjective?

- With a few of your peers, list some appropriate objectives for each of the test types discussed in this chapter.

- What commonalities did you find among the item types?

Assessing Performance and Products

Many areas of student achievement are more effectively assessed with a performance-based assignment than with a test question. Knowing *how* is often as important as knowing *that*. Language arts teaches speech and listening, both of which are assessed most directly by observing students' performances. The same is true of science lab procedures, social studies community projects, and reports of observations in health or earth science class. Physical education, music, art, home and family living, and the industrial arts are all based on knowing *how*.

Performance-based items do not have a single best response. Instead, students are required to organize and present the material in their own way within the stated bounds of the task. In essence, performance-based assessments ask the student to do whatever will reasonably demonstrate competence. These assessments do, however, require expert judgment from the teacher in what constitutes competence, and they are time consuming. Performance-based assessment can use the evaluation of either actual student performances (demonstrations) of a task or authentic student products (original creations).

Performances are active demonstrations that assess student learning, such as oral presentations, musical and dramatic performances, and kinesthetic activities. Students can demonstrate mastery of objectives in numerous ways. Oral explanations, for instance, are a key way to improve students' learning and understanding. The more time students spend explaining what they have learned to the teacher or other students, the more effective their learning will be. A mix of formal and informal presentations will provide many opportunities for students. Music, drama, and physical education teachers can give you some excellent suggestions and models.

At all grade levels, students produce **products**—book reviews, term papers, homework assignments, display boards, murals, and posters. The key to assessment is to specifically inform students of what will be assessed—form, content, spelling, design—and then to provide models or rubrics so students will know what an acceptable or superior product looks like.

Several tools are basic to performance and product assessment: rating scales, checklists, anecdotal records, observations, portfolios, and the rubrics that guided the project.

Rating Scales and Checklists   In general, rating scales provide a list of characteristics to be observed and a scale showing the degree to which they are present. To the extent that it is keyed to learning outcomes that can be observed and is used appropriately to evaluate processes or products, a rating scale is a useful assessment tool. See Figure 10.6 for examples.

Checklists, or "yes-no" rating scales, are useful when a process can be divided into steps and each one checked for its presence. Figure 10.7 gives an example.

Rating scales and checklists have widespread utility in the classroom. They identify specific tasks and portions of tasks and point out strong and weak areas, giving students the information they need to improve their learning. If used carefully, they provide the student with a model or rubric that

Find out what students can do, not just what they know.

Checklists and rating scales give students specific feedback.

FIGURE 10.6

Examples of a Rating Scale

Instructions: Rate the presenter on the following characteristics by placing an "X" anywhere on the line under each item. In the comment space, add any thoughts that will clarify your rating.

1. **Presenter spoke loudly and clearly so all could understand.**

1	2	3	4	5
Difficult to understand		Understood most of presentation		Clearly understood entire presentation

Comments:

2. **Presenter maintained eye contact with class.**

1	2	3	4	5
Read notes instead of looking at class		Made eye contact about half the time		Maintained eye contact through most of presentation

Comments:

3. **Presenter made biography interesting.**

1	2	3	4	5
Very few "humanizing" details		Quite a few interesting details		Made subject come to life. We learned what this person was like

Comments:

---

specifies what an acceptable performance looks like and what its important parts are, as does the checklist in Figure 10.7.

A second value of these performance assessments is their utility in grading. Learning must include the freedom to experiment and make mistakes, but you must grade enough of the students' work to monitor and sustain progress. Also, when it is time to make a summative judgment of a student's achievement, you will use every indicator available so as to make the most accurate assessment possible. Your assessments of achievement can recognize and record that the student did outstanding work on a project, made acceptable scores on three speeches, is improving in penmanship, contributes readily and usefully to class discussions, functions well as a work-group member, and so on. Like all the other forms of assessment, however, rating scales and checklists have limitations. They can be unreliable—giving varying results when used by different teachers or at different times by the same teacher. A clear statement of the objective to be assessed and the criteria to judge by can alleviate this problem.

FIGURE 10.7

Example of a Checklist

Homework Grading Guide

	Yes	No
1. Is the handwriting legible?	_____	_____
2. Is the response correct?	_____	_____
3. Are the statements clear?	_____	_____
4. Were all necessary data included?	_____	_____

Anecdotal Records and Observations   **Anecdotal records** are recorded observations of student behaviors made during routine class work and perhaps in the halls or on the playground. What do you observe? Primarily, those behaviors that you can't assess any other way—John seems slow in responding to requests; Cheryl is never asked into groups; Archie doesn't seem well much of the time. A single notice of any of these, and similar behaviors, probably means little, but repeated and recorded over time, these observations can provide insights that will allow you to help students in areas you might otherwise overlook.

Four keys govern the effective use of anecdotal records (summarized in the Instructional Strategies box below). First, don't try to record everything about everybody. Record the unusual, but do it systematically, briefly, and nonjudgmentally: what, where, and when (and your response, if appropriate). Make the note quickly in a couple of minutes during lunch or after school: "Date of 4/3/06. Jack hit Sam in the face during recess. This is the 2nd fight between them in 3 days. Each accuses the other of initiating it. I have sent both boys to the vice principal, as per school policy for fighting."

INSTRUCTIONAL STRATEGIES

Four Keys to Keeping Effective Anecdotal Records

1. Don't record too much.
2. Be consistent.
3. Record positive as well as negative indicators.
4. Don't draw inferences from a single incident.

Second, be consistent, in both watching and recording. Make a few observations each day, recording them on index cards or notepaper and keeping the notes in your files or some other private place. Although the practice may seem tedious at first, it soon becomes a habit and is quickly done. The first time you alert a parent to a possible medical problem on the basis of anecdotal records, you'll become an enthusiastic recorder.

When you have discipline difficulties with a student—defiance, abusive language, fighting in class—such records can become very important.

Anecdotal records can help you get needed assistance for a student.

Obtaining help for the student (and you) generally depends on following due process for student rights and is greatly facilitated by dated records of all incidents relevant to the problem.

Third, record positive indicators of growth, not just evidence of problems. A surly student's voluntary class contribution, the class bully's politeness to a substitute teacher—these and more can be indicators of growth and should be part of your assessments.

Fourth, don't draw inferences about student behavior from a single incident. The unusual may be simply that—unusual. Patterns, observed over time, are necessary for drawing inferences about health or behavioral problems (Mamchak and Mamchak 1993).

Portfolios **Portfolios** are collections of student work. The concept of assembling these collections to monitor student progress and to share with parents and administrators is not new. Many elementary school teachers, and some middle school and high school teachers, have done so for years.

VIDEO CASE ⏪ ▶ ⏩

Teacher Fred Park helps his young students develop new pieces for their writing portfolios in the Video Case "Portfolio Assessment: Elementary Classroom." What do students learn in the course of this video? How does it differ from what they would learn from a paper-and-pencil test? Also read the interview with Fred.

What is new is the idea that much student achievement can be more effectively demonstrated by a product than by scores on a paper-and-pencil test alone. A collection of these products, if carefully and purposefully assembled, can be a valuable assessment tool.

For assessment use, a portfolio cannot be just a collection of student papers. Instead, it must be a demonstration of student effort and progress toward achieving particular learning objectives. (The Instructional Strategies box below lists the characteristics of a carefully planned portfolio.) Many classes or particular units within a class contain objectives that are readily and effectively assessed with work samples. In social studies and history, maps and charts are basic tools. Students produce these as aids to understanding. Oral presentations are part of most classes, and rating sheets from these can document student improvement. The more you think of objectives, the more ways you will find to use a portfolio to document progress.

Focus portfolio on specific learning objectives.

INSTRUCTIONAL STRATEGIES

Designing Student Portfolios

1. Establish how the portfolios will be used.
2. Center the content of portfolios on instructional goals.
3. Translate instructional goals into student performance.
4. Plan the student into the assessment process.
5. Take steps to make review of portfolios more efficient.
6. Use multiple observations to increase generalizability.

SOURCE: Oosterhof 2003, pp. 186–193.

To grade a portfolio, assess the student's entries in relation to the objectives specified. Rating scales and checklists are useful here, particularly when the student has them as guides while constructing the entries.

Portfolios are increasingly used in mathematics classes, partly as a result of the standards adopted by the National Council of Teachers of Mathematics

**Formative assessment
is a positive
experience.**
© Royalty-Free / Corbis

in 1989. Most other content areas have also adopted national standards (see Chapter 3). All the new standards emphasize problem solving and thinking skills, which are more accurately reflected by portfolios than by standardized achievement tests (Far West Laboratory 1992). In fact, since 1990, Lewis and Clark College of Portland, Oregon, has allowed academically talented prospects to submit portfolios of their work in place of the usual SAT scores and admission essay (Stiggins 1994, pp. 421–422).

Sharing portfolios with parents on special occasions can reinforce a positive link between home and school. Additional perspectives on performance and alternative assessments can be found in the following: Eisner 1999; Haertel 1999; Herman et al. 1997; and Madaus and O'Dwyer 1999.

Rubrics   Especially when students are involved in the construction of the rubrics, this assessment tool can provide readily comprehensible feedback to students. **Rubrics** contain two primary components—*criteria*, which are really categories that describe *what* is being evaluated, and *standards*, which describe the level of achievement and tasks involved in reaching that level.

Rubrics: criteria + standards

Table 10.1 demonstrates what one kind of rubric might look like (both from Roe, Smith, and Burns, 2005). Some guidelines for writing rubrics are listed below.

- Base standards on samples of student work that represent each level of proficiency.
- Use precise wording that describes observable behaviors in terms that students can understand.

- Avoid negative statements, such as "cannot make predictions."
- Construct rubrics with 3-, 4-, or 5-point scales, with the highest number representing the most desirable level.
- Limit criteria to a reasonable number.

TABLE 10.1

Rubric for Evaluating Research Reports			
Criteria	Standards		
	3	2	1
Content	This report covers all major aspects of the topic and is focused. It shows evidence of higher-order thinking and is based on three or more references.	This report covers several aspects of the topic but omits some important information. It makes use of two or more references.	This paper is limited to one or two aspects of the topic. Only one source (or no source) of information is given.
Organization	This report is logically organized and easy to follow. The introduction presents the topic, the content follows in reasonable order, and the conclusion pulls information together.	This report shows some evidence of organization, but it lacks a clearly constructed beginning, middle, and end. Connections among subtopics are sometimes unclear.	This report is difficult to follow because it lacks a logical organizational plan. It shifts from one idea to another without making logical connections.
Use of conventions	This paper shows consistent use of standard English and correct spelling, punctuation, capitalization, and paragraphing. It is neat and legible.	This paper indicates a general observance of conventions, but several errors exist in spelling, mechanics, and form.	This paper shows little awareness of writing conventions. Neatness and legibility are minimal.

SOURCE: Paul C. Burns, Betty D. Roe, and Elinor P. Ross. *Teaching Reading in Today's Elementary Schools,* 11th edition. Copyright © 1999 by Houghton Mifflin Company. Reprinted with permission.

TECHNOLOGY INSIGHT

Sharing Too Much: Internet Identity, Security, and Copyright Issues

There is a famous cartoon of two dogs using a computer. One is saying to the other, "On the Internet, no one knows you're a dog." This phrase has become a common one among computing experts. It is used to remind people that it is very easy to be someone or something false using a networked computer and that it is easy to copy someone else's identity or work. Using the Internet and incorporating it into your teaching can be very rewarding, but certain challenges must be met as well. Many of these challenges are related to identity, security, and copyright—all of which have some bearing on issues of evaluation.

The Internet is generally not a secure environment; information that is sent using e-mail or http (the standard method of sending and receiving webpages) may be intercepted and read by others. There are myriad cases of people sending e-mail under another person's name and misrepresenting themselves in public or semiprivate forums (such as chat rooms). Teachers need to be aware that students may send messages using another student's name and that students cannot always trust the identity of someone they meet in cyberspace.

Teachers should keep in mind that the Internet was originally a place for academics to share their work (the World Wide Web was originally designed for physicists to share unpublished papers and in-progress research). Most scholars currently generate their work on networked computers in academic settings, and most scholarly work is intended for public dissemination. This suggests that a huge amount of scholarly "product" is freely available on the Internet. Add to this that these scholarly products are usually in some word-processed form that is easy to copy and adapt, and it becomes obvious that plagiarism can be dangerously easy. With cell phone scanning devices, transmission of test items to friends may become a problem.

When allowing (or encouraging) the use of networked computing tools for classroom projects, a teacher must be aware of the potential for misrepresentation.

reflect

- Ask a teacher to share some anecdotal records and portfolios that might be available without invading anyone's privacy. Examine them for objectivity.

- Create a portfolio rating scale for some class attribute, such as completion of seat-work. Then surf the Net to locate any information about portfolio rating scales.

- Locate two books or articles on portfolio assessment and summarize the pros and cons of this technique.

SECTION 5: GRADING TO IMPROVE STUDENT LEARNING

We end this chapter by considering the summative judgments you make about student achievement (that is, grades) and how you report those judgments to students, parents, administrators, and others.

As an instructional tool, grading and reporting should focus on improving student learning and development by clarifying instructional objectives, indicating students' learning strengths and weaknesses, showing students' personal and social development, and adding to students' motivation (Linn and Miller 2005, p. 367). This is certainly more than can be included in the traditional letter grade, but supplementing the nine-week or semester grade with other periodic reports can help achieve these goals. Periodic reports can also establish a positive climate of communication between you and parents, further reinforcing learning and adding to your students' motivation.

> The point of grades is student development and learning.

We know several teachers, at both the elementary and middle school levels, who send weekly class newsletters to parents. Groups of three or four students prepare them, on a rotating schedule, and the newsletters highlight learning objectives and their accompanying activities. The teachers report that most students enjoy working on the newsletters, and parents appreciate the communication.

Some elementary and secondary schools use checklists containing descriptive statements about students' academic skills, behavior, and attitudes in place of or as a supplement to letter grades, and others use narrative descriptions as a supplement (Oosterhof 2003, p. 219). Also, generally below grade 4, it is unlikely that children understand what an abstract letter grade means (Newman and Spitzer 1998). In addition, some schools hold "portfolio nights" routinely, allowing students to share their efforts with their parents. This adds more reinforcement to students' learning and motivation.

All of the above ideas are attempts to provide more and better information about student achievement than a letter grade communicates. Even so, it seems unlikely that letter grades will be replaced very soon. Besides being traditional, they are a convenient administrative tool—for determining honors, promotion, scholarships, and athletic eligibility and for reporting to other schools—which is not readily duplicated by other means.

Principles of Grading

Never Too Much Data One of the first principles of grading is that you can't have too much data. No matter how many test scores, homework exercises, and class activities you have assessed, you will likely feel that you need more information to make summative evaluations. By giving your students many opportunities to show achievement, you provide yourself with more data for a fair, professional judgment, and you also provide each student with every possible chance to succeed.

> Follow the inclusion principle in grading.

The range of activities you can include in grading is limited only by your imagination. Most teachers include at least the following (not listed in order of importance):

- Unit tests
- Periodic quizzes
- Assigned work done in class
- Homework
- Projects—both group and individual
- Papers and reports

The goal is to use a large enough variety that every student finds several areas in which to operate at his or her preferred learning mode and to achieve success.

Some teachers also include conduct and participation in grading. They argue that, especially in elementary and middle school, these are important learning areas—we expect students to learn how to behave and participate in social situations, so we should evaluate students on their progress in these areas. The choice is yours (depending, of course, on your school's policy), but if you intend to include these areas in grading, you should inform all students and keep systematic data on them. This can be done quite easily with checklists, rating scales, and anecdotal records.

Which Assessment Tools?   Having decided on areas and activities on which to base grades, your next step is to determine what instruments—portfolios, objective tests, attitude inventories, checklists—will best provide valid, reliable data. Whatever instruments you choose, use a number system to record data. (Many teachers assign point values to every piece of student work.) This will greatly simplify your efforts to convert all your data to a letter grade.

Where to record data may puzzle beginning teachers. School districts usually provide a grade book, but the books don't typically provide enough space to include everything. Many teachers make grade sheets on large sheets of paper, with sections labeled for each type of data, such as Unit Tests, Quizzes, Projects, and Homework. That way, all scores are recorded as you collect them. This, too, is a convenience when you assign term grades. Many teachers also use (and some districts require) a computer grading program, which records whatever you enter, does calculations, and prints out results. With this system, you can tell a student at any time what his or her grade is, at least that portion represented by numbers. Teachers who use a computer grade book often keep a backup, either on another disk, on paper, or both.

Devising a Grading System   Deciding what to record and how to record it are your first steps. Next is adopting a system for assigning grades. Several systems are used, but authorities in the field suggest that the *percent* or *absolute* system is common (Kim and Kellough 1995; Ornstein 1989). It works like this: Each graded activity is assigned a total numerical or point value. Student points are recorded for each activity, and at the end of the grading period, the student's grade is based on the percentage of the possible points he or she obtained. A typical example of grades and percentages follows:

Having decided what to grade, the next step is to determine the proportion each activity will contribute to the total grade. In other words, do you want homework to count 90 percent or 15 percent or some other portion of the grade? (Authorities differ, by the way, on whether homework should be

---

Keep all your data in numerical form.

Determine grade/point relationship, then weight each activity.

A   =   90% or higher
B   =   80–89%
C   =   70–79%
D   =   60–69%
F   =   below 60%

included in a grade. See Cooper 1989 and Nottingham 1988 for a discussion.) Teachers commonly use approximations of the following weightings:

Tests and quizzes: 50–60%
Classwork: 15–30%
Projects and papers: 10–15%
Homework: 10–15%

If you include participation and conduct, these, too, must be assigned a weight. Conduct in a shop class, for instance, where dangerous machinery is used, would be a reasonably important part of achievement.

Avoiding Grading Errors   There are five errors you should try to avoid in testing and grading (Daniel and King 1998):

1. *Using pretest scores in determining grades.* Such scores should indicate only where to begin instruction.
2. *Not adequately informing students of what to expect on a test.* This leaves students trying to decide what's important, which is the teacher's responsibility.
3. *Assigning a zero for missing or incomplete work.* A zero misrepresents achievement and has a profound effect on an average. One alternative is to use the median (middle-ranking) score as an indicator rather than using the average.
4. *Using grades for rewards or punishment.* Achievement of learning objectives should be the only consideration in assigning grades.
5. *Assigning grades contingent on improvement.* You might determine other errors after a few years of teaching

Communicating Your Intentions

Whatever your system, you must explain it clearly—with appropriate handouts and examples—to your students during the first days of class. Students can and should be taught to keep track of their own grades, and a few minutes can be spent one day a week to be sure each student has recorded his or her current scores. At this time, students can discuss questions and difficulties and calculate their grades. Students will know at all times what their progress is, where their achievement is strong, and what areas need attention. There should be no surprises at report card time. Many secondary and middle school teachers distribute a course outline or syllabus that includes a description of the grading system for the class and then have each student and parent or guardian sign it to indicate that they received, read, and understood the contents. This type of communication prevents unnecessary confusion and disagreement and meets our intended goal of making grading more objective in a very subjective business.

With the advent of school reform, report cards have evolved into monumental checklists that parallel various state or local standards. One school district's newly distributed fourth-grade "Student Progress Report" has eleven different categories with a total of ninety items to be evaluated on a five-point scale. A teacher will make a minimum of 450 decisions for each student!

Have parents buy in to grading system.

Another school district is field-testing an eleven-page report card. We leave any reflections on this to you. The sequence of steps we've outlined in this chapter and that we recommend you use as you develop your own classroom assessment approach is outlined in the Instructional Strategies box below. In conclusion, we refer you to our website, **http://education.college. hmco.com/students**, where you may be surprised to learn that appropriate uses of assessments as feedback mechanisms have positive effects on learning.

INSTRUCTIONAL
STRATEGIES

Guidelines for Selecting and Using Classroom Assessments

1. Be clear about the learning targets you want to assess.
2. Be sure that the assessment techniques you select match each learning target.
3. Be sure that the selected assessment techniques serve the needs of the learners.
4. Whenever possible, be sure to use multiple indicators of performance for each learning target.
5. Be sure that when you interpret the results of the assessments you take their limitations into account.

SOURCE: Nitko 2004, p. 6.

REFLECT

A Closing Reflection

- Examine a sample of the Iowa Test of Basic Skills. How do the various questions align with various curricula you have studied for K–12? (Be sure to select the appropriate version of the test.)

- Examine the fall issues of *Phi Delta Kappan*. Each fall this journal publishes the annual PDK/Gallup poll about what people think about U.S. schools. What trends do you observe relating to achievement or assessment?

- Select any school district's policy handbook and then examine the section on testing and grading. How do the policies compare to what we have discussed?

- Devise a plan for communicating to parents about class efforts and activities. What information will you share? In what way? How often?

summary

1. Assessment is a continuous process whose primary purpose is to improve student learning.

2. Classroom assessments are used for four primary purposes: to determine placement; to diagnose persistent problems; to monitor progress, provide feedback, and correct errors; and to assign grades.

3. Using various methods, you can assess students' behaviors, skills, knowledge, thinking, and attitudes.

4. Curricular alignment can best be obtained if you plan assessment at the same time you plan instruction.

5. Teachers have many choices of assessment methods and should select the one that best matches their particular goals of instruction.

6. Standardized tests provide comparative data on a broad scale.

7. Formative assessment is devoted entirely to the enhancement of student learning and achievement.

8. Performance assessment tools include rating scales, checklists, observations and anecdotal records, portfolios, and rubrics.

9. Objective test items include true-false, matching, short-answer and completion, and multiple-choice questions.

10. Essay items are an excellent means of assessing students' higher-level thinking processes.

11. The purpose of grading is to improve student learning by clarifying learning objectives, indicating each student's strengths and weaknesses, evaluating the student's personal and social development, and motivating the student.

12. Fairness and objectivity are two grading criteria that teachers and students typically infer.

13. Assessing instructional outcomes is a very complex craft and scientific skill that requires a high degree of technical proficiency.

print resources

The field of student assessment has a plethora of publications to aid the novice in learning more about the process. However, we attempted to identify four that would be of immediate and practical use.

Marzano, R. J. "An Array of Strategies for Classroom Teachers." *Momentum* 28(2) (1997): 6–10.

This journal article provides a quick summary of five assessment methods with examples to aid the teacher.

Salvia, J., and J. E. Ysseldyke. *Assessment* (9th edition). Boston: Houghton Mifflin, 2004, 816 pp.

We suggest this textbook as a handbook on the topic. The authors wrote the book with novices in mind. Everything you want to know about assessment is here in one source.

Taggart, G. L., S. J. Phifer, J. A. Nixon, and M. Woods. *Rubrics: A Handbook for Construction and Use.* Lancaster, PA: Technomic, 1998, 152 pp.

The authors provide a detailed compilation of rubric examples, models, designs, and scoring techniques.

Taylor, C. S., and Nolen, S. B. *Classroom Assessment: Supporting Teaching and Learning in Real Classrooms.* Upper Saddle River, NJ: Pearson, 2005, 423 pp.

This book, written by professionals who truly wish to support classroom assessment, is a wonderful resource for any educator. It is full of classroom-tested assessment ideas, and each technique is realistically connected to student learning.

InTerneT Resources

Go to the website for this book to find live links to resources related to this chapter.

> On-line resources to help you obtain the information you need to evaluate standardized tests can be found in the Buros Institute of Mental Measurements, University of Nebraska.
> **http://www.unl.edu/buros**

> Information about standardized tests and other related products developed by the Educational Testing Service may be found at the ETS website.
> **http://www.ets.org**

> A memorandum from the Family Policy Compliance Office of the U.S. Department of Education notes that a parent has the right under the Family Educational Rights and Privacy Act (FERPA) to examine both the test question booklet and the child's test answer sheet for any test, including high-stakes state assessments. You can view the full document at **http://www.fetaweb.com/04/ferpa.rooker.ltr.protocols.htm**

References

Black, P., C. Harrison, C. Lee, B. Marshall, and D. Wiliam. "Working Inside the Black Box: Assessment for Learning in the Classroom." *Phi Delta Kappan* 86(1) (2004): 8.

Black, P., and D. Wiliam. "Assessment and Classroom Learning." *Assessment in Education: Principles, Policy and Practice* 5(1) (1998): 7.

Bloom, B. S., et al., editors. *Handbook on Formative and Summative Evaluation of Student Learning.* New York; McGraw-Hill, 1971.

Cooper, H. "Synthesis of Research on Homework." *Educational Leadership* 47(3) (1989): 85–91.

Daniel, L. G., and D. A. King. "Knowledge and Use of Testing and Measurement Literacy of Elementary and Secondary Teachers." *Journal of Educational Research* 91(6) (1998): 331.

Davies, A., C. Cameron, C. Politano, and K. Gregory. *Together Is Better: Collaborative Assessment, Evaluation and Reporting.* Courtney, British Columbia, Canada: Classroom Connections International, 1992.

Dempster, F. N., and P. G. Perkins. "Revitalizing Classroom Assessment: Using Tests to Promote Learning." *Journal of Instructional Psychology* 20(3) (1993): 197.

Eisner, E. W. "The Uses and Limits of Performance Assessment." *Phi Delta Kappan* 80(9) (1999): 658.

Far West Laboratory. "Using Portfolios to Assess Student Performance." *Knowledge Brief.* San Francisco: Number Nine, 1992.

Gronlund, N. E. *Assessment of Student Achievement* (8th edition). Boston: Allyn and Bacon, 2006.

Haertel, E. H. "Performance Assessment and Education Reform." *Phi Delta Kappan* 80(9) (1999): 662.

Hattie, J. E. "Measuring the Effects of Schooling." *Australian Journal of Education* 36(1) (1992): 5–13.

Herman, J. L., P. Aschbacher, and L. Winters. *A Practical Guide to Alternative Assessment.* Alexandria, VA: Association for Supervision and Curriculum Development, 1992.

Herman, J. L., et al. "American Students' Perspectives on Alternative Assessment: Do They Know It's Different?" *Assessment in Education: Principles, Policy and Practice* 4(3) (1997): 339.

Kim, E. C., and R. D. Kellough. *A Resource Guide for Secondary School Teaching* (6th edition). New York: Macmillan, 1995.

Linn, R. L. *Assessments and Accountability. CSE Technical Report 490.* University of California, Los Angeles: Center for the Study of Evaluation, November 1998.

Linn, R. L., and M. D. Miller. *Measurement and Assessment in Teaching* (9th edition). Englewood Cliffs, NJ: Merrill, 2005.

Madaus, G. "The Distortion of Teaching and Testing: High-Stakes Testing and Instruction." *Peabody Journal of Education* 64(1) (1998): 29–46.

Madaus, G. F., and T. Kellaghan. "The British Experience with Authentic Testing." *Phi Delta Kappan* 74(6) (1993): 458–469.

Madaus, G., and L. M. O'Dwyer. "A Short History of Performance Assessment." *Phi Delta Kappan* 80(9) (1999): 688.

Mamchak, S., and S. R. Mamchak. *Teacher's Time Management Survival Kit.* Englewood Cliffs, NJ: Prentice Hall, 1993.

Marzano, R. J., D. J. Pickering, and J. E. Pollock. *Classroom Instruction That Works: Research-Based Strategies for Increasing Student Achievement.* Alexandria, VA: Association for Supervision and Curriculum Development, 2001.

Newman, R. S., and S. Spitzer. "How Children Reason About Ability from Report Card Grades: A Developmental Study." *Journal of Genetic Psychology* 159(2) (1998): 133.

Nichols, S., and D. C. Berliner. *The Inevitable Corruption of Indicators and Educators Through High-Stakes Testing.* Tempe: College of Education, Arizona State University, Education Policy Studies Laboratory, March 2005.

Nitko, A. J. *Educational Assessment of Students* (4th edition). Englewood Cliffs, NJ: Merrill, 2004.

Nottingham, M. "Grading Practices: Watching Out for Landmines." *NASSP Bulletin* 72(507) (1988): 24–28.

Oosterhof, A. *Developing and Using Classroom Assessments* (3rd Edition). Englewood Cliffs, NJ: Prentice Hall, 2003.

Ornstein, A. C. "The Nature of Grading." *Clearing House* 62(8) (1989): 365–369.

Popham, W. J. "Why Standardized Tests Don't Measure Educational Quality." *Educational Leadership* 56(6) (1999): 8.

Roe, B., D., Smith, S. H., and P. C. Burns. *Teaching Reading in Today's Elementary Schools* (9th edition). Boston: Houghton Mifflin, 2005

Sadler, D. R. "Formative Assessment: Revisiting the Territory." *Assessment in Education: Principles, Policy and Practice* 5(1) (1998): 77.

Salvia, J., and J. E. Ysseldyke. *Assessment* (9th edition). Boston: Houghton Mifflin, 2004.

Stiggins, R. J. *Student-Centered Classroom Assessment.* New York: Macmillan, 1994.

Stiggins, R. J. *Student-Involved Assessment for Learning* (4th edition). New York: Macmillan, 2005.

U.S. Department of Education. *No Child Left Behind.* Retrieved at January 22, 2002, http://www.ed.gov.

Verma, M., and J. Chhatwal. "Reliability of Essay Type Questions—Effect of Structuring." *Assessment in Education: Principles, Policy and Practice* 4(2) (1997): 265.

Weber, L. J., and R. B. Frary. "Allowing Students a Choice of Items on Objective Examinations." *Assessment and Evaluation in Higher Education* 20(3) (1995): 301.

Wiggins, G., and J. McTighe. *Understanding by Design, Expanded, 2nd edition.* Alexandria, VA: Association for Supervision and Curriculum Development, 2005.

Worthen, B. R. "Critical Issues That Will Determine the Future of Alternative Assessment." *Phi Delta Kappan* 74(6) (1993): 444–454.

Glossary

acculturation   The combination of processes that introduce a child to the culture, including customs and social patterns.

active learning   Any of a wide range of teaching strategies that engage the learner in the instruction taking place, such as working on problems in small groups, as opposed to passive methods such as seat work or listening to a lecture.

advance organizer   A frame of reference for a lesson, such as a chart, study guide, list, or graph, that presents the main facts, concepts, or generalizations to be learned.

affective domain   The area of learning that encompasses ethical, emotional, attitudinal, and social knowledge.

algorithm   A special method of solving a specific problem; for example, a formula.

alternatives   The different possible responses to a multiple-choice test question.

analysis   The process of discovering relationships, interactions, and causality among ideas, concepts, and situations.

analytic scoring   The assessment of student performance by means of a rating system.

anecdotal records   Notes written objectively on a periodic basis to track student performance, which may include checklists, student self-reports, and teacher observations.

application   The process of employing abstract ideas and concepts in real-world situations, such as hands-on learning and problem solving.

artificial intelligence   The mechanical simulation of human or animal thought processes, usually by computers.

assertive discipline   A structured approach designed to assist teachers in running an organized, teacher-in-charge classroom environment, including a discipline plan, classroom rules, positive recognition, and consequences.

assessment   The process of evaluating student performance using a variety of measurements, such as tests, observations, ratings, portfolios.

asynchronous learning   Learning or responses that are usually associated with computer-aided instruction but not do not occur within a structured class period.

awareness   The ability of a teacher to recognize student needs and demands and adjust the classroom environment to meet them.

behavior modification   The process of changing behavior by rewarding desired actions and ignoring or punishing undesired actions.

behavioral perspective   An educational approach that stresses changing student actions by rewarding and reinforcing desired actions and outcomes.

bilingual education   The teaching of students in both their first and their second language (often Spanish and English) simultaneously.

brainstorming   A discussion process in which the leader presents a topic or problem and solicits open-ended ideas about it from all group members.

character development   An aspect of schooling that includes discussion of ethical issues and moral dilemmas, with the goal of developing characteristics such as trustworthiness, respect, responsibility, and citizenship.

checklist   List-format assessment tools used by a teacher or student to document work completed or skills learned.

classroom clarifier   The role the teacher takes during inquiry learning to guide students toward developing logical thinking skills.

classroom management   The methods of organization, disciplinary procedures, and routines established by the teacher to ensure positive student behaviors that are conducive to learning and social interaction.

cognitive domain   The area of learning encompassing intellectual aspects, such as information processing, memorization, and thinking skills.

cognitive psychology   An area of psychology that focuses on inner mental processes rather than behavior.

cohesion   The tendency of a group to stick together and support all members.

completion items   Test items that contain an incomplete statement and require the student to fill in a missing word, phrase, or symbol.

concept   An expression or abstraction based on observations of a group of stimuli, facts, or objects having common characteristics; for example, the concept "animal" encompasses and describes dogs, cats, and elephants.

concept analysis   The process of identifying the components of a concept to be taught and deciding whether to teach it inductively (from underlying specific examples to broader generalizations) or deductively (from broader generalizations to underlying specific examples).

concept review questioning technique A teaching strategy that consists of inserting review questions throughout the recitation period.

concrete operational stage A stage of cognitive development (ages 8–11) in which children learn best through visual and hands-on activities.

content differentiation The process of isolating each fact, concept, or generalization within a hierarchy of knowledge so that it can be learned independently.

content hierarchy A sequence of learning matter that may be closely interrelated and requires a series of definite steps to achieve.

content The subject matter, substance, or materials of a lesson, consisting of facts, concepts, and generalizations.

convergent questions Questions that require students to give factual or specific answers.

cooperative learning Learning based on a small-group approach to teaching, in which students are held accountable for both individual and group achievement.

correlation A relationship between two factors, but not necessarily one of cause and effect.

criteria Characteristics used to categorize or rate ideas or products.

criterion measure The third element of a performance objective, which defines the minimum level of acceptable performance.

curriculum guides Sets of goals and objectives published by a school district to guide teachers in developing instruction by stating what students should learn at each grade level and in each content area.

declarative knowledge Knowledge of content (*what*), such as facts, definitions, and concepts, as opposed to knowledge of processes (*how*). Also called *content knowledge*.

deductive reasoning The process of discovering specific examples or facts from a generalizing framework; a thinking process that moves from the general to the specific.

democratic discipline A classroom management approach that treats diverse students equally and expects them to take responsibility for their own behavior.

dependent skills Those items of information that are typically taught in a carefully structured or linear manner. For example, one teaches decimals before introducing percents.

desist strategy Discipline technique in which the teacher systematically communicates his or her desire for a student to stop a particular behavior, using either private or public communication.

diagnostic test Assessment tool that pinpoints students' strengths and weaknesses, specifically what students need to learn in designated fields.

direct instruction Teacher-initiated whole-class learning.

discipline The setting of behavioral parameters for the classroom, both by the teacher alone and in response to teacher-student interactions and situational factors.

discovery learning An inquiry process in which learners pose questions and seek explanations.

discussions Interactive learning processes involving the exchange of information, perceptions, and ideas in a small group.

distractors The incorrect alternative answers on a multiple-choice test.

divergent questions Questions that encourage students to give complex, creative, longer answers.

eclectic Made up of a mix of varied approaches or teaching models.

effect size A statistical notation of comparing independent samples to show evidence of the impact an educational treatment or intervention has on student achievement.

efficacy Effectiveness; the ability to reach a goal or complete a task.

empirical epistemology The process of knowing or learning through observation or experimentation.

enabling skills Facts, concepts, and processes students must be taught before they can learn more complex facts, concepts, and processes.

entry skills The knowledge and perceptions students possess at the beginning of a given lesson.

equity A moral rationale that all children should be given the same opportunities to succeed in school.

evaluation The process of making judgments and supporting one's viewpoints with specific criteria, facts, and values. In education, determining the effectiveness of a lesson or unit in terms of student outcomes.

evaluative criteria Parameters for questioning that ask students to make a choice about where they stand on a given issue or question.

evaluative question Question that asks students to make a personal judgment and then defend their position with criteria that support the position taken.

example A concrete or specific form of a more abstract concept.

exceptionality A condition in which a student qualifies for special services by virtue of his or her physical, cognitive, or emotional characteristics and abilities.

experience The totality of the events and activities in which a student has participated as part of planned learning processes.

expert training Education that provides skills and proficiency in a given area and creates a very proficient person.

extrinsic motivation Desire to perform based on the reward provided for engaging in an activity.

facilitator   The supportive role a teacher takes by giving students the skills, materials, and opportunities they need to direct their own learning experiences.

fact   The most fundamental piece of information, which is singular in occurrence, occurs or exists in the present time, does not help the learner predict other facts, and is acquired solely through the process of observation.

formal operations stage   A stage of cognitive development (ages 11–15 and above) in which adolescents develop knowledge through systematic reasoning.

formative assessment   A type of classroom assessment devoted entirely to the enhancement of student learning and achievement via specific feedback.

framing   The technique of asking a question very precisely, pausing, then calling on a student.

general instructional objectives   Statements of what is to be learned that are broad and encompassing.

generalization   An inferential statement that expresses relationships between concepts and has predictive value.

goals   The broad, general outcomes students should reach as the result of a learning experience, lesson, or unit of study; for example, "Students will learn to appreciate and interpret drama."

graphic organizers   Pictures, outlines, sketches, or some pictorial display that help the learner to obtain a quick mental perception or image of the topic.

guided inductive inquiry   A learning process in which the teacher provides specific facts or ideas, from which students make their own generalizations.

halo effect   The tendency of a teacher to assess a student's later performance based on the quality of earlier performance rather than being totally objective.

hemisphericity   The study of where in the brain—in the left hemisphere or the right hemisphere—different types of mental functions occur.

heuristics   "Rules of thumb" used to find solutions.

higher-level thinking   A multistage construction of meaning that employs analysis and synthesis. Also called *critical thinking*.

high-stakes tests   Tests that are administered to children to determine some prescribed level of competence and in which penalties or rewards are provided to children or teachers.

holistic instructional view   A model for instructional planning that considers many social and educational factors simultaneously.

holistic scoring   The assessment of a student's work in its entirety rather than judgment of specific parts.

humanistic orientation   An outlook that views all students as unique individuals deserving acceptance and respect.

idiosyncrasies   Teacher behaviors and habits that interfere with effective classroom interaction.

imposed-discipline systems   Approaches to discipline in which the teacher dictates appropriate classroom behaviors and consequences for misbehavior.

inclusion   The practice of lacing and serving all children, including those with special cognitive, affective, or psychomotor needs, in regular classrooms. See also *mainstreaming*.

inclusionary classroom   A classroom in which any learner with a disability is educated alongside students without disabilities.

independent skills   Learning that can be taught without any prerequisite skills.

independent study   Situation in which teachers allow students options of what to study and where the work is done.

individual education plan (IEP)   An agreement between a student with special learning needs and his or her classroom teachers, special education staff, and parents that outlines educational goals, procedures, and expected outcomes.

Individuals with Disabilities Education Act (IDEA)   Federal act which states that all children with disabilities must have access to a free and appropriate public education.

induction   The process of analyzing specific ideas to form more general concepts.

inductive inquiry   The process of inferring generalizations from a set of specific ideas or facts.

inductive reasoning   The process of studying examples or facts in order to develop generalizations or concepts; a thinking process that moves from the specific to the general.

information processing   A means used to learn and remember knowledge.

information-processing psychology   A branch of psychology that holds that learning is an interactive process between learners and their environment.

inquiry discussion group   A specific kind of small group in which students develop questioning and problem-solving skills through a process of discovery and analysis.

inquiry process   An investigative learning process that includes skills such as classifying, predicting, and experimenting.

inquiry teaching   An investigative process of learning in which students are asked to pose questions, analyze data, and develop conclusions or generalizations.

instructional equity   The provision of equal learning opportunities to students of both genders and from diverse backgrounds and cultures.

integration The third step in the advance organizer model, in which students see how main concepts and underlying facts are related (vertical integration) or how underlying facts are similar or different (horizontal integration).

interdisciplinary thematic unit A unit of instruction that incorporates various content areas while covering an overall topic or theme, such as "Dinosaurs" or "Seeds."

internalize To make something part of one's unconscious, automatic learning processes.

interpersonal Occurring between people.

interpretation Giving meaning to a new concept by relating it to another, known concept.

interpretive exercise A means of assessment in which students analyze data, charts, maps, or written passages, using higher-level thinking skills.

intrapersonal Occurring within an individual.

intrinsic motivation An incentive, such as pride, self-esteem, and the desire to learn, that comes from within the student.

Kaplan matrix A curriculum planning chart that includes the different levels of thinking in Bloom's taxonomy.

knowledge Recognition and recall of facts and explicitly stated concepts.

learned helplessness A state of being in which students quit trying because they have repeatedly had their efforts neglected.

learning activities Hands-on, interactive classroom experiences.

learning community The concept of a school as a social unit that supports all members—students, teachers, administrators, staff, and parents.

learning deficits Skills students must acquire before they begin learning new concepts.

learning modality A way of gaining knowledge or expression through one of the senses—for example, auditory, tactile, visual, or kinesthetic.

learning style The set of cognitive, affective, and physiological traits that a learner exhibits as he or she interacts in the classroom environment and which determines the manner in which they will solve problems. Also called *learning preference*.

least restrictive environment The classroom setting that is as close to the "regular" classroom as possible and still provides the learning opportunities needed to address a student's special needs.

lesson A piece of a unit, in which a given set of objectives or concepts is taught.

mainstreaming Placing and serving children with special cognitive, behavioral, or psychomotor needs in regular classrooms. See also **inclusion.**

Maslow's hierarchy of needs A theory that an individual's behavior at any time is determined by his or her needs, ranging from basic physiological needs such as hunger and thirst to the highest needs of self-actualization and transcendence.

master teacher A teacher who possesses much experience and expertise and may serve as a role model or mentor for other teachers.

matching exercises Test items that require students to match words or concepts in one column to statements listed in another column; for example, identifying a word with its definition.

measurement The process of assigning numerical achievement indicators to student performance.

metacognition Conscious awareness of one's own thinking and learning process.

metaphor A figure of speech describing something with implied terms.

mnemonics A strategy for remembering facts by using a device, such as having the first letter of each fact make up a word or sentence.

motivation The desire or incentive to learn something or to behave in a given way.

multiculturalism The practice of including and honoring diverse cultures within school curricula and instruction.

multimethodology The teaching practice of using a wide variety of techniques during lessons so that every student will benefit from at least one mode of every presentation.

multiple intelligences The concept that intelligence does not take just one form but exists in eight facets: verbal/linguistic, bodily/kinesthetic, intrapersonal, logical/mathematical, musical/rhythmic, visual/spatial, interpersonal, and naturalistic.

multiple-choice item Test item that contains a question and asks students to choose an answer from a list of provided alternatives.

multiple-response questions An instructional technique in which the teacher asks multiple students to respond to a single question, thus encouraging divergent thinking.

negative interdependence A management system that encourages students to work against one another in competition for academic resources and recognition.

norm An unwritten behavioral rule, pattern, or habit accepted by a particular culture or group of people.

objective items Test items that have a single best or right answer.

objectives The specific steps that must be achieved to realize a broader goal.

outcome A description of some product or other tangible evidence that learning has occurred.

performance objective A specific observable outcome students should reach as the result of a learning experience or lesson; for example, "After reading the play, students will write an essay naming and describing five characters." Also called *performance statement*.

performance   An active demonstration used to assess student learning, such as oral presentations, musical and dramatic performances, and kinesthetic activities.

physical diversity   The variety of individuals' physical traits, such as height, weight, appearance, and physical ability.

planning   The process of choosing instructional goals, content, materials, and activities prior to teaching.

pluralism   The idea that a society should reflect the diverse mix of racial and other groups of which it is composed.

portfolio   A collection of student work that can be used to demonstrate student effort and progress toward particular learning objectives.

positive interdependence   A management system that encourages students to work together, with the assumption that the success of each student enhances the quality of learning for all students.

power   The influence teachers have over students by virtue of their age, authority, role, or physical strength.

preoperational stage   A early stage of cognitive development (ages 2–8) in which children learn through intuition, experience, and concepts.

prerequisite skills   The skills or knowledge students must have before they begin a new learning experience.

pretest   An assessment given before instruction begins to determine students' entry skills.

problem solving   An inquiry learning process in which students seek answers to a question that is relevant to themselves and their culture.

procedural knowledge   Knowledge of processes (*how*), as opposed to knowledge of content (*what*). Also called *process knowledge*.

process objectives   Statements that focus on the way students learn (*how*) rather than the specific outcomes of learning (*what*).

programmed instruction   A teaching method in which skills are presented in small segments, with immediate feedback and continual practice.

progressive differentiation   The second step in the advance organizer model, in which the basic facts, details, and concepts underlying a main concept or generalization are identified.

psychomotor domain   The area of learning encompassing physical movement, including gross and fine motor skills and coordination.

rationale   A reason or purpose.

readiness   The willingness and ability of a student to begin learning.

reality therapy   An approach to discipline in which individuals take responsibility for solving their own problems and begin to reshape their own behaviors to meet selected needs without any threats or implied punishments.

reciprocal teaching   A cooperative learning model used to improve reading, in which students play the teacher's role.

recitation   A learning technique in which the teacher calls on a different student to answer each factual or knowledge-based question, thus limiting students to one "correct" response.

reflection   An active mental process that teachers use consistently as they interact with students and the curriculum, including mental rehearsal prior to teaching, careful consideration of instructional options, anticipation of classroom problems, and quick daily evaluations of which methods worked and did not work.

reflective questions   Questions requiring students to develop higher-order thinking. A reflective question attempts to elicit motives, inferences, speculations, impact, and contemplation.

regional diversity   The differences in beliefs, values, and practices among people living in different parts of the same country.

regulatory agency   An office or board that sets standards, rules, and regulations.

reinforcement   A system of rewards that encourages students to repeat positive behaviors.

reliability   The degree to which a test consistently measures a given attribute.

ripple effect   The negative effects felt by all class members when a teacher responds negatively to a student.

role   An assigned set of responsibilities given to a student as a member of a group; for example, group leader, group recorder, group timekeeper, group evaluator.

role playing   A learning process in which students act out or simulate a real-life situation.

routines   Daily organizational tasks, such as taking attendance and checking papers, that must be part of a classroom time management plan.

rubrics   Examples of different types, models, illustrations, or levels of possible responses that are used as guidelines for assessing student work.

schema   A mental scaffold for learning, made up of previously learned concepts to which new concepts are attached.

schema theory   An assumption that learners have internal, cognitive frameworks into which they fit new knowledge, concepts, and experiences.

school culture   The environment of a school, including its values, management systems, communication styles, and interpersonal relationships.

school ethos   The tone of the interactions within a school's environment.

self-discipline   A classroom management system that emphasizes student goal setting, individual responsibility, and self-monitoring.

sensorimotor stage   A period of cognitive development (ages 0–2) during which children learn through sensations and movement.

sequencing   The process of organizing instruction by placing curricula or learning tasks in order.

sex-role stereotyping   Making assumptions about students' abilities based on their gender.

short-answer items   Test items that pose a question and require students to give a brief, two- to three-sentence response.

simulation   An artificial setting or situation that parallels a real-world setting or situation and allows students to practice problem-solving skills.

small groups   Purposefully constructed sets of four to eight students who work together to learn.

small-group discussions   Verbal exchanges of ideas and information in groups of four to eight students.

social capital   The sum of interpersonal relationships that provide support or encouragement.

standardized test   A nationally normed test that compares a student's performance to that of other students across the nation (if norm referenced) or to expected levels of achievement (if criterion referenced).

standards   Criteria for what knowledge and learning processes students should be taught in a given subject area, or how teachers should be trained to perform.

stem   The part of a multiple-choice test item that poses the question or problem.

strategic learning   Student development of critical thinking skills that accelerate learning.

student-initiated learning   An instructional technique in which students decide the content, means, and pace of the learning process.

summative assessment   A manner of making evaluative judgments and certifying completion of projects, classes, and programs, most often using a letter grade.

synergism   The increased energy created when individual elements work together as a whole, smooth-functioning, creative system.

synthesis   A process of creatively combining facts, concepts, and learning processes into new knowledge.

task analysis model   The process of subdividing the content, concepts, or processes of a lesson into smaller, sequential steps that begin with the least complex and progress to the most complex.

task group   A small group of students who work together to complete a particular assignment or job.

taxonomy   A set of standards for classifying ideas or objects into hierarchical categories; for example, Bloom's taxonomy of cognitive skills.

test   An assessment instrument that requires students to answer questions to demonstrate learning.

thinking   A complex act comprising attitudes, knowledge, and skills that allows the individual to shape his or her environment more effectively than intuition alone.

topics   Various subjects used by teachers to help organize their lesson plans.

transcendence   The highest level of Maslow's hierarchy of needs, in which one helps others find self-fulfillment and realize their potential.

transfer of learning   The application of knowledge or behaviors learned in one setting to a new situation.

translation   A thinking skill in which one form of expression is changed into another form.

true-false question   A test item that requires students to determine whether a given statement is correct or not.

tutorial discussion group   A group of two to four students being taught skills not mastered in large group class instruction.

two-way interactive television   A form of broadcast between distant sites, in which a teacher in one location interacts with students in another location.

unguided inductive inquiry   A learning process in which students discover specific facts or ideas themselves and then make their own generalizations based on them.

unit   A block of lessons grouped together based on related skills, concepts, or themes.

unit plan   A detailed plan for providing instruction on a skill, concept, or theme.

validity   The degree to which a test measures what it is intended to measure.

virtual reality   A computer-generated environment designed to create the illusion of a real setting or situation.

wait time 1   The time between when a teacher poses a question and then calls on a student to answer it.

wait time 2   A silent period that occurs after a student responds to a teacher's question.

zone of proximal development   The difference between the intellectual level a child can reach on his or her own and the level that can be reached with expert assistance.

Index

▶ HOW THIS TEXT HELPS MEET PROFESSIONAL TEACHING STANDARDS

Much is expected of professional teachers, both from within the occupation and outside it. Here is a list of teacher education standards most frequently cited by accrediting and professional associations along with key sections in this textbook where you will gain the entry-level knowledge to meet those standards.

Standard	Chapter Number and Title	Some Key Sections
Developing collegiality	Chapter 1, The Professional Challenges of Teaching	The Collegial Context; Incentives of the Teaching Culture
Developing professionalism	Chapter 1, The Professional Challenges of Teaching	Criteria for Professionals; Professional Obligations; Professionalism and Diversity; Meeting Mandated Professional Standards
Understanding students	Chapter 1, The Professional Challenges of Teaching Chapter 2, The Big Picture in Your Classroom Chapter 6, Managing the Classroom Environment	Facilitating the American Dream; Key Contexts of Schooling Developmental Perspective; Behavioral Perspective; Cognitive Perspective Changing Definitions of Discipline; Managing Interruptions; Dealing with Abusive Attitudes and Behaviors
Promoting social understanding	Chapter 1, The Professional Challenges of Teaching Chapter 2, The Big Picture in Your Classroom Chapter 8, Small-Group Discussions and Cooperative Learning	The Social Context Racial and Socioeconomic Diversity; Language Diversity; Ability Diversity: Who Is Exceptional? Cohesion: The "We" Attitude; Development of Social Skills; Setting Academic and Social Goals
Promoting diversity, equity, and fairness	Chapter 1, The Professional Challenges of Teaching Chapter 2, The Big Picture in Your Classroom Chapter 3, Objectives, Taxonomies, and Standards for Instruction Chapter 6, Managing the Classroom Environment Chapter 7, The Process of Classroom Questioning Chapter 8, Small-Group Discussions and Cooperative Learning Chapter 10, Classroom Assessment	Professionalism and Diversity Educational Equity as the Big Picture Using Objectives to Guide Learners Engendering Cooperation and Equity; Gender and Race Issues; Educational Equity and Student Tracking Promoting Multiple Responses; Encouraging Volunteers; Avoiding Teacher Idiosyncrasies Teaching Good Listening Skills; Features of Cooperative Learning Principles of Grading
Connecting with families	Chapter 6, Managing the Classroom Environment	The Importance of Parental Involvement; Meeting Effectively with Parents
Working with students who have special needs	Chapter 2, The Big Picture in Your Classroom Chapter 4, Instructional Design Chapter 5, Sequencing and Organizing Instruction Chapter 6, Managing the Classroom Environment	Ability Diversity: Who Is Exceptional? Constructing IEPs Task Analysis Model; Diversity and Learning Styles; Multiple Intelligences Engendering Cooperation and Equity
Planning instruction	Chapter 3, Objectives, Taxonomies, and Standards for Instruction Chapter 4, Instructional Design Chapter 5, Sequencing and Organizing Instruction Chapter 7, The Process of Classroom Questioning Chapter 8, Small-Group Discussions and Cooperative Learning Chapter 9, Inquiry Teaching and Higher-Level Thinking	Planning for Successful Instruction; Elements of Planning; Reflecting on Planning Factors Affecting Planning; Planning Resources; Preplanning; Unit Planning; Lesson Planning; How Expert Teachers Plan Models of Lesson Organization; Including Creativity in Instructional Plans Questioning Strategies; Preparing Yourself and the Students Choice of Topics and Applications; Selecting Student Groups; Planning Cooperative Activities Structuring Instruction for Success in Teaching Thinking
Forming and conveying expectations for students	Chapter 3, Objectives, Taxonomies, and Standards for Instruction Chapter 4, Instructional Design Chapter 6, Managing the Classroom Environment Chapter 7, The Process of Classroom Questioning Chapter 8, Small-Group Discussions and Cooperative Learning Chapter 9, Inquiry Teaching and Higher-Level Thinking Chapter 10, Classroom Assessment	Writing Performance Objectives; Curriculum Alignment; Converting Standards to Objectives Defining Goals and Objectives Establishing Usable Rules; Systems Based on Self-Discipline Aiming for Critical and Higher-Level Thinking; Preparing Yourself and the Students; Leading the Way with Questioning Teaching Good Listening Skills; Roles and Responsibilities; Leadership; Individual Accountability; Setting Academic and Social Goals Helping Students Become Better Thinkers Student-Led Conferences; Principles of Grading; Communicating Your Intentions